# Harriet Tubman

# Significant Figures in World History

*Charles Darwin: A Reference Guide to His Life and Works*,
by J. David Archibald, 2019.

*Leonardo da Vinci: A Reference Guide to His Life and Works*,
by Allison Lee Palmer, 2019.

*Michelangelo: A Reference Guide to His Life and Works*,
by Lilian H. Zirpolo, 2020.

*Robert E. Lee: A Reference Guide to His Life and Works*,
by James I. Robertson Jr., 2019.

*John F. Kennedy: A Reference Guide to His Life and Works*,
by Ian James Bickerton, 2019.

*Florence Nightingale: A Reference Guide to Her Life and Works*,
by Lynn McDonald, 2019.

*Napoléon Bonaparte: A Reference Guide to His Life and Works*,
by Joshua Meeks, 2019.

*Nelson Mandela: A Reference Guide to His Life and Works*,
by Aran S. MacKinnon, 2020.

*Winston Churchill: A Reference Guide to His Life and Works*,
by Christopher Catherwood, 2020.

*Catherine the Great: A Reference Guide to Her Life and Works*,
by Alexander Kamenskii, 2020.

*Golda Meir: A Reference Guide to Her Life and Works*,
by Meron Medzini, 2020.

*Karl Marx: A Reference Guide to His Life and Works*,
by Frank Elwell, Brian Andrews, and Kenneth S. Hicks, 2020.

*Eva Perón: A Reference Guide to Her Life and Works*,
by María Belén Rabadán Vega and Mirna Vohnsen, 2021.

*Adolf Hitler: A Reference Guide to His Life and Works*,
by Steven P. Remy, 2021.

*Sigmund Freud: A Reference Guide to His Life and Works*,
by Alistair Ross, 2022.

*Henry VIII: A Reference Guide to His Life and Works*,
by Clayton Drees, 2022.

*Harriet Tubman: A Reference Guide to Her Life and Works*,
by Kate Clifford Larson, 2022.

# Harriet Tubman

## A Reference Guide to Her Life and Works

Kate Clifford Larson

ROWMAN & LITTLEFIELD
*Lanham • Boulder • New York • London*

Published by Rowman & Littlefield
An imprint of The Rowman & Littlefield Publishing Group, Inc.
4501 Forbes Boulevard, Suite 200, Lanham, Maryland 20706
www.rowman.com

86-90 Paul Street, London EC2A 4NE, United Kingdom

Copyright © 2022 by Kate Clifford Larson

*All rights reserved.* No part of this book may be reproduced in any form or by any electronic or mechanical means, including information storage and retrieval systems, without written permission from the publisher, except by a reviewer who may quote passages in a review.

British Library Cataloguing in Publication Information Available

**Library of Congress Cataloging-in-Publication Data**

Names: Larson, Kate Clifford, author.
Title: Harriet Tubman : a reference guide to her life and works / Kate Clifford Larson.
Description: Lanham : Rowman & Littlefield, [2022] | Series: Significant figures in world history | Includes bibliographical references and index. | Summary: "Harriet Tubman: A Reference Guide to Her Life and Works captures her life, her works, and her legacy. It features a chronology, an introduction offers a brief account of her life, a dictionary section includes entries on people, places, and events related to her. A comprehensive bibliography offers a list of works about her life"—Provided by publisher.
Identifiers: LCCN 2021056018 (print) | LCCN 2021056019 (ebook) | ISBN 9781538113561 (cloth) | ISBN 9781538197622 (paper) | ISBN 9781538113578 (epub)
Subjects: LCSH: Tubman, Harriet, 1822–1913—Encyclopedias. | Tubman, Harriet, 1822–1913—Friends and associates. | Tubman, Harriet, 1822–1913—Bibliography. | Abolitionists—United States—Biography—Dictionaries. | African American Abolitionists—Biography—Dictionaries. | Underground Railroad—Dictionaries. | Antislavery movements—United States—History—19th century—Dictionaries.
Classification: LCC E444.T82 L375 2022 (print) | LCC E444.T82 (ebook) | DDC 326/.8092 [B]—dc23/eng/20211122
LC record available at https://lccn.loc.gov/2021056018
LC ebook record available at https://lccn.loc.gov/2021056019

# Contents

| | |
|---|---|
| Preface | vii |
| Maps of Harriet Tubman's Underground Railroad Routes | xi |
| Genealogy of the Ross Family | xiii |
| Chronology | xv |
| Introduction | xxiii |
| **THE DICTIONARY** | 1 |
| Appendixes | |
|     A  Harriet Tubman's Underground Railroad Rescue Missions | 161 |
|     B  Anthony Thompson's Inventory of Slaves, Recorded by Dr. Anthony C. Thompson, January 1839 | 163 |
|     C  Famous Harriet Tubman Quotes and Speech Fragments | 165 |
|     D  Earliest Published Interviews and Biographical Essays about Harriet Tubman | 169 |
|     E  Underground Railroad Myths | 185 |
|     F  Myths about Harriet Tubman | 189 |
| Bibliography | 191 |
| Index | 209 |
| About the Author | 225 |

# Preface

I have been researching and writing about Harriet Tubman for more than twenty-five years. She first captured my attention as a biographical subject while I was a master's degree student at Simmons University in the early to mid-1990s. Though she had been famous for well over one hundred years, it was surprising to discover that there were only three full adult biographies of her—two nineteenth-century books published while Tubman was still alive and a twentieth-century biography published in 1943—and scores of mostly fictionalized books written for children and young readers. How strange, I thought, that such a famous American woman had received such little scholarly and critical attention. I would come to learn, however, through my graduate work in women's and African American studies, that the lives and contributions of women and people of color are often overlooked in history books. I was convinced that Tubman deserved a serious modern biography.

As I began my research, I quickly realized that there were many myths surrounding Tubman's long life, making it difficult to discern truth from fakelore and exaggeration from hagiography. As an enslaved person in Maryland, a formal education was denied her—she could not read or write and left no personal papers or memoirs for historians to mine for her views, deeds, and aspirations. Fortunately, some of the people who knew her wrote about her, documented conversations with her, wrote letters for her, and recorded their own thoughts, memories, and impressions of her. In their personal letters, diaries, and memoirs, they expressed profound admiration, deep wonder, and amazement at the power and courage of the petite—she was just five feet tall—Black woman who refused to give up. They loved her, sincerely and genuinely. The organizations they belonged to and supported—Underground Railroad and antislavery societies, women's rights groups, refugee and war relief associations, and educational institutions—recorded their work with her. Descendants of those friends, colleagues, and admirers deposited those primary sources in numerous northern archives and libraries. Fortunately, they had the foresight to recognize that the records of their ancestors were worth preserving. Those collections provided a solid foundation for my work on uncovering Harriet Tubman the woman, Underground Railroad conductor, soldier, activist, and humanitarian. They also helped me document Tubman the daughter, sister, aunt, wife, mother, and friend.

While working on my dissertation in New England archives, one of my academic advisors suggested that I explore the physical landscapes of the Eastern Shore of Maryland where Tubman was born and raised as an enslaved person and the place from which she escaped to freedom. They felt that I would gain a valuable perspective of her life if I could see the region and imagine her in those fields and forests and on the water. I needed to find ways to record her presence there. I had long understood that finding documentary evidence of Tubman's life in Dorchester and Caroline counties in Maryland would be difficult. She was not a famous person then. She was invisible, like many enslaved people, to slaveholders. Her enslaver, Edward Brodess, cared little about her growth and development other than what she could do for him and how much money she could earn for him. He did not care about her interior life—what she thought, hoped for, or dreamed about. Compounding my research hurdles was the fact that the Dorchester County courthouse in Cambridge, Maryland, which held the majority of legal documents associated with local slavery, burned in May 1852, three years after Tubman had escaped to freedom. Any official records that might have recorded her existence would have burned that night. But, when I arrived in Cambridge, I discovered that on the night of the fire, the townspeople rushed into the burning building and saved records. While much was indeed lost, some significant documents survived, including court testimony taken during a lawsuit over the legal ownership of Tubman, her mother, and her siblings. Through that testimony and other records, I was able to piece together Tubman's family and, just as importantly, the community of free and enslaved people around her who helped raise her, protect her, educate her, and secure freedom for herself and many others.

The State of Maryland, through its State Archives, has made a commitment to preserving local, county, and state records that provide evidence of the institution of slavery and the lives of the enslaved. Without that preservation ethic and the work of the extraordinary staff at the archives who have worked tirelessly to make the records available, we would know little about Tubman's world. Their *Legacy of Slavery Project* is a vital resource for any researcher digging for genealogical, social, political, and legal records for the enslaved. Newspapers, many now digitized, have been a vital source, too. Finding the people who escaped slavery with Tubman's help during the 1850s, for instance, was possible because of reward notices advertising for their recapture and return to their enslavers. Later, newspapers published some of Tubman's speeches and interviews, making her well known to the public. After she died in 1913, the *New York Times* included her as one of the most important people in the world to have died that year.

Together, these sources expose a historical record that reveals an extraordinary life far greater than the myths. In the nearly twenty years since I published my book, *Bound for the Promised Land: Harriet Tubman, Portrait of an American Hero*, many more records have been discovered, advancing our knowledge of this remarkable woman. Her life and legacy have inspired two new national parks, a state park, an interstate Byway and All-American Road, numerous public memorials, books, animation, a feature-length film, and plans to have her image featured on a newly designed $20 U.S. bill.

This guide begins with maps of the general paths of the Underground Railroad that Tubman used to bring freedom seekers to Northern states and Canada during the 1850s. A genealogy of Tubman's immediate family provides a segue to a chronology highlighting significant experiences and turning points in Tubman's life. A brief overview then introduces the reader to the basic contours of her life. The encyclopedia entries focus on the people, places, and events associated with Tubman during her lifetime, concepts and specific language particular to the institution of slavery and its practice, organizations and institutions, social and political movements, as well as entries associated with Tubman's legacy and the memorialization of her contributions to this nation. Four appendixes capture selected significant historical records, which include a list of approximate dates for Tubman's thirteen missions via the Underground Railroad to Maryland with the names of the individuals she rescued, if known; the probate record for Anthony Thompson, who enslaved Tubman's father, Ben Ross, containing an estate inventory of all of Thompson's enslaved people and their family relations—a rare and exciting genealogical source for researchers; a select list of Tubman's most famous quotes; and lastly, a collection of early primary unpublished and published interviews and biographical details recorded by Tubman's colleagues and friends. The bibliography provides a selective list of primary and secondary sources concerning Tubman's life and the context for her times.

Through this guide I have been able to share my passion for Harriet Tubman and honor the people, places, and events that shaped and inspired her. Some of the information presented in this encyclopedia has not been published before, offering researchers opportunities for further exploration, interrogation, and interpretation. In order to facilitate the rapid and efficient location of information in this encyclopedia and encourage its use as a reference tool, extensive cross-references are provided in the entries. Within the body of each entry, terms that have their own individual and separate entry are in boldface type. Related terms that are not in the entry are indicated by "see also" references, and "see" references refer to other entries that relate to this topic. Dollars are in US currency denominations for the time period. For comparative purposes, a dollar in 1850 would be worth about thirty-two dollars in 2021.

# Maps of Harriet Tubman's Underground Railroad Routes

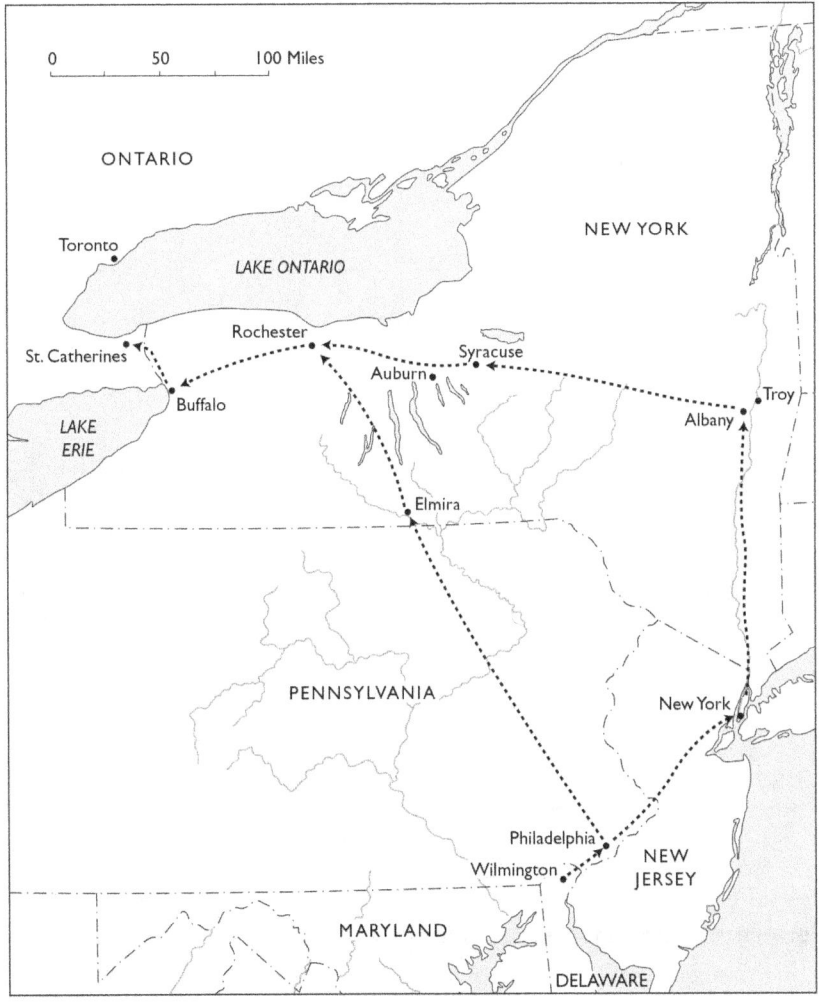

Northern Underground Railroad routes. *Bill Nelson Maps*

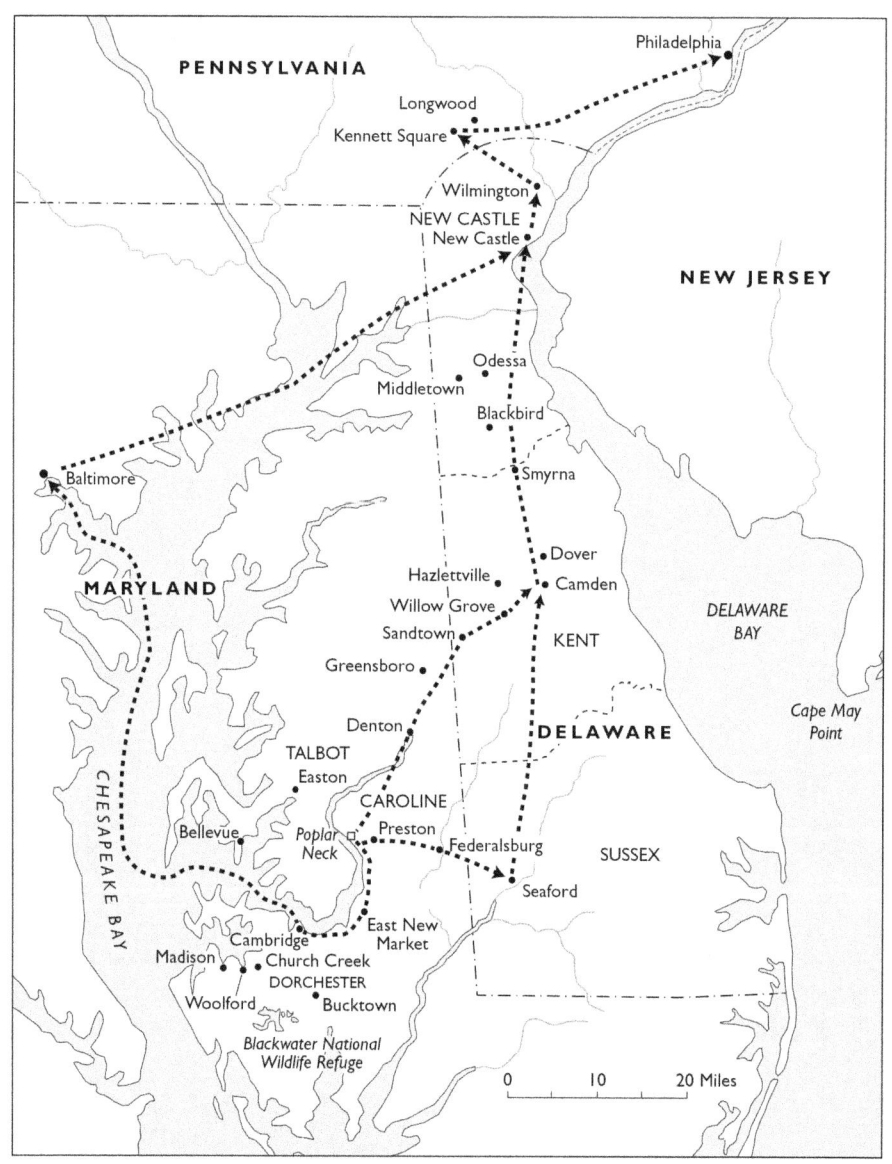

Southern Underground Railroad routes

# Genealogy of the Ross Family

## TUBMAN'S GRANDPARENTS

Only named/known grandparent is Modesty—Tubman's maternal grandmother, born in Africa; died between 1810 and 1820.

## TUBMAN'S PARENTS

**Benjamin "Ben" Ross**—born circa 1785; left Caroline County, Maryland, 1857; died in Auburn, New York, 1871.

**Harriet "Rit" Green Ross**—born circa 1785; left Caroline County, Maryland, 1857; died in Auburn, New York, 1879.

## TUBMAN'S SIBLINGS

**Linah Ross Jolly**—born circa 1808; sold between 1834 and 1840. Fate unknown.

**Mariah Ritty**—born circa 1811; sold 1825. Fate unknown.

**Soph**—born circa 1813; sold circa 1845. Fate unknown.

**Robert Ross**—born circa 1816; escaped slavery 25 December 1854; died in Auburn, New York, 14 November 1889. Changed name to John Stewart.

**Ben Ross Jr.**—born 1823; escaped slavery 25 December 1854; died in Buffalo, New York, or St. Catharines, Ontario, Canada, circa 1860–1863. Changed name to James Stewart.

**Rachel Ross**—born 1825; died in Bucktown, Maryland, circa 1859, leaving behind two children, Ben and Angerine. Fates unknown.

**Henry Ross**—born 1830; escaped slavery 25 December 1854; died in Auburn, New York, 1912. Changed name to William Henry Stewart.

**Moses Ross**—born 1832; escaped slavery circa 1851; died before 1865. Fate unknown.

# Chronology

**Pre-1785** A captive female African child or young woman is brought to Maryland and sold. Planter Atthow Pattison of Little Blackwater Bridge in Dorchester County, Maryland, enslaves her. She is called Modesty.

**Circa 1785** Modesty gives birth to Harriet Tubman's mother, Harriet "Rit" Green, whose father is unknown. Harriet Tubman's father, Benjamin Ross, is born to an unidentified enslaved mother and unknown father. He is enslaved six miles to the west of the Pattison farm, along the Blackwater River, by planter and slaveholder Anthony Thompson of Peter's Neck, south of Madison (formerly Tobacco Stick), in Dorchester County, Maryland.

**1793** Congress passes the Fugitive Slave Act of 1793, the first of its kind to address the rising numbers of enslaved people fleeing bondage.

**1797 ca. 18 January:** Atthow Pattison dies, passing legal ownership of young Rit Green to his granddaughter, Mary Pattison. The status and whereabouts of Modesty are unknown.

**1800 2 March:** Mary Pattison marries a neighbor, farmer Joseph Brodess, and they live with Mary's mother, Elizabeth Pattison, at Little Blackwater Bridge on Atthow Pattison's former farm.

**1801 14 June:** Edward Brodess, child of Mary and Joseph Brodess, is born.

**1802 June:** Joseph Brodess dies.

**1803 11 October:** Widow Mary Pattison Brodess marries widower Anthony Thompson, bringing her young son, Edward Brodess; enslaved young woman Rit; and at least three enslaved men she inherited from Joseph Brodess to Thompson's plantation at Peter's Neck, south of Madison in Dorchester County.

**Circa 1808** Living together on the Thompson plantation, Ben Ross and Rit Green welcome their first child, Linah Ross.

**1810** Mary Pattison Brodess Thompson dies, leaving young Edward and several enslaved people, including Rit and her daughter Linah, under the guardianship of Anthony Thompson. Modesty is still alive, and her presence during Mary Thompson's last illness and death is noted by a Thompson relative in court testimony in 1853.

**1811** Ben and Rit Ross's second child, Mariah Ritty, is born.

**1813** Ben and Rit Ross's third child, Soph Ross, is born.

**1816** Ben and Rit Ross's fourth child, Robert Ross, is born.

**1822 15 March:** Anthony Thompson pays a midwife two dollars for helping Rit Ross give birth to her fifth child, Araminta "Minty" Ross, later known as Harriet Tubman, sometime in early to mid-March.

**1823** Ben and Rit Ross's sixth child, Ben Ross Jr., is born. **14 June:** Edward Brodess turns twenty-two years old and becomes legally independent of Anthony Thompson, his stepfather and former guardian.

**1824 2 March:** Edward Brodess marries Eliza Ann Keene and moves to a small farm he inherited from his deceased father, Joseph, near Bucktown, Maryland, ten miles east of Peter's Neck. It is unclear when he brings Rit and her children to live on his farm with him, but it is likely sometime between 1825 and 1829. This forced separation from Ben and the enslaved community at the Thompson plantation begins years of harsh treatment for the Ross children. Linah Ross marries Harkless Jolly, a man enslaved by Dorothy Staplefort at Little Black Water Bridge. Their daughter, Kessiah Jolly, is born in this year.

**1825 July:** Ben and Rit Ross's seventh child, Rachel Ross, is born. Edward Brodess sells fourteen-year-old Mariah Ritty to Mississippi slave trader Dempsey P. Kane, fracturing the Ross family forever.

**1828–1832** Young Minty is hired out by Brodess to nearby farmers, including James Cook, who neglects and abuses her, and she suffers from frequent whippings and ill health.

**1830** Ben and Rit Ross's eighth child, Henry Ross, is born.

**1831 21–23 August:** Nat Turner's Rebellion in Southampton, Virginia, sends shock waves throughout the South. Restrictions on free and enslaved African Americans intensify.

**1832** Ben and Rit Ross's ninth and last child, Moses Ross, is born.

**1833–1844** Brodess sells Minty's sister Linah sometime during these years. Her whereabouts remain unknown.

**1833 12 November:** The Leonid Meteor Shower explodes in the night sky, making it seem like daytime and frightening people around the world. Minty witnesses the celestial event after sneaking out at midnight to visit with her mother, Rit; little brothers Henry and Moses; her sister Linah; and Linah's second child, Harriet Jolly, who have been leased to Brodess's neighbor, Polish Mills.

**1834–1836** Minty is leased to Thomas Barnett, a farmer in the Bucktown area, to work in his fields. She is nearly killed when struck on the head by an iron weight thrown by an angry overseer at a fleeing enslaved man at the Bucktown Village Store. Tubman would suffer from sudden seizures and debilitating headaches, likely temporal lobe epilepsy, for the rest of her life.

**1836 November:** Anthony Thompson, Ben Ross's enslaver, dies. His will instructs his heirs to gradually manumit all of his forty-three enslaved people, including Ross.

**1836–1842** Brodess leases Tubman to John T. Stewart of Madison, Maryland, bringing her closer to her father. She works as a domestic, field hand, dockworker, and logger. Her work assignments and nearness to her father help her acquire skills she would later need on the Underground Railroad.

**1840** Ben Ross is manumitted and given ten acres of land through a provision in Anthony Thompson's will. Rit, Minty, and some of her siblings are able to live with Ben in his home at Peter's Neck.

**1844** Soph Ross gives birth to a daughter, Ann Ross, before Brodess sells her. Her whereabouts remain unknown. Ann's father remains unidentified. Minty marries freeman John Tubman, changing her name to Harriet in honor of her mother. She pays Brodess $60 per year to hire herself out, which allows her to keep some of her earnings for herself. She purchases two oxen to help maximize her work options and income. Tubman's niece Kessiah Jolly marries freeman John Bowley. Their son, James Alfred Bowley, is born in this year.

**1846** Ben Ross moves to Poplar Neck near Preston in neighboring Caroline County to manage timbering operations on a 2,200-acre plantation owned by Anthony Thompson's son, Dr. Anthony C. Thompson. Rit moves to Caroline County with him.

**1847** Harriet Tubman hires herself out to Dr. Anthony C. Thompson and lives with her parents at Poplar Neck. Rachel Ross's daughter, Angerine, is born. Tubman learns that a provision in Atthow Pattison's 1797 will instructed his heirs to set Rit free when she turned forty-five years old (circa 1830), but Brodess kept her enslaved. Tubman hires a lawyer to document the Pattison bequest.

**1849 7 March:** Edward Brodess dies, leaving his widow Eliza burdened with debt and six of their eight children dependent upon her. She begins selling some of her enslaved people. **17 September:** Harriet Tubman runs away from Poplar Neck with her brothers Henry and Ben. Eliza Brodess posts a $100 reward for Tubman's return, but the three siblings return voluntarily because of confusion over where to go and whom to trust. **Late October/early November:** Fearful she is about to be sold, Tubman flees alone and successfully reaches freedom in Philadelphia. Rachel Ross's son, Ben Ross Jr., is born this year.

**1850 October:** The Fugitive Slave Act of 1850 is passed. **December:** Tubman conducts her first rescue mission by coordinating the escape of her niece Kessiah Jolley Bowley and Kessiah's two children, James Alfred and baby Araminta, through the assistance of Kessiah's free husband, John Bowley.

**1851** Tubman assists several other individuals escape enslavement on the Eastern Shore of Maryland, including her youngest brother, Moses. When she returns to Dorchester County in the fall of 1851 to bring her husband John to Philadelphia to live with her, he refuses to leave. He has married a free woman and moved on with his life. Tubman is devastated.

**1852** Tubman works as a domestic in Philadelphia and then in hotels in Cape May, New Jersey, during the summer. She conducts a rescue mission from the Eastern Shore of Maryland that fall, bringing nine people to freedom.

**1854 10 June:** Tubman helps Winnebar Johnson escape from his enslaver, Samuel Harrington of Madison (née Tobacco Stick), Maryland. **August:** Sam Green Jr., the son of Reverend Samuel Green, escapes from Dr. James Muse of Cambridge, Maryland, with the help of instructions passed along by Tubman. **25 December:** Tubman succeeds in rescuing her brothers Robert, Ben, and Henry Ross and several other individuals from Poplar Neck in Caroline County, Maryland, bringing them to Philadelphia and then St. Catharines, Ontario, Canada. By now Harriet has attracted the attention of abolitionists and Underground Railroad operators Thomas Garrett, William Still, Lucretia Mott, and others. Her brothers shed the Ross surname and take the new name "Stewart." Ben and Rit stay behind. Ben declares that he will not leave Maryland until all of his children and grandchildren are free.

**1855 11 June:** Ben Ross purchases Rit's freedom from Eliza Brodess for $20. **December:** Tubman assists in the escape of Henry Hooper or Cooper. She may have assisted Joseph Cornish flee from Cambridge, Maryland, that same month.

**1856 26 April:** Benjamin Jackson, James Coleman, William Andrew Conoway (aka Cook), and Henry Hopkins flee from Cabin Creek, Dorchester County, with Tubman's help. **21 October:** Tubman rescues Tilly, a young enslaved woman, from Baltimore. **15 November:** Josiah Bailey, Bill Bailey, Peter Pennington, and Eliza Manokey escape from enslavement on the Eastern Shore of Maryland with Tubman's assistance.

**1857** **7 March:** Using information given to them by Tubman, Henry Predeaux, Thomas Elliott, Denard Hughes, James and Lavinia Woolford, Bill and Emily Kiah, and an unidentified man named Tubman escape from Dorchester County, Maryland. They are betrayed by a Black Underground Railroad conductor named Thomas Otwell, who lures them into the Dover, Delaware, jail. They successfully break out of the jail and reach freedom. Newspapers across the country report on the group's escape, calling them the "Dover Eight." **4 April:** Reverend Sam Green, who helped the Dover Eight, is arrested. **April–May:** Tubman rescues her parents from Poplar Neck in Caroline County before her father, under suspicion for aiding in the escape of the Dover Eight, is arrested. She settles them in St. Catharines, Ontario, Canada. **17 October:** Sixteen enslaved people flee from the greater Cambridge, Maryland, area. **24 October:** Twenty-eight enslaved people escape from the same area. They become known as the Cambridge 28. Tubman does not lead these two groups to freedom herself, but she facilitates their flights through instructions on where to go and whom to trust on the route to Philadelphia, Pennsylvania. The escapes of these two large groups within one week shock the country. Newspaper headlines call the escapes a "stampede of slaves." The U.S. Supreme Court decision in the *Dred Scott* case denies African Americans their citizenship.

**1858** Tubman rents a log house on North Street in St. Catharines for her parents. **April:** John Brown meets Tubman at her home and discusses his plans to attack the South and liberate the slaves. He admires her courage and great intelligence and calls her General Tubman. She thinks he is the greatest white man she has ever met because he is willing to die for her. She promises to help recruit men to join in his effort. **May–December:** Tubman tours throughout New York and Massachusetts, giving public lectures and private talks at gatherings of abolitionists to raise money to support her parents and fund more rescue missions to Maryland. Newspaper editor and abolitionist William Lloyd Garrison of Boston calls her Moses, the leader of her people.

**1859** **May:** Tubman purchases a home and seven acres of land from William H. Seward, President Abraham Lincoln's future secretary of state, near Auburn, New York. She appears frequently at public antislavery conventions and forums in New England and becomes widely known as an Underground Railroad heroine. Her parents and other family members move into her home in the fall. **16 October:** John Brown begins his raid on the arsenal at Harpers Ferry, Virginia. **18 October:** Brown and his surviving men are captured by the U.S. Army. Tubman is supposed to join him but is either sick in New Bedford, Massachusetts, or attempting to rescue more family members in Maryland and therefore unable to fight at his side. **2 December:** Brown is hanged. Tubman flees to Canada because authorities discover her name among Brown's papers and seek to arrest her. Her family is no longer safe at her home in Auburn, New York, so they return to Canada. Rachel Ross dies in Bucktown, Maryland, sometime during this year.

**1860** **24 April:** Tubman is involved in the dramatic rescue of a freedom seeker, Virginian Charles Nalle, who was being held by federal marshals in Troy, New York. **4 July:** Tubman makes a speech during a public women's suffrage meeting in Boston, Massachusetts. **November–December:** Tubman makes another trip to the Eastern Shore of Maryland to rescue her sister Rachel and Rachel's children, Ben and Angerine. She discovers Rachel is dead. She tries to bring the children north, but she lacks the $30 to pay a bribe to someone who can bring the children to her hiding place. Deeply saddened by her loss, Tubman leads the Ennals family and others to freedom in late December. This is her last rescue mission.

**1861** **February–March:** Tubman's parents and other family members resettle into her home in Auburn, New York. **12 April:** The Civil War starts with the firing on Fort Sumter in Charleston Harbor by a South Carolina Confederate militia.

**1862** **10 January:** John A. Andrew, governor of Massachusetts, sends Tubman to Hilton Head district in South Carolina, to work as a scout and spy for the U.S. Army. She recruits eight Black men, most formerly enslaved, to work with her conducting special operations and intelligence-gathering missions in enemy territory.

**1863** **2 June:** Under the command of Colonel James Montgomery, Tubman becomes famous for her role as the first woman to conduct an armed raid. Using intelligence gathered with her team of scouts, she leads Montgomery's forces, the Second South Carolina Colored Troops, up the Combahee River, where they rout rebel forces, liberate more than 750 enslaved people, and burn buildings, crops, and stockpiles of munitions and food. **18 July:** Tubman witnesses the battle of Fort Wagner, where the famous all-Black Massachusetts Fifty-fourth Regiment fights bravely and ferociously. Their commander, Colonel Robert Gould Shaw, is killed. Hundreds in the regiment are wounded, and hundreds more would die. Tubman helps bury the dead and nurse the wounded.

**1864** Tubman continues spying for the U.S. Army while also working as a nurse, cook, and launderer. Between late November and December, Tubman takes a leave of absence and travels to Washington, D.C. She begins working in the Colored Women's and Orphans Home in Georgetown with Harriet Jacobs and other abolitionist and reform-minded women.

**1865** **9 April:** Confederate general Robert E. Lee surrenders to U.S. Army general Ulysses S. Grant at Appomattox Courthouse, Virginia, ending the Civil War. **14 April:** President Abraham Lincoln is assassinated at Ford's Theater in Washington, D.C., by John Wilkes Booth. **July:** Tubman begins work in the Colored Hospital at Fortress Monroe, Hampton, Virginia. She complains to U.S. surgeon general Joseph K. Barnes about the poor treatment given to Black soldiers, and her orders change to the administration of care at the facility. **October:** On her way home to Auburn, New York, Tubman is severely injured when a racist conductor violently ejects her from a passenger train because she is an African American. Tubman returns to a household full of family and friends. **6 December:** The Thirteenth Amendment to the U.S. Constitution is ratified by Congress, ending slavery.

**1867** **30 September:** John Tubman, Harriet's husband, is killed by Robert Vincent after a dispute on a country road near John's home in Dorchester County, Maryland.

**1868** **9 July:** The Fourteenth Amendment to the U.S. Constitution is ratified, guaranteeing citizenship, due process, and equal protection under the law for African Americans, who had been denied these rights under the *Dred Scott* decision. **November:** Sarah H. Bradford publishes Tubman's first biography, *Scenes in the Life of Harriet Tubman*. Tubman petitions the federal government for wages never paid for her service as a spy and scout during the war. Congress denies her petition, though her male fellow Black spies are paid for their service to the U.S. Army.

**1869** **18 March:** Forty-seven-year-old Tubman marries twenty-five-year-old Civil War veteran Nelson Charles Davis at Central Presbyterian Church in Auburn, New York. Albert Thompson, a fellow soldier in Company G, Eighth U.S. Colored Troop Regiment, had encouraged Davis to move to Auburn and find employment in the city's booming manufacturing industries.

**1870** **3 February:** The Fifteenth Amendment to the Constitution is ratified, guaranteeing that the right to vote "shall not be denied or abridged by the United States or by any State on account of race, color, or previous condition of servitude." The amendment applies only to men. Women of every race are still denied the franchise.

**1871** **19 November:** Ben Ross dies in Tubman's home on South Street in Auburn. Tubman continues to care for her mother, orphans, the homeless, the sick and disabled, and elderly people with no place to go.

**1873 September:** Tubman becomes involved in a mysterious gold swindle perpetrated by two con men from South Carolina, who convince her to borrow $2,000 to purchase a trunk full of gold from them. When she delivers the money, they beat her unconscious and steal the cash.

**1874** Tubman and Davis adopt a baby girl who was born to an unidentified woman living nearby. They name her Gertrude "Gertie" Davis.

**1879 13 October:** Rit Green Ross, Tubman's mother, dies. Tubman continues to farm her seven-acre property and run a small brick-making business with Davis.

**1880 10 February:** Tubman's wood-frame home burns to the ground. With the help of the community, she rebuilds a new brick residence, which still stands in Auburn today.

**1886** Sarah Bradford publishes a second biography of Tubman called *Harriet Tubman, the Moses of Her People*.

**1888 14 October:** Nelson Davis dies of tuberculosis and is buried at Fort Hill Cemetery in Auburn, New York.

**1890** Tubman becomes more actively involved in the women's suffrage movement, attending both Black and white suffrage conventions. Tubman applies for a widow's pension as the wife of Civil War soldier Nelson Davis. She begins helping raise funds to build the Thompson Memorial African Methodist Episcopal Zion (AMEZ) Church on Parker Street in Auburn, New York.

**1895** After five years of appeals and documentation, Tubman is finally awarded an eight-dollars-per-month widow's pension. She uses a portion of her pension to support Thompson AMEZ Church. **May:** Tubman purchases the twenty-five-acre parcel next to her property on South Street to establish the Harriet Tubman Home for the Aged and the John Brown Hall hospital for indigent, aged, and sick African Americans.

**1896 21 July:** Tubman is a featured speaker at the founding of the National Association of Colored Women at the 19th Street Baptist Church in Washington, D.C. **November:** Tubman attends a suffrage convention in Rochester, New York, where she gives a speech and utters her famous words: "I was a conductor on the Underground Railroad and I can say what most conductors can't say—I never ran my train off the track and I never lost a passenger."

**1897 31 May:** Tubman attends the unveiling of the memorial to Robert Gould Shaw and the Massachusetts Fifty-fourth Regiment, a large bronze sculpture by Auguste Saint-Gaudens, in Boston. Another edition of *Harriet, the Moses of Her People* is released to raise money to help Tubman pay for the twenty-five-acre property she acquired in 1895.

**1899** Through the efforts of friends in Auburn, Tubman is finally awarded her own pension at twelve dollars per month for her work as a Civil War nurse, which is combined with her eight-dollar widow's pension for a total of twenty dollars per month.

**1901** A final edition of *Harriet, the Moses of Her People*, with additional information and stories gleaned from new interviews with Tubman, is published.

**1903** Tubman transfers ownership of the twenty-five-acre property with the Harriet Tubman Home for the Aged and John Brown Hall to the African Methodist Episcopal Zion Church.

**1905** Tubman remains actively involved in suffrage politics. She attends ceremonies in Boston celebrating the service of Colonel Robert Gould Shaw and the men of the Massachusetts Fifty-fourth Regiment.

**1908 23 June:** The Harriet Tubman Home for the Aged officially opens for residents.

# CHRONOLOGY

**1911** Sick and disabled, Tubman enters the home she helped establish.

**1913 10 March:** Harriet Tubman dies. **13 March:** Hundreds of people, including dignitaries from around the country, attend Tubman's funeral at the Thompson Memorial African Methodist Episcopal Zion Church. She is buried next to her brother William Henry Stewart at Fort Hill Cemetery in Auburn, New York. **13 December:** The *New York Times* includes Tubman on its list of the 250 most important people in the world who died during the year.

**1920** American women win the vote with the passage of the Nineteenth Amendment.

**1944 3 June:** The U.S. Liberty ship SS *Harriet Tubman* is launched at the New England Ship Building Company in South Portland, Maine.

**2003–2005, 2017** The State of Maryland in partnership with Dorchester and Caroline counties create and launch the 125-mile Harriet Tubman Underground Railroad Scenic Byway and All-American Road on the Eastern Shore. By 2017 partnerships extend the byway more than another 120 miles through Delaware and on to Philadelphia, Pennsylvania.

**2013** President Obama creates the Harriet Tubman Underground Railroad National Monument in Dorchester County, Maryland, through a provision in the Antiquities Act, the 399th park in the U.S. national park system.

**2016** U.S. secretary of the treasury Jack Lew determines that a new $20 bill will feature Harriet Tubman's image, replacing Andrew Jackson.

**2017 10 January:** The Harriet Tubman National Historical Park in Auburn, New York, is established, marking the first time two national park units are named in honor of a Black woman.

**2022 March:** The bicentennial of Harriet Tubman's birth is held in Dorchester County, Maryland.

# Introduction

On 15 March 1822, Anthony Thompson paid a midwife two dollars for helping an enslaved woman named Rit Green Ross give birth. The baby, originally called Araminta, or Minty for short, grew up to become Harriet Tubman, one of the most famous women in American history and certainly its most celebrated Underground Railroad and civil rights hero. But when Minty was born there was no inkling as to the lives she would save, the world she would change, and the legacy she would leave behind.

Minty was the fifth of nine enslaved children of Rit and Ben Ross. They lived together on Thompson's plantation in Dorchester County, Maryland, a land rich in fields, forests, and marshes. His property, more than one thousand acres, sat along the Blackwater River, south of Madison in an area known as Peter's Neck. Thompson's wealth was also derived from his ownership of nearly forty people of African descent, including Ben.

Rit and their children, however, were the legal property of Thompson's stepson, Edward Brodess, who claimed them through the estate of his dead mother, Mary Pattison Brodess Thompson. The Ross family was allowed to live together while Brodess was a child and under the guardianship of his stepfather. Tragically, their lives as a nuclear family were permanently shattered sometime in 1823 or 1824, when Brodess exercised his rights as an adult and left his stepfather's home and moved to a small farm of his own near Bucktown, ten miles to the east. He separated Rit and her then five children, including Minty, from Ben in what would become the first of many cruel and heartless actions. He sold Rit's fourteen-year-old daughter, Mariah Ritty, to a Mississippi slave trader in 1825. He rented some of Rit's children to temporary masters for a yearly fee, tearing them away from their mother to live with strangers who were often abusive and violent. He started leasing Minty to neighbors when she was six years old. She once told an interviewer, "I use' to sleep on the floor in front of the fireplace an' there I'd lie and cry an' cry. I use to think all the time if I could only get home and get in my mother's bed, an' the funny part of that was, she never had a bed in her life. Nothing but a board box nailed up against the wall and straw laid on it."

Her first forced labor work included setting muskrat traps in cold marshes during the winter months. With no protective clothing to protect her from icy riverbanks, she frequently fell ill. Nursed back to health by her mother, she was repeatedly returned to the labor market. She endured beatings, whippings, and food insecurity and was denied basic clothing and medical treatment. "Slavery," she said, "is the next thing to hell."

Working as a field hand while a young teen, Minty was nearly killed by a blow to her head from an iron weight, thrown by an angry overseer at a young enslaved man who had left his work assignment in the fields. The severe injury left her suffering from headaches and epileptic seizures, most likely temporal lobe epilepsy, which afflicted her for the rest of her life. The injury also coincided with an explosion of religious enthusiasm, deeply rooted in Evangelical Protestantism and spiritual footings rooted in vestiges of West African belief systems still manifest in everyday life in communities of African descent on the Eastern Shore of Maryland.

During the late 1830s and early 1840s, Minty was leased to John T. Stewart, a Madison merchant and shipbuilder, bringing her back to the familial and social community near where her father lived and where she had been born. She worked on the docks and learned about the communication and transportation networks, sometimes secret, of Black mariners known as Black Jacks. She learned to read the night sky, a form of literacy well known to seamen. She grew strong and worked at jobs often reserved for men.

Her father, Ben, was set free in 1840 in accordance with the wishes of Anthony Thompson, who died in 1836. Thompson instructed his heirs to manumit all of his enslaved people according to a specific schedule of dates set in the future. Ben was also given ten acres to farm for himself. A skilled ship carpenter and lumberjack and renowned timber inspector, Ben was able to earn wages enabling him to hire Rit and some of their children so they could live together. Minty learned survival in the woods from her father and foodways and folk medicines from her mother.

About 1844 Minty married a local free African American named John Tubman, shedding her childhood name Minty in favor of Harriet in honor of her mother. They settled in a predominantly Black community on White Marsh Road south of Madison, where they hoped to build a life together. Tubman negotiated a contract with Brodess that allowed her to pay him $60 per year for the privilege of working for herself. With extra income she earned hiring herself to employers of her own choosing, she purchased a pair of oxen and maximized her earnings. No doubt she and John hoped to buy her freedom from Brodess.

Those years, though, were also marred by more tragedy. Brodess was frequently in debt and turned to his most liquid assets to stave off creditors. He sold Tubman's sisters, Linah and Soph, during the 1830s and 1840s. Both women were separated from their children and never heard from again. The shock and horror stayed with Tubman. She later told an associate that "she never closed her eyes that she did not imagine she saw the horsemen coming, and heard the screams of women and children, as they were being dragged away to a far worse slavery than that they were enduring there." When Brodess later tried to sell Tubman's youngest brother, Moses, Rit threatened to kill anyone who tried to take him from her with a knife. It was an act of defiance that could have resulted in her own death. Moses was not sold that day.

In 1846, Ben Ross moved to Poplar Neck, near Preston, Caroline County, to manage a lumber business established by Anthony Thompson's son, Dr. Anthony C. Thompson, on a 2,200-acre estate along the Choptank River. Within a year, Tubman, her mother, and possibly her husband and one or more of her brothers joined him there.

Sometime during the late 1840s, Tubman hired a lawyer to check the probate records of Atthow Pattison, Rit's first enslaver, who had died in 1797 when Rit was about twelve years old. Paying for the lawyer with money she earned by hiring herself out, Tubman learned that Pattison had directed his heirs to manumit his enslaved women and their children when they reached the age of forty-five. Tubman was enraged. Rit had been entitled to her freedom around 1830. She was now over sixty years old. Edward Brodess, Pattison's great-grandson, had not honored the legal stipulations in the will. He did nothing; the courts were likely to ignore the terms of a fifty-year-old will in favor of a white citizen and he knew it.

Forty-seven-year-old Brodess fell ill during the late winter of 1849 and died on 7 March. Deeply in debt, Brodess's widow, Eliza, turned to one of the most liquid assets she possessed: Rit and her children and grandchildren. Auctions began within months of Edward's death.

To avoid an unknown fate on the auction block, Tubman took her own liberty. On 17 September 1849, she fled with her brothers Ben Jr. and Henry from Poplar Neck. Eliza Brodess posted a $300 reward advertisement for their capture and reenslavement. The siblings argued about which way was the safest route to freedom. Before they could be caught, they returned to Poplar Neck.

Tubman knew she could not bear being sold away from her loved ones, so, sometime that October or November, she escaped by herself. She tapped into an Underground Railroad network that was already functioning well in the region. Traveling by night, using the North Star and instructions from Black and white collaborators, she found her way to freedom in Philadelphia.

Her husband John refused to join her. A free man from a free family, he risked being killed, imprisoned, or sold into slavery if they were caught during her escape. He soon married a free woman named Caroline, destroying Tubman's dream of sharing a free life with him in the North. She channeled that heartbreak into a liberation strategy, and over the next eleven years she returned to Maryland approximately thirteen times to personally liberate about seventy or so enslaved family and friends. She also provided instructions to about sixty to seventy more who found their way to freedom independently. Her rescue and escape missions earned her the nickname "Moses."

Tubman relied heavily upon an intricate and secretive web of communication and support among African Americans to effect her rescues. The collective efforts of free and enslaved Blacks operating beyond the scrutiny of whites along the various routes to freedom were crucial to her success. In collusion with like-minded white abolitionists, the networks to freedom called the Underground Railroad were an extraordinary biracial operation. Underground Railroad "agents," "stationmasters," and "conductors" facilitated the movement of "passengers," marshaled financial resources, and provided the protection that sustained Tubman.

Ben Ross was an Underground Railroad agent, too, and he risked arrest when he was threatened with exposure in the spring of 1857. At enormous risk, Tubman returned to the Eastern Shore to rescue him and Rit, bringing them safely to Canada. That fall, after the escapes of two large groups of enslaved people from Dorchester County, the slaveholders on the Eastern Shore became aware of the possibility that a person or several people were helping the enslaved flee bondage. They redoubled their efforts to root out any abolitionist or Underground Railroad agents in their midst. They had no idea, however, that one of the people responsible was Harriet Tubman.

She rented a log cabin on North Street in St. Catharines, Ontario, Canada, for her parents to live comfortably. Her brothers Robert and Henry lived nearby. She had rescued them, and her brother Ben, on Christmas Day 1854. When they traveled through the offices of Underground Railroad agent William Still in Philadelphia during their flight north, the brothers told him that they wanted to take new names. Robert Ross became John Stewart, Henry became William Henry Stewart, and Ben Jr. became James Stewart. They were free, but Tubman struggled to execute the rescue of her sister Rachel and Rachel's children, Ben and Angerine. Tragically, Rachel died in 1859 before Tubman reached her, and the children remained enslaved by the Brodesses.

Tubman's remarkable ability to travel undetected over hostile landscapes piqued the interest of John Brown, a radical abolitionist and fierce freedom fighter. He met with her at her home in St. Catharines in the spring of 1858, and they discussed his plans to attack the federal arsenal at Harpers Ferry, Virginia; distribute the stolen weapons to enslaved people; and lead a revolt against slaveholders. He was so impressed by her great intelligence that he called her "General Tubman." She thought he was the greatest white man to have ever lived, and after he was arrested and hanged in December 1859, she knew his sacrifice to end slavery and the political and financial systems that supported it would spark a revolution.

Her total commitment to destroying slavery eventually led her to the battlefield during the Civil War. Governor John Andrew of Massachusetts sent her to South Carolina to work as a spy and a scout. In cooperation with Colonel James Montgomery and his Second South Carolina Colored Regiment, she became the first American woman to lead an armed raid into enemy territory. On 2 June 1863, she led Montgomery and his men up the

Combahee River, where they routed out Confederate forces, looted and burned plantations, and liberated more than 750 enslaved people. They called her the "Black She-Moses." Tubman's skills earned her the respect and admiration of Union Army officers. She worked as a nurse and a cook, too, contributing whatever resources she had to the war effort. She witnessed the Second Battle of Fort Wagner where the heroic Fifty-fourth Massachusetts Voluntary Infantry Regiment fought so boldly.

During the war, her family moved from St. Catharines to a seven-acre farm she had purchased in 1859 in Fleming, outside the city of Auburn, New York, from William Henry Seward. When she returned home after the war, she was greeted by a house full of dependents, including her aged parents. Petitions to the federal government to pay her for her service during the war were denied. She struggled to feed and care for everyone in her care, but with the support of allies in the city, including Martha Coffin Wright, the Sewards, Eliza Wright Osborne, and many others, Tubman and her family thrived. She welcomed scores of orphaned children, destitute and sick formerly enslaved people, the homeless, and others in need.

Tubman met and fell in love with Nelson Davis, a young veteran who had come to Auburn to work in its mills and factories after the war. Her husband John was murdered in Dorchester County in 1867, releasing her to wed again. She and Davis were married in March 1869 at Central Presbyterian Church in Auburn, and they adopted a baby girl whom they named Gertie. Her parents passed—Ben in 1871 and Rit in 1879. Her house was destroyed by fire in 1880, forcing her to move in with her brother John and his wife. Over the next three years, Tubman, Davis, and other family and friends rebuilt her home using bricks manufactured on her property. Davis lived just a few more years, succumbing to tuberculosis in 1888.

Maintaining her relationships with a multitude of former abolitionists, Tubman became active in women's suffrage and civil rights movements. After Davis's death, she became a fixture at suffrage meetings and conventions throughout New York and New England, sometimes appearing with her longtime friend, Susan B. Anthony. Her dream of opening a nursing home and assisted living center for aged and ill African Americans was realized in 1896 when she purchased the twenty-five acres abutting her own seven-acre farm. After transferring the property to the African Methodist Episcopal Zion Church in 1903, the buildings on the property were reconfigured to serve the sick and elderly. One brick structure was retrofitted into a nursing facility and named after Tubman's hero, John Brown.

She continued to travel to visit friends and attended ceremonies honoring deceased friends from the Underground Railroad and Civil War days in Boston, Canada, New York, and elsewhere. Her fame only grew greater as she aged. Several editions of her biography, written by Sarah H. Bradford, were published, reintroducing her to younger generations. Her allies helped her claim a pension as the widow of Civil war veteran Nelson Davis, and eventually, after a long campaign, the federal government awarded her a pension for her work as a nurse during the war.

The years of hard labor took their toll, though, and by 1911 she moved into John Brown Hall where nurses and staff could care for her. Though frail and confined to a wheelchair, she welcomed reporters who wrote feature articles about her life and adventures. She often took the opportunity to speak up and advocate for equality, justice, and civil rights. She died on 10 March 1913. The *New York Times* claimed she was one of the most important people in the world to have died that year.

In the years following Tubman's death in 1913, the Black community maintained Tubman's memory, mostly in segregated classrooms. Highly fictionalized accounts of her life started appearing in the late 1920s and early 1930s, specifically in young adult and juvenile works highlighting the history of the Underground Railroad. In 1938, reporter Earl Conrad began researching a full-length biography of Tubman. After five years of research and writing, Conrad published *Harriet Tubman*. A modestly successful book, it influenced the decision by the United States

Maritime Commission to build a World War II Liberty Ship in honor of Tubman. In print for decades, it served to educate generations of Americans and inspired scores of fictionalized biographies for children and adults. During the 1990s and early 2000s, new information and fresh sources, hidden and long forgotten in private and public records, emerged that offered a more accurate life history of Harriet Tubman. This dictionary is the compendium of that work.

# The Dictionary

**ABBOTT, WILLIAM E. (1821–?).** Treasurer of the **Fugitive Aid Society of Syracuse, New York**, who aided **Harriet Tubman** on her way through central New York with **freedom seekers** to Rochester and Niagara Falls, New York, to the suspension bridge over the Niagara River to Ontario, Canada. He worked directly with other **Underground Railroad** agents, including **Stephen** and **Harriet Myers**, **Jermain Loguen**, **Frederick** and **Anna Douglass**, and others in central and western New York State.

**ABOLITION MOVEMENT.** A political and social movement to end slavery.

**ABOLITIONIST.** An individual dedicated to abolishing slavery.

**ADAMS, NEHEMIAH (19 February 1806–6 October 1878).** A Boston Congregational minister, Adams wrote *A Southside View of Slavery* (1854) defending the institution of slavery as beneficial to people of African descent. The book and the author's proslavery views were roundly denounced by abolitionists, including **William Lloyd Garrison**, who wrote a scathing critique in the antislavery newspaper *The Liberator*.

**ADAMS, SAMUEL HOPKINS (26 January 1871–16 November 1958).** The great nephew of **Sarah Hopkins Bradford**, Hopkins was born in Dunkirk, New York, and spent many hours with his grandparents, who were friends with **Harriet Tubman** in Auburn, New York. He later wrote *Grandfather Stories* (1955), a collection of memories of his childhood, which included reminiscences of listening to Tubman's stories rescuing enslaved people on the **Underground Railroad** and spying during the **Civil War**.

**ADKINS ARBORETUM.** A native garden and arboretum located within Tuckahoe State Park in Ridgely, Maryland, and along the **Harriet Tubman Underground Railroad Byway**. Its gardens focus exclusively on plants native to the Mid-Atlantic coastal plain. Visitors can experience native plants in a natural setting and in cultivated gardens. This Arboretum offers an audio tour, *A Journey Begins: Nature's Role in the Flight to Freedom*, that guides visitors through its landscapes and explores the little-known relationship between nature and the **Underground Railroad**.

**AFRICAN AMERICAN SPIRITUAL.** A Christian hymn, an African American spiritual is a particular genre of religious music closely associated, originally or figuratively, with enslaved people in America during the eighteenth and nineteenth centuries before the end of slavery during the **Civil War**. Some of these spirituals were originally Methodist and other Christian hymns whose words held particular importance for enslaved people. Some spirituals are original compositions embodying the experiences of the enslaved. African American spirituals became very popular, particularly after the Civil War, and many scholars view them as original American folk songs.

**AFRICAN METHODIST EPISCOPAL (AME) CHURCH.** An African American religious denomination founded for Black people in America by Reverend Richard Allen in 1793. Seeking independence from white Methodist and other Protestant denominations, Allen gathered disaffected Black Christians to join together and establish their first church in Philadelphia. With a focus on racial equality and civil rights, the denomination grew quickly in the south and west. Since the Civil War, the AME Church has grown to become the largest African American religious denomination in the world. It is generally called the AME Church or AME.

**AFRICAN METHODIST EPISCOPAL ZION CHURCH (AMEZ).** An African American religious denomination founded for Black people in America by a group of disaffected Black Christian worshipers in New York City. Led by abolitionist William Hamilton, the congregants established Zion Church in 1800. The church's association with abolition earned it the designation "Freedom Church." Like the **AME Church**, the AMEZ's roots in fostering racial equality and civil rights fueled its growth in the decades before and after the Civil War. Its ministers and congregations played a powerful role during the civil rights movement of the 1960s. Today, it maintains an active international ministry. **Harriet Tubman**'s parents attended St. Mark's AME Church in Auburn, New York, during the **Civil War**, and her second husband, **Nelson Davis**, was a member. Tubman helped fund and establish **Thompson Memorial AMEZ Church** in 1892 in Auburn, New York. Her funeral service was held there on March 13, 1913.

**AGNEW, ALLEN AND MARIA (ca. 1810–1870).** The Agnews were Presbyterian abolitionists and **Underground Railroad** agents and were part of an active community secretly aiding **freedom seekers** escaping slavery. They lived in Pennsbury Township near other prominent antislavery activists and Underground Railroad operators, including Isaac and Dinah Mendenhall and **John and Hannah Cox** from Longwood and Kennett Square in Chester County, Pennsylvania. The couple sheltered **Tubman** and her brothers, **Robert, Ben,** and **Henry Ross**, on 29 December 1854, after their escape from Maryland on **Christmas Day 1854**.

**ALCOTTS, OF CONCORD, MASSACHUSETTS.** Amos Bronson Alcott, his wife, and their daughters, Anna, Elizabeth, Abby May, and author Louisa May, were **abolitionists** and **women's rights** activists. They welcomed **Harriet Tubman** into their home when she was visiting Boston, Massachusetts, before the **Civil War**.

**AMBY, ELIZABETH "LIZZY" AND NAT (ca. 1830s–dates unknown).** Born into slavery in **Dorchester County, Maryland**, the Ambys were enslaved by different enslavers: Nat Amby was held by **John Muir**, but Lizzy Amby was enslaved by **Dr. Alexander Bayly**, both of Cambridge, Maryland. The couple conspired to escape together and successfully fled on 17 October 1857 with a group of thirteen other **freedom seekers**, including **Caroline and Daniel Stanley** and their six children and six other adults: Hannah Peters, William Griffen, Henry Moore, James Camper, Noah Ennals, and Levin Parker. **John Augusta**, an African American barber and **Underground Railroad** agent in Norristown, Pennsylvania, hid them before sending them to **William Still** in Philadelphia. The Ambys reached Auburn, New York, where they were sheltered by **Morgan Luke Freeman**, a descendent of one of the very first black families to settle in Auburn in the early nineteenth century.

**AMERICAN AND FOREIGN ANTI-SLAVERY SOCIETY (1840–1860).** Founded in May 1840 by Arthur Tappan and his brother **Lewis Tappan** after a schism in the **abolition movement** in the United States. The Tappans were founding members of the **American Anti-Slavery Society (AASS)** with **William Lloyd Garrison** and others. Rifts occurred over the participation of women in the organization and in public as questions about women's rights began attracting attention. The Tappans and other conservative abolitionists grew uncomfortable with Garrison's more radical positions regarding the dismantling of the slave system, and when the AASS membership elected a woman, Abby Kelley, to its executive committee, the Tappans and their followers defected from the organization. The new organization established a weekly newspaper, the *National Era*. Though the organization had some influence in the abolition movement, it never gained the power and influence of the AASS and Garrison with his newspaper, *The Liberator*.

**AMERICAN ANTI-SLAVERY SOCIETY (AASS) (1833–1870).** Founded by **William Lloyd Garrison** and **Lewis Tappan**, the AASS was formed in response to expanding slavery in the United States. In December 1833, Garrison and Tappan called for a convention of **abolitionists** in Philadelphia to create an organization dedicated to the immediate abolition of slavery, condemning the **American Colonization Society**, and advocating pacifist methods of resistance. **Frederick Bailey Douglass** became a member and lectured widely for the society. In the spring of 1840, after electing the first woman, Abby Kelley, to the society's executive committee, Garrison, **Lucretia Coffin Mott**, **Elizabeth Cady Stanton**, and other society members were invited to the World Anti-Slavery Convention in London, England. Female attendees were not allowed to sit on the convention floor, creating a crisis for the Americans. Garrison chose to sit with the women in the gallery to watch the convention proceedings separately. This became one of the seminal moments for the fledgling **women's rights movement**. Founding member Arthur Tappan and his brother **Lewis Tappan** disagreed with Garrison and the women. As conservative abolitionists, the Tappans believed in the subjugation of women. The election of Kelley and the active participation of women strained relationships over growing disagreements over tactics. The society split, and the Tappans and their followers established the **American and Foreign Anti-Slavery Society** in 1840. The society remained a powerful antislavery voice throughout the 1840s and 1850s. It disbanded after the **Civil War** and **emancipation**.

**AMERICAN COLONIZATION SOCIETY (1816–1964).** Founded to encourage the forcible removal and voluntary repatriation of African Americans, slave and free alike, to Africa from the United States. The society encountered powerful criticism from abolitionists like **William Lloyd Garrison**, editor of *The Liberator*, and free people of color. Its efforts resulted in the immigration of several thousand African Americans, by the outbreak of the **Civil War**, to **Liberia** in Africa, where many immigrants died of disease.

**AMERICAN FREEDMEN'S INQUIRY COMMISSION.** Established in March 1863 by the federal government and led by Dr. **Samuel Gridley Howe**, the commission was charged with determining the status of newly freed people in the South, as well as **freedom seekers** then living in Canada. The commission interviewed hundreds of Black and white people for its final report, published in May 1864. On 8 November 1863, Howe and his staff interviewed **Harriet Tubman**'s brother **William Henry Ross Stewart** and others in St. Catharines, Ontario, Canada. The interviews are available at the National Archives Records Administration.

**AMERICAN WOMAN SUFFRAGE ASSOCIATION (AWSA).** One of two national woman's suffrage organizations, the AWSA was founded in Boston in 1869 in response to the disagreements over support for the Fourteenth and Fifteenth Amendments, which secured voting rights for African American men but no women of any race. **Elizabeth Cady Stanton** and **Susan B. Anthony** rejected the more conservative AWSA, which supported the amendments. They formed the **National Woman Suffrage Association**, a rival organization. The NWSA and the AWSA remained in opposition until the 1890s, when both organizations reunited to form the **National American Woman Suffrage Association (NAWSA)**. Harriet Tubman supported Susan B. Anthony in her views.

**ANDERSON, OSBORNE P. (1830–1872).** Born free in Chester County, Pennsylvania,

Osborne moved to Chatham, Ontario, Canada, in 1850 and opened a printing shop and advocated for the end of slavery. He met revolutionary **John Brown** and attended Brown's meetings to plan an attack on the federal arsenal at **Harpers Ferry**, Virginia. Anderson was the only survivor out of the five African American men who joined Brown in his assault on the arsenal. He escaped capture after the raid through help from **Underground Railroad** operatives, who sent him to Canada. He enlisted in the Union Army during the **Civil War**. He died in Washington, D.C., in 1872.

**ANDREW, JOHN ALBION (31 May 1818–30 October 1867).** Born in Windham, Maine, Andrew became a lawyer and radical abolitionist, having been deeply inspired by **William Lloyd Garrison**. He moved to Boston in 1837 and became involved with the **Boston Vigilance Committee**. He aided in the legal defense of **freedom seekers** and free Blacks arrested under the 1850 **Fugitive Slave Act**. Active in politics, he was elected governor of Massachusetts in 1861. An admirer of **Harriet Tubman**, he made arrangement for her to be appointed as a spy and scout for the Union Army and sent her to **Hilton Head, South Carolina**, in May 1862 to begin her service. Andrew was also one of the leading advocates for the enlistment of Black men into the Union Army, leading to the creation of the **Fifty-fourth Massachusetts Infantry Regiment**, and fought for equal pay for Black and white soldiers (which did not happen until 24 September 1864). He died in Boston.

**ANTEBELLUM PERIOD (OR ERA).** The period of American history from the Early Republic (last quarter of the eighteenth century) to the beginning of the Civil War. The antebellum era is characterized by the growth of the southern plantation economy and expansion of slavery. It is also framed by the rise in southern states' political power in opposition to a rapid increase in antislavery and abolitionist activity in northern states. The eventual polarization of the country led to the Civil War in 1861, bringing the antebellum period to an end.

**ANTHONY, KIT AND LEAH (ca. 1830s–dates unknown).** Born into slavery in **Dorchester County, Maryland**, the Anthonys were enslaved by **Samuel Pattison**, on his plantation near **Cambridge, Maryland**. They escaped with their three small children, Adam, Mary, and one-year-old Murray, and twenty-three other people on Saturday, 24 October 1857. The group, later known as the **Cambridge 28**, successfully eluded arrest and made their way through Delaware, Pennsylvania, and New York. They safely settled in St. Catharines, Ontario, Canada. This escape came just one week after the escape of **Lizzie and Nat Amby**, **Caroline and Daniel Stanley**, Hannah Peters, William Griffen, Henry Moore, James Camper, Noah Ennals, and Levin Parker on 17 October 1857. Together, these two large escapes became known as the Stampede of Slaves.

**ANTHONY, SUSAN B. (15 February 1820–13 March 1906).** Abolitionist, women's rights activist, and social reformer, Anthony was close friends with **Harriet Tubman** for more than forty years. Introduced during the late 1850s in central New York, possibly through other **abolitionists** like **Amy** and **Isaac Post**, **Anna** and **Frederick Douglass**, **Maria Porter**, and **Martha Coffin Wright**, Tubman and Anthony shared speaking platforms on occasion, arguing for suffrage and civil rights. In 1861, Anthony sheltered Tubman and some **freedom seekers** in her home in Rochester.

**ANTISLAVERY MOVEMENT.** A moral, social, and political crusade to end the institution of slavery and the enslavement of human beings. *See also* ABOLITION MOVEMENT.

**ASANTE/ASHANTE.** An ethnic group and part of West African Akan-speaking people from present-day Ghana. A highly spiritual culture that believed in the sacredness of land and water, Asante society was rooted in the power of female ancestors and their roles as advisors and leaders in the community. The Asante were known for their skills clearing dense forests to create productive agricultural fields. **Harriet Tubman**'s grandmother **Modesty** may have been Asante. Similar to other

West and West Central African peoples, the Asante believed in a variety of deities linked to both the natural and spiritual worlds. The most powerful were associated with bodies of water, but the land, or mother earth, was the link between the dead and the living, through which all Asante individual and communal values rest. Their ancestors were buried but continued to live in a parallel world and could be sought out in times of need. As a loosely defined coalition of small chiefdoms, the Asante defended themselves against British colonial rule far longer than most African states, finally succumbing to defeat in 1896. They failed in protecting themselves from capture and enslavement, however. Years of conflict between the Asante and their neighbors offered a steady supply of Akan, Fante, Asante, and other Gold Coast captives to New World markets.

**ASSOCIATED PUBLISHERS.** Founded in 1920 by Carter G. Woodson to publish works by Black authors and for African American readers. An American historian and journalist, Woodson also founded the Association for the Study of African American Life and History (1915); published the *Journal of Negro History* (1916), now called the *Journal of African American History*; and created Black History Month. Associated Publishers published **Earl Conrad**'s 1943 biography of Harriet Tubman.

**AUGUSTA, JOHN (1819–before 1900).** An African American barber and **Underground Railroad** agent in Norristown, Pennsylvania, who helped **freedom seekers** before sending them to **William Still** in Philadelphia. He was instrumental in helping several members of the famous **Cambridge 28** and Stampede of Slaves escape in October 1857.

**AVERILL, HORATIO F. (4 February 1834–12 May 1887).** Born in Sand Lake, Rensselaer County, New York, Averill was a lawyer and a Democrat who supported the **Fugitive Slave Act**. He betrayed **Charles Nalle**, a **freedom seeker** who had settled in Sand Lake and was a frequent visitor to Averill's neighborhood. Hoping to secure a bounty for the capture of **Nalle**, he secretly wrote a letter to **Nalle**'s Virginia enslaver, **Blucher Hansbrough**, and revealed **Nalle**'s whereabouts. **Harriet Tubman** helped rescue **Nalle** from capture by Hansbrough.

# B

**BAILEY, FREDERICK.** *See* DOUGLASS, FREDERICK BAILEY.

**BAILEY, JOSIAH "JOE"** (ca. 1828–unknown). Born enslaved in **Dorchester County, Maryland**, Joe and his brother **William "Bill" Bailey**, **Peter Pennington**, and **Eliza Manokey** fled slavery with the help of **Harriet Tubman** in mid-November 1856. Joe Bailey knew about **Harriet Tubman** and her rescue missions to the region to bring **freedom seekers** north. After being assaulted and whipped by his enslaver, **William Hughlett** of Talbot County, Joe decided to escape. A skilled timber foreman who managed the harvesting and hauling of ship timber from Hughlett's land along the **Choptank River** at Jamaica Point, Bailey was well connected to the Black maritime, timbering, and shipping networks in that region.

One evening in the fall of 1856, Joe rowed six miles up the river to **Poplar Neck** in **Caroline County** where **Harriet Tubman**'s free father, **Ben Ross**, lived and worked as timber foreman for Dr. **Anthony C. Thompson**. Bailey informed him that he was ready to escape the next time Tubman arrived from the North. Joe's brother **Bill Bailey** was enslaved by **John Campbell Henry** of **Cambridge, Maryland**, but had been leased to Hughlett. Their friend **Peter Pennington** was enslaved by **Turpin Wright** on Wright's farm at Oyster Shell Point, across the **Choptank River** from Jamaica Point. **Eliza Manokey** was enslaved by Ann Martin Staplefort Grieves, who lived at **Church Creek** in Dorchester County. On 15 November 1856, Tubman led the group north into Delaware. Bounty hunters chased the group, eager to collect the $2,600 reward for their arrest, including **William Hughlett**'s offer of $1,500 for the capture of twenty-eight-year-old **Joe Bailey**. Such high rewards increased the danger of capture for the runaways. It took the group ten days to reach **Thomas Garrett** in Wilmington, Delaware, a trip that typically took only three days. **Slave catchers** forced them to proceed cautiously and remain hidden. They were "passed along by friends in various disguises" and were "scattered and separated" and led "roundabout" to a variety of **Underground Railroad** safe houses to avoid detection. Garrett learned they were trapped on the other side of the Christiana River, unable to cross the bridge into Wilmington because the authorities were watching. Garrett engaged the services of two Black bricklayers, who loaded their wagon and rode across the bridge in the morning, "singing and shouting" and greeting the police and others looking for the group. The bricklayers located Tubman and the **freedom seekers** and concealed them in a hidden compartment built into the wagon. The bricklayers proceeded back over the bridge, still "singing and shouting," successfully evading detection by the police and **slave catchers**.

One day later, on 26 November, the party arrived in Philadelphia at **William Still**'s office, who instantly sent them to **Sydney Howard Gay** of the New York Vigilance Committee and his associate **Oliver Johnson** at the offices of the *National Anti-Slavery Standard* newspaper in New York City, who forwarded them by train to the **Fugitive Aid Society of Syracuse, New York**. The Treasurer of the Syracuse society, **W. E. Abbott**, sent them to Samuel D. Porter of Rochester, New York, who immediately put them on a train to the suspension bridge over the Niagara River just north of **Niagara Falls**. Joe Bailey had been terrified for much of the trip. Bounty hunters had continued to track them. A deep scar on his face, described in the runaway reward advertisement, made him easily recognizable and compromised the group's safety. As they approached the suspension bridge, Tubman called out to her companions to look at the roaring falls. Joe was too nervous to look. When the train reached the Canadian side of the bridge, Tubman shouted out, "Joe, you're free!" Overcome with relief, Joe's shouts of joy and singing drew a crowd. Praising God for his good fortune, Joe told Tubman the next trip he planned would be to heaven. "You might have looked at the Falls first," Tubman replied, "and then gone to Heaven afterwards." The **freedom seekers** settled in Ontario. In the spring of 1858, Tubman introduced the Bailey brothers, **Peter Pennington**, and other **freedom seekers** from **Dorchester County** to **John Brown**. Though they initially agreed to join Brown on his raid on **Harpers Ferry**, they decided not to follow him in the fall of 1859. Joe and his brother Bill stayed in the St. Catharines area for an undetermined amount of time.

**BAILEY, WILLIAM "BILL"** (ca. 1824– unknown). Born enslaved in **Dorchester County, Maryland**, Bill and his brother **Josiah "Joe" Bailey**, **Peter Pennington**, and **Eliza Manokey** fled slavery with the help of **Harriet Tubman** in mid-November 1856. The Bailey brothers knew about **Harriet Tubman** and her rescue missions to the region to bring **freedom seekers** north. After Joe was assaulted and whipped by his enslaver, **William Hughlett** of **Talbot County**, the brothers decided to escape. Bill was enslaved by **John Campbell Henry** of **Cambridge, Maryland**, but had been leased to Hughlett to operate his steam mill.

One evening in the fall of 1856, Joe rowed six miles up the **Choptank River** from Hughlett's plantation on Jamaica Point to **Poplar Neck** in **Caroline County** where **Harriet Tubman**'s free father, **Ben Ross**, lived and worked as timber foreman for Dr. **Anthony C. Thompson**. Joe informed him that he and his brother were ready to escape the next time Tubman arrived from the North. Their friend **Peter Pennington** was enslaved by **Turpin Wright** on Wright's farm at Oyster Shell Point, across the **Choptank River** from Jamaica Point. **Eliza Manokey** was enslaved by Ann Martin Staplefort Grieves, who lived at **Church Creek** in Dorchester County. On 15 November 1856, Tubman led them North into Delaware. Bill was forced to leave behind his twenty-five-year-old wife and four small children. Bounty hunters chased the group, eager to collect the $2,600 reward for their arrest, including **John Campbell Henry**'s offer of $300 for the capture of thirty-two-year-old **Bill Bailey**. Such high rewards increased the danger of capture for the runaways. It took the group ten days to reach **Thomas Garrett** in Wilmington, Delaware, a trip that typically took only three days. **Slave catchers** forced them to proceed cautiously and remain hidden. They were "passed along by friends in various disguises" and were "scattered and separated" and led "roundabout" to a variety of **Underground Railroad** safe houses to avoid detection. Garrett learned they were trapped on the other side of the Christiana River, unable to cross the bridge into Wilmington because the authorities were watching. Garrett engaged the services of two Black bricklayers, who loaded their wagon and rode across the bridge in the morning, "singing and shouting" and greeting the police and others looking for the group. The bricklayers located Tubman and the **freedom seekers** and concealed them in a hidden compartment built into the wagon. The bricklayers proceeded back over the bridge, still "singing and shouting," successfully evading detection by the police and **slave catchers**.

One day later, on 26 November, the party arrived in Philadelphia at **William Still**'s office, who instantly sent them to **Sydney Howard Gay** of the New York Vigilance Committee and his associate **Oliver Johnson** at the offices of the *National Anti-Slavery Standard* newspaper in New York City. Before forwarding them by train to the **Fugitive Aid Society of Syracuse, New York**, Gay recorded an interview with Bill, who told him his alias would be William Smith. It does not appear that Bill took the new name once he reached freedom in Canada. The Treasurer of the Syracuse society, **W. E. Abbott**, sent them to Samuel D. Porter of Rochester, New York, who immediately put them on a train to the suspension bridge over the Niagara River just north of **Niagara Falls**. **Joe Bailey**'s prominent facial scar, described in the runaway reward advertisement, made him easily recognizable and compromised the group's safety. Bounty hunters had continued to track them. They safely made it across the suspension bridge to freedom. The **freedom seekers** settled in Ontario. In the spring of 1858, Tubman introduced the Bailey brothers, **Peter Pennington**, and other **freedom seekers** from **Dorchester County** to **John Brown**. Though they initially agreed to join Brown on his raid on **Harpers Ferry**, they decided not to follow him in the fall of 1859. Bill and his brother Joe stayed in the St. Catharines area for an undetermined amount of time.

**BANKS, WILLIAM "BILL"** (ca. 1807–unknown). Born in **Dorchester County, Maryland**, Banks was enslaved by **Anthony Thompson** of **Peter's Neck**, near **Madison**. He worked with **Ben Ross**, **Harriet Tubman**'s father, who was also enslaved by Thompson. Banks was married to **Eliza Manokey**, who was enslaved by Ann Martin Staplefort Grieves through an inheritance from her first husband, John Staplefort of the **Little Blackwater Bridge** area. Anthony Thompson died in 1836, and his son, Dr. **Anthony C. Thompson**, inherited Banks. Through a provision in **Anthony Thompson**'s estate, Banks was set free on 23 February 1846. He and Manokey had two enslaved children, Catherine and an unnamed boy who was sent to Missouri. When his wife escaped to freedom in the North in January 1856, he stayed in **Dorchester County, Maryland**.

**BARNES, JOSEPH K.** (21 July 1817–5 April 1883). Appointed surgeon general by Secretary of War Edwin Stanton in 1863, Barnes was instrumental in enforcing reforms in the recruitment of doctors for the army hospitals and mandated guidelines for the treatment of soldiers during the **Civil War**. At the close of the **Civil War** in the spring of 1865, Secretary of State **William Henry Seward** referred **Harriet Tubman** to Barnes, who appointed her "Nurse or Matron at the colored hospital" at **Fortress Monroe** in Hampton, Virginia. She soon reported on the poor medical care and high fatality rate for African American soldiers, which was two and half times greater than for whites.

**BARNETT, THOMAS** (1792–1849). A white farmer and slaveholder who managed several farms in and around **Bucktown, Maryland**. Sometime around 1835, **Harriet Tubman** was leased to Barnett to work in his fields. In the fall, Tubman had been assigned the chore of breaking flax, necessary to transform the outer shell of the flax shaft to release the fibers to make linen thread. Pieces of broken flax, Tubman later told interviewers, flew up into the air with dust and dirt and settled onto her unwashed hair. Called by the house cook to go to the local **Bucktown Village Store** to buy goods for the kitchen, Tubman took a shawl from the kitchen and wrapped her hair to hide the dirt. When she approached the store, one of Barnett's enslaved men, who was fleeing from Barnett's overseer, ran into the store. The overseer called to Tubman to stop the young man, but Tubman refused and stepped aside to let the man exit the door. The overseer threw a two-pound scale weight at the young man, but it hit Tubman in the head, cracking her skull and rendering her unconscious. The near-fatal head injury left her with epileptic seizures for the rest of her life.

**BAYLEY, MARIA** (ca. 1820–unknown). Born in Dorchester County, Maryland, Bayley was enslaved by **Anthony Thompson**. According to Thompson's will, executed after his death in 1836, Maria was to be set free when she turned thirty-seven years old. In 1842, **Ben Ross** purchased Maria's freedom from Thompson's son, Dr. **Anthony C. Thompson**

for ten dollars. Maria was married to freeman Isaac Bayley.

**BAYLY, ALEXANDER** (3 March 1814–14 March 1892). Born and raised in Cambridge, Maryland, Dr. Bayly lived on High Street where he practiced medicine and was involved in county politics. Bayly enslaved **Elizabeth "Lizzie" Amby**, who fled with her husband **Nat Amby** as part of the Stampede of Slaves in October 1859. Bayly placed a runaway reward advertisement in the *Cambridge Democrat* newspaper on 4 November 1857, offering a reward of $300 for her capture.

**BAYLY, JOSIAH, JR.** (5 May 1811–6 September 1888). Born and raised in Cambridge, Maryland, Bayly was a lawyer, a teacher, and the older brother of Dr. **Alexander Bayly**. Josiah Bayley married Mary Jane Thompson, the daughter of Dr. **Anthony C. Thompson**, in 1837. He was constantly in debt, likely from gambling. Early in his marriage, Bayly mortgaged the enslaved people his wife had been gifted by her father and quickly spent all the money. He was physically and emotionally abusive to Mary, so she divorced him in 1847. He died penniless in Alexandria, Virginia, in 1888.

**BAYLY, MARY ANN THOMPSON** (March 1821–unknown). Born in Talbot County, Maryland, Mary was the daughter of Dr. **Anthony C. Thompson**. In 1837, at the age of sixteen, Mary married **Josiah Bayly Jr.** of Cambridge. She divorced him in 1847 citing physical and emotional abuse. Mary would have known the Ross family, including **Harriet Ross Tubman**. On 21 October 1856, Mary's enslaved woman named "Laura" escaped from Baltimore. Bayly offered a $250 reward for her capture. Scholars believe Tubman planned the escape aboard the steamer *Kent* sailing from **Dugan's Wharf** in Baltimore. The rescue mission was well documented by **Thomas Garrett** of Wilmington, who identified the woman with Tubman as **Tilly**. Bayly later married Samuel Haddaway of Talbot County.

**BAZEL METHODIST EPISCOPAL CHURCH.** Located on Bestpitch Ferry Road, **Bucktown, Maryland**, this church sits in a one-acre clearing edged by the road and cultivated fields and the forested boundary of **Blackwater Wildlife Refuge**. Organized in 1876 as a Methodist Church by formerly enslaved African Americans in the Bucktown area, the building did not exist during **Harriet Tubman**'s time, though oral tradition suggests open-air worship services for free and enslaved Blacks occurred here during the antebellum period. Thomas Meredith, a landowner with sizable holdings in the area and the owner-operator of the **Bucktown Village Store** during the 1860s and 1870s, sold the quarter-acre lot for five cents to the local Black community for a church. The 21 February 1876 deed listed these church trustees: Moses Blake, Emory Pinder, Levin Cephas, Henry Cephas, Robert Standly, Samuel Hollis, Westly Brooks, Alexander Bazel, Nathaniel Bazel, and James W. Standly. The church halted services a few decades ago, but until recently, it remained open for special services and Juneteenth celebrations. The current building, constructed in 1911, replaced an earlier 1876 structure.

**BELL, DINAH.** *See* JACKSON, DINAH BELL.

**BELL, ROBERT** (ca. 1800–unknown). Bell was sheriff of Dorchester County during the 1850s and 1860s. He served an arrest warrant on Reverend **Samuel Green** at his home on 4 April 1857. After searching Green's home, Bell discovered letters from Green's fugitive son, **Sam Green Jr.**; train schedules; maps; and a copy of *Uncle Tom's Cabin*. Bell arrested Green under suspicion of aiding the **Dover Eight** and other freedom seekers escaping slavery.

**BENSON, STEPHEN ALLEN** (21 May 1816–24 January 1865). Born free to free parents in **Cambridge, Maryland**, Benson moved to **Liberia** in Africa with his family in 1822 as part of a scheme developed by the **American Colonization Society** to move free Blacks back to Africa. They were joined by several families from **Maryland**. He eventually was elected vice president in 1853 and president of **Liberia** in 1856. He died on his coffee plantation in 1865.

**BESS (dates unknown).** Likely born in Africa, Bess was enslaved by John Pattison, **Atthow Pattison**'s father. When John Pattison died in 1776, he gifted Bess to Atthow. When Atthow died, he gave Bess and another enslaved woman named **Suke** to his daughter, **Elizabeth Pattison**. It is likely these enslaved women were related to **Harriet Tubman**'s mother, **Harriett "Rit" Green Ross**. According to Pattison's will, his heirs were legally bound to set Bess, Suke, and Rit free when they reached the age of forty-five years old. It is not known if they were **manumitted**.

**BIG DIPPER.** A group of seven bright stars in the constellation **Ursa Major** in the Northern Hemisphere night sky. The configuration of the stars is similar to a ladle or dipper with a handle. The two stars forming the outer edge of the dipper bowl, Merak and Dubhe, are known as the pointer stars because they direct viewers to **Polaris**, also known as the North Star. Tracing a line from Merak to Dubhe, the tip of the dipper, points one directly to the North Star. The North Star is the last star on the tip of **Ursa Minor**, also known as the **Little Dipper**. The North Star is an important navigational tool, and **Harriet Tubman** used it to guide her on her **Underground Railroad** rescue missions.

**BLACK JACKS.** Slang in the eighteenth and nineteenth centuries for free and enslaved African and African American seamen. **Harriet Tubman** relied on their vast, trusted networks of communication and transportation during her years operating on the **Underground Railroad**.

**BLACKWATER AND PARSONS CREEK CANAL COMPANY.** Organized in about 1809 and authorized by the Maryland state legislature, the canal company was established to raise funds to cut a canal through the forests and marshes to connect Parson's Creek with the headwaters of the **Blackwater River** in **Dorchester County, Maryland**, for the purpose of easing the transportation of timber and agricultural goods from that area of the county. *See also* STEWART'S CANAL.

**BLACKWATER NATIONAL WILDLIFE REFUGE (BWNWR).** Established in 1933 in South Dorchester County as a haven for migratory birds, the refuge manages 28,000 acres of tidal marsh, forest, fields, and freshwater wetlands and shares some boundaries and significant landscapes within the **Harriet Tubman Underground Railroad National Park and Monument**. The **Harriet Tubman Underground Railroad State Park and Visitor Center** and National Park headquarters is on Key Wallace Drive within a mile of BWNWR Visitor Center.

**BLACKWATER RIVER, DORCHESTER COUNTY, MARYLAND.** The Blackwater River and the Little Blackwater River flow through three local swamps, the Gum, the Kentuck, and the Moneystump, and they sit at the heart of the **Blackwater National Wildlife Refuge**. They provided navigable water in the region for transportation of people and goods, as well as serving as important food resources. **Anthony Thompson** enslaved **Harriet Tubman**'s father, **Ben Ross**, on his plantation along this river, where Tubman herself was born. During the early 1800s, the **Blackwater and Parsons Creek Canal Company** built **Stewart's Canal** through the forests and marshes to connect Parson's Creek with the headwaters of the Blackwater River for the purpose of easing the transportation of timber and agricultural goods from that area of the county. Tubman and her family traveled along this river to visit with family and friends. It also facilitated numerous escapes by **freedom seekers**. Today, the river and its estuarine marshland ecosystem is an important stop along the Atlantic Flyway, a migratory bird route from Canada to Florida.

**BLAKE, MOTT (ca. 1840–unknown).** Born enslaved in Santee, South Carolina, Blake was a member of **Harriet Tubman**'s group of men who spied on Confederate forces and relayed information to Union officers during the **Civil War**. The other scouts were **Isaac Hayward, Peter Burns, Gabriel Cahern, Sandy Sellers, George Chisholm, Solomon Gregory, Walter**

D. Plowden, and river pilots **Charles Simmons** and **Samuel Hayward**. Under Tubman's command, the group was considered by **General Rufus Saxton** to be among "the most valued scouts and pilots in the Gov't employ in" Hilton Head, South Carolina. How Blake escaped slavery or came to work on Hilton Head Island is unknown. He was working as a groomsman and stableman, managing the horses of Union soldiers on Hilton Head Island, South Carolina, when he joined Company B of the Twenty-first USCT on 21 October 1864. He mustered out on 25 April 1866 in Charleston, South Carolina.

**BLONDO, RICHARD A.** Author of "Samuel Green: A Black Life in Antebellum Maryland," a master of arts thesis written for a graduate degree program in history at the University of Maryland in 1988. The thesis documents of the life of Reverend **Samuel Green**, an **Underground Railroad** agent who assisted more than twenty-five **freedom seekers** who escaped from Dorchester County, Maryland, including **Harriet Tubman** and at least twelve of her refugees. A copy is available online at the Maryland State Archives.

BLOOMER, AMELIA (27 May 1818–30 December 1894). An American **abolitionist**, women's rights advocate, and newspaper publisher, Bloomer created a style of women's wide-legged pants known as "Bloomers." Derided by men and women of her time, her goal was to create clothing less restrictive and cumbersome than the full and heavy dresses of the 1850s. **Harriet Tubman** requested a pair of Bloomers in a letter to **Franklin Sanborn** after her famous **Combahee River Raid** during the **Civil War**. She thought they would be more practical in the battlefields of the South than a dress.

BOSTON VIGILANCE COMMITTEE (1841–1861). An antislavery organization established in Boston to provide resources, including money, jobs, housing, medical care, and transportation, to **freedom seekers** who arrived in the city. They formed subcommittees to provide protection to self-liberators who were being followed by **slave catchers** and bounty hunters, through physical force or legal aid to prevent the kidnapping or arrest of a formerly enslaved person. Over a twenty-year period, the committee secured help for hundreds of individuals. They also colluded with Underground Railroad agents and vigilance committees in other communities, including New York City, and were involved in several violent confrontations with slaveholders, **slave catchers**, and the authorities. The committee aided several **freedom seekers** from the Eastern Shore of Maryland.

"BOUND FOR THE PROMISED LAND." A Methodist spiritual, also known as the "Goodbye Song," that **Harriet Tubman** sang on the evening of her escape in the fall of 1849 as a signal to her family that she was escaping. She tried to tell them herself, but their enslaver, Dr. Anthony Thompson, rode up to the yard when Tubman was trying say good-bye to her family because she was running away to freedom. Desperate to leave, she sang this song in the hopes that her family would realize her song was a code and that the doctor would not. The spiritual is also known as "**On Jordan's Stormy Bank,**" and it was written and composed by Samuel Stennett and first published in 1787.

When that thar ole chariot comes,
I'm goin' to leave you;
I'm boun' for the promised land,
I'm goin' to leave you.
I'm sorry I'm goin' to leave you,
Farewell, oh farewell;
But I'll meet you in the mornin',
Farewell, oh farewell.
I'll meet you in the mornin',
Safe in the promised land,
On the other side of Jordan,
Boun' for the promised land.

*BOUND FOR THE PROMISED LAND: HARRIET TUBMAN, PORTRAIT OF AN AMERICAN HERO.* (New York: Random House, 2004.) Written by Kate Clifford Larson, *Bound* was one of several Harriet Tubman biographies written by historians in the early twenty-first century. Using newly unearthed documents and other historical resources, the biography reveals a more accurate history of Tubman's life.

**BOUNTY HUNTERS.** *See* SLAVE CATCHERS.

**BOWLEY, ARAMINTA (ca. 1850–after 1890).** Born enslaved in **Dorchester County, Maryland**, Araminta escaped with her parents, **John** and **Kessiah Jolly Bowley**, and her brother, **James A. Bowley**, in December 1850. When she returned to Dorchester County after the Civil War, she married a man named Hayes.

**BOWLEY, BINAH (ca. 1789–ca. 1885).** Born in **Dorchester County, Maryland**, she and her children, **John**, Richard, Major, Harriet, and Terry Bowley, were enslaved by **Levin Stewart**, a merchant and shipbuilder from Tobacco Stick, Maryland. Stewart set them free through a deed of **manumission** on 17 July 1817, which required the Bowley family to serve a set term of years for Stewart and his heirs before being freed. Binah became free in 1827, at the age of thirty-eight. She was in her nineties when she died sometime around 1885 in **Dorchester County**.

**BOWLEY, HARKLESS (1856–December 1942).** Born free in Chatham, Ontario, Canada, Bowley was the fifth child of **Kessiah Jolly Bowley** and **John Bowley** and the grandson of **Harriet Tubman**'s sister **Linah Ross Jolly**. After Tubman helped **John Bowley** rescue Kessiah from the auction block in **Cambridge, Maryland**, in 1850, the Bowley family fled to safety and freedom in Canada. After the **Civil War** in 1867, Harkless and his family moved to Auburn, New York. They lived with **Harriet Tubman**, and Harkless worked in the brickyard behind her house. They moved back to **Cambridge, Maryland**, in 1869.

During the late 1870s, Harkless, who had been well educated in Canada and Auburn, operated a grocery store and taught in a segregated Black school. Harkless married Rachel (surname unknown) before 1880; they had several children. She died before 1895 when Bowley married Mary J. (surname unknown). He lived in Washington, D.C., for several years from the 1890s through the early 1900s, then settled near Baltimore, Maryland. His correspondence with **Earl Conrad** in 1938 and 1939 offered firsthand accounts of **Harriet Tubman** and her family during the 1850s and 1860s.

**BOWLEY, JAMES ALFRED (ca. 1844–30 January 1891).** Born enslaved in **Dorchester County, Maryland**, James was the son of **Kessiah Jolly Bowley** and **John Bowley** and was the grandson of **Harriet Tubman**'s sister **Linah Ross Jolly**. It was Tubman's deep love for her family that propelled her to return to slave territory in Maryland to rescue them. The Bowleys were the first people Tubman helped escape. In December 1850, six-year-old James; his infant sister, **Araminta Bowley**; and their mother, Kessiah, were set to be sold at auction at the county courthouse. Through a bold and daring plan contrived by Tubman and their free father, John, James and his family escaped in broad daylight from the courthouse steps—a feat so remarkable that rare testimony from shocked white witnesses remains preserved in a Maryland archive.

Once free in Philadelphia, Tubman worked long hours as a domestic to secure James a coveted education while his parents and baby sister moved on to Chatham in Ontario, Canada. Denied the right to learn to read and write letters herself, Tubman knew that formal literacy was its own liberation. Slave hunters roaming Philadelphia's streets eventually forced James to join his refugee family in Canada, while Tubman stepped up her missions of emancipation in Maryland. At age nineteen, Bowley left Canada and joined the U.S. Navy and waged battle against slavery during the **Civil War**.

Like his aunt, Bowley committed himself to a life of service, settling in Georgetown, South Carolina, in 1866, where he worked with newly freed people as a teacher. Supported by the **Freedmen's Bureau** and resources raised by Tubman and her allies nearly one thousand miles away in Auburn, New York, Bowley expanded educational opportunities for many. Elected to South Carolina's House of

Representatives, he served his Georgetown constituents from 1869 to 1873. He also served as a trustee of the University of South Carolina. After passing the bar, he became the second African American lawyer to appear in Georgetown's courts. He founded and published the *Georgetown Planet*, an African American newspaper, in 1873. He married Laura Clark, a formerly enslaved woman and a teacher, and they raised their family in Georgetown. He died there in 1891. A National Register of Historic Places Historical Marker commemorates Bowley's life and legacy outside his former home, now private, on King Street in Georgetown.

**BOWLEY, JOHN (ca. 1816–before 1897).** Born in **Dorchester County, Maryland**, Bowley was enslaved by **Levin Stewart** of **Madison, Maryland**. Bowley; his mother, **Binah Bowley**; and siblings Richard, Major, Harriet, and Terry Bowley were set free through a deed of **manumission** on 17 July 1817, which required the Bowley family to serve a set term of years for Stewart and his heirs before being freed. The Bowley brothers were apprenticed as ship carpenters, a skill that enabled them to earn high wages. John married **Kessiah Jolly** around 1844. In 1847 he was **manumitted** by Stewart's heirs. Though legally free, his wife, Kessiah, and children, **James Alfred** and **Araminta Bowley**, remained enslaved by **Edward Brodess** and his family. With **Harriet Tubman**'s help, John was instrumental in planning and executing the rescue and escape of his family from slavery in December 1850.

The Bowleys settled in Chatham, Ontario, Canada, in 1851. After a brief stay in Auburn, New York, in 1867, the Bowleys moved back to **Dorchester County, Maryland**. In 1868, Bowley rescued the sons of **Harriet Tubman**'s brother, **John Stewart**, who were **indentured** against their will by **Thomas Haddaway** and **Sarah Thompson Haddaway** in Talbot County. **John Ross Stewart Jr.** and **Moses Ross Stewart** moved to Auburn, New York, to live with their father. Bowley died sometime between 1888 and 1897.

**BOWLEY, KESSIAH JOLLY (ca. 1824–1897).** Born enslaved, Bowley was the eldest daughter of **Linah Ross Jolly** and **Harkless Jolly**. Her enslaver, **Edward Brodess**, frequently separated the Jolly family when he leased them to labor for other **Dorchester County** farmers. She married **John Bowley** before 1844, when their son, **James Alfred Bowley**, was born. **John Bowley** was **manumitted** in 1847, but Kessiah and their son remained enslaved. **Edward Brodess's** widow, **Eliza Keene Brodess**, advertised to sell Kessiah in the *Cambridge Democrat* at the **Dorchester County Courthouse** on 10 September 1849. The sale was postponed while Brodess petitioned the court to allow the sale to move forward. It is believed that **John Bowley** negotiated a delay until December 1850, giving him time to plan their escape from slavery. At the auction, Bowley bid on Kessiah, son James, and newborn child **Araminta Bowley**. He won the bidding but fled with his family before the auctioneer called for payment. He sailed his family in a small boat to Baltimore, where **Harriet Tubman** met them and secreted them among friends and relatives living along the city's busy waterfront. Tubman secured passage for them along the **Underground Railroad** from Baltimore to Philadelphia and then to Chatham, Ontario, Canada, where they stayed until 1867. Kessiah and John had six more children. She died in **Cambridge, Maryland**, in 1897.

**BOYCE, HENRY (1797–1 March 1873).** Born in Ireland, Boyce settled in Rapides Parish, Louisiana, to practice law and run a vast cotton plantation with his wife, Irene. Typical of **Deep South** planters in need of labor, Boyce traveled to the Chesapeake to purchase enslaved people directly from **Upper South** enslavers to avoid paying higher prices commanded by professional **slave traders**. In October 1828, Boyce purchased twelve enslaved people in **Dorchester County, Maryland**, including men, women, and children as young as eighteen months old. By 1860, he owned 6,000 acres of land with 332 slaves on his Louisiana plantations. A supporter of the

Confederacy, his property was burned during the **Civil War**. He died in his rebuilt home in 1873.

**BRADFORD, SARAH HOPKINS (20 August 1818–25 June 1912).** A writer, poet, and avocational historian, Bradford wrote fiction, nonfiction, poetry, children's books, and short stories, often under the pen name Cousin Cicely. A resident of Geneva, New York, she interviewed **Harriet Tubman** in Auburn, New York, for a biography published that year as *Scenes in the Life of Harriet Tubman*. This biography also included "Essay on Woman Whipping," written by her brother, Reverend **Samuel Miles Hopkins Jr.** The success of the biography provided desperately needed income to Tubman. In 1886 Bradford rewrote the biography and added new information gleaned from additional interviews with Tubman and published it under the title *Harriet, the Moses of Her People*. This biography was reprinted in 1897 and again in 1901 with even more stories she gathered from Tubman.

**BRADSHAW HOTEL.** Located on High Street in **Cambridge, Maryland**, the hotel was established by John Bradshaw during the 1840s and served as a popular inn for **slave traders** from Maryland, Virginia, Kentucky, Georgia, and other southern states. Boarding for weeks at a time, traders had easy access to **slave auctions** at the **Dorchester County District Courthouse** across the street. Perched on the hotel's veranda, traders haggled with private sellers or bid on enslaved people placed for sale on the courthouse steps. The county jail, also located on High Street and across from the hotel, served as a holding area for recently purchased enslaved people.

**BRAINARD, DORSEY (ca. 1842–unknown).** Born in Maryland, Brainard, a farmer by trade, joined Company G, Eighth United States Colored Troops (USCT) on 23 September 1863 in Utica, New York. He served during the **Civil War** with **Harriet Tubman**'s second husband, **Nelson Charles Davis**. Brainard, then living in East Syracuse, New York, served as a witness on 16 October 1894, in support of Tubman's widow application for Davis's veteran's pension.

**BRANNOCK, WILLIS (1819–3 February 1884).** Born in **Dorchester County**, Brannock was a farmer and one of the slaveholders whose enslaved persons, **Solomon Light** and **George Light**, escaped with twenty-six others during the Stampede of Slaves, on 24 October 1857. Brannock died in **Dorchester County**.

**BRICKLER, ALICE LUCAS (21 October 1899–19 December 1990).** Born and raised in Auburn, New York, by her parents **Margaret Woolford Stewart** and **Henry Lucas**, Alice was a great-niece of **Harriet Tubman**. On 12 June 1914, at a memorial celebration, Alice was chosen to unveil a memorial plaque in Tubman's honor, donated by the residents of Auburn "in recognition of her unselfish devotion to the cause of humanity." The bronze tablet, bearing the likeness of Tubman in her later years, was inscribed with the following: "In Memory of Harriet Tubman. Born a slave in Maryland about 1821. Died in Auburn, New York, March 10, 1913. Called the 'Moses' of her people during the Civil War, with rare courage, she led over three hundred Negroes up from slavery to freedom and rendered invaluable service as nurse and spy. With implicit trust in God, she braved every danger and overcame every obstacle; withal she possessed extraordinary foresight and judgment so that she truthfully said – 'On my Underground Railroad I nebber run my train off de track and I nebber lost a passenger.' This tablet erected by the citizens of Auburn, 1914." After leaving Auburn and marrying Dr. Alexander Brickler, Alice continued her own career as a teacher and librarian. Her correspondence with **Earl Conrad** in 1939–1941 provided unique, firsthand accounts of Tubman and her family. The family owns one of Tubman's pistols and her Grand Army of the Republic Woman's Relief Corps medal, which Tubman wore proudly during her lifetime.

**BRINKLEY, NATHANIEL (1818–1875).** Born in Kent County, Delaware, Brinkley was a farmer and entrepreneur who owned property at Brinkley Hill, a free Black community on the north side of Camden in Kent County. He and his brother **William Brinkley**, and neighbor **Abel Gibbs**, were **Underground Railroad** agents who helped **Harriet Tubman**, among others. She later said she felt "safe and comfortable" hiding in their homes during her escape missions. He died in 1875.

**BRINKLEY, WILLIAM (1815–5 January 1887).** Born in Kent County, Delaware, Brinkley was a farmer and entrepreneur who owned property at Brinkley Hill, a free Black community on the north side of Camden in Kent County. He and his brother **Nathanial Brinkley**, and neighbor **Abel Gibbs**, were **Underground Railroad** agents who helped **Harriet Tubman**, among others. She later said she felt "safe and comfortable" hiding in their homes during her escape missions. He wrote letters to Underground Railroad agent **William Still** in Philadelphia recording his activities helping **freedom seekers**. He drove members of the **Dover Eight** to Wilmington after they had escaped **Thomas Otwell** at the Dover jail. He was also responsible for bringing members of the Stampede of Slaves, who escaped slavery in **Dorchester County, Maryland**, during October 1857. He died in 1887.

**BRODESS, EDWARD (14 June 1801–March 1849).** Born in **Dorchester County, Maryland**, on the small plantation of **Elizabeth Pattison**, his maternal grandmother, on the banks of the **Little Blackwater River**, he was the first and only child of **Joseph Brodess** and Mary Pattison Brodess. Edward's father, Joseph, died in 1802, and his mother, Mary, married widow **Anthony Thompson** of **Peter's Neck** in 1803. Mary and Edward moved six miles west of the Pattison farm to Thompson's thousand-acre plantation along the **Blackwater River**. Mary brought several enslaved people with her, including **Harriet "Rit" Green**, **Harriet Tubman's** mother, whom Mary had inherited from her grandfather, **Atthow Pattison**, in 1797, and four men she inherited from **Joseph Brodess**: Samuel, Frederick, Shadrack, and an unknown fourth man.

Thompson was wealthier and more successful than Joseph Brodess. In addition to his large plantation, he enslaved nine people, including **Ben Ross**, Harriet Tubman's father. After Mary's death around 1810, Edward inherited **Rit Green**, who had married **Ben Ross** in 1808; a small, unimproved 250-acre farm near **Bucktown** once owned by his father, **Joseph Brodess**; and four enslaved men. Thompson raised young Edward, providing him with fine clothing and a private education. Between 1820 and 1822, Thompson used Brodess's small inheritance to build a small house in anticipation of Brodess's impending adulthood and need to establish his own home. A rift between Brodess and his stepfather soured their relationship, and they parted on bitter terms sometime between the summer of 1822 and the winter of 1824.

In March 1824, Brodess married **Eliza Anne Keene**. They settled into Brodess's small cottage on his farm near **Bucktown** and raised eight children together: John E., Joseph, Richard, Charles, Benjamin, Thomas, Mary Ann Eliza, and Henrietta Mariah. Brodess was never a successful farmer, and when he died in March 1849, he left Eliza in deep debt.

**BRODESS, ELIZA ANN KEENE (ca. 1806–ca. 1859).** Born in **Dorchester County, Maryland**, Eliza was the third daughter of John and Catherine Keene. She married **Edward Brodess** in March 1824. They had eight children together: John E., Joseph, Richard, Charles, Benjamin, Thomas, Mary Ann Eliza, and Henrietta Mariah. After her husband's death in 1849, Eliza found herself in debt. She petitioned the **Dorchester County** court to allow her to sell her enslaved people to raise funds to pay her debtors. This compelled **Harriet Tubman** and her brothers **Henry Ross** and **Ben Ross Jr.** to escape slavery on 17 September 1849. On 3 October 1849, Eliza posted a reward advertisement in the local newspaper offering a $300 payment for the capture and return of the three siblings. Eliza died at the age of fifty-three in 1859.

**BRODESS FARM.** Near Bucktown, Maryland. **Edward Brodess** inherited this property and lived here during the second quarter of the nineteenth century, moving here after **Harriet**

**THREE HUNDRED DOLLARS REWARD.**

RANAWAY from the subscriber on Monday the 17th ult., three negroes, named as follows: HARRY, aged about 19 years, has on one side of his neck a wen, just under the ear, he is of a dark chestnut color, about 5 feet 8 or 9 inches hight; BEN, aged about 25 years, is very quick to speak when spoken to, he is of a chestnut color, about six feet high; MINTY, aged about 27 years, is of a chestnut color, fine looking, and about 5 feet high. One hundred dollars reward will be given for each of the above named negroes, if taken out of the State, and $50 each if taken in the State. They must be lodged in Baltimore, Easton or Cambridge Jail, in Maryland.

ELIZA ANN BRODESS,
Near Bucktown, Dorchester county, Md.
Oct. 3d, 1849.

☞The Delaware Gazette will please copy the above three weeks, and charge this office.

Runaway reward advertisement for Harriet Tubman (Minty) and her two brothers. The three siblings returned shortly after this ad was posted because they were confused about which way to go and fearful of being caught. Tubman fled again, alone, shortly afterward. *Cambridge Democrat* newspaper, 3 October 1849. *Courtesy Bucktown Village Foundation, Bucktown, Maryland*

Tubman's birth. Situated on the south side of Greenbriar Road about a mile west of the **Bucktown Village** crossroads and the **Bucktown Village Store**, the Brodess farm is one of the most significant sites of the Tubman landscapes on the Eastern Shore. Tubman spent little time here with her family because Brodess leased Tubman, her mother, and siblings to area farmers throughout her childhood. After Brodess's death in 1849, his farm passed to his wife, **Eliza Ann Keene Brodess**, and then his sons. The Brodess family maintained control of the farm into the early twentieth century. The original circa 1823 house is no longer extant. An early twentieth-century structure located at the south end of a dirt lane from Greenbriar Road is a private hunting lodge. A public roadside pull-off and Harriet Tubman Underground Railroad Byway signage offer visitors interpretation at the private, gated entrance to the farm.

**BRODESS, JOSEPH.** Married to Mary Pattison Brodess and the father of **Edward Brodess**. He died on his mother-in-law's farm on the **Little Blackwater River** in 1802.

*BRODESS V. THOMPSON.* In June 1820, the Orphans Court of Dorchester County gave authorization to **Anthony Thompson** to proceed with the construction of a house, "a single story 32 by 20 [ft.] two rooms below with two plank floors and brick chimney, and also a barn of good material" for his stepson and ward, **Edward Brodess**, on the Brodess's inherited farm in **Bucktown, Maryland**. At a cost of thirteen hundred dollars, the improvements to Brodess's property exceeded the value of his inheritance. In 1823, when Thompson demanded reimbursement for funds spent to build the house, purchase expensive clothing, and manage Brodess's enslaved people, the court found in Thompson's favor, but Brodess appealed. In 1828, Maryland's Court of Appeals agreed with Brodess, charging the Orphans Court had exceeded its legal authority and had, in effect, encumbered Brodess's estate beyond what was legally allowed. *Brodess v. Thompson* is still referred to in legal matters related to guardianship.

**BROOKS, ELIZABETH (1867–1951).** Born in New Bedford, Massachusetts, to a formerly enslaved mother. A teacher, civic rights activist, suffragist, and social reformer, Brooks was a lifelong advocate of African American education and the first African American teacher in New Bedford. She attended the founding convention meeting of the suffrage organization **National Association of Colored Women's Clubs** in Washington, D.C., in 1896, with **Harriet Tubman**. Brooks later recalled hearing the story of Tubman using a pistol to threaten **freedom seekers** giving up hope and wanting to return to slavery because of exhaustion. She recalled that **Henry Carrol**, a runaway from Maryland who took flight with Tubman, wanted to stop for a rest, even though **slave catchers** were closing in quickly. Harriet told him, "Go on or die," and he quickly moved along.

**BROOKS, E. U. A.** Reverend Brooks spoke at **Harriet Tubman**'s funeral service. He also coauthored, with James E. Mason, *Tribute to Harriet Tubman, the Modern Amazon* (Auburn, NY: Tubman Home, 1914).

**BROWN, JOHN (9 May 1800–2 December 1859).** A radical American **abolitionist** and insurrectionist. Born in Torrington, Connecticut, Brown was raised in an antislavery household. A deeply religious man, he publicly denounced and pledged his life to destroying slavery. Convinced that slaveholders would not give up their financial, political, and social power, he realized that only through bloodshed would slavery be rooted out of American soil. In 1849 he moved his wife, Mary, and their thirteen children to a farm in North Elba, New York, where industrialist and philanthropist **Gerrit Smith** had distributed thousands of acres to African Americans in support of self-sufficiency and land ownership that enabled Black men in New York to vote.

After the passage of the Kansas-Nebraska Act in 1854, which opened up Nebraska and Kansas territories to development and future statehood and repealed the Missouri Compromise of 1820 that banned slavery above latitude 36°30' north, pro- and antislavery settlers raced to establish residency. The act gave settlers "popular sovereignty" to vote on whether to allow slavery or not. Brown traveled to Kansas and joined his sons and other antislavery settlers determined to create a free state. The war on slavery there became known as "Bleeding Kansas." In response to proslavery violence, Brown led antislavery forces to exact retribution at both Pottawatomie Creek and Osawatomie in the summer of 1856, earning him the nickname "Osawatomie Brown." Brown's son Frederick, however, was killed.

**James Montgomery**, later a colonel in the Union Army during the **Civil War**, worked with Brown and admired him. During this time, Brown began formulating plans for an armed raid on the federal arsenal at **Harpers Ferry**, Virginia, to take control of thousands of guns and supplies of munitions. He hoped to inspire an insurrection by liberating enslaved people, arming them, and overthrowing the governments of slave states. With support from a small group of wealthy and powerful northern abolitionists known as the **Secret Six**, Brown began planning and recruiting followers, and in the spring of 1858, he traveled to St. Catharines, Ontario, Canada, to meet **Harriet Tubman** and ask for her advice and support. She readily embraced his plans and recruited some of the **freedom seekers** she had brought north from the **Eastern Shore of Maryland**, including **Thomas Elliott, Peter Pennington, Denard Hughes, Josiah Bailey,** and **William Bailey**. Brown was so impressed with Tubman's genius and courage he referred to her as "General Tubman." Brown expected her to join him when he attacked the arsenal in October 1859, but she was traveling in Massachusetts and may have fallen ill in New Bedford, precluding her participation in his raid. Her recruits failed to join Brown as well.

The attack commenced on 16 October and was initially successful—Brown and his men seized arms from the arsenal, cut telegraph lines, and took hostages. By the morning of the 18th, Brown and his men were surrounded by U.S. Marines. When an offer to surrender was made, it was ignored, and the soldiers shot and killed Brown's sons Watson and Oliver. During the brief battle that ensued, Brown's men killed four and wounded nine, while eight more of his died. Five escaped, including his son Owen, and seven were captured with Brown. A brief investigation revealed evidence implicating the **Secret Six** and **Harriet Tubman**, and she was secretly rushed to Canada for protection and avoid arrest. Brown was hanged on 2 December 1859. Tubman told her friend **Edna Dow Littlehale Cheney**, "I've been studying and studying upon it, and its clar to me, it wasn't John Brown that died on that gallows. When I think how he gave up his life for our people, and how he never flinched, but was so brave to the end; its clar to me it wasn't mortal man, it was God in him. When I think of all the groans and tears and prayers I've heard on the plantations, and remember

John Brown shortly before his raid on Harpers Ferry, Virginia, in the fall of 1859. He called Harriet Tubman "General Tubman." She thought he was the greatest white man who ever lived. Martin M. Lawrence, photographer. *Library of Congress Prints and Photographs Division*

that God is a prayer-hearing God, I feel that his time is drawing near."

**BROWN, WILLIAM WELLS (ca. 1814–6 November 1884).** Brown, a prominent **abolitionist**, author, part-time homeopathic healer, and former **freedom seeker**, was born enslaved in Kentucky and escaped in 1838. In 1860, he went to Canada and interviewed some of **Harriet Tubman**'s friends and family members who had fled north with her during the 1850s. They told him that Tubman had the "charm." The "whites can't catch Moses," they told Brown, "cause you see she's born with the charm. The Lord has given Moses the power." He published these quotes in his 1873 book *The Rising Son or The Antecedents and Advancements of the Colored Race*. He died in Massachusetts in 1884.

**BUCHANON, MRS. [LIKELY SARAH] (1815–unknown).** Though not specifically identified in historical records, Mrs. Buchanon is likely Sarah Buchanon, a free Black boarding-house owner on Lombard Street in Philadelphia during the 1840–1860s. **William Still** paid Mrs. Buchanon to board **freedom seekers** who arrived at his office in Philadelphia.

**BUCKTOWN VILLAGE, DORCHESTER COUNTY, MARYLAND.** Organized as a village with town lots in the 1780s, the village became a small but important crossroads in the heart of south **Dorchester County**. In the early to mid-nineteenth century, the village was a larger community than today, with a general dry goods store at its center, a blacksmith and wheelwright, and numerous residences and small farms.

**BUCKTOWN VILLAGE STORE.** A general dry goods store at the center of commercial and social activity in **Bucktown Village** at the intersection of Greenbrier and Bestpitch Ferry roads. The store is one of the most significant and still-extant buildings associated with **Harriet Tubman** in the region. The site features one of Tubman's first acts of defiance, when, circa 1835, she endured a severe blow to her head that fractured her skull and nearly killed her. This injury caused lifelong health problems, leaving her suffering from epileptic seizures and headaches for the rest of her life.

A store at this location dates to at least 1826 and possibly earlier. The Bucktown store sold china, kitchenware, textiles, various flours, sugar, seeds, corn meal, tobacco, medicines like Worm Pills, and other goods. The store remained the only merchant business at the crossroads until the late 1840s or 1850s. The store was renovated and expanded during the 1860s, the 1890s, and several times during the twentieth century. **Harriet Tubman Underground Railroad Scenic Byway** interpretive signage welcomes visitors, and the store is open to visitors most days and by appointment.

**BURNS, PETER (dates unknown).** Born enslaved in South Carolina, Burns became a scout for the U.S. Army during the **Civil War**. He was a member of **Harriet Tubman**'s group of men who spied on Confederate forces and relayed information to Union officers. The other scouts were **Isaac Hayward**, **Mott Blake**, **Gabriel Cahern**, **Sandy Sellers**, **George Chisholm**, **Solomon Gregory**, and **Walter D. Plowden**, along with river pilots **Charles Simmons** and **Samuel Hayward**. Under Tubman's command, the group was considered by General **Rufus Saxton** to be among "the most valued scouts and pilots in the Gov't employ in" Hilton Head, South Carolina.

**BUSTILL, CHARLES (ca. 1815–ca.1890).** A member of the prominent Black Bustill family of Philadelphia, Bustill was a painter and plasterer. An **abolitionist**, Bustill was a member of the **Philadelphia Vigilance Committee** and worked as an **Underground Railroad** agent. He sheltered **Sam Green Jr.** in his home on 28 August 1854.

**BUTTONS CREEK.** Located in **Church Creek, Maryland**, Buttons Creek flows through Button's Neck south to the **Blackwater River** and is situated between Buttons Neck Road and Golden Hill Road, just west of the **Harriet Tubman Underground Railroad State Park Visitor Center** and east of the **Anthony Thompson** plantation site. The area hosts the site of **Jane Kane**'s escape from the former Horatio Jones plantation on Christmas Eve 1854.

# C

**CABIN CREEK.** A stream in **Dorchester County, Maryland**, that flows into the Choptank River, north of East New Market. Landowners on either side of the creek could transport their harvests of wheat, corn, and peaches to markets around the Chesapeake Bay. The creek is the site of the 26 April 1856 escape of four freedom seekers: Benjamin Jackson, **Henry Hopkins, William A. Cook**, and **James Coleman**. They were led to freedom by **Harriet Tubman**.

**CAHERN, GABRIEL** (dates unknown). Born enslaved in South Carolina, Cahern became a scout for the U.S. Army during the **Civil War**. He was a member of **Harriet Tubman**'s group of men who spied on **Confederate** forces and relayed information to Union officers. The other scouts were **Isaac Hayward, Mott Blake, Peter Burns, Sandy Sellers, George Chisholm, Solomon Gregory**, and **Walter D. Plowden**, along with river pilots **Charles Simmons** and **Samuel Hayward**. Under Tubman's command, the group was considered by General **Rufus Saxton** to be among "the most valued scouts and pilots in the Gov't employ in" Hilton Head, South Carolina.

**CAMBRIDGE 28.** A group of **freedom seekers** who escaped from several enslavers in and near **Cambridge, Maryland**, on the night of Saturday, 24 October 1857. The self-liberators included fifteen who fled from **Samuel Pattison**. They were **Kit and Leah Anthony** and their three small children, Adam, Mary, and one-year-old Murray; **Sarah Jane Hill**; her brother **Joseph Hill**; **Susan and Joe Viney** and their four young children, Lloyd, Frank, Albert(a), and nine-month-old J. W.; and Joe's three older sons, Henry, Joe, and Tom. Joseph Hill's free wife and son, Alice and Henry, joined them. They escaped together with seventeen more people from neighboring plantations, including **Aaron and Daffney Cornish** and six of their eight surviving children, Solomon, George Anthony, Joseph, Edward James, Perry Lake, and a two-week-old infant; **Solomon Light; George Light; Marshall Dutton**; and **Silas Long**. The freedom seekers were chased by **slave catchers** seeking to cash in on the thousands of dollars in reward money posted for their capture. They successfully eluded arrest and made their way through Delaware, Pennsylvania, and New York. They safely settled in St. Catharines, Ontario, Canada. The group was later known as the **Cambridge 28**. This escape came just one week after the escape of **Lizzy and Nat Amby, Caroline and Daniel Stanley**, Hannah Peters, William Griffen, Henry Moore, James Camper, Noah Ennals, and Levin Parker on 17 October 1857. Together, these two large escapes became known as the Stampede of Slaves.

**CAMBRIDGE, MARYLAND.** Established in 1663 as the county seat for **Dorchester County, Maryland**.

**CAMP MEETING.** Camp meetings were a form of outdoor communal worship in Methodist religious services. Generally held during the late spring through early fall, thousands of Christian believers gathered for days- or weeks-long events, which featured itinerant preachers, singing, baptisms, conversions, and other social and spiritual connections. Congregants traveled for miles to attend meetings, staying in tents, wagons, or temporary structures wherever they were held. In the Chesapeake region, camp meetings were well attended by both whites and Blacks (free and enslaved). On the **Eastern Shore**, camp meetings were often held in the **Choptank River** region at sites in **Dorchester** and **Caroline counties**, including **Madison**, Taylor's Island, Ennals Springs, **Bucktown**, and **Marsh Creek**. Attendees from Baltimore and the western shore of Maryland eagerly traveled to meetings in the area. Meeting sites needed to have access to fresh drinking water, shade trees, and transportation by water and roads. Notices appeared in newspapers announcing the next camp meeting site, usually on land owned by devout and well-to-do Methodist plantation owners. **Harriet Tubman**'s family attended meetings. Enslaved people sometimes took advantage of such gatherings to escape. **William Cornish**, an enslaved man from **Madison** who later escaped to Canada while attending a meeting at **Marsh Creek** in **Caroline County**, was allowed by his confident enslaver to travel as far away as Baltimore and "stay a week or two ... to go to a camp meeting." Tubman reportedly tried to rescue her brothers during "Camp Meeting time" in the summer of 1854, but they could not escape at that time.

CANNON, PATTY (ca. 1765–11 May 1829). Born Martha "Patty" Handley in **Dorchester County, Maryland**, she married carpenter Jesse Cannon in 1787. For twenty years, the Cannons engaged in kidnapping and selling free and enslaved people, a practice known as the Reverse **Underground Railroad**. Their home sat on a crossroads nestled between three counties: Sussex County, Delaware, and **Caroline** and **Dorchester counties** in Maryland. They engaged several family members and in-laws in their illegal business, too, and became known as the Cannon-Johnson Gang. Long suspected of multiple crimes, including murder, Patty was finally arrested in the spring of 1829 after several bodies, including two enslaved infants, a six-year-old boy, and a Georgia slave trader, were unearthed on her farm. She died in prison awaiting trial in Delaware. Two of her associates were imprisoned, but her Johnson and Cannon relatives fled to Alabama and elsewhere, avoiding prosecution. The kidnapping of free and enslaved Blacks continued throughout the antebellum period, striking fear in Black communities throughout the **Upper South** and free states in the North. The criminal history of the Cannon-Johnson gang became mythologized over the decades after Patty's death, but twenty-first-century research has revealed the scope of the criminal enterprise engaged in by the Cannon-Johnson family.

CAPE MAY, NEW JERSEY. A seaside resort town on the northside outlet of the Delaware Bay on the southwest coast of New Jersey in Cape May County. It became a popular summer destination for middle- and upper class whites and Blacks during the 1830s through the mid-1900s. **Harriet Tubman** worked in one of the hotels in the town during the summer of 1852 and possibly other times as well. Cape May offered opportunities and resources that benefited Tubman: Black maritime networks that helped provide clandestine communication and transportation crucial to successful escape missions; higher wage-earning opportunities in the summer resort's bustling hotels; and access to Black antislavery elites and Underground Railroad supporters from Philadelphia, Pennsylvania, and New York who summered in the resort community's Black neighborhood. She could blend easily with other Black hotel and restaurant employees. Tubman earned about $16 a month. She conducted one rescue mission while in residence in Cape May during the fall of 1852. No more information is known about this event.

CAROLINE COUNTY, MARYLAND. A county on the **Eastern Shore of Maryland**. It was created out of **Dorchester** and Queen Anne's counties in June 1773. It is bound by the **Choptank River** to the west, **Dorchester**

County to the south, and Kent and Sussex counties in Delaware.

**CARROL, HENRY (dates unknown).** A **freedom seeker** whose history remains obscure. According to **Elizabeth Brooks** of New Bedford, Massachusetts, Carrol escaped from Maryland with **Harriet Tubman**'s help. He grew tired and footsore and wanted to stop for a rest, even though **slave catchers** were closing in quickly. Tubman told him, "Go on or die," and he quickly moved along.

**CARTER, FLORENCE (ca. 1865–ca. 1942).** A friend and supporter of **Harriet Tubman**'s during her older years in Auburn, New York. Carter corresponded with **Earl Conrad** in 1939–1940 and provided important information to Conrad about Tubman's life and family.

**CATOR, JANE (ca. 1837–unknown).** Cator and her family enslaved dozens of people in **Dorchester County, Maryland**. On 28 October 1857, twenty-eight enslaved men, women, and children escaped away from the homes near **Cambridge, Maryland**. Cator and her stepfather, Reuben E. Phillips, enslaved **Daffney Cornish** and her six children she took with her that night. The following summer, in July 1858, Daffney's son **William Henry Cornish** fled but was captured and reenslaved.

**CATT, CARRIE CHAPMAN (9 January 1859–9 March 1947).** Catt was an American woman suffragist, who, as the president of the **National American Woman Suffrage Association**, helped push the movement to the final passage of the **Nineteenth Amendment** giving American women the right to vote. She was notable, also, for her racism. In 1939, **Earl Conrad** contacted Catt to inquire about **Harriet Tubman**'s role in the suffrage movement. Catt's shameful, dismissive attitude toward Tubman and the contributions of any woman of color stands in marked contrast to the true history of Black women's role in the movement.

**CENTRAL PRESBYTERIAN CHURCH, AUBURN, NEW YORK.** Central Presbyterian Church was founded in 1861 when sixty-six antislavery members walked out of the Second Presbyterian over the issue of slavery. The congregation built its church on land behind **William Henry Seward**'s home in Auburn, New York. Harriet Tubman and **Nelson Charles Davis** were married there on 18 March 1869 in a ceremony officiated by Reverend Henry Fowler.

**CHAPMAN, MARIA WESTON (25 July 1806–12 July 1885).** Born in Weymouth, Massachusetts, Chapman was an active **abolitionist** and one of the founding members of the Boston Female Anti-Slavery Society with **Lydia Maria Francis Child**. She worked for the *National Anti-Slavery Standard* and **William Lloyd Garrison**'s *Liberator*. In early June 1859, Chapman wrote a letter of introduction for **Harriet Tubman** to fellow **abolitionist** Sarah Arnold of New Bedford. Tubman was hoping to raise money to help support her family in the home she had just purchased in Auburn, New York, from **William Henry Seward**. In the same letter, Chapman suggested that Tubman could be persuaded to help rescue the children of an unidentified man named Charles.

**CHARLES, NELSON.** *See* DAVIS, NELSON CHARLES.

**CHASE, JOHN (ca. 1844–unknown).** Born in Dorchester County, Maryland, Chase was enslaved by **John Campbell Henry**. Chase fled with **Harriet Tubman** and her brothers **Ben Ross Jr., Robert Ross,** and **William Henry Ross** and friends **Jane Kane, Peter Jackson,** and others on **Christmas Day 1854**. While hiding on Christmas Eve in the fodder house on the **Poplar Neck** plantation belonging to **Dr. Anthony C. Thompson**, where **Ben** and **Rit Ross** lived, Tubman told Chase and Jackson to go to her parents' cabin and ask Ben to secretly bring them some food without alerting Rit of their escape plans. When Chase and the others made their way to **William Still**'s office, an **Underground Railroad** agent in Philadelphia, Chase told Still his new name was Daniel Lloyd. They reached Canada and freedom, though no more information is known of Chase's fate.

**CHENEY, EDNAH DOW LITTLEHALE (27 June 1824–19 November 1904).** A Boston abolitionist, writer, reformer, and suffragist. Active in antislavery activism, Cheney met Harriet Tubman in the late 1850s at a meeting in the city. She was involved in the Freedmen's Aid Society and traveled to South Carolina after the Civil War to help support Freedmen's Schools. She wrote a lengthy biographical essay about Tubman titled "Moses" for the *Freedmen's Record* in 1865. *See* appendix D for the article.

**CHILD, LYDIA MARIA FRANCIS (11 February 1802–7 July 1880).** Born in Medford, Massachusetts, and raised in a home that valued the education of women, Child grew up aspiring to be a writer and reformer. After marrying abolitionist and lawyer David Child in Boston, she became intimate with a circle of powerful abolitionists, including William Lloyd Garrison. Her writing featured arguments in favor of emancipation of both women and enslaved people. She was a founding member of the Boston Female Anti-Slavery Society and became one of the most prolific antislavery writers of the antebellum period. During the early 1840s, Child and her husband became coeditors of the *National Anti-Slavery Standard*, the official publication of the American Anti-Slavery Society. After John Brown's death in 1859, Child helped raise funds to support his grieving family. In 1861, Child edited and published *Incidents in the Life of a Slave Girl*, a memoir by formerly enslaved Harriet Jacobs. Child knew Harriet Tubman from her visits to Boston and connections with New England abolitionists like William Lloyd Garrison and Ednah Dow Littlehale Cheney. She quoted Tubman in a letter to author and poet John Greenleaf Whittier in 1862. She continued to advocate for equal rights for African Americans and women until her death in 1880.

**CHION, EMILY.** *See* KIAH, EMILY.

**CHION, WILLIAM.** *See* KIAH, WILLIAM "BILL."

**CHISHOLM, GEORGE (dates unknown).** Born enslaved in South Carolina, Chisholm became a scout for the U.S. Army during the Civil War. He was a member of Harriet Tubman's group of men who spied on Confederate forces and relayed information to Union officers. The other scouts were as follows: Isaac Hayward, Mott Blake, Peter Burns, Sandy Sellers, Solomon Gregory, Gabriel Cahern, and Walter D. Plowden, along with river pilots Charles Simmons and Samuel Hayward. Under Tubman's command, the group was considered by General Rufus Saxton to be among "the most valued scouts and pilots in the Gov't employ in" Hilton Head, South Carolina.

**CHOPTANK INDIAN TRIBE.** Long before Europeans and Africans arrived in the Chesapeake region, the Eastern Shore of Maryland was home to Algonquin-speaking peoples, including the Choptank, Nanticoke, Manokin, and Pokomoke people. During the mid-seventeenth century, these Indians fought European intrusion and struggled to maintain community and cultural independence. The Choptanks included subgroups called (by English colonizers) the Ababco, Hatsawap, and Transquaking, a subgroup of the Ababcoes.

When Europeans arrived in the early 1600s, the largest Choptank village was located just north of present-day Cambridge, with large and significant burial and ceremonial sites just northwest of Cambridge at Sandy Hill and at the current site of the Dorchester County Courthouse on High Street in Cambridge. Colonists recognized "Choptank lands" encompassing landscapes along the Choptank River, from Jenkins Creek (Sandy Hill) northeast to at least Secretary Creek, if not farther north. These lands extended from the Choptank River south to the Little Blackwater River and east to the Transquaking River and include another ossuary (burial mound) site known as Indian Bone about three miles northeast of Bucktown. Smaller villages were located farther north near present-day Choptank Village, Potters Landing, and Denton in Caroline County.

Though living near each other, the Nanticoke and Choptank Indians recognized that they were distinctly different people and worked to maintain a fragile peaceful coexistence. They negotiated for separate, independent reservations that contained thousands of acres along the Choptank and Nanticoke Rivers during the early to mid-seventeenth century. The Choptank tribe faced extinction due to European plunder, inequitable treaties, and attrition through disease, famine, and out-migration. Those who stayed faced constant efforts to Christianize them. By the mid-eighteenth century, the few remaining Choptanks had intermarried with white colonists and enslaved Africans, and eventually their presence on the landscape declined.

**CHOPTANK LANDING, MARYLAND.** Also known as **Medford's Wharf** during the nineteenth century, the landing is located along the **Choptank River** near Preston in **Caroline County, Maryland**. The small river port is situated between the former **Dr. Anthony C. Thompson** plantation at **Poplar Neck** along **Marsh Creek** to the northwest and Hunting Creek to the southeast.

**CHOPTANK RIVER.** A major tributary of the Chesapeake Bay, the Choptank River was an important pathway and barrier for **freedom seekers** making their way from the **Eastern Shore of Maryland** to free soil in states to the north and beyond. During the antebellum period, the Choptank was traversed by only three bridges, all located upriver in **Caroline County**. The towns and villages along the river were devoted to merchant shipping, shipbuilding, and slave trading. The sixty-eight-mile long river, from its headwaters near the Delaware border in **Caroline County, Maryland**, to the Chesapeake Bay between **Dorchester** and Talbot counties, was the site of numerous escape attempts—some successful, others unsuccessful—during the seventeenth, eighteenth, and nineteenth centuries. Rivers and streams served as guides for people seeking freedom in the north. Following the Choptank northeast to the Delaware border brought **freedom seekers** within a day's travel to freedom in Pennsylvania. Using their own maritime skills, relying on the aid of other mariners, or secreting themselves aboard vessels sailing along the river, **freedom seekers** used a variety of resources to utilize the river as their means of escape from slavery. Some simply sailed, rowed, swam, or waded across the river to continue their land-based journey to freedom, while others used the waterway itself as a significant resource to facilitate their escapes via maritime networks throughout the greater Chesapeake and Atlantic world.

**CHRISTMAS DAY 1854, ESCAPE OF HARRIET TUBMAN'S BROTHERS.** Three brothers, **Ben Ross Jr.**, **Robert Ross**, and **William Henry Ross**, and friends **Jane Kane**, **Peter Jackson**, and others escaped slavery with **Harriet Tubman**'s help on Christmas Day 1854. While hiding on Christmas Eve in the fodder house on the **Poplar Neck, Caroline County, Maryland** plantation belonging to Dr. **Anthony C. Thompson** and where parents **Ben Ross Sr.** and **Rit Green Ross** lived, Tubman told Chase and Jackson to go to her parents' cabin and ask Ben Sr. to secretly bring them some food without alerting Rit of their escape plans. Ben did so without arousing Rit's suspicions. The next night, Christmas Day, Ben wrapped a scarf around his eyes and accompanied his children and the others down the road on their first part of their journey on the **Underground Railroad**. He did not want to see them so that if asked by the **slave catchers** if he had seen his sons he would not have to lie. When the group made their way to **William Still**'s office in Philadelphia, each of the brothers took freedom names. Ben Jr. became **James Stewart**, Robert became **John Stewart**, and Henry became **William Henry Stewart**. They reached Canada and freedom.

**CHURCH CREEK, MARYLAND.** Situated on a tributary of the same name on the Little Choptank River, seven miles west of **Cambridge**, the town was the original settlement site of the **Anthony Thompson** family in 1681 on a tract of land called White Haven. The town, with its sheltered cove and access to the Chesapeake, supported early shipbuilding and merchant shipping. One of the oldest Episcopal churches in America, Trinity P.E. Church, was built here in 1696.

**CIVIL WAR, AMERICAN (1861–1865).** Began in April 1861, with the firing on Fort Sumter, a U.S. federal property in the Charleston, South Carolina, harbor, by a newly created confederacy of separatist states organized as the **Confederate States of America**. Their goal was to preserve the right to enslave people of African descent. Decades of tension with the more industrialized, free Northern states over the expansion or limitation of slavery in territories to the west culminated in a bloody civil war. After the election of **Abraham Lincoln** in 1860, thirteen Southern slave states seceded from the United States. The war ended in April 1865 when the Union Army soundly defeated the **Confederate** forces. The war cost nearly 800,000 lives and left much of the South in ruin. More than four million enslaved people were liberated, and slavery was abolished.

**CLARKE, JAMES B. (1888–unknown).** Born in the West Indies, Clarke was a student at Cornell University when he interviewed **Harriet Tubman** in Auburn, New York. He was actively soliciting funds to help support the **Harriet Tubman Home for the Aged**, and he hoped to encourage giving with an article, "An Hour with Harriet Tubman," he published in 1911. He captured some of Tubman's last recorded words and stories.

**COBB, HARRIET (24 May 1839–1932).** In August 1897, **Harriet Tubman** met with Wilbur Siebert in **Cambridge**, where she was staying with Dr. Harriet Cobb. Siebert was compiling evidence for his lengthy volume on the **Underground Railroad**. During his interview with Tubman at Cobb's residence, he noted that Tubman was "considerably aged and worn," but he wrote, "Her mind was still clear." He noted at that time that she would often doze off at "frequent intervals" of every half hour or so for a few minutes, then regain consciousness and carry on "without losing the thread of the conversation." Little is known of Cobb's life.

**CODED MESSAGES.** On the Underground Railroad, freedom seekers, station masters, conductors, and others along paths to freedom from slavery used codes to conceal communication. **Harriet Tubman** used a code when communicating by letter to **Jacob Jackson** when she referenced a Christian spiritual, "Old Ship of Zion," telling Jackson to inform her brothers to "be ready to step aboard the old ship of Zion" when it comes by. Her brothers understood she was returning to Maryland to rescue them. Tubman also sang specific spirituals, including "**Hail, oh Hail Ye Happy Spirits**," "**Moses Go Down to Egypt Land**," and "**Bound for the Promised Land**," to signal her intentions or inform **freedom seekers** in her care that it was safe or not safe to follow her. **Underground Railroad** participants sometimes wrote letters to each other using railroad terminology to hide their true intent. For instance, they referred to freedom seekers as "bales" of cotton or wool or as "packages." During the twentieth century, the history of coded messages on the Underground Railroad became corrupted by myths, which inflated the use and types of coded messages beyond historical reality.

**COHEN, EARL.** *See* CONRAD, EARL.

**COLEMAN, JAMES (dates unknown).** One of four men who escaped from **Cabin Creek** north of East New Market, Maryland, with **Harriet Tubman** on 26 April 1856. Coleman and Benjamin Jackson were enslaved by Isaac Henry Wright, whose plantations included some of the largest peach farms in the region. The third **freedom seeker**, **Henry Hopkins**, was enslaved by John Houston, and the fourth, **William A. Cook**, was enslaved by Levin Hodson. Tubman had led them safely to New Castle, Delaware, but bounty hunters eager for the high rewards for their capture slowed them down, forcing them to stay hidden for several days. **Thomas Garrett** in Wilmington, Delaware, was able to finally forward them to **William Still**, an **Underground Railroad** agent in Philadelphia. Still noted their arrival after they sought shelter with **Mrs. Buchanon** and forwarded them on to agent **Sydney Howard Gay** of New York City, who wrote that "Captain Tubman" had arrived safely with the men on May 14th. He sent them on to Syracuse, New York, where they received help getting to Canada, where they settled among other freedom seekers they knew.

**COLONIZATION MOVEMENT.** A scheme developed by the **American Colonization Society** beginning in 1817 that promoted the idea that all free African Americans should move to Africa. Popular among conservative whites and Blacks and slaveholders, the movement had some success in convincing a few free Blacks to emigrate. The society provided transportation and resettlement costs to a few thousand individuals. The movement was instrumental in establishing the colony of Liberia in Africa. Ultimately, the movement proved ineffective. Most free African Americans preferred to stay in America. **Harriet Tubman**, Rev. **Samuel Green**, and many Northern **abolitionists** opposed the movement.

**COLORED CONVENTIONS.** Established in 1830 as a national movement to organize African Americans. These conventions—both national and state-wide meetings—addressed political and social issues specific to the needs of Black communities, including the immediate end to slavery. In 1855, **Harriet Tubman** attended the Colored National Convention held at Franklin Hall in Philadelphia, along with Reverend **Samuel Green** and his wife, **Catherine (Kitty)**, and numerous Northern Black **abolitionist** leaders. While there, Tubman, the Greens, and many other convention attendees visited Passmore Williamson at the nearby Moyamensing Prison. For more information on Colored Conventions, see https://coloredconventions.org/.

**COLORED PEOPLES CHURCH.** In East New Market, Maryland.

**COMBAHEE RIVER.** Named for a local indigenous tribe living in the area during the colonial contact period, the Combahee River in South Carolina flows forty miles southeast through Colleton and Beaufort counties and empties into St. Helena Sound near Beaufort, South Carolina. The river supported thousands of acres of rice plantations before the **Civil War** and was the route for **Harriet Tubman's** famous **Combahee River Raid** with Colonel **James Montgomery** in June 1863.

**COMBAHEE RIVER RAID (2 June 1863).** A well-executed and successful raid into **Confederate**-held territory in southeastern South Carolina during the **Civil War**. Using intelligence she gathered with the male scouts who worked for her, **Harriet Tubman** led Colonel **James Montgomery** and his **Second South Carolina Colored Volunteers** regiment up the **Combahee River** in two steamboats. They disabled mines placed in the water, routed out enemy forces, raided plantation warehouses, burned homes, flooded rice fields, and liberated 727 enslaved people. Newspapers later reported that Harriet Tubman, "the Black She-Moses," conducted the successful raid.

**"COME ALONG, COME ALONG."** This song, also known as "Uncle Sam's Farm," was written and performed by the famous abolitionist performers the Hutchinson Family Singers and was popular during the 1850s. Harriet Tubman sang "Come Along, Come Along" during the **Combahee River Raid** in June 1863 to calm anxious enslaved people fleeing plantations for the protection of the Union Army steamboats. Their frantic efforts to escape threatened to sink the rowboats lined up on shore to take them to safety downriver. The lyrics include:

"Of all the mighty nations in the East or in the West,
O this glorious Yankee nation is the greatest and the best.
We have room for all creation and our banner is unfurled,
Here's a general invitation to the people of the world.
Then come along, come along, make no delay;
Come from every nation, come from every way.
Our lands, they are broad enough—don't be alarmed,
For Uncle Sam is rich enough to give us all a farm."

RAID OF SECOND SOUTH CAROLINA VOLUNTEERS (COL. MONTGOMERY) AMONG THE RICE PLANTATIONS ON THE COMBAHEE, S. C.—[SEE PAGE 427.]

Harriet Tubman and her team of scouts guided Colonel James Montgomery through the mined waters of the Combahee River during a successful raid in June 1863. From *Harper's Weekly*, 4 July 1863. *National Portrait Gallery, Smithsonian Institution*

***COMMONWEALTH, THE*** **(1862–1880).** An antislavery newspaper published in Boston during the **Civil War**. **Franklin B. Sanborn**, one of **John Brown**'s co-conspirators and a member of Brown's **Secret Six**, became its second editor (1862–1867) within months of its founding. Sanborn wrote the first biographical sketch of **Harriet Tubman**, publishing it in the 17 July 1863 issue of *The Commonwealth*. After the **Civil War**, the newspaper continued to publish works by famous reformers and civil rights advocates. In 1880, the newspaper changed hands and became known as *The Boston Commonwealth*. It ceased publication in 1896.

**CONFEDERACY, THE.** *See* CONFEDERATE STATES OF AMERICA.

**CONFEDERATE STATES OF AMERICA.** Commonly referred to as the Confederacy, the Confederate states seceded from the United States over the issue of slavery and started the **Civil War**. Between 8 February 1861 and the end of May 1861, the following states broke away and formed the Confederacy: South Carolina, North Carolina, Virginia, Georgia, Alabama, Florida, Mississippi, Louisiana, Arkansas, Kentucky, Tennessee, Missouri, and Texas.

**CONNOWAY (CONOWAY), WILLIAM A.** *See* COOK, WILLIAM ANDREW.

**CONRAD, EARL (17 December 1906–17 January 1986).** Born Earl Cohen in Auburn,

New York, to a large Jewish family, Conrad's early interest in writing emerged when he became a high school reporter for the local *Auburn Citizen-Advertiser* newspaper. In 1932 he moved to New York City, where he worked as a journalist under the name Conrad so that his articles would not be rejected because of rampant anti-Semitism in the publishing industry. Working as a teamster union organizer in Harlem, he became the Harlem bureau chief for the *Chicago Defender*, a national African American newspaper for which he investigated lynchings in the south. Conrad worked as a Federal Writer's Project author and held strong socialist and communist political views and sympathies during the 1930s.

In 1938 he began researching a full-length biography of Tubman. He told Tubman's nephew, **Harkless Bowley**, that through his work organizing truck drivers on New York City's waterfront during the Great Depression and after studying Black history, he determined **Harriet Tubman** was the greatest African American historical figure who deserved a modern biography. Numerous mainstream publishers turned down his manuscript. Finally, **Associated Publishers** in Washington, D.C., founded by the African American historian and creator of Black History Month, **Carter G. Woodson**, agreed to publish the biography. Because Conrad was able to interview individuals who knew Tubman when she was alive, he documented many lost and forgotten stories of her life. Conrad was critical of Tubman's first biographer, **Sarah H. Bradford**, but he also perpetuated some of Bradford's exaggerations and myths.

Released as *Harriet Tubman* in 1943, Conrad's book laid the foundation for fictionalized juvenile biographies that emerged during the late 1940s and 1950s, including Dorothy Sterling's *Freedom Train: The Story of Harriet Tubman* and Ann Petry's *Harriet Tubman, Conductor on the Underground Railroad*. Later, Conrad donated all of his Tubman research and writing materials to two institutions where the collections remain accessible to the public: the **Earl Conrad Papers**, Cayuga Community College, Bourke Memorial Library, Auburn, New York, and the **Earl Conrad/Harriet Tubman Collection**, at the Schomburg Center for Research in Black Culture, New York Public Library. His collections remain some of the most important archival collections related to documenting Harriet Tubman's life, and his work proved to be integral to twenty-first century biographies by Jean Humez, Kate Clifford Larson, Milton Sernett, and **James McGowan**. Conrad wrote more than twenty books and pamphlets in addition to articles and essays for newspapers and magazines over his fifty-year career as a journalist. Conrad died on 17 January 1986 in La Jolla, California, from complications of lymphoma. His life and work is celebrated for his contributions to Tubman studies at the Memorial Garden at the **Harriet Tubman Underground Railroad State Park and Visitor Center** in **Church Creek, Maryland**.

**COOK, JAMES (dates unknown).** When **Harriet Tubman** was a small child, Cook, a yeoman farmer, hired her from **Edward Brodess** to learn weaving and collect muskrats from his traps in the nearby marsh. His home site is presumed to be at the intersection of Maple Dam Road and Greenbriar Road near the Little Blackwater River. Tubman may have stayed with the Cooks for as long as two years. Tubman became sick from being forced to manage Cook's traps in the cold winter marsh and was physically abused by Cook and his family.

**COOK, WILLIAM ANDREW (ca. 1831–unknown).** Formerly enslaved by Levin Hodson, Cook escaped slavery on 26 April 1856, with three other men and accompanied by **Harriet Tubman**. They left from a plantation along **Cabin Creek**, Maryland. Cook's companions were Benjamin Jackson and **James Coleman**, both enslaved by Isaac Henry Wright, whose plantation abutted **Cabin Creek** and included a large peach orchard, among the largest on the **Eastern Shore**. The fourth **freedom seeker**, **Henry Hopkins**, was enslaved by John Houston, from nearby Secretary, Maryland.

Hodson offered a $300 reward for Cook's capture. Tubman had led them safely to New Castle, Delaware, but bounty hunters eager for the high rewards for their capture slowed them down, forcing them to stay hidden for several days. **Thomas Garrett** in Wilmington, Delaware, was able to finally forward them to **William Still**, an **Underground Railroad** agent in Philadelphia. Still noted their arrival after they sought shelter with **Mrs. Buchanon** and forwarded them on to agent **Sydney Howard Gay** of New York City, who wrote that "Captain Tubman" had arrived safely with the men on May 14th. He sent them on to Syracuse, New York, where they received help getting to Canada, where they settled among other **freedom seekers** they knew.

CORNISH, DAFFNEY AND AARON (dates unknown). Members of a group of twenty-eight **freedom seekers** who escaped from enslavers in and near **Cambridge, Maryland**, on the night of Saturday, 24 October 1857. Aaron and Daffney took six of their eight children with them: Solomon, George Anthony, Joseph, Edward James, Perry Lake, and a two-week-old infant. Reverend **Levi D. Travers** enslaved Aaron, but **Jane Cator** and her stepfather, **Rueben Elliot Phillips**, enslaved Daffney and her children. Two of the Cornishes' children had to be left behind; as young teenagers, they had been leased to another white farmer, making it difficult for Aaron or Daffney to retrieve them the night of the escape.

The group of **freedom seekers**, later known as the **Cambridge 28**, successfully eluded arrest and made their way through Delaware, Pennsylvania, and New York. They safely settled in St. Catharines, Ontario, Canada. This escape came just one week after the escape of **Lizzy and Nat Amby**, **Caroline and Daniel Stanley**, Hannah Peters, William Griffen, Henry Moore, James Camper, Noah Ennals, and Levin Parker on 17 October 1857. Together, these two large escapes became known as the Stampede of Slaves. The Cornishes' son, **William Henry Cornish**, was captured after trying to escape the following July.

CORNISH, DELIA ANN (dates unknown). Wife of **William Cornish**. Delia escaped sometime after William fled in September 1856. She brought their two children with her and settled with William in St. Catharines, Ontario, Canada. By the fall of 1863, Delia had died along with three of their six children.

CORNISH, ESTHER. Born in Maryland and enslaved by Anne M. Dixon, Esther escaped on Saturday night, 24 July 1858, with **Mary Light, Charles Anthony Light, William Henry Cornish** (possibly related), **Solomon Cornish** (possibly related), **Thomas Rideout**, and **John Green**. Their white **Underground Railroad** conductor was an Irish immigrant and wood sawyer named **Hugh Hazlett**. The group was caught a few days later in **Caroline County, Maryland**, and brought to **Cambridge** via a steamboat, but a mob had gathered to await their arrival at Long Wharf. The sheriff feared a lynching, so he ordered the steamboat to leave Long Wharf and dock at another location upriver. Hazlett and the others were later safely secured in the Cambridge jail. Cornish was reenslaved by Dixon.

CORNISH, JOSEPH (ca. 1815–unknown). Born in Maryland, Cornish was enslaved by **Samuel W. LeCompte** of **Cambridge, Maryland**. A skilled blacksmith and a part-time minister in the **African Methodist Episcopal Church**, Cornish learned he was going to be sold. In December 1855, probably with the instructions provided by **Harriet Tubman**, Cornish escaped. He boarded a ship at Gilpin's Point in **Caroline County, Maryland**, and sailed to Philadelphia, where he was interviewed by **Underground Railroad** agent **William Still**. He successfully made his way to St. Catharines, Ontario, Canada. He left behind a free wife and five children. Their fates remain unknown.

CORNISH, SOLOMON. Born in Maryland and enslaved by Anne M. Dixon, Solomon escaped on Saturday night, 24 July 1858, in company with **Mary Light, Charles Anthony Light, William Henry Cornish** (possibly related), **Esther Cornish** (possibly related), **Thomas Rideout**, and **John Green**. Their white **Underground Railroad** conductor was an Irish immigrant and wood sawyer named **Hugh Hazlett**. The group was caught a few days later in **Caroline County, Maryland**, and brought to **Cambridge** via a steamboat, but a mob had gathered to await their arrival at Long Wharf. The sheriff feared the mob would lynch Hazlett, so he ordered the steamboat to leave Long Wharf and dock at another location upriver. Hazlett and the others were later safely secured in the **Cambridge** jail. Cornish was reenslaved by Dixon.

**CORNISH, WILLIAM** (ca. 1819–unknown). Born enslaved in **Dorchester County, Maryland**, William was a timber foreman, much like **Ben Ross**. His enslaver, Thomas Dail, died in May 1853, leaving his estate in debt and the Dail heirs arguing over assets, including Cornish and dozens of other enslaved people. Cornish believed he would be set free when Dail died, but he was deceived. Dail had not instructed his heirs to **manumit** Cornish as he had promised. At the time, Cornish was leased to **Dr. Anthony C. Thompson** at **Poplar Neck** and worked closely with **Ben Ross**. Ross used **Marsh Creek** to float timber to the **Choptank River**, where waiting vessels loaded milled boards and felled trees for market. Cornish had long hoped to be free and considered escaping, but his familial and community relationships made him hesitate when he had opportunities. He was able to earn additional income, which he used to make installment payments to the Dails for his freedom. In the summer of 1856, William's mother told him she heard he was going to be sold in spite of his payments. An unidentified Quaker, possibly **Arthur Leverton** or **Jonah Kelley**, advised him to escape, which he did, during a **Camp Meeting** at **Marsh Creek** in late August. Cornish took advantage of the Dails' trust in him—they allowed him, on occasion, to go as far away as Baltimore and "stay a week or two, or to go to a camp meeting," so they did not suspect he would run away. During his escape, he was helped by **Underground Railroad** agents in Maryland and Delaware. Cornish arrived in **William Still**'s office in Philadelphia on September 5th with **George Wilmer**, an enslaved **Underground Railroad** conductor from Kent County, Maryland, where they were both interviewed. Within days, Cornish was in Canada. His wife, **Delia Cornish**, and his two daughters joined him soon thereafter. Cornish was interviewed in 1863 by the **American Freedmen's Inquiry Commission**. He told them that his wife and three of his children (born in Canada) had died during an epidemic.

**CORNISH, WILLIAM HENRY** (dates unknown). Born in Maryland and enslaved by **Jane Cator**, William was likely the son of **Aaron and Daffney Cornish** who was left behind when the couple escaped from slavery in October 1857. William escaped on Saturday night, 24 July 1858, in company with **Mary Light, Charles Anthony Light, Esther Cornish** (possibly related), **Solomon Cornish** (possibly related), **Thomas Rideout**, and **John Green**. Their white **Underground Railroad** conductor was an Irish immigrant and wood sawyer named **Hugh Hazlett**. The group was caught a few days later in **Caroline County, Maryland**, and brought to **Cambridge** via a steamboat, but a mob had gathered to await their arrival at Long Wharf. The sheriff feared the mob would lynch Hazlett, so he ordered the steamboat to leave Long Wharf and dock at another location upriver. Hazlett and the others were later safely secured in the **Cambridge** jail. Cornish was reenslaved by Cator.

**COURSEY CREEK.** *See* STEWART'S CANAL.

**COWGILL, HENRY** (4 April 1812–27 October 1881). Oral tradition indicates that Cowgill, a Quaker **abolitionist**, and his family sheltered **freedom seekers** at his farm on Willow Grove Road between Sandtown and Camden, Delaware. During her 1897 interview with historian **Wilbur Siebert, Harriet Tubman** mentioned that she passed through Sandtown and "Will Grove" on her way to Camden and other Delaware towns on her escape missions north. **Underground Railroad** agent Samuel D. Burris lived near the Cowgills. At Camden, Tubman trusted free Blacks **Abraham Gibbs** and brothers **Nathaniel** and **William Brinkley**, who worked together to bring her and other **freedom seekers** further north, often by way of Dover, Smyrna, Blackbird, Odessa, New Castle, and Wilmington, Delaware.

**COX, JOHN (1786–1880) AND HANNAH (1797–1876).** **Underground Railroad** operators in the Longwood and Kennett Square community in Chester County, Pennsylvania. The Coxes sheltered members of the **Cambridge 28** during their escape in October 1857.

**CRAIG, ANN E. (ca. 1787–ca. 1862).** Born in Dorchester County, Maryland, Craig enslaved **Emily Kiah**, who fled slavery with her husband, **William Kiah**, and other members of the famous **Dover Eight** in March 1857.

# D

**D. M. OSBORNE & CO.** Founded in Auburn, New York, by David Munson Osborne and his business partner, William Kirby, the company manufactured agricultural tools and machinery. During the **Civil War** and afterward, the company employed many formerly enslaved people and **freedom seekers**, including **Harriet Tubman**'s brother **John Stewart**, as well as her second husband, **Nelson Charles Davis**, a **Civil War** veteran. The company became part of International Harvester Company.

**DAIL, THOMAS J. (1816–unknown).** Enslaved man **William Cornish** identified Dail and his brothers as heirs to their father's estate, which held Cornish in bondage. Cornish paid the Dail brothers several payments toward purchasing his freedom, but soon discovered the brothers schemed instead to sell him to pay estate debts. Cornish escaped while attending a **Camp Meeting** at **Marsh Creek** in **Caroline County, Maryland**, in late August 1856, denying the Dail brothers the proceeds of an impending sale.

**DAVIS, GERTRUDE "GERTIE" (ca. 1874–ca. 1900).** Adopted daughter of **Harriet Tubman** and her second husband, **Nelson Charles Davis**. Possibly of mixed-race heritage, little is known about her life. In November of 1892, she gave birth to a son, whom she named Nelson Charles Davis Jr. in honor of her father. The child died at two months old on 9 January 1893 from complications of syphilis. Gertie's fate remains unknown, although it is likely she died of the same disease.

**DAVIS, HARRIET ROSS TUBMAN.** *See* TUBMAN, HARRIET ROSS.

**DAVIS, NELSON CHARLES (ca. 1844–18 October 1888).** Born near Elizabeth City, North Carolina, Davis was enslaved by Frederick "Fred" M. Charles, a well-to-do farmer. Nelson was the son of Milford Davis, who was enslaved by another farmer, and an unidentified woman also enslaved by Charles. Nelson escaped slavery circa 1860 and reached central New York sometime in 1861. He enlisted in the Eighth United States Colored Troop Regiment in September 1863 at Rome, Oneida County, New York. The regiment participated in many significant battles and endured heavy losses during the **Civil War**. Nelson was spared serious injury and mustered out of the army at Brownsville, Texas, in November 1865.

He traveled immediately to Auburn, New York, where a friend and fellow soldier from his regiment, **Albert Thompson**, was living and working. Nelson boarded at **Harriet Tubman**'s home and fell in love. On 18 March 1869, Tubman, then a widow, and Davis were married at **Central Presbyterian Church** in Auburn by former abolitionist and friend Reverend Henry Fowler. News of the wedding was featured in all the local newspapers. Tubman and Davis adopted an orphaned baby girl in 1874. They named her **Gertrude "Gertie" Davis**.

Nelson worked as a brick maker and general laborer. There were several brickmaking operations in Auburn, including at least two abutting Tubman's property. Nelson became a Trustee of the local St. Mark's AME Church on

Harriet Tubman, circa 1870s, possibly around the time she and her husband Nelson Davis adopted a baby girl, Gertie Davis. Photo by Harvey B. Lindsley, Auburn, New York. *Collection of the National Museum of African American History and Culture and the Library of Congress Prints and Photographs Division*

Washington St. in Auburn. Though Davis was not seriously wounded during the **Civil War**, he contracted tuberculosis and died in 1888 at the age of forty-four years old. He is buried at Fort Hill Cemetery in Auburn, New York, with his grandson, two-month-old Nelson Davis Jr. (November 1892–9 January 1893), the son of Gertie Davis, and Tubman's nephew John Isaac Stewart (ca. 1856–3 March 1893). There is a **Civil War** veteran marker at his grave. He is not buried with Tubman, but her grave is close by.

**DAY, WILLIAM HOWARD (16 October 1825–3 December 1900).** Born in New York City, Day was educated in Northampton, Massachusetts. An **abolitionist**, publisher, minister, and teacher, Day traveled with some of the most important and powerful leaders of his day, including **Henry Highland Garnet** and **John Brown**. Day graduated from Oberlin College in 1847 and later received a DD from Livingston College. During the 1850s he worked as a reporter and editor for various newspapers in Ohio and published his own newspaper, the *Aliened American*, from 1852 to 1855. He moved to Canada in 1857, setting up a print shop in St. Catharines where he printed Brown's pamphlet outlining the Provisional Constitution for his visionary free state in May 1858. Brown corresponded with Day that spring regarding **Harriet Tubman**'s whereabouts. Day spent the **Civil War** in England but returned in 1865 to work with the **Freedman's Bureau**. He was committed to establishing schools throughout the South for black children. He later became a minister in the **African Methodist Episcopal Zion Church** and was in Auburn, New York, to preside over the dedication ceremonies for **Thompson Memorial African Methodist Episcopal Zion Church** in 1892. Day remained a lifelong friend with Tubman.

**DEEP SOUTH.** A region of the United States that generally includes South Carolina, Georgia, Florida, Alabama, Mississippi, Louisiana, Texas, and Arkansas.

**DENTON, MARYLAND.** Situated along the **Choptank River**, Denton is the county seat and largest town in **Caroline County, Maryland**. During the eighteenth and nineteenth centuries, Denton was the center of commerce on the upper **Choptank River**.

The earliest known photograph of Harriet Tubman, aged about forty-six years old, taken in the Auburn, New York, studios of Benjamin F. Powelson ca. 1868. It is likely that Tubman posed for this portrait on the eve of the publication of her first biography, *Scenes in the Life of Harriet Tubman* by Sarah H. Bradford, in November 1868, a few months before she married veteran Nelson Charles Davis. Collection of the National Museum of African American History and Culture and the Library of Congress Prints and Photographs Division

**DEPARTMENT OF THE SOUTH.** A military zone established by the US armed forces during the American **Civil War** that encompassed South Carolina, Georgia, and Florida. On 7 November 1861, the Union Navy captured two forts at the mouth of Port Royal Bay, on the southeastern coast of South Carolina.

Confederate forces and many civilians fled from the area, leaving behind plantations, storehouses, and enslaved people. Claiming the Sea Islands and the whole Port Royal district, including Hilton Head Island, St. Helena's Island, and Beaufort districts, Union forces secured a vital position from which to launch offensive raids throughout the region. **Harriet Tubman** arrived there to begin her work as a spy and scout in late January 1862.

**DEPEE, NATHANIEL W.** (ca. 1810–unknown). Lived in Philadelphia, Pennsylvania, and was a member of the Acting Committee of the **Philadelphia Vigilance Committee**, along with **William Still** and **James Miller McKim**. Depee sheltered **freedom seekers** in his home on Lombard Street. He aided **Harriet Tubman** and the four men she rescued in May 1856. *See also* COLEMAN, JAMES; HOPKINS, HENRY; AND COOK, WILLIAM ANDREW.

**DEPENDENT PENSION ACT OF 1890.** Passed by the U.S. Congress, the act provided benefits to any disabled **Civil War** veterans or their widows and dependents. It greatly expanded the original pension plan that provided compensation only to veterans suffering with disabilities related to war service. **Harriet Tubman** was able to apply for a Dependent Pension as the widow of veteran **Nelson Charles Davis**. It took Tubman five years to navigate the approval process because Davis had changed his surname from Charles, which he used when he joined the Eighth United States Colored Troops during the war. Dozens of friends, family members, and Union officers testified as to the veracity of Davis's identity and Tubman's claim. She was finally awarded $500 retroactively in October 1895.

**DOMESTIC SLAVE TRADE.** *See* SLAVE TRADE, U.S. INTERSTATE.

**DORCHESTER COUNTY, MARYLAND.** Established in 1669, Dorchester is the largest county on the **Eastern Shore of Maryland**. The county is bordered by the **Choptank River** to its north, the Chesapeake Bay to the west, the **Nanticoke River** to the south, **Caroline County** to the northeast, and Sussex County, Delaware, to the east. Its county seat is **Cambridge, Maryland**. **Harriet Tubman** and her family lived and worked here for a portion of their lives.

**DORCHESTER COUNTY COURTHOUSE.** On High Street in **Cambridge, Maryland**. Built in 1852 after a fire destroyed an earlier building, the courthouse was the site of numerous slave auctions and court cases related to **Harriet Tubman**, her family, and **Underground Railroad** associates and events. The fire, set by an unknown arsonist in May 1852, destroyed a great portion of the county's historical records. The documentary gaps in the historical past created by that fire have hampered efforts to chronicle Tubman's family story—and the cultural and historical accounts of African American families before that date—more fully. These records include probate, tax, chattel, **manumission**, and other court proceedings from 1778 to 1852, confounding an already difficult task tracking the conveyance of enslaved individuals to slaveholders' descendants or to purchasers. A few documents survived the fire—residents entered the burning building and carried out what they could, and later families contributed their personal copies of probate and estate records, deeds, mortgages, tax assessments, bills of sale, **manumissions**, and certificates of freedom, helping replace badly damaged and lost papers. The bulk of colonial-era records prior to 1778 survive in Annapolis, Maryland, the state capital, at the Maryland State Archives.

At this courthouse in December 1850, **John Bowley** made the winning bid on his enslaved wife, **Kessiah Jolly Bowley**, and children, who were being sold by **Eliza Brodess**. In 1857, Underground Railroad agent Rev. **Samuel Green** was tried and convicted here, and in 1858, **Hugh Hazlett** was convicted and sentenced here to forty-four years in prison for aiding enslaved people escape.

**DORCHESTER COUNTY HISTORICAL SOCIETY.** Located in **Cambridge, Maryland**, the society was founded in 1953 to collect, preserve, restore, and interpret artifacts and historic records. They operate a museum and maintain an archive of historic artifacts and documents. The society conducts educational programming and special events focused on historical events, people, and places in the region.

**DOUGLASS, ANNA MURRAY** (ca. 1815–4 August 1882). Born free in **Denton, Caroline County, Maryland**, Anna was the seventh of twelve children born to formerly enslaved parents Bambara and Mary Murray. On 29 May 1832, Anna and three siblings, Elizabeth, Phillip, and Charlotte, obtained certificates of freedom so they could move to Baltimore for work. In 1837, Anna met the young, enslaved **Frederick Bailey** and they fell in love. When he decided to escape slavery, Anna sold her belongings to pay for train tickets to New York City and sewed a sailor's uniform for him to wear as a disguise. He successfully escaped in September 1838, and she soon followed him to New York, where they married on 15 September 1838. They had five children together. Once settled in Rochester, New York, by the late 1840s, Anna managed their household as a family home and a station on the **Underground Railroad**, providing **freedom seekers** with food, shelter, and medicine. She and Frederick moved to Washington, D.C., in 1872 after their Rochester home was set on fire by an arsonist. She suffered a stroke and died at their home, Cedar Hill, on 4 August 1882.

**DOUGLASS, FREDERICK BAILEY** (February 1818–20 February 1895). Born enslaved in Talbot County, Maryland, to an enslaved mother, Harriet Bailey, and an unknown white man, though it has been long suspected that he was Aaron Anthony, Harriet's enslaver. Named Frederick Augustus Washington Bailey, Douglass later escaped from slavery in Baltimore, Maryland, at the age of twenty years old. Assisted by his free fiancée, **Anna Murray**, Douglass disguised himself as a sailor, boarded a train, and rode to freedom in New York City. Anna followed him, and on 15 September 1838, they were married and adopted the new name Douglass. They lived in New Bedford and Lynn, Massachusetts, then settled in Rochester, New York, where the couple ran an **Underground Railroad** station and raised money to help **freedom seekers** make their way to Canada.

Douglass became one of the most famous **abolitionists**, orators, and public figures of the nineteenth century. Within ten years of his escape, **abolitionist** allies purchased his freedom from his enslaver, Thomas Auld, whose wife had inherited Douglass when Aaron Anthony died. Douglass published three autobiographies, highlighting the atrocities endured in slavery. **Harriet Tubman** sought shelter in their home during some of her rescue missions from Maryland, and the Douglass children remembered her fondly. Two of the Douglass sons, Lewis and Charles, joined the **Fifty-fourth Massachusetts Voluntary Infantry Regiment** and saw Tubman when they served in South Carolina during the **Civil War**. When **Sarah Bradford** was preparing to publish *Scenes in the Life of Harriet Tubman* in 1868, Douglass wrote a glowing letter of support attesting to Tubman's great bravery and work on the **Underground Railroad**. In 1872, Frederick and Anna moved to Washington, D.C., where he carried on a career in civil rights activism and publishing. After Anna died in 1882, Frederick married Helen Pitts, a white woman. He was appointed U.S. minister to Haiti in 1889. He died at his estate, Cedar Hill in Washington, D.C., on 20 February 1895.

**DOVER EIGHT.** The nickname given to a group of eight enslaved people who fled their enslavers in **Dorchester County, Maryland**, on the evening of 8 March 1857. **Thomas Elliott** and **Denard Hughes** fled the **Bucktown, Maryland**, farm of their enslaver, **Pritchett Meredith**. **Henry Predeaux**, enslaved by Ara Spence but hired to a farmer, possibly Meredith, in the **Bucktown** area, joined them. **James and Lavinia Woolford**, **Bill** and **Emily Kiah**, and an unidentified man named Tubman rounded out the group of eight.

They followed instructions to follow a particular **Underground Railroad** route given to them by **Harriet Tubman**, first seeking help and shelter from Reverend **Samuel Green** in East New Market, Maryland, and then from Tubman's father, **Ben Ross**, at **Poplar Neck** in **Caroline County**. The group was instructed to contact a Black **Underground Railroad** agent, **Thomas Otwell**, then living somewhere outside of Dover, Delaware, who was supposed to guide them to the next stops on the **Underground Railroad** north to Wilmington, Delaware. Otwell betrayed them when he conspired with a white man, **James Hollis**, and lured the group into the Dover jail so they could collect the $3,000 reward for the **freedom seekers'** capture. The group became suspicious and, after an altercation with the sheriff, made a bold and dangerous escape from the jail. A trustworthy Black **Underground Railroad** agent, **William Brinkley**, successfully ferried the group in his wagon thirty-eight miles to **Thomas Garrett's** home in Wilmington, Delaware. Garrett forwarded them to **William Still** in Philadelphia. They eventually made their way to freedom in Canada where they joined **Harriet Tubman** and other friends from **Dorchester County, Maryland**.

DREW, BENJAMIN (1812–1903). A Boston **abolitionist** and journalist, Drew embarked on an investigative journey to Canada to record the testimonies of **freedom seekers** who had settled there. He interviewed **Harriet Tubman**, her brothers **John** and **James Stewart**, and James's wife, **Catherine Kane Stewart** (though he erroneously used the surname "Seward"). Drew was determined to record the true experiences of the enslaved under slavery in the South. He published his findings in *The Refugee: A Northside View of Slavery* as a deliberate counterpoint to the Southern apologists George Fitzhugh's *Sociology for the South; or, the Failure of Free Society* and Reverend Nehemiah Adams's *A Southside View of Slavery*, both of which argued that slavery was far more beneficial and less oppressive to enslaved people than **abolitionists** had led the public to believe. Drew's work reinvigorated the antislavery efforts to challenge Southern slaveholders' rhetoric.

DUGAN'S WHARF. Baltimore Harbor, Maryland. On 21 October 1856, **Harriet Tubman** helped a young woman named "Tilly" flee enslavement. Unable to safely bring Tilly to Philadelphia via a northeasterly route out of Baltimore, Tubman cleverly devised a scheme to take Tilly south, via the steamboat *Kent* to Seaford, Delaware. The steamer *Kent* docked at Dugan's Wharf in Baltimore's Inner Harbor, which is now the site of the National Aquarium Marine Mammal Pavilion at Pier 4.

DURRANT, HENRY K. (dates unknown). Acting assistant surgeon at the Freedmen's or "Colored Hospital" in Beaufort, South Carolina, during the **Civil War**. In August 1862, Durrant ordered that Tubman be given a "little Bourbon whiskey for medicinal purposes" and later testified on 3 May 1864 as to her character and work during the war for her petition to secure her protection and access to resources while working in the field: "I have been acquainted with Harriet Tubman for nearly two years; and my position as Medical Officer in charge of 'contrabands' in this town and in hospital, has given me frequent and ample opportunities to observe her general deportment; particularly her kindness and attention to the sick and suffering of her own race. I take much pleasure in testifying to the esteem in which she is generally held."

DUTTON, CHARLES (ca. 1832–unknown). Born in **Dorchester County, Maryland**, Dutton was enslaved by Mary Hurley of Cambridge. Dutton fled on 20 September 1856 in company with four other men, including **Francis Molock**, **Joshua Handy**, **Ephraim Hudson**, and **Cyrus Mitchell**. They followed instructions likely given to them by **Harriet Tubman**. After passing through **Thomas Garrett's** home in Wilmington, Delaware, the men arrived in Philadelphia, where they were interviewed on the 29th by **William Still**. Still noted that Dutton used William Robinson as an alias. Mary Hurley posted a $200 reward advertisement for Dutton's capture. The **freedom seekers** reached Canada safely.

DUTTON, MARSHALL. Born enslaved in Maryland, Dutton fled on 24 October 1857 with twenty-seven other people famously known as the **Cambridge 28**. He was interviewed by **Underground Railroad** agent **William Still** in Philadelphia. He successfully made his way to freedom and settled in St. Catharines, Ontario, Canada.

# E

**EARL CONRAD PAPERS.** Cayuga Community College, Bourke Memorial Library, Auburn, New York. This collection contains manuscript materials including early drafts of **Earl Conrad**'s 1943 biography *Harriet Tubman*, Tubman research materials, and photographs. This collection also contains an original transcript from an interview with Albert Einstein, original manuscripts about the Civil Rights Party, and poetry on the topic of civil rights. This collection also contains original manuscripts and research materials related to Errol Flynn and correspondence between Conrad and prominent people, including Richard Nixon, Lyndon Johnson, Langston Hughes, Eleanor Roosevelt, and Rudy Vallee.

**EARL CONRAD/HARRIET TUBMAN COLLECTION.** Schomburg Center for Research in Black Culture, New York Public Library. The Earl Conrad/Harriet Tubman Collection represents years of research by historian-journalist Earl Conrad into the life of **Harriet Tubman**. The collection consists of correspondence between Conrad and archivists; government agencies; Tubman relatives; Auburn, New York residents; and others across the country who knew Tubman or were in possession of primary resource material and documentation about her. The collection includes voluminous notes on his research, telephone or in-person interviews with relatives and people knowledgeable about Tubman's life, photographs, newspaper clippings, and drafts of portions of his biography. Interviews include Tubman relatives **Harkless Bowley**, Aida and Henry Johnson, and **Alice Lucas Brickler** and friends **Florence Carter**, **Charles** and **Frances Smith**, and **Helen Tatlock**.

**EASTERN SHORE OF MARYLAND.** The nine Maryland counties—**Dorchester**, **Caroline**, Talbot, Kent, Queen Anne's, Worcester, Cecil, Wicomico, and Somerset—on the east side of the Chesapeake Bay.

**ELLIOTT, ANN MARIE STEWART (ca. 1844–ca. 1880).** Born in Maryland, Ann Marie was an infant when her mother and **Harriet Tubman**'s sister, **Soph Ross**, was sold by **Edward Brodess** in 1844. Soph's brother **William Henry Ross Stewart** later testified for the **American Freedmen's Inquiry Commission** that when Brodess lay dying in the winter of 1849, he could not look at five-year-old Ann out of shame. Ann lived with her grandparents **Ben** and **Rit Ross** in their home in **Poplar Neck** in **Caroline County** in 1850. How and when she was brought to Auburn, New York, is unknown, but it was before or during the **Civil War**. In July 1864 she married **Thomas Elliott**, who had escaped with the **Dover Eight** in 1857. The couple lived with **Harriet Tubman** until they moved to their own home in Auburn. They raised three children together. Ann died between 1879 and 1880.

**ELLIOTT, THOMAS (ca. 1829–2 October 1884).** Born near **Bucktown** in **Dorchester County**, Elliott was sold by his enslaver Margaret Keys Elliott and her husband, Benjamin, to farmer **Pritchett Meredith** in April 1841.

Meredith's home farm was situated about a mile from the **Bucktown** crossroads and less than two miles from the **Edward Brodess** farm where **Harriet Tubman** spent portions of her childhood.

On the evening of 8 March 1857, Elliott and **Denard Hughes** escaped from Meredith. **Henry Predeaux** joined them; he was enslaved by Ara Spence but probably leased to Meredith. **James and Lavinia Woolford, Bill** and **Emily Kiah**, and an unidentified man named Tubman rounded out the group of eight. They followed instructions to follow a particular **Underground Railroad** route given to them by Tubman, first seeking help and shelter from Reverend **Samuel Green** in East New Market, Maryland, and then from Tubman's father, **Ben Ross**, at **Poplar Neck** in **Caroline County**. The group was instructed to contact a Black **Underground Railroad** agent named **Thomas Otwell**, then living somewhere outside of Dover, Delaware, who was supposed to guide them north to **Wilmington, Delaware**. Otwell betrayed them when he conspired with a white man, **James Hollis**, and lured the group into the Dover jail so they could collect the $3,000 reward for the **freedom seekers'** capture. The group became suspicious and, after an altercation with the sheriff, made a bold and dangerous escape from the jail. A trustworthy Black **Underground Railroad** agent, **William Brinkley**, successfully ferried the group in his wagon thirty-eight miles to **Thomas Garrett's** home in Wilmington, Delaware. Garrett forwarded them to **William Still** in Philadelphia. They eventually made their way to freedom in Canada, where they joined Tubman in St. Catharines, Ontario.

The 1861 census reveals Elliott was living with another man named Abraham Elliott, whose relationship to Thomas remains unknown. Hughes and Elliott were recruited by **John Brown** to serve in his provisional army when he attacked **Harpers Ferry**, Virginia, but the two men did not follow Brown in the fall of 1859. Elliott later moved to Auburn, where he married Harriet Tubman's niece, **Ann Marie Stewart**. The couple lived with **Harriet Tubman** until they moved to their own home in Auburn. They raised three children together.

Ann died between 1879 and 1880. Thomas remarried, but in 1881 he experienced a nervous breakdown and was institutionalized at the Willard Asylum for the Insane, a state psychiatric hospital in Ovid, New York. He died there in 1884.

**EMANCIPATION.** The process of setting free, **manumitting**, or liberating someone from slavery.

**EMANCIPATION IN MARYLAND, NOVEMBER 1864.** Slavery in Maryland ended with the rewriting of the state's constitution in the fall of 1864. After a slim victory during a contested vote on November 1, enslaved people were set free. Former enslavers found ways to keep their formerly enslaved people working for them by legally indenturing the children and employing many other legal and extra-legal tactics to maintain control over African American labor.

**EMANCIPATION PROCLAMATION (1 January 1863).** President **Abraham Lincoln** issued a preliminary emancipation proclamation on 22 September 1862, which declared that enslaved people in those parts of the country in rebellion against the United States would be "thenceforward and forever free." The proclamation did not liberate enslaved people in the border states that stayed in the Union, nor did it free those in Union-occupied Louisiana and Tennessee. Lincoln officially signed the proclamation on 1 January 1863 to much fanfare and excitement, ensuring that the **Civil War** was indeed a battle for freedom over slavery.

**EMPIRE STATE FEDERATION OF WOMEN'S CLUBS.** Founded in New York in 1908, the federation had two goals—to provide social and educational "uplift" resources for African American girls and women and support an aging **Harriet Tubman** at her home in Auburn, New York. **Mary Burnett Talbert**, one of the founders of the Niagara Movement and the NAACP and a founding member of the Empire State Federation, became close with Tubman. She was responsible for the organization's

Members of the Empire State Federation of Women's Clubs installed a memorial on Harriet Tubman's grave at Fort Hill Cemetery in Auburn, New York. Photo from *Tribute to Harriet Tubman, the Modern Amazon*, by James E. Mason and Edward U. A. Brooks, 1915. *Courtesy of the author*

attention to Tubman's needs as she aged. After Tubman's death, the federation raised the funds to commission a large headstone designed by a Mrs. Jackson Stewart for her grave in 1915.

**ENNALS, STEPHEN AND MARIA (dates unknown).** Stephen and Maria Ennals and their three children, Harriet, Amanda, and a three-month-old infant, escaped with **Harriet Tubman**'s help in November 1860. It was one of the longest and most dangerous of Tubman's rescue missions. She had returned to **Dorchester County, Maryland**, to liberate her sister **Rachel Ross** and Rachel's two children, Ben and Angerine. Tubman was unaware that Rachel had died the year before, and she lacked $30 to pay someone to bring the two children to her hiding place. Tubman rescued the Ennals family instead. Stephen was enslaved in the Parson's Creek area, and Maria and her children were enslaved by **Algernon S. Percy**, of Vienna, Maryland. Another man, John Wesley Cornish Reed from **Church Creek**, **Maryland**, accompanied the group north.

By 1860, the **Underground Railroad** network that Tubman relied upon had collapsed after the authorities arrested several agents. The group hid in swamps and wooded areas and endured snow and high winds. Tubman administered paregoric—an opiate—to the baby to keep it from crying and revealing their hiding place to **slave catchers**. An unnamed Quaker found them and helped them along the route to Wilmington, Delaware, where, on 1 December 1860, **Thomas Garrett** gave them food, shelter, and clothing. Tubman brought them further north to Auburn, New York, where **Martha Coffin Wright** and her husband, **David**, welcomed them a few days after Christmas. Tubman suffered frostbite during this mission, which was her last attempt to rescue friends or family from Maryland.

**ESCAPEE.** Once commonly used to describe a **freedom seeker**. According to the **National Park Service Network to Freedom Program**, terms "such as 'runaway' and 'escapees' refer to freedom seekers. These terms tend to disparage the freedom seeker. 'Runaway' conjures up the image of a discontent adolescent, while 'escapee' is linked to 'fugitive,' evoking the image of a guilty law breaker deserving of capture and punishment" (https://www.nps.gov/subjects/undergroundrailroad/language-of-slavery.htm).

**"ESSAY ON WOMAN-WHIPPING."** A critical essay written by Professor Reverend **Samuel M. Hopkins**, **Sarah H. Bradford**'s brother, criticizing the violent practice of whipping enslaved people by both white women and men. The essay appeared in the earliest editions of Bradford's 1868 *Scenes in the Life of Harriet Tubman*.

# F

**FIFTEENTH AMENDMENT TO THE CONSTITUTION.** Passed by Congress on 26 February 1869, the amendment was ratified by the states a year later on 3 February 1870. The amendment guaranteed that the "right of citizens of the United States to vote shall not be denied or abridged by the United States or by any State on account of race, color, or previous condition of servitude." At that time, the right to vote was restricted to men. Women could not vote in federal elections until 1920. *See also* NINETEENTH AMENDMENT TO THE CONSTITUTION.

**FIFTY-FOURTH MASSACHUSETTS VOLUNTARY INFANTRY REGIMENT (1863–1865).** The second official African American regiment established by the U.S. Army during the **Civil War**. Resistance to recruitment of Black men prevented the authorization of African American units for two years. The **Emancipation Proclamation** (1 January 1863) included the authorization to establish Black regiments.

Gov. **John Andrew** of Massachusetts had been campaigning the U.S. government to establish African American units, and in February he rushed to recruit Black men for the Fifty-fourth. The Black community in Boston led recruitment efforts, lending a powerful voice and support to the fighting force. Andrew appointed twenty-five-year-old **Robert Gould Shaw**, the son of a wealthy **abolitionist** family from Boston, as commander of the regiment. In May, the regiment shipped out to Beaufort, South Carolina, where they joined the command of General **David Hunter**. They were involved in a few skirmishes early that summer, but on 18 July 1863, they participated in the assault known as the Second Battle of Fort Wagner. The Fifty-fourth suffered extensive casualties, including the death of Shaw. **Harriet Tubman** later recalled watching the battle from Morris Island: "And then we saw the lightning, and that was the guns; and then we heard the thunder, and that was the big guns; and then we heard the rain falling, and that was the drops of blood falling; and when we came to get in the crops, it was the dead that we reaped."

In 1864, the Fifty-fourth Massachusetts took part in the Battle of Olustee, where Tubman's second husband, **Nelson Charles Davis**, fought with his regiment, the Eighth United States Colored Troops. The courage and service of the Fifty-fourth, especially their attack at Fort Wagner, is remembered as one of the most celebrated and important moments of the war. The Fifty-fourth Massachusetts achieved near cult status through its portrayal in the 1989 award-winning film *Glory*, starring Denzel Washington.

**"FOLLOW THE DRINKING GOURD."** A song erroneously credited as a **coded message** used on the **Underground Railroad**. It is an **Underground Railroad myth**. Versions of "Follow the Drinking Gourd" first appeared circa 1928 but became popularized in 1947 when Lee Hayes and the Weavers, a white folk group, reworked the song. The song gained more popularity during the civil rights movement of the 1950s and 1960s. The words describe escaping from

Mobile, Alabama, during the spring and following the North Star through Mississippi, Tennessee, and Kentucky to the Ohio River and freedom. See http://www.followthedrinkinggourd.org/.

**FORTEN-GRIMKE, CHARLOTTE (17 August 1837–23 July 1914).** Born in Philadelphia to a well-to-do Black **abolitionist** family, Forten grew up to be a prominent writer, educator, and antislavery activist. She taught newly free people in South Carolina during the **Civil War** where she met **Harriet Tubman** on 31 January 1863. Forten wrote about her meeting with Tubman in her diaries and letters.

**FORTRESS MONROE.** Hampton, Virginia. Heavily fortified by federal forces, the fort remained in Union control when Virginia seceded and joined the **Confederate States of America** in May 1861. A medical complex at Fort Monroe expanded rapidly throughout the **Civil War**, emerging as the United States' second-largest military hospital. Segregated placement of Black and white sick and wounded soldiers resulted in fewer resources available to treat African Americans and death rates soared. At the end of the war, Dr. **Joseph K. Barnes** assigned **Harriet Tubman** as a nurse in charge of the "colored hospital" at the fort. Tubman's complaints about the facility's neglect and abuse of Black soldiers and high number of fatalities were reported to Barnes and published in the *New York Independent* newspaper on 3 August 1865.

**FOURTEENTH AMENDMENT TO THE CONSTITUTION.** Passed on 13 June 1866 and ratified by Congress on 9 July 1868, the Fourteenth Amendment was one of three post–**Civil War** amendments to the U.S. Constitution that secured freedom and some civil rights for African Americans. The Fourteenth Amendment conferred citizenship on all people "born or naturalized in the United States" and prevented any state from depriving "any person of life, liberty, or property, without due process of law; nor deny to any person within its jurisdiction the equal protection of the laws."

**FOWLER, HENRY (17 October 1824–4 August 1872).** A radical **abolitionist** and Presbyterian minister, Fowler refused to stop condemning slavery and slaveholders from his Second Presbyterian Church pulpit in Auburn, New York, when his conservative superiors demanded that he do so. He led a group of **antislavery** defectors to establish the **Central Presbyterian Church** in Auburn. He officiated at **Harriet Tubman** and **Nelson Charles Davis**'s wedding in March 1869.

**FREDERICK.** A man enslaved by Mary Pattison Brodess Thompson. He is identified in **Anthony Thompson**'s guardian's account for the years 1821–1822 for his stepson, **Edward Brodess**. Frederick's full identity and fate remain unknown.

**FREEDMEN'S BUREAU.** Established in the U.S. War Department in 1865 as the Bureau of Refugees, Freedmen, and Abandoned Lands, the Freedmen's Bureau offered financial, legal, social, and political assistance to hundreds of thousands of formerly enslaved people in the South. The Bureau provided relief; built and operated hospitals, schools, and temporary refugee camps; and invested in helping newly freed people secure the protection and benefits of full citizenship. It ceased its work in 1872, leaving many Black communities vulnerable to renewed forms of discrimination and violence by whites.

*FREEDMEN'S RECORD.* Published by the **New England Freedmen's Aid Society** from January 1864 to April 1874, the *Record* reported on conditions for the newly free people in the South during and after the **Civil War**. The *Record* helped raise charitable funds in support of the Freedmen's Aid Society's food and clothing distribution, educational programs, medical care, and efforts to confront and dismantle discrimination and subjugation of African Americans.

**FREEDOM SEEKER.** Also known as a self-liberator or self-emancipator. According to the **National Park Service Network to Freedom Program**, freedom seeker "reflects the freedom of spirit by referring to escaping African Americans as 'freedom seekers,' rather than runaways, fugitives, or escapees. The labels 'fugitive,' 'runaway,' and 'escapee' were constructs of the Southern slave-holding societal structure and patronizing abolitionists. These terms reflect how slave-holding society viewed African American efforts toward freedom and ultimately, takes away their agency. 'Freedom seekers' demonstrates what was in the hearts of freedom-seeking African Americans who acted to make liberty a reality" (https://www.nps.gov/subjects/undergroundrailroad/language-of-slavery.htm).

*FREEDOM TRAIN: THE STORY OF HARRIET TUBMAN.* A creative nonfiction juvenile biography by **Dorothy Sterling** published by Doubleday & Company of New York in 1954. A very successful children's book, it is still in print.

**FREEMAN, MORGAN LUKE.** A gunsmith and barber, Freeman was born in 1803 to enslaved parents Harry and Kate Freeman. Their enslaver, John Hardenburgh, founded the city of Auburn, New York. Once free, the Freeman family formed the core of what became known as the "Negro Settlement" or **New Guinea**, along the Owasco River outlet in Auburn. Luke and his wife, Catherine, managed an **Underground Railroad** station in their home at 3 Court Street in Auburn, New York, for twenty-nine years, from the 1830s to the **Civil War**. They sheltered **Nat and Lizzy Amby** in 1858. Highly respected, Freeman's funeral attracted hundreds of mourners. A plaque honoring his **Underground Railroad** work and community activism was placed on a building located at the intersection of Genesee Street and State Street in Auburn and unveiled by local Genesee Elementary School children who sponsored its placement in 2016.

**FRIBLEY, CHARLES (ca. 1835–20 February 1864).** Fribley was appointed colonel of the Eighth United States Colored Troops regiment, of which **Nelson Charles Davis** was a member, on 18 November 1863 at Camp William Penn. He was killed in action during the Battle of Olustee, Florida, on 20 February 1864. At the time of his death, he was being investigated for "conduct unbecoming an officer." His body was never recovered.

**FRIEND, GABRIEL (ca. 1800–19 June 1869).** Born enslaved in **Caroline County, Maryland**, Friend was set free in 1815 by his enslavers Henry A. Black and Caleb Connelly. He married **Gracie Chase**, a freed woman, and they had nine children, including **Harrison Friend**. They lived near Preston, Maryland, and were neighbors with **Ben Ross** and **Rit Green Ross** and **Harriet Tubman** when the Rosses lived and worked on Dr. **Anthony C. Thompson**'s plantation at **Poplar Neck**. A farmer, Friend was ordained a minister at the segregated Bethesda Methodist Episcopal Church in Preston in 1850, reportedly the congregation's first Black preacher. He died in Preston on 19 June 1869.

**FRIEND, GRACIE CHASE (ca. 1805–aft. 1870).** Born free or **manumitted** in **Dorchester County, Maryland**, Gracie married **Gabriel Friend** around 1821 in **Caroline County**, and they had nine children together, including **Harrison Friend**. They lived near Preston, Maryland, and were neighbors with **Ben Ross, Rit Green Ross**, and **Harriet Tubman** when the Rosses lived and worked on Dr. **Anthony C. Thompson**'s plantation at **Poplar Neck**. Sometime between 1861 and 1864, Gracie took in abandoned child and neighbor **Moses Woolford**, whose mother, **Mary Woolford**, and siblings **James** and **Sarah** had died and whose father, **Isaac Woolford**, had joined the U.S. Army. Moses's sister, **Margaret Woolford Stewart Lucas**, was taken from the Woolford family in 1861 by Harriet Tubman. Margaret searched for her father and young brother in 1885 by placing an advertisement in the *Christian Recorder*, where she described her father as having left "my youngest brother with an old lady in Caroline county." In 1870, Moses was recorded as living with Gracie and **Harrison Friend** in **Caroline County, Maryland**. His fate is unknown.

**FRIEND, HARRISON (ca. 1835–aft. 1880).** Born free in **Caroline County, Maryland**, to free Black parents, **Gabriel Friend** and **Gracie Chase Friend**. He would have known neighbors **Ben Ross** and **Rit Green Ross** and **Harriet Ross Tubman**. After his father's death in 1869, Harrison took care of his elderly mother. He also helped raise orphaned **Moses Woolford**, the son of Harriet Tubman's close friends **Isaac** and **Mary Woolford**. Harrison died sometime after 1880.

**FRYMAN, EDGAR J. (ca. 1839–unknown).** Born in Columbia County, New York, Fryman, a cooper by trade, joined the Company G, Eighth United States Colored Troops (USCT) on 4 August 1863 in Oswego, New York. He served during the **Civil War** with **Harriet Tubman**'s second husband, **Nelson Charles Davis**. Fryman served as a witness on 25 January 1895 in support of Tubman's widow application for Davis's veteran's pension.

**FUGITIVE.** A term once used to describe **freedom seekers**. Escape from slavery by an enslaved person was against the law, making that person a "fugitive." The term is no longer in common use to describe freedom seekers, self-liberators, or self-emancipators. According to the **National Park Service Network to Freedom Program**, the term "fugitive" is "linked to the various Fugitive Slave Laws (1793, 1850) passed by the U.S. Congress, and suggests that the 'fugitive' was criminal to escape from bondage. This language was key in attempts to preserve the view that the law was on the side of the slaveholding society—which it was—while reinforcing the view that the 'fugitive' was incapable of acting responsibly in a society governed by the rule of law" (https://www.nps.gov/subjects/undergroundrailroad/language-of-slavery.htm).

**FUGITIVE AID SOCIETY OF ST. CATHARINES.** A relief organization for **freedom seekers** established in St. Catharines, Ontario, Canada, in 1861 by **Harriet Tubman**. She was frustrated by the slow response of existing humanitarian organizations in the area, so she organized her own and staffed it with people she knew and trusted; many had fled slavery in Maryland and Delaware. Charles H. Hall, the president, had run away from Maryland twenty-five years before; Benjamin Fletcher, the vice president, had only arrived in 1859; Christopher "Kit" Anthony, the secretary, was one of the **Cambridge 28**; H. W. Wilkins, assistant secretary, had escaped Dorchester in February 1858, with a party of five other men, all of whom settled in the St. Catharines area. A fifth man, William Hutchinson, served as treasurer for the newly formed society. Tubman, her brother **William Henry Stewart**, John Jones, and Hutchinson's wife, Mary, served as the society's committee.

**FUGITIVE AID SOCIETY OF SYRACUSE, NEW YORK.** Syracuse became an active center for the **abolitionist** movement due in large part to the influence of **Gerrit Smith**, Rev. **Jermain Loguen**, and Rev. **Samuel May**, among others. The society was established after the passage of the **Fugitive Slave Act of 1850**. The society helped hundreds of **freedom seekers** in defiance of the law. **Underground Railroad** agent **Sydney H. Gay** of New York City and **Stephen** and **Harriet Myers** of Troy, New York, sent self-liberators to Syracuse. By the late 1850s, Loguen was so confident that he advertised his address in local newspapers advising freedom seekers needing assistance could come directly to him for help. Loguen and others often sent **freedom seekers** via train to Rochester, New York, where **Frederick Douglass**, his associates, and members of the **Rochester Ladies' Anti-Slavery Sewing Society** helped them to Canada.

**FUGITIVE SLAVE ACT OF 1850.** The U.S. Congress passed this law on 18 September 1850 as part of a larger piece of legislation called the Compromise of 1850. Southern slaveholders who were fearful that the admission of California in 1850 into the union as a free state—meaning, slavery was illegal there—would dilute their voting power in Congress demanded some measure of restitution. The admission of California meant that free states had more votes in Congress than slaveholding states. Northern antislavery interests had hoped to stop the expansion of slavery into the western territories, and slaveholders wanted to protect their rights to their human property and prevent escapes to friendly northern communities. The Fugitive Slave Act required northern law enforcement officers and everyday citizens to assist **slave catchers** in capturing and returning **freedom seekers** to their legal enslavers. The Fugitive Slave Act of 1850 strengthened federal enforcement in fugitive slave laws already in use, including the Fugitive Slave Act of 1793. The new law denied the **freedom seekers** the right to a jury trial and to testify in their own defense. It levied heavy fines on those who failed to assist in the capture of self-liberators and paid bounties to those who helped capture them.

# G

**GARNET, HENRY HIGHLAND** (23 December 1815–13 February 1882). Born enslaved, Garnet was the son of George and Henny Trusty. When their enslaver, William Spencer of Chesterville, Kent County, Maryland died in 1822, the family escaped to avoid being sold. They settled in New York City, where they changed their surname to Garnet. Well educated, Henry became an ordained minister. A radical **abolitionist**, he became famous after delivering a fiery speech in 1843 entitled "Address to the Slaves," which advocated armed resistance to enslavement. He was friends with **Harriet Tubman**, **John Brown**, and **Gerrit Smith**. Garnet aided **freedom seekers** and encouraged Black men to enlist in the U.S. Army during the **Civil War**. President Abraham Lincoln chose Garnet to deliver a speech on the floor of the House of Representatives in honor of the anniversary of the **Emancipation Proclamation** in February 1865, the first Black man to appear in front of Congress. Appointed ambassador to **Liberia** in Africa in 1881, he died there in 1882.

**GARRETT, THOMAS** (21 August 1789–24 January 1871). A Quaker and **abolitionist**, Garrett was raised on a farm outside of Philadelphia in Upper Darby. His family supported the **antislavery movement** and assisted **freedom seekers** fleeing bondage, many of them from nearby Maryland. A merchant specializing in hardware, he moved to Wilmington, Delaware, in 1822 with his wife and children and from there ran an **Underground Railroad** station from his office and home. After his wife Mary died, he married Rachel Mendenhall in 1830. Together they sheltered and supported many freedom seekers. In 1845, Garret was charged with aiding in the escape of the Hawkins family, and after a brief trial in 1848, he was fined $1,500. He told the judge and jury, "I now pledge myself . . . to use all lawful and honorable means to lessen the burdens of this oppressed people, and . . . to burst their chains asunder, and set them free."

During the 1850s, he helped **Harriet Tubman** on several of her rescue missions and wrote about her often in his letters to other **abolitionists**. He worked with a large network of mostly Black **Underground Railroad** agents in Delaware, Maryland, and Pennsylvania, including **William Still** in Philadelphia, and some whites, including **John** and **Hannah Cox** and **Allen** and **Maria Agnew**, among others. Garrett is credited with giving aid to 2,500 to 3,000 freedom seekers over a forty-year period between 1820 and the **Civil War**. He died at his home on Shipley Street in Wilmington in 1871.

**GARRISON, AGNES** (14 June 1866–31 March 1950). The granddaughter of **William Lloyd** and **Helen Garrison** of Boston and **David** and **Martha Coffin Wright** of Auburn, New York, Agnes was a woman suffragist. She knew **Harriet Tubman** from childhood visits to relatives in Auburn. In 1899, Agnes sat down with Tubman and interviewed her. She encouraged Tubman to tell "stories of her youth which a stenographer took down as best she could," though it was "impossible to unravel the chronology," Agnes later wrote to her mother, **Ellen**

Wright Garrison. Hoping to glean more interesting details from Tuman, Agnes interviewed her again a few days later. "We had another bout with Harriet," Agnes wrote again, "she got warmed up to her narrative yesterday and acted out parts of it, crawling on the floor, gesticulating and singing one of the old songs in a curious, nasal, mournful voice." According to Agnes, Tubman, nearly eighty at the time, was caring for three orphaned children. Agnes, like all Garrison family members, remained devoted to Tubman until her death in 1913.

**GARRISON, ELLEN WRIGHT (19 August 1840–12 February 1931).** The daughter of woman suffragist **Marth Coffin Wright** and **David Wright**, Ellen grew up in Auburn, New York, surrounded by her parents' **abolitionist** friends, family, and colleagues. The Wrights welcomed **freedom seekers** into their home and advocated for women's suffrage and equal rights. Ellen married **William Lloyd Garrison**'s son **William Lloyd II** in Boston in 1864, bringing the two families together. Ellen met **Harriet Tubman** through her mother, Martha, a close friend and ally, and she remained devoted to Tubman for the rest of her life.

**GARRISON, GEORGE (13 February 1836–24 January 1904).** Eldest son of **William Lloyd Garrison** and his wife, **Helen**, George grew up in a busy activist household in Brookline, a suburb of Boston, Massachusetts, with six siblings. **Harriet Tubman** was an admired guest in the Garrison home in the 1850s. During the Civil War, George accepted a commission as the second lieutenant of the Fifty-fifth Massachusetts Black regiment. While stationed on Folly Island outside of Charleston, South Carolina, he ran into Tubman. Writing to his brother, William "Willie" Lloyd Garrison II, George described Tubman's surprise upon seeing him: "When we entered where she was at work ironing some clothes, Mrs. Severance went to introduce me by saying here is George Garrison, she no sooner saw me than she recognized me at once, and instantly threw her arms around me, and gave me quite an affectionate embrace, much to the amusement of those with me." She was cooking and washing clothes for Union Army officers, Garrison wrote, and wanted to go home, but the army would not allow her to go. "Her services are too valuable to loose. She has made it a business to see all contrabands escaping from the rebels and is enable to get more intelligence from them than anybody else." George noted that she was trying to save money to send to her family in Auburn, New York, and that Tubman had "a chance of making a good deal of money here, and can easily get fifty times more work than she can do," stressing Tubman's value as a scout and spy, nurse, and domestic worker.

**GARRISON, HELEN BENSON (23 February 1811–25 January 1876).** Born in Providence Rhode Island to **abolitionist** parents, Helen married **William Lloyd Garrison** in 1834. They had seven children, including two who died at a very young age. Helen was active in antislavery activities and helped raise money for the Boston Female Anti-Slavery Society, which supported her husband's newspaper, *The Liberator*. Helen and her husband were devoted to progressive politics including women's suffrage, equal human rights, abolition, and many other reform causes of the period. She and **Harriet Tubman** became close friends during the 1850s. Helen suffered a paralyzing stroke in 1863 and died in their home in Roxbury, Massachusetts in 1876.

**GARRISON, WENDELL PHILLIPS (4 June 1840–27 February 1907).** The son of **William Lloyd Garrison** and his wife, **Helen**, Wendell became a journalist and newspaper editor. In 1864, during the **Civil War**, he started working as a writer for the *New York Independent*, which supported **abolition** and women's suffrage. In 1865, he went on to help found *The Nation*, a progressive political literary magazine published weekly, and served as literary editor. It replaced *The Liberator*, which had ceased publication in 1865 when the **Civil War** and the **Thirteenth Amendment** to the U.S. Constitution ended slavery. The same year he married Lucy McKim, the daughter of Philadelphian **abolitionist** and **Underground Railroad** agent **James Miller McKim**. She documented and published songs sung by enslaved people in the South Carolina Sea Islands during the **Civil War**. In the 1880s, Wendell became editor of *The Nation*. He met **Harriet Tubman** in Boston during the 1850s and remained friends with her until his death in 1907.

**GARRISON, WILLIAM LLOYD (10 December 1805–24 May 1879).** Born in Newburyport, Massachusetts, Garrison, his mother, and his siblings were abandoned by their father and lived in abject poverty. Apprenticed as a young teenager to the publisher of the *Newburyport Herald* newspaper, Garrison acquired important skills as a writer. He became involved in the **abolition movement** during the 1820s in Baltimore, Maryland. In 1829, he started working as a writer and editor for the antislavery newspaper the *Genius of Universal Emancipation* in Baltimore, Maryland. He railed against slave trading in the pages of *Genius*, drawing the condemnation of powerful **slave traders**. He was arrested, fined, and thrown in jail.

Upon release in 1831, he moved to Boston, Massachusetts, and began publishing *The Liberator*. A radical **abolitionist**, Garrison denounced the **colonization movement** and called for the immediate end to slavery. His brand of antislavery politics was called "immediatist." He espoused peaceful protest, and he frequently quoted the Bible to argue against slavery. He married **Helen Benson** in Connecticut in 1834. They had seven children, including two who died very young. He helped found the **New England Anti-Slavery Society** in 1832 and the **American Anti-Slavery Society** in 1833. With Helen, they supported the emerging women's suffrage movement, and he published many articles on women's rights and featured women writers. Garrison's support for women's equality alienated some of his followers, who formed rival antislavery societies that forbade women from speaking in public. Garrison faced violent attacks from proslavery forces and frequently experienced threats to his life.

One of the most powerful abolitionists of his day, Garrison was friends with **Frederick Douglass, John Brown, Harriet Tubman**, and many, many others. He disagreed with Brown's use of violence, and he and Douglass became hostile to each other over differing views on how the U.S. government should dismantle slavery. *The Liberator* was the most influential antislavery and progressive publication of the period. Garrison closed the newspaper in December 1865 after the U.S. Congress approved the **Thirteenth Amendment** to the U.S. Constitution, which ended slavery in the country. He continued to fight for equality and justice until he died in 1879.

**GARRISON, WILLIAM "WILLIE" LLOYD, II (21 January 1838–12 September 1909).** The namesake of **William Lloyd Garrison** and son of Garrison and his wife, **Helen**, Willie became a political activist and social reformer like his parents and siblings. He married **Ellen Wright**, the daughter of **abolitionist** and women's suffrage advocate **Martha Coffin Wright** of Auburn, New York, in 1864 in Boston. A businessman and wool trader, Garrison fought racism and campaigned against the Chinese Exclusion Act, which barred Chinese immigrants from entering the United States during the 1880s. He supported women's suffrage and other progressive causes. He met **Harriet Tubman** in Boston during the 1850s, and they remained friends until his death in 1909.

**GAY, SYDNEY HOWARD (26 May 1822–25 June 1888).** Born in Hingham, Massachusetts, Gay became an ardent **abolitionist** as a young adult. He wrote articles for the local newspaper, following **William Lloyd Garrison**, and joined the **American Anti-Slavery Society** (AASS). He moved to New York City in 1843 to become editor of the *National Anti-Slavery Standard*, the newspaper of the AASS. In 1845 he married Elizabeth Neall, a Quaker, **abolitionist**, and women's suffrage activist.

Gay welcomed **freedom seekers** into the *Standard*'s offices in the city with the help of his assistant editor, **Oliver Johnson**. He worked as an **Underground Railroad** agent with **Louis Napoleon**, an African American conductor from Staten Island. Gay kept records of some of the freedom seekers he helped. Two surviving journals, similar to those kept by **William Still** of Philadelphia, include the names of two hundred individuals that Gay, Johnson, and Napoleon helped in 1855–1856. The record is preserved at Columbia University.

Gay assisted **Harriet Tubman**. On 16 May 1856, Gay interviewed Tubman when she brought four men—**William Andrew Cook**, **Henry Hopkins**, Benjamin Jackson, and **James Coleman**—through his office. His report on Tubman spans five pages in the journal. He called her "Captain Harriet Tubman" in honor of her successful rescue missions bringing **freedom seekers** north. Gay also worked closely with **William Still** of Philadelphia and other agents in Boston and central New York state, including **Frederick Douglass**, **Jermain Loguen**, and **Stephen Myers**. He left the *Standard* in 1857 and worked as an editor and writer for numerous newspapers. He died after complications from a fall in 1888.

*GENERAL HARRIET TUBMAN*. Book by **Earl Conrad**. *See also* HARRIET TUBMAN.

*GEORGETOWN PLANET* (1873–1875). Established by **Harriet Tubman**'s nephew **James A. Bowley** in Georgetown, South Carolina, in 1873 as a Republican newspaper for African Americans. The newspaper promoted the ideologies of equality of the races and political and social advancement of Blacks in the state. Lacking financial resources, the newspaper folded after two years.

**GIBBS, ABEL** (ca. 1810–aft. 1879). Born in Kent County, Delaware, Gibbs was a mason. Living in the free Black community of Brinkley Hill on the north side of Camden during the 1840s and 1850s, he and his neighbors **Nathaniel Brinkley** and **William Brinkley** were **Underground Railroad** agents who helped **Harriet Tubman**, among others. She later said she felt "safe and comfortable" hiding in their homes during her escape missions. He built the Whatcoat Methodist Episcopal Church in the Brinkley Hill community during the late 1850s. Before he died, he changed his name to Abraham.

**GIBBS, ABRAHAM.** *See* GIBBS, ABEL.

**GIBBS, JACOB R.** (ca. 1805–unknown). Born enslaved in Maryland around 1805, Gibbs purchased his freedom and established a successful house-painting business in Baltimore. He managed an **Underground Railroad** station in the city for decades, often using forged certificates of freedom, which were required for African Americans to travel safely outside the state. After his partner Charles Torrey was arrested for smuggling **freedom seekers** in 1844, Gibbs fled to New York City, where he continued his work with **Sydney H. Gay** and the New York Vigilance Committee. Gibbs likely helped Tubman and her refugees during the 1850s. He sent **freedom seekers** along the same route Tubman frequently used—New York City to Albany, Syracuse, Rochester, and **Niagara Falls**.

**GILPIN POINT, MARYLAND.** A peninsula extending into the **Choptank River** southwest of **Denton, Maryland**. During the nineteenth century, it was one of the busiest wharves along the river, serving merchant and passenger vessels. On 8 December 1855, **Joseph Cornish** escaped from his enslaver in **Cambridge**. He joined the crew of a vessel docked at Gilpin Point. He sailed with them to Philadelphia, where he fled further north to freedom.

**GOLD SWINDLE (September–October 1873).** Three con artists arrived in Auburn, New York, claiming they had a chest of gold and silver worth $5,000 in U.S. dollars, which one of them found in South Carolina. They approached Harriet Tubman and agreed to sell her the contents of the chest for $2,000. She convinced a local real estate developer, Anthony Shimer, to provide the funds. With the money in hand, Tubman met the con men in a nearby cemetery. They knocked her unconscious, tied her up, and stole her money. The trunk contained only rocks. Shimer tried to reclaim his loss by demanding restitution from Tubman, but the loss was his to bear alone.

**"GOODBYE SONG."** *See* "BOUND FOR THE PROMISED LAND."

**GREEN, BERIAH** (dates unknown). Founder and charismatic leader of the Oneida Institute. The school accepted African American students and held integrated classes for Black and white students, making the institute America's first racially desegregated institution of higher education.

**GREEN, CATHERINE "KITTY"** (ca. 1806–bef. 1889). Born enslaved, Kitty was the wife of Rev. **Samuel Green**. He purchased her freedom from Ezekiel Richardson in 1842, but their children, **Sam Jr.** and **Sarah**, remained enslaved. She died in Baltimore between 1886 and 1889. *See also* GREEN, SAMUEL.

**GREEN, HARRIET "RIT."** *See* ROSS, HARRIET "RIT" GREEN.

**GREEN, JOHN.** Born in Maryland and enslaved by Samuel Hooper, John escaped on Saturday night, 24 July 1858, in company with **Mary Light, Charles Anthony Light, William Henry Cornish, Esther Cornish, Solomon Cornish**, and **Thomas Rideout**. Their white **Underground Railroad** conductor was an Irish immigrant and wood sawyer named **Hugh Hazlett**. The group was caught a few days later in **Caroline County, Maryland**, and brought to **Cambridge** via a steamboat, but a mob had gathered to await their arrival at Long Wharf. The sheriff feared the mob would lynch Hazlett, so he ordered the steamboat to leave Long Wharf and dock at another location upriver. Hazlett and the others were later safely secured in the **Cambridge** jail. Green was reenslaved by Hooper.

**GREEN, SAMUEL** (ca. 1802–28 February 1877). Preacher, farmer, and **Underground Railroad** agent, Green was born enslaved on the **Eastern Shore of Maryland**. He spent his childhood and young adulthood laboring for whites in **Caroline** and **Dorchester counties**, eventually settling near Indian Creek and near the town of East New Market with his enslaver, Henry Nichols (Nicols). Sam purchased his freedom in 1832 after Nichols's death. Green married an enslaved woman named **Kitty**, and they had two children who survived to adulthood, **Sam Jr.** and **Sarah**, born between 1828 and 1830. Though Kitty and their children were enslaved by Ezekiel Richardson, it appears that they were allowed to live with Green. By 1842, Sam had earned enough money as a farm laborer and part-time preacher to purchase Kitty's liberty. Unfortunately, the children remained enslaved, and Richardson sold the children to Dr. **James Muse** of **Cambridge** in 1847.

Literate, Green became a highly respected lay preacher and exhorter in the Methodist Episcopal Church in **Dorchester County**. In spite of severe restrictions on African American ministers in the slave states throughout the antebellum period, Green preached to both free and enslaved African Americans in his community. In August 1844, Green became a member of the Board of Trustees of the Colored Peoples United Methodist Episcopal Church. Under the board's leadership, they accepted a gift of land in East New Market from freed woman Sarah Young and her children, Clem, George, and Rosette, and built a church.

Green's stature within the community grew during the 1840s, and by the early 1850s Green had taken on a leadership role among **Dorchester County** African Americans. In 1852, Green traveled to Baltimore as a delegate to the Convention of the Free Colored People of Maryland. The meeting was convened to discuss the present condition of civil rights and future prospects for free African Americans living in the state. The issue of colonization and emigration to **Liberia** was hotly debated during the convention. Green opposed the idea and left the convention and returned home.

When and for how long Green acted as an **Underground Railroad** agent is unknown, but **Harriet Tubman** said that she sometimes stayed with Green when she returned to Maryland on her rescue missions. He aided in the escapes of his son, **Sam Green Jr.**, in 1854; **Josiah** and **William Bailey** and **Peter Pennington** in November 1856; and the **Dover Eight** in March 1857. He was betrayed by a member of the community after he sheltered the **Dover Eight**; he was arrested and tried for aiding in the escape of enslaved people. The all-white jury refused to convict him, but white slaveholders demanded justice. Green was arrested again for owning a copy of Harriet Beecher Stowe's *Uncle Tom's Cabin*, which was considered **abolitionist** material and therefore illegal for Maryland Blacks to have in their possession. He was convicted and sentenced to ten years in prison. Green's literacy spared him from hard labor, and he was assigned to work in the warden's office. Kitty found work as a domestic when she moved to Baltimore to be near Sam in prison. In March 1862, after continued pressure from northern abolitionists, powerful Baltimore Quakers, and Methodist Episcopal church officials, newly elected Governor Augustus W. Bradford pardoned Green on the condition that he leave Maryland immediately. On 21 April 1862 Sam Green was freed.

Sam and Kitty left Maryland for a speaking tour through Philadelphia, New York, and New England. Harriet Beecher Stowe gave him a new copy of *Uncle Tom's Cabin*. They moved to Canada to live with Sam Jr. After the **Civil War**, the Greens returned to Maryland. They eventually settled in Baltimore, where Green became actively involved in the Centenary Biblical Institute, which trained young men for the ministry and in time became known as Morgan State University. He and Kitty were members of the Orchard Street United Methodist Church. Sam died on 28 February 1877 and is buried in the South Baltimore Cemetery.

**GREEN, SAMUEL, JR.** (ca. 1829–1875). Born enslaved in **Dorchester County, Maryland**, Sam Jr. was the son of Rev. **Samuel Green** and **Catherine "Kitty" Green**. His sister, **Sarah Ann Green**, was born three years later in 1832. Sam Jr.'s father purchased his own freedom in 1832 and then bought Kitty in 1842. The family lived together near East New Market, Maryland. Dr. **James Muse** of **Cambridge** enslaved young Sam, a blacksmith, and his sister. Sam Jr. described Muse as cruel and violent, "the worst man" in Maryland. Aided by **Harriet Tubman** and possibly his father, young Green escaped on 28 August 1854 and made his way safely to **William Still**'s office in Philadelphia, Pennsylvania. The **Underground Railroad** agent then forwarded him on to the home of **Charles Bustill**, a member of one of the most important Black **Underground Railroad** families in the region. Sam Jr. was quickly sent to Canada. He settled temporarily in Chippawa, Ontario, Canada, just across the United States border near **Niagara Falls**, New York, where he joined other **Eastern Shore of Maryland freedom seekers**.

On 10 September 1854, young Green wrote to his father, reassuring him that he had found not only a safe and easy passage to Canada but that he had seen Tubman in Philadelphia. He revealed that his successful journey to freedom included "plenty of friends, plenty to eat, and to drink." He told his father to tell **Peter Jackson** and **Joseph "Joe" Bailey**, both locally enslaved men, to come to Canada as soon as they could. Within four months, Jackson fled to Canada with Tubman and her brothers during their escape in December 1854. **Joe Bailey** and his brother, **William "Bill" Bailey**, escaped two years later. Tragically, Sam Jr.'s sister, Sarah, was unable to escape. Muse, angry over the flight of Sam Jr., sold her to a Missouri family, cruelly separating her from her family forever. Sam Jr. married a woman named Louisa Gray, the daughter of Virginia-born **freedom seekers** who fled to Canada after the **Fugitive Slave Act** was passed in 1850. The Greens had five children: Vesta, Oliver, James, Annie, and Joseph. Sam Jr. died 20 April 1875, and Louisa died 23 December 1884 in Ontario, Canada.

**GREEN, SARAH ANN** (ca. 1832–unknown). Enslaved daughter of Rev. **Samuel Green** and his wife, **Kitty**. Her father purchased his freedom in in 1832, but Sarah, her mother, and her brother, **Sam Green Jr.**, remained enslaved. Sarah and her brother were allowed to live with their parents at Indian Creek near East New Market, Maryland, until about 1847, when their enslaver, Dr. **James Muse**, moved them to his home in **Cambridge**. Sarah likely worked in the house as a domestic, while Sam Jr. was trained as a blacksmith. After Sam Jr. fled in 1854, Muse sold Sarah to an unidentified Missouri buyer, forever separating her from a husband, two children, and her parents. Her fate remains unknown.

**GREGORY, SOLOMON.** Born enslaved in South Carolina, Gregory became a scout for the U.S. Army during the **Civil War**. He was a member of **Harriet Tubman**'s team who spied on **Confederate** forces and relayed information to Union officers. The other scouts were: **Isaac Hayward**, **Mott Blake**, **Peter Burns**, **Sandy Sellers**, **George Chisholm**, **Gabriel Cahern**, and **Walter D. Plowden**, along with river pilots **Charles Simmons** and **Samuel Hayward**. Under Tubman's command, the group was considered by General **Rufus Saxton** to be among "the most valued scouts and pilots in the Gov't employ in" Hilton Head, South Carolina.

# H

**HADDAWAY, SARAH CATHERINE THOMPSON (1832–1888).** The daughter of Dr. **Anthony C. Thompson**, Sarah married **Thomas Haddaway** in Talbot County in 1853. After **Harriet Tubman**'s brother **Robert Ross** escaped on **Christmas Day 1854**, Dr. Thompson immediately forced Ross's enslaved wife, **Mary Manokey**, and her three children to move from **Dorchester County** to the Haddaway plantation. Thompson may have believed that it would have been more difficult for Manokey to escape from his daughter's property. Manokey and her children remained enslaved by the Haddaways until they were freed when Maryland abolished slavery on 1 November 1864.

**HADDAWAY, THOMAS (1831–1876).** A merchant and farmer born in Talbot County, Haddaway married **Sarah Catherine Thompson**, the daughter of Dr. **Anthony C. Thompson**, in 1853. The couple enslaved **Mary Manokey**, the wife of **Robert Ross**, and their children after Ross escaped on **Christmas Day 1854**. *See also* HADDAWAY, SARAH CATHERINE THOMPSON.

**"HAIL, OH HAIL YE HAPPY SPIRITS."** Spiritual sung by **Harriet Tubman** to signal to her companions on the **Underground Railroad**. Author **Sarah H. Bradford** recorded two versions of this spiritual in her early Tubman biographies. Bradford noted that Tubman sang this song as a **coded message** to fellow **freedom seekers**. Tubman changed the tempo or the words to inform them that it was either safe to come out of hiding or that there was danger nearby and to stay hidden. The song includes these famous lyrics:

Oh go down, Moses,
Way down into Egypt's land, Tell old Pharaoh,
Let my people go.
Oh Pharaoh said he would go across,
Let my people go,
And don't get lost in the wilderness,
Let my people go.

Oh go down, Moses,
Way down into Egypt's land,
Tell old Pharaoh,
Let my people go.

You may hinder me here, but you can't up there,
Let my people go,
He sits in the Heavens and answers prayer,
Let my people go!

Oh go down, Moses,
Way down into Egypt's land,
Tell old Pharaoh,
Let my people go.

**HANDY, JOSHUA (ca. 1835–unknown).** Born in **Dorchester County, Maryland**, Handy was enslaved by Isaac Harris. Handy fled on 20 September 1856 in company with four other men: **Cyrus Mitchell**, **Francis Molock**, **Charles Dutton**, and **Ephraim Hudson**. They followed instructions likely given to them by **Harriet**

Tubman. After passing through **Thomas Garrett**'s home in Wilmington, Delaware, the men arrived in Philadelphia, where they were interviewed on the 29th by **William Still**. Still noted that Handy used Hambleton Hamby as an alias. The **freedom seekers** reached Canada safely. Handy settled in Owen Sound, Ontario, Canada.

**HANSBROUGH, BLUCHER (1817–1873).** Born in Culpeper County, Virginia, Hansbrough was a wealthy farmer. One of his enslaved men and his half-brother, **Charles Nalle**, escaped in October 1858 and settled in the small city of Troy, New York. Hansbrough discovered Nalle's whereabouts in April 1860 from a lawyer who befriended Nalle in Troy and was eager to claim the reward for informing on Nalle. Empowered by the laws embedded in the **Fugitive Slave Act**, Hansbrough sent **slave catchers** to capture Nalle and bring him back to Virginia. On 7 April 1860, Nalle was caught and secured in a jail cell. A large crowd gathered and with the help of **Harriet Tubman** freed Nalle from custody. The authorities battled the crowd and recaptured Nalle, only to have him liberated again and hurried off to Canada for his safety. Local **abolitionists** raised $650 and paid Hansbrough for Nalle's legal freedom.

**HARPERS FERRY RAID (16–18 October 1859).** An armed insurrection and raid on the federal arsenal in Harpers Ferry, Virginia, by militant **abolitionist** and revolutionary **John Brown** and a group of eighteen men, including two of Brown's sons. After fighting proslavery forces in Kansas territory in 1856, Brown spent two years among **abolitionist** circles in New England raising money and interest in his scheme to build the Provisional Army of the United States to attack the federal arsenal in **Harpers Ferry**, arm enslaved people, and defend their right to freedom. Brown recruited **Harriet Tubman** into his provisional army when he met her in St. Catharines, Ontario, Canada, in the spring of 1858. With money secured from supporters, including a small group called the **Secret Six**, Brown rented the Kennedy Farm in Sandy Hook, Maryland, four miles from Harpers Ferry, in July 1859 and began planning and training for the eventual attack with his group of twenty-two volunteers—fifteen white and seven Black men. Tubman did not join him, despite his efforts to find her and encourage her to come fight with him.

On the night of 16 October 1859, Brown and eighteen of his recruits staged their assault. Though he expected hundreds, if not thousands of enslaved people to join him, they did not. By the 18th, Brown and his men were trapped in the arsenal and surrounded by federal troops commanded by Colonel Robert E. Lee, the future commander of the army of the **Confederate States of America**. Ten of Brown's men, including his sons Watson and Oliver, were killed, and six more were captured with Brown. Quickly tried and then convicted on 2 November 1859, Brown was led to the gallows on 2 December 1859 and hanged. In a note he left behind, he wrote, "I, John Brown, am now quite certain that the crimes of this guilty land will never be purged away but with blood. I had, as I now think, vainly flattered myself that without very much bloodshed it might be done." The other six men were also executed, while five escaped and fled north. Tensions between the free North and slaveholding South increased, eventually leading to a breakdown in any compromise over the expansion of slavery into the western U.S. territories. The secession of Southern states from the United States began in January 1861, with the first shots of the Civil War fired on 19 April 1861 in South Carolina. *See also* BROWN, JOHN; SECRET SIX.

*HARRIET.* A commercial biographical film about **Harriet Tubman** directed by Kasi Lemmons and based on a script written by Gregory Allen Howard and Lemmons. Filmed in Virginia in the late fall of 2018, it featured actors Cynthis Erivo as Tubman, Leslie Odum Jr., Janelle Monae, Vondie Curtis-Hall, Henry Hunter Hall, Joe Alwyn, and Clarke Peters, among others. Produced by Stay Gold Features, New Balloon, and Perfect World Pictures, *Harriet* was distributed by Focus Features Films. Released in November 2019, the film earned good reviews and several industry award nominations and more than tripled its $17 million production budget.

**HARRIET ON THE HILL DAY.** On 14 September 2011, more than one hundred Tubman parks supporters from Maryland to New York gathered in Washington, D.C., for Harriet on the Hill Day to pressure Congress to pass Senate Bill S. 247, the **Harriet Tubman National Historical Parks Act**, which would establish the Harriet Tubman National Historical Park and the Harriet Tubman Underground Railroad National Historical Park. The legislation eventually failed to pass at that time.

Harriet Tubman circa 1885, Auburn, New York. In 1886, Sarah H. Bradford published an updated edition of Tubman's biography in *Harriet, the Moses of Her People*. Photo by H. Seymour Squyer, ca. 1885. *National Portrait Gallery, Smithsonian*

*HARRIET, THE MOSES OF HER PEOPLE.* Book by **Sarah Hopkins Bradford**. Published by George R. Lockwood & Sons of New York in 1886, this biography of Harriet Tubman is more than a reprint of the 1868 *Scenes in the Life of Harriet Tubman*, also written by Bradford. The author reworked scenes from the earlier biography, added new details about Tubman's life, eliminated some details, and modified Tubman's speech to reflect a more caricatured plantation dialect. The tone of this version of Tubman's life is more bigoted, including racist stereotypes. A second edition of this biography was published in 1896 to help raise money for Tubman's support. A third edition, with an appendix with additional stories from Tubman's life, was published by Little & Company of New York in 1901.

*HARRIET TUBMAN.* Book by **Earl Conrad**. A biography, published by **Associated Publishers** of Washington, D.C., in 1943. Conrad interviewed people who had known Tubman during her lifetime, adding significant details to Tubman's life story not previously published. Conrad reveals Tubman in a more militant balanced light than **Sarah Hopkins Bradford**'s nineteenth-century biographies. Later editions were published as *General Tubman*.

**HARRIET TUBMAN ASSOCIATION.** *See* HARRIET TUBMAN ORGANIZATION, INC.

*HARRIET TUBMAN, CONDUCTOR ON THE UNDERGROUND RAILROAD.* A book for young readers by Ann Petry (New York: Crowell, 1955). A partially fictionalized portrayal of Harriet Tubman, the popular juvenile biography is still in print more than sixty years after its debut. Petry was a famous best-selling American author, earning accolades for her adult novels, including *The Street*, published in 1946, which sold more than a million copies and made her the first African American female author to achieve that goal.

**HARRIET TUBMAN HOME FOR THE AGED AND INFIRM NEGROES.** Officially opened in 1908 in Auburn, New York, the Home for the Aged was located on a twenty-five-acre

Harriet Tubman's wood-framed house burned in January 1881 and was replaced by this residence, built with bricks made on the property, in 1883. *Harriet Tubman Home, Inc., and Harriet Tubman National Historical Park*

parcel of land that **Harriet Tubman** purchased at auction in 1896 and that abutted Tubman's seven-acre farm on the Auburn and Fleming municipal boundaries. The wood-framed Home building served aging African Americans in need of assisted living services. **John Brown Hall**, a brick structure that provided more advanced nursing care, was also located on the property. Tubman transferred ownership and management of the property and buildings to the **African Methodist Episcopal Zion Church** (AME Zion) in 1903. Fundraising events and donations from Tubman relatives, the community, and supporters around the country helped furnish and financially secure the facilities for its opening in 1908. By the late 1920s, the Home for the Aged and John Brown Hall were no longer in active use and eventually closed. During the late 1940s, after John Brown Hall was destroyed by fire and vandals had nearly destroyed the Home, a group of Harriet Tubman relatives and community members established the Harriet Tubman Boosters, a nonprofit organization dedicated to restoring the twenty-five-acre property and the Home for use as a historic site. Still run and operated by the AME Zion church through a separate nonprofit 501(c)(3) entity called the **Harriet Tubman Home, Inc.**, the site is now a National Park. *See also* HARRIET TUBMAN NATIONAL HISTORICAL PARK (HART); JOHN BROWN HALL.

**HARRIET TUBMAN HOME, INC.** is an independent nonprofit established by the **African Methodist Episcopal Zion Church** to manage, preserve, and operate Harriet Tubman's thirty-two-acre homestead in Auburn, New York.

The property includes Tubman's brick residence and historic barn, **John Brown Hall**, and the **Harriet Tubman Home for the Aged and Infirm Negroes**. The Harriet Tubman Home, Inc., is charged with sharing Harriet Tubman's core values with visitors through guided tours of the property. On 10 January 2017 the **Harriet Tubman National Historical Park** was established on the property and shares management of the site.

**HARRIET TUBMAN MEMORIAL AND LEGACY GARDEN.** Located on Route 50 in **Cambridge, Maryland**, the garden features interpretive signage and murals painted by local artist Charles Ross that pay tribute to Tubman, her family, and members of the community who escaped to freedom. The garden is part of the **Harriet Tubman Underground Railroad Scenic Byway and All-American Road**.

**HARRIET TUBMAN MURAL.** Located beside the Harriet Tubman Museum and Educational Center in **Cambridge, Maryland**, the mural "Take My Hand" was created and painted by Michael Rosato, a renowned **Dorchester County, Maryland**, artist in May 2019. The 14-by-28-foot mural features Tubman with an outstretched hand, beckoning visitors to follow her. The mural was commissioned by the Dorchester Center for the Arts in a partnership project with Alpha Genesis CDC, the Maryland State Arts Council, and the **Harriet Tubman Organization**, with additional support from Downtown Cambridge. An early photo of a little girl reaching up to touch Tubman's hand on the mural went viral in 2019, bringing thousands of visitors to the small Maryland city to seek out the site.

**HARRIET TUBMAN MUSEUM AND EDUCATIONAL CENTER.** *See* HARRIET TUBMAN ORGANIZATION, INC.

**HARRIET TUBMAN NATIONAL HISTORICAL PARK (HART).** During the 110th, 111th, and 112th Congresses, legislation cosponsored by delegates from both Maryland and New York to create the Harriet Tubman National Historical Park in Auburn, New York, and the Harriet

During the final two years of her life, Harriet Tubman lived in John Brown Hall, the nursing home she established on her property in Auburn, New York. She died on 10 March 1913. Photo ca. 1912. *National American Woman Suffrage Association Collection, Library of Congress Rare Book and Special Collections*

Tubman Underground Railroad National Historical Park in **Dorchester County, Maryland**, failed to reach a vote during all sessions. Through Executive Order on 25 March 2013, President Barack Obama designated the **Harriet Tubman National Monument** in **Dorchester County**, under provisions in the Antiquities Act, in honor of Tubman and the site's historic and cultural significance. The creation of the National Monument did not satisfy the recommendations set forth in the **Harriet Tubman Special Resources Study** (SRS)—two National Parks in Tubman's honor. Maryland senator Benjamin L. Cardin and three cosponsors—New York senator Charles E. Schumer, Maryland senator Barbara A. Mikulski, and New York senator Kirsten E. Gillibrand—reintroduced the **Harriet Tubman National Historical Parks**

Harriet Tubman Barn and Brick Residence, Auburn, New York. Harriet Tubman Home, Inc., and Harriet Tubman National Historical Park. *Courtesy of the author*

Act, S. 247, in February 2013. In July 2014, the U.S. Senate passed the bill. Five months later, on 3 December 2014, the House and Senate leaders unveiled a final agreement on the 2015 National Defense Authorization Act (NDAA), which included language establishing national parks in Auburn and in Maryland. After the 2015 NDAA passed both the House and Senate, President Barack Obama signed it on 19 December 2014, authorizing the two national parks, including Harriet Tubman National Historical Park (HART) in Auburn. On 10 January 2017, Secretary of the Interior Sally Jewell formally established the park at a signing ceremony at the Department of the Interior's headquarters in Washington, D.C. The Tubman National Historical Park includes Tubman's former thirty-two-acre farm, brick residence, the **Harriet Tubman Home for the Aged**, the ruins of **John Brown Hall** on South Street, and **Thompson Memorial African Methodist Episcopal Zion Church** and Rectory on Parker Street in Auburn. The National Park Service owns and operates the church and rectory and will comanage the Tubman property with the **Harriet Tubman Home, Inc.**, a 501(c)(3) organization established by the AME Zion Church. The park also features a visitor center, library, and an audio tour.

**HARRIET TUBMAN NATIONAL HISTORICAL PARKS ACT, S. 247.** In the 112th Congress (2011–2012), Senator Ben Cardin (D-Maryland) sponsored S. 247, the Harriet Tubman National Historical Parks Act, which was cosponsored by Senator Mikulski (D-Maryland), Senator Schumer (D-New York), and Senator Gillibrand (D-New York). This Act would establish the Harriet Tubman National Historical Park in Auburn, New York, and the Harriet Tubman National Historical Park in **Caroline, Dorchester**, and Talbot counties, Maryland. A similar bill was introduced in the 111th Congress, in the U.S. Senate and U.S. House, but never made it out of committee. The legislation authorized the establishment of the park as a unit of the National Park System. It also provided an authorization of appropriations for the National Park Service to administer, interpret, and acquire the park. On 11 May 2011, the Senate Energy and Natural Resources Committee Subcommittee on

National Parks held a hearing to review S. 247. The Subcommittee voted favorably to support the legislation. The committee referred the legislation to "mark up" (debate, amend, or rewrite) the bill and hold a vote to move the bill to the floor of the U.S. Senate. **Harriet on the Hill Day** was sponsored by various Maryland state agencies and lawmakers to bring activists, supporters, stakeholders, and others to Capitol Hill to meet with Congresspeople and encourage passage of S. 247. It failed to pass. S. 247 was reintroduced in February 2013, and in July 2014, the U.S. Senate passed the bill. Five months later, on 3 December 2014, the House and Senate leaders unveiled a final agreement on the 2015 National Defense Authorization Act (NDAA), which included language establishing national parks in Auburn and in Maryland. After the 2015 NDAA passed both the House and Senate, President Barack Obama signed it on 19 December 2014, creating the Harriet Tubman Underground Railroad National Historical Park (HATU) in Maryland and the **Harriet Tubman National Historical Park** (HART) in Auburn, New York.

## HARRIET TUBMAN ORGANIZATION, INC. (1983–present).

The Harriet Tubman Organization, Inc. (HTO) is a community-based historical, cultural, and preservation association in **Cambridge, Maryland**. Officially founded in 1983, the HTO began as a small informal group who gathered together in 1974 and were known as the Harriet Tubman Association. By 1983, cofounders Addie Clash Travers and Reverend Edward Jackson called an organizational meeting at Waugh Chapel United Methodist Church in **Cambridge**, which included the following community members: Richard Bailey, Woodrow A. Pinder, Elaine Bennett, Myrtle Cromwell, Elsie M. Pinder, Louise Stanley, Mary S. Elliott, Reverend Edwin Ellis, Marvel Travis, Linda P. Wheatley, and Loretta P. Young. They collaborated with **Bazel United Methodist Church** in **Bucktown, Maryland**, to create an annual community event celebrating the life and legacy of **Harriet Tubman**. Though many members of the Black community had been unofficially celebrating Harriet Tubman Day for more than a decade, it became formalized in an annual June gathering. The organization developed a plan to fund and create a civic center to provide cultural, historical, social, economic, and educational resources in support of the community through mirroring Tubman's values and sharing her history and legacy. The HTO and its members have been one of the driving forces behind the establishment of the **Harriet Tubman Underground Railroad Byway and All-American Road**, the **Harriet Tubman Underground Railroad State Park**, and the **Harriet Tubman Underground Railroad National Historical Park**. Its headquarters, the Harriet Tubman Museum and Educational Center, is located at 424 Race Street, **Cambridge, Maryland**. Operated completely by volunteers, it hosts a small educational museum with exhibits, educational resources, and step-on-guided tours and promotes local activities and events associated with Tubman.

## HARRIET TUBMAN SPECIAL RESOURCES ACT.

In the late 1990s, through the encouragement of Vincent DeForest, special assistant to the director of the National Park Service, and Addie Richberg (International Network to Freedom Association), a meeting was held to discuss the idea of a Harriet Tubman National Park. Present at this meeting were Mike Long from the Auburn, New York, City Planning Office; AME Zion Church bishop George Herbert Walker; and Reverend Paul G. Carter, resident director of the **Harriet Tubman Home** and then-minister at **Thompson Memorial AME Zion Church** in Auburn. The group continued their discussions in Washington, D.C., with National Park Service director Robert Stanton. They tentatively approved the idea of turning Tubman's thirty-two-acre property in Auburn into a national park through a public-private partnership with the AME Zion Church and its nonprofit management entity, the **Harriet Tubman Home, Inc.**, similar to the partnership that operates the Martin Luther King Jr. Center for Nonviolent Social Change. Initial legislation for a **Harriet Tubman Special Resources Study** was drafted. This legislation primarily focused on the Tubman property, her Fort Hill Cemetery gravesite, Thompson Memorial AME Zion Church, and the **William Henry Seward**

House in Auburn, and St. Catharines, Canada, where Tubman spent time during the 1850s. Sponsored by Congressman Amo Houghton in 1997, the legislation did not include any sites related to Tubman's formative years in Maryland. Lacking broad congressional support, the bill failed to pass.

In April 2000, New York's Senator Charles Schumer reintroduced legislation for the Harriet Tubman Special Resources Study. The original group of supporters and leaders from Auburn, the NPS, and the AME Zion Church coordinated their efforts with members of the **Harriet Tubman Organization** in **Cambridge, Maryland** and other community and state supporters. The new legislation amended and expanded the former Houghton effort to include three sites in **Dorchester County—Bazel Church**, the former **Brodess Farm**, and the **Bucktown Village Store**. The legislation passed both the House and the Senate, and in November 2000, President Clinton signed the Harriet Tubman Special Resources Act. The act authorized the National Park Service to begin its study to determine the suitability and feasibility of establishing a national park in honor of Tubman.

**HARRIET TUBMAN SPECIAL RESOURCES STUDY (SRS) (2000–2008).** Established as a result of directives to the National Park Service in the **Harriet Tubman Special Resources Act**. The Harriet Tubman Special Resources Study took eight years to complete—one of the longest special resource studies ever conducted by the National Park Service. The study revealed that initial sites designated by the legislation were inadequate to represent Tubman's life history and contributions. With the help of historians, researchers, and local supporters in New York, Maryland, and from across the nation and Canada, new details of Tubman's life and activities expanded the scope of the resource study far beyond its original intent. The study identified significant sites in Maryland, South Carolina, Florida, New York, and New England. Maryland's Office of Business and Economic Development and the tourism and economic development offices in the city of **Cambridge** and in **Dorchester** and **Caroline** counties urged the National Park Service to expand its scope to include nearly two dozen historically and culturally significant sites on the **Eastern Shore of Maryland** in its proposed park boundaries. These sites, they argued, represented unique examples of a surviving nineteenth-century agrarian working landscape where people pursued traditional uses of farming, timbering, hunting, fishing, and trapping during Tubman's time. These landscapes included sites where she lived and worked as an enslaved person and where she conducted clandestine **Underground Railroad** activities. Many of the sites were already part of the **Harriet Tubman Underground Railroad Scenic Byway and All-American Road**.

In response, the National Park Service narrowed its focus to just sites in New York and Maryland. The **Harriet Tubman Organization**, Dorchester and Caroline County Historical Societies, state and local tourism, other local museums, site owners and partners, Blackwater NWR, Maryland State Parks, the NAACP, and numerous other local, regional, and national organizations and stakeholders joined in support of the National Park Service and its expanded study. The study, completed in November 2008, determined that resources (buildings and landscapes) in Auburn, New York, and in **Dorchester**, **Caroline**, and Talbot counties in Maryland met criteria for units of the park system. The secretary of the interior transmitted the study and its recommendations to Congress on 12 January 2009, with support for establishing two units of the National Park System—one in New York and one in Maryland—to honor Tubman.

**HARRIET TUBMAN UNDERGROUND RAILROAD NATIONAL HISTORICAL MONUMENT (HATU).** Eastern Shore, Maryland. In September 2012, the State of Maryland requested that President Barack Obama designate the **Harriet Tubman National Monument** in **Dorchester County**. The Conservation Fund owned a 480-acre parcel near **Madison**, which once contained the farm of **Jacob Jackson**, a free Black farmer and veterinarian who helped Tubman plan the rescue of her brothers during **Christmas Day 1854**. The Fund transferred the land to the Department of the Interior for the National Park Service, which enabled the president, under provisions in the Antiquities Act, to designate the site a National Monument in honor of Tubman and the site's historic and cultural significance. President Obama designated the Harriet Tubman National Monument through an Executive Order on 25 March 2013, during a signing ceremony in the Oval Office.

The creation of the National Monument did not satisfy the recommendations set forth in the **Harriet Tubman Special Resources Study** (SRS)—two National Parks in Tubman's honor. Maryland senator Benjamin L. Cardin and three cosponsors—New York senator Charles E. Schumer, Maryland senator Barbara A. Mikulski, and New York senator Kirsten E. Gillibrand—reintroduced the **Harriet Tubman National Historical Parks Act, S. 247**, in February 2013. In July 2014, the U.S. Senate passed the bill. Five months later, on 3 December 2014, the House and Senate leaders unveiled a final agreement on the 2015 National Defense Authorization Act (NDAA), which included language establishing national parks in Auburn and in Maryland. After the 2015 NDAA passed both the House and Senate, President Barack Obama signed it on 19 December 2014. Though the previous Presidential Proclamation in 2013 created the 480-acre **Harriet Tubman Underground Railroad National Monument** in **Dorchester County**, the Harriet Tubman Underground Railroad National Historical Park included more than eleven thousand acres in **Dorchester County** and additional authorized acquisition areas in **Caroline** and Talbot counties. The National Park Service administers the Harriet Tubman Underground Railroad National Monument and the Harriet Tubman Underground Railroad National Historical Park as one unit. NPS manages the park unit from offices at the separately owned and operated seventeen-acre **Harriet Tubman Underground Railroad State Park and Visitor Center** in Church Creek, Maryland.

**HARRIET TUBMAN UNDERGROUND RAILROAD NATIONAL HISTORICAL MONUMENT HISTORIC RESOURCE STUDY (HRS) (December 2019).** A study commissioned by the National Park Service Northeast Region History Program in Partnership with the Organization of American Historians and researched and written by Dr. Kate Clifford Larson. Based on guidelines developed by the National Park Service Office of Policy: *NPS-28 Cultural Resource Management Guidelines*, the HRS provides a historical overview of the monument and park and identifies and evaluates a park's cultural resources within historic contexts. The HRS is used by the Tubman park managers, planners, interpreters, cultural resource specialists, and the interested public as a reference for the history of the region and its resources within the park boundaries.

**HARRIET TUBMAN UNDERGROUND RAILROAD NATIONAL HISTORICAL PARK.** *See* HARRIET TUBMAN UNDERGROUND RAILROAD NATIONAL HISTORICAL MONUMENT (HATU).

**HARRIET TUBMAN UNDERGROUND RAILROAD SCENIC BYWAY AND ALL-AMERICAN ROAD.** The Tubman Byway winds through 125 miles of beautiful historic landscapes of Maryland's **Eastern Shore** and then another 98 miles through Delaware and into Pennsylvania. It includes forty-five historically significant sites related to **Harriet Tubman**, African American history and culture, and the **Underground Railroad**. The **Harriet Tubman Underground Railroad State Park Visitor Center** and **Bucktown Village Store** are sights along the Byway. A free self-guided, scenic driving tour—with a map and guide, audio, and Augmented Reality offerings—includes outdoor markers and interpretive signs that share the story of that place. Other highlights include the **Harriet Tubman Memorial and Legacy Garden**, the Harriet Tubman Museum and Educational Center, the **Harriet Tubman Mural**, **Long Wharf**, the **Brodess Farm**, the **William Still Center**, and the Leverton House. https://harriettubmanbyway.org/.

**HARRIET TUBMAN UNDERGROUND RAILROAD STATE PARK.** Church Creek, Maryland. In 2004, efforts to establish a Harriet Tubman State Park in **Dorchester County**

Harriet Tubman Underground Railroad State Park and Visitor Center and National Park headquarters, Church Creek, Maryland. *Photo, Acroterion. Wikimedia Commons*

began in earnest. At the urging of the Dorchester County Office of Tourism, the Heart of the Chesapeake Heritage Area Committee, and the **Harriet Tubman Organization**, the Maryland Department of Budget and Economic Development's (Maryland DBED) Office of Tourism responded. Recognizing the rising interest and advocacy to commemorate Tubman and the **Underground Railroad**, and the need to protect the significant Maryland sites identified by the **Harriet Tubman Special Resources Study** (SRS), county and state officials launched a working group of interested people and organizations to coordinate efforts and advise on a potential state park project. In 2007, the transfer of a seventeen-acre site known as the Linthicum Tract on Key Wallace Drive owned by **Blackwater National Wildlife Refuge** (BNWR) to the State of Maryland and facilitated by a land exchange coordinated by the Conservation Fund officially established the Harriet Tubman Underground Railroad State Park. The years-long process to build out the park involved a broad cross-section of community members; local, county, and state elected officials; tourism, business, and state and local heritage organizations; Maryland State Parks and Department of Natural Resources; the Conservation Fund; historians; family members; the National Park Service; interpretive specialists; and other Tubman stakeholders. A visitor center was completed in early 2017 on the seventeen-acre site. Considered the trailhead for the **Harriet Tubman Underground Railroad Byway and All-American Road**, the **Harriet Tubman Underground Railroad State Park Visitor Center** opened on 10 March 2017 and has hosted more than 250,000 visitors from all fifty states and sixty countries.

**HARRIET TUBMAN UNDERGROUND RAILROAD STATE PARK VISITOR CENTER. Church Creek, Maryland.** Opened to the public on 10 March 2017, the Visitor Center was designed by GWWO Architects, Baltimore, Maryland. The 6,000-square-foot Center is LEED Certified, with indoor and outdoor exhibits, orientation theater, library, multipurpose room, gift shop, offices, break room, exhibit storage space, memorial garden, walking paths, and a picnic pavilion. These features express the importance of traveling northward to escape the circumstances of slavery through an integrated site, building, and exhibit design. The Center immerses visitors in the story of Tubman's life. The Center's LEED Silver Certification includes many sustainable design strategies including vegetative roofs, skylights and sun tubes, rainwater capture for plant watering, bio-retention ponds, low-flow toilet room fixtures, and geothermal heat exchange system.

**HARRINGTON, SAMUEL (6 February 1803–2 July 1878).** A merchant and farmer in **Madison, Maryland**, Harrington enslaved **Winnebar Johnson**; his sisters Ann, Charlotte, and Ellen; two male children; and an adult man named Joe in 1852. Johnson successfully escaped with the help of **Harriet Tubman** on 10 June 1854. Harrington was so angry he sold the three Johnson sisters. Ann later escaped from the man who purchased her in Maryland, but Charlotte and Ellen were sold to out-of-state buyers and never heard from again.

**HART, ALBERT BUSHNELL (1 July 1854–16 July 1943).** Born in Mercer County, Pennsylvania, Hart graduated from Harvard University in 1880 and received his doctorate in history in 1883 from Freiberg University in Germany. He secured a professorship at Harvard and taught there for forty-three years and wrote several histories of the United States. He interviewed **Harriet Tubman** sometime in the late 1890s or early 1900s, recording her memory of the Battle of Fort Wagner during the **Civil War** and publishing it in the sixteenth volume of his twenty-seven-volume series *American Nation*. He died in Boston in 1943.

**HASKINS, MARGARET (ca. 1814–unknown).** Enslaved by William Willoughby in **Dorchester County, Maryland**. According to Willoughby's 1827 will, Haskins was to be set free on 1 January 1858 when she would have been forty-four years old. Haskins was purchased by Dr. Francis Phelps of Dorchester in 1838. Haskins's husband, name unknown, was enslaved by a farmer named James Hall who lived near Phelps. On 31 December 1857, within hours of her legal freedom, Haskins, her husband, and their four enslaved children escaped with the help of **Daniel Hubbard** and **Arthur Leverton**, who lived in nearby **Caroline County, Maryland**. The family was captured within days near Greensboro, Maryland. Haskins was tried in court for illegally helping enslaved people to run away and found not guilty. Her fate remains a mystery. Her husband was sold, and the children remained the property of Phelps.

**HAYDEN, LEWIS (ca. 1811–7 April 1889).** Born enslaved in Lexington, Kentucky, Hayden was sold at the age of ten to a traveling salesman who traveled widely and gave Hayden a view of a world beyond slavery. He married a woman named Esther in the 1830s, but she and their son were sold to the **Deep South** and he never saw them again. After marrying a woman named Harriet Bell in 1842, he conspired to escape with her and her son. With the assistance of **abolitionists** Calvin Fairbanks and Delia Webster in Lexington, and later John Rankin of Ripley, Ohio, the Haydens successfully made it to Canada and freedom in the fall of 1844. Webster and Fairbanks were subsequently arrested and jailed for aiding in the Haydens' escape.

Two years later, the family moved to Boston, where Hayden opened a used clothing store and became active in the city's **abolitionist** community. He lectured for the **American Anti-Slavery Society** and was a member of the **Boston Vigilance Committee**. The Hayden home on Beacon Hill became the center of **Underground Railroad** activity, boldly defying **slave catchers** roaming the city in search of **freedom seekers**, and Hayden on at least one occasion threatened to blow up his house to scare off bounty hunters. **Harriet Tubman** stayed with the Haydens on one or more of her trips to the city during the 1850s. Lewis recruited men to fill the ranks of the **Fifty-Fourth Massachusetts Voluntary Infantry Regiment**, and after the **Civil War** he became active in state politics and voter registration.

He died in 1889 and is buried in Woodlawn Cemetery in Everett, Massachusetts, with his wife Harriet, who died in 1894.

**HAYWARD, ISAAC (dates unknown).** Born enslaved in South Carolina, Hayward became a scout for the U.S. Army during the **Civil War**. He was a member of **Harriet Tubman**'s team who spied on **Confederate** forces and relayed information to Union officers. The other scouts were **Mott Blake, Peter Burns, Sandy Sellers, George Chisholm, Solomon Gregory, Gabriel Cahern, Walter D. Plowden**, and river pilots **Charles Simmons** and **Samuel Hayward**. Under Tubman's command, the group was considered by General **Rufus Saxton** to be among "the most valued scouts and pilots in the Gov't employ in" Hilton Head, South Carolina.

**HAYWARD, SAMUEL (dates unknown).** Born enslaved in South Carolina, Hayward was a river pilot who aided the U.S. Army during the **Civil War**. He was a member of **Harriet Tubman**'s team who spied on **Confederate** forces and relayed information to Union officers. The other scouts were **Isaac Hayward, Mott Blake, Peter Burns, Sandy Sellers, George Chisholm, Solomon Gregory, Gabriel Cahern, Walter D. Plowden**, and **Charles Simmons**, also a river pilot. Under Tubman's command, the group was considered by General **Rufus Saxton** to be among "the most valued scouts and pilots in the Gov't employ in" Hilton Head, South Carolina. Hayward and Simmons were vital to safe navigation along heavily mined waters in the Hilton Head district.

**HAZLETT, HUGH (ca. 1825–unknown).** Born in Ireland, Hazlett immigrated to the United States in 1844. By 1855, Hazlett moved to **Dorchester County** and began working as a lumberjack and sawyer. He may have been involved in **Underground Railroad** activity in Pennsylvania, but on the night of Saturday, 24 July 1858, he helped **William Henry Cornish, Mary Light, Charles Anthony Light, Esther Cornish, Solomon Cornish, Thomas Rideout**, and **John Green** flee their enslavers in the Town Point and **Cambridge** areas in **Dorchester County, Maryland**. He may have harbored the **freedom seekers** in his home for an unknown amount of time.

The group made slow progress north. Over the course of six days, they had only traveled northeast about fifty miles to an area between Henderson and Templeville, in **Caroline County**, near the border of Queen Anne's County, Maryland, and Kent County, Delaware. It was there that the group was betrayed by a local free Black man named Jesse Perry, who, in collusion with several white men, including John Walls, Titus West, William Wicks, Mr. Tarr, Mr. Knotts, Henry Johnson, Edward C. Johnson of Caroline County, and William H. Grace and Samuel R. Vinton of Dorchester County, captured them. These men shared in the $1,000 reward offered for the enslaved people and an additional reward for the arrest of Hugh Hazlett. Hazlett and the **freedom seekers** were lodged in the **Denton** jail, located next to the county courthouse on the square in **Denton**. The following Monday, August 2, they were taken to the wharf on the West Denton side of the **Choptank River** from the courthouse and jail, where the steamboat *Kent* waited for its weekly departure down the river and up the Chesapeake Bay for Baltimore. By seven o'clock that morning, the group had boarded the steamer not knowing what fates awaited them back in **Dorchester County**. On the morning of August 2, Hazlett and the **freedom seekers** traveled on the steamboat *Kent* from Denton via the **Choptank River** to **Cambridge**, where a mob had gathered to await their arrival at **Long Wharf**. The sheriff feared the mob would lynch Hazlett, so he ordered the steamboat to leave **Long Wharf** and dock at another location upriver. Hazlett was later safely secured in the **Cambridge** jail. The **freedom seekers** were reenslaved, and Hazlett was tried and convicted and sent to prison for forty-four years. He was pardoned and released from prison on 21 December 1864, several weeks after the State of Maryland outlawed slavery.

**HENRY, JOHN CAMPBELL (21 April 1808–1 April 1857).** A wealthy planter and merchant in **Cambridge, Maryland**, Henry enslaved more than two dozen people when **John Chase** escaped from Henry's estate on the **Choptank River** and made his way to **Caroline County, Maryland**, and joined **Harriet Tubman** and her brothers **Henry Ross, Benjamin Ross Jr.,** and **Robert Ross** on **Christmas Day 1854**. Two years later, Henry's enslaved man **William "Bill" Bailey** escaped with **Joseph "Joe" Bailey, Peter Pennington,** and **Eliza Manokey** on 15 November 1856. Henry offered a $300 reward for the capture of Bailey.

**HICKS, THOMAS H.** (2 September 1798–13 February 1865). Born in **Dorchester County, Maryland**, Hicks held various local and state political offices, including governor from 1858 to 1862. He was a Unionist and devoted his energies to preventing Maryland from joining the Confederacy in the early years of the **Civil War**. Elected as a U.S. senator in 1863, he died in office in 1865. He is buried in the Cambridge Cemetery.

**HIGGINSON, THOMAS WENTWORTH** (22 December 1823–9 May 1911). Born in Cambridge, Massachusetts, Higginson's family was among the original European settlers of New England and influential American patriots of the American Revolution. Trained as a minister, Higginson became a radical **abolitionist** and was a member of the **Boston Vigilance Committee**, helping in the escape of several high-profile **freedom seekers** during the 1850s, including Thomas Sims and Anthony Burns. Activists **William Lloyd Garrison** and **Lydia Maria Child** deeply influenced Higginson's antislavery views. Higginson met **Harriet Tubman** in Boston in 1858 and reported on her speeches in his letters and diaries. He was a strong supporter of **John Brown** and was a member of Brown's **Secret Six**. During the **Civil War** Higginson was the colonel of the First South Carolina Colored Volunteers, one of the first African American regiments formed early in the war. While in service in South Carolina, he saw Tubman at work as a spy and scout. He disapproved of Colonel **James Montgomery**, the leader of the Second South Carolina Colored Volunteers who worked with Tubman, because he burned plantations and destroyed crops as punishment to rebel forces. Higginson was a staunch supporter of women's rights.

**HILL, JOSEPH "JOE"** (ca. 1837–unknown). Born in Maryland and enslaved by **Samuel Pattison**, Hill escaped on 24 October 1857 with twenty-six other people, including his sister **Sarah Jane Hill**. The group famously became known as the **Cambridge 28**. His free wife and son, Alice and Henry, joined him, too. The Hills were interviewed by **Underground Railroad** agent **William Still** in Philadelphia. Hill and his family successfully made their way to freedom and settled in Canada.

**HILL, SARAH JANE** (ca. 1832–unknown). Born in Maryland and enslaved by **Samuel Pattison**, Hill escaped on 24 October 1857 with twenty-six other people, including her brother **Joseph Hill**. The group famously became known as the **Cambridge 28**. Sarah may have been hired off the Pattison plantation at the time she ran away with the rest; it was not until a few days after the escape that Pattison realized that she, too, was gone. The Hills were interviewed by **Underground Railroad** agent **William Still** in Philadelphia. They all made their way to freedom and settled in Canada.

**HILTON HEAD, SOUTH CAROLINA.** A barrier island along the Atlantic Coast of South Carolina on the southwest side of Port Royal Sound. In November 1861, during the **Civil War**, the U.S. Army and Navy seized the island and surrounding area from the Confederacy and used it as a base of operations in the region throughout the war. **Harriet Tubman** was stationed there while working as a scout and spy for the Union Army.

**HIRING OUT OF SLAVES.** *See* LEASING OF SLAVES.

**HOLLEY, SALLIE** (17 February 1818–12 January 1893). Born in Canandaigua, New York, Holley was an abolitionist, writer, suffragist, educator, and friend of **Harriet Tubman**. Holley published a letter to the *National Anti-Slavery Standard* on 30 November 1867, highlighting Tubman's petition to receive back pay as a scout and spy during the **Civil War** and efforts to gain restitution for her injuries from the train incident two years earlier. Holley exaggerated some of Tubman's accomplishments and fraudulently claimed that there was a $40,000 reward posted for Tubman's capture during the 1850s.

**HOLLIS, JAMES.** Colluded with **Thomas Otwell** in March 1857 to capture eight **freedom seekers** known as the **Dover Eight**. Hollis and Otwell lured the group into the Dover, Delaware, jail on the pretext that the group would be safe there for the night before they continued their journey north to freedom. The two men hoped to share in the more than $3,000 reward for the capture of the **Dover Eight**.

**HOLT, ROSA BELLE (1856–unknown).** Born in Buffalo, New York, Holt traveled around the world beginning at a young age. A writer who published dozens of articles and books, she was also a women's suffrage activist and friends with Auburn's women's rights activists, including **Eliza Wright Osborne**. During a visit with Osborne in 1896, Holt interviewed Tubman and published an article in the July 1896 issue of *Chautauquan* about their conversations called "A Heroine in Ebony." Though Holt relied heavily on **Sarah Hopkins Bradford**'s biographies, Holt's interviews yielded fresh Tubman quotes and some new biographical information. Holt's travels and deep interest in antique carpets led to a later career in buying and selling rare examples for clients during her travels abroad.

**HOOPER, JOHN H. (ca. 1811–ca. 1890).** Born enslaved on the **Eastern Shore of Maryland**, Hooper escaped sometime in 1844 and fled to Troy, New York. There, he joined his wife, Mary Ann, who had escaped in 1841. Working as a painter, he and Mary, a washerwoman, owned their own home in Troy and were active in the antislavery and **Underground Railroad** activities along with other Black Maryland **freedom seekers**. He told associates that he grew up near **Frederick Bailey Douglass** in Talbot County, Maryland.

**Harriet Tubman** claimed John was her cousin. She stayed with him when she visited Troy and was there on 27 April 1860 when **Charles Nalle** was captured by **slave catchers** looking for him in the city and turned over to federal marshals to be returned to Virginia and his enslaver, **Blucher Hansbrough**. Her proximity to the courthouse enabled Tubman to rescue Nalle that day.

**HOPKINS, HENRY (dates unknown).** One of four men who escaped from **Cabin Creek** north of East New Market, Maryland, with **Harriet Tubman** on 26 April 1856. Hopkins, enslaved by John Houston, escaped with **James Coleman** and **Benjamin Jackson**, who were enslaved by **Isaac Henry Wright**, a wealthy planter. The fourth **freedom seeker**, **William A. Cook**, was enslaved by **Levin Hodson**. Tubman had led them safely to New Castle, Delaware, but bounty hunters eager for the high rewards for their capture slowed them down, forcing them to stay hidden for several days. **Thomas Garrett** in Wilmington, Delaware, was able to finally forward them to **William Still**, an **Underground Railroad** agent in Philadelphia. Still noted their arrival after they sought shelter with **Mrs. Buchanon** and forwarded them onto agent **Sydney Howard Gay** of New York City, who wrote that "Captain Tubman" had arrived safely with the men on May 14th. He sent them on to Syracuse, New York, where they received help getting to Canada, where they settled among other **freedom seekers** they knew.

**HOPKINS, SAMUEL M., JR. (8 August 1813–29 October 1901).** Presbyterian minister and theologian. He was a professor at the Auburn Theological Seminary in Auburn, New York. His sister, Sarah Hopkins Bradford, wrote and published biographies of Harriet Tubman. Samuel wrote the "Essay on Woman-Whipping" for the 1868 edition of *Scenes in the Life of Harriet Tubman* and wrote the introduction to the 1886 *Harriet, the Moses of Her People*. He hosted Tubman at his home on Owasco Lake, where Sarah interviewed Tubman for another edition of the biography published in 1901.

**HOWE, FRANCIS EDWARD (1828–1883).** Born in Brookline, Massachusetts, Howe moved to New York City and established a store selling business equipment in the 1850s. At the outbreak of the American **Civil War** in 1861, he offered resources and the use of the store rooms in his business to take care of sick and wounded Massachusetts soldiers who passed through the city on their way home from the battlefields. His work was organized into the New England Soldiers' Relief Association. Governor **John A. Andrew** of Massachusetts appointed Howe to a position on the governor's staff with the rank of lieutenant colonel. At Andrew's request, Howe made arrangements for **Harriet Tubman** to travel from New York City to Washington, D.C., in early January 1862 during her journey from Boston to Hilton Head, South Carolina, to work as a spy and scout for the Union Army.

**HOWE, SAMUEL GRIDLEY (10 November 1801–9 January 1876).** A Boston, Massachusetts, physician and married to Julia Ward Howe, Howe was a staunch **abolitionist**. He supported and funded **John Brown** and was a member of the **Secret Six**. He helped **freedom seekers** escape through his work with the **Boston Vigilance Committee**. In 1863, the **American Freedmen's Inquiry Commission** sent Howe on a fact-finding mission in Canada and several Southern states under Union Army control to interview freedom seekers and newly freed people. He recorded the economic and social conditions formerly enslaved people were experiencing in freedom. He noted the continued problem of anti-Black racism and discrimination, as well as the many benefits of living in a free society.

In the fall, Howe interviewed **Harriet Tubman's** brother William Henry Stewart and fellow **freedom seeker** from Maryland **William Cornish** in St. Catharines, Ontario, Canada. He may have seen Tubman in Canada at that time, as she was visiting family there while on leave from her work in Hilton Head. Howe's work was published as *The Refugees from Slavery in Canada West* in 1864 by the commission. During the **Civil War**, Howe worked with the U.S. Sanitary Commission to help improve conditions in the field that contributed to infections and to diseases like dysentery and then with the **Freedmen's Bureau** to help provide resources to newly freed people. He spent the rest of his life devoted to politics and charitable work. His wife, Julia Ward Howe, wrote the famous "Battle Hymn of the Republic" at the start of the **Civil War**. He died in 1876 and is buried in Mount Auburn Cemetery in Cambridge, Massachusetts.

**HOWLAND, EMILY (20 November 1827–29 June 1929).** Born in Sherwood, New York, to wealthy Quaker parents, Emily was a devoted **abolitionist**, teacher, woman suffragist, and philanthropist. She devoted much of her adult life to financially supporting Black schools and paid for the college education of several young Black women and men. She likely met **Harriet Tubman** through **Frances Seward** in Auburn, New York, in the fall of 1863. They became fast friends. After Tubman suffered injuries during the **Gold Swindle** incident in the fall of 1873, Emily Howland took her into her home in Sherwood and nursed her back to health. Howland acquired a copy of a carte de visite (photograph) of forty-six-year-old Tubman, taken in Auburn by **Benjamin Powelson** in 1868. That photograph was among a group of images of Black and white friends stored in one of Howland's photo albums, which sold at auction in March 2017 for $160,000. Howland outlived many of her activist friends and passed away at the age of 101 in 1929 in her family home in Sherwood.

**HUBBARD, DANIEL (ca. 1795–unknown).** A free Black farmer and skilled millwright in **Caroline County, Maryland**. His wife, Phoebe, and children, Mary, Elizabeth, and Solomon, were enslaved though allowed to live with him on his fifty-five-acre farm near **Preston, Maryland**. Hubbard leased his family from their enslaver so that he could raise his children. Though Hubbard managed his own farm, he likely worked at the nearby **Linchester Mill**, as wages for millwrights were good and would have provided the financial resources enabling Hubbard to keep his family with him. Hubbard's farm was situated along the border between **Dorchester** and **Caroline County** in a Quaker community of **Underground Railroad** activists, including **Jonah** and **Hester Kelley**, **Jonah** and **Hannah Leverton**, and **Arthur W. Leverton**. Jonah Kelley's son, William T. Kelley, later wrote that some "**fugitives** coming to the home of my father . . . were directed to Daniel's house." Hubbard was involved in the escape of **Margaret Haskins**, who fled with her husband and five children on New Year's Eve, 31 December 1857. Within the week, the Haskins family was caught, and Hubbard and Arthur Leverton were implicated in their escape. Soon, a lynch mob threatened to exact extra-legal revenge and hang them, so the two men fled. What happened to Hubbard remains unknown. His family remained enslaved until **Emancipation in Maryland** in November 1864.

**HUDSON, EPHRAIM** (ca. 1832–unknown). Born in **Dorchester County, Maryland**, Hudson was enslaved by **John Campbell Henry** of **Cambridge**. Hudson fled on 20 September 1856 in company with four other men: **Francis Molock, Joshua Handy, Charles Dutton**, and **Cyrus Mitchell**. They followed instructions likely given to them by **Harriet Tubman**. After passing through **Thomas Garrett**'s home in Wilmington, Delaware, the men arrived in Philadelphia, where they were interviewed on September 29 by **William Still**. Still noted that Hudson used John Spry as an alias. The **freedom seekers** reached Canada safely.

**HUGHES, DENARD (DANIEL DENWOOD)** (ca. 1827–unknown). Enslaved by **Pritchett Meredith** near **Bucktown, Maryland**, Hughes escaped in early March 1857 with **Thomas Elliott, Henry Predeaux, James** and **Lavinia Woolford, Bill** and **Emily Kiah**, and an unidentified man named Tubman. The group used instructions given to them by **Harriet Tubman** and followed her **Underground Railroad** route through Delaware. Their near capture but successful breakout in Dover, Delaware, earned them the nickname the **Dover Eight**. Meredith posted a reward advertisement for Hughes, offering $600 for the capture of both Hughes and Elliott. Hughes made it to Canada, where he settled in St. Catharines. Tubman recruited Hughes and Elliott to fight with **John Brown** during his raid on **Harpers Ferry**, Virginia. Hughes changed his mind and did not follow Brown to Virginia.

**HUGHLETT, WILLIAM (1816–1885).** A Talbot County, Maryland, merchant, farmer, and shipbuilder. His extensive holdings included thousands of acres of forest and fields and waterfront properties used for shipping and ship construction. He enslaved scores of people and leased many more from regional slaveholders to work for him. Two of his enslaved people, **Josiah "Joe" Bailey** and **William "Bill" Bailey**, whom Hughlett had leased for a year, escaped from Hughlett in November 1856 in company with **Peter Pennington** and **Eliza Manokey**. They were helped to freedom by **Harriet Tubman**. Hughlett posted a $1,500 reward for Joe Bailey's capture.

**HUNTER, DAVID** (21 July 1802–2 February 1886). Born in Troy, New York, Hunter spent more than four decades in the U.S. Army. During the **Civil War**, he was appointed major general in command of the **Department of the South** and stationed in Hilton Head in March 1862. An **abolitionist**, he advocated for the enlistment of Black men into the U.S. Army and formed the First South Carolina (African Descent) to fulfill that mission. Ordered to disband the regiment by his superiors, Hunter refused and on 11 May 1862 issued General Order 11, which declared that all enslaved people in South Carolina, Georgia, and Florida were free. President **Abraham Lincoln** rescinded Hunter's order. Hunter effectively ignored the revocation in practice and continued to recruit and drill his newly emancipated soldiers. Lincoln's policy officially remained in effect until the **Emancipation Proclamation** was inaugurated on 1 January 1863.

**Harriet Tubman** served under Hunter while working as a scout and spy for the Union. He admired her greatly and trusted her judgment and military intelligence work explicitly. Francis Jackson Merriam, an **abolitionist** and one of the men who followed **John Brown** to **Harpers Ferry** but escaped, witnessed Hunter and Tubman together. In a 13 June 1863 letter to

Harriet Tubman worked under Major General David Hunter during the Civil War as a scout and spy. She is pictured in her Civil War Union great coat, with haversack and a specialty sharpshooter rifle. Frontispiece to *Scenes in the Life of Harriet Tubman*, 1868. Artist, John G. Darby. *National Portrait Gallery, Smithsonian Institution*

Governor **John A. Andrew** of Massachusetts, Merriam wrote of Hunter, "I have seen this Major General, commanding a Department, go and fetch a pitcher of water and stand waiting with it in his hand while a black woman drank, as if he had been one of his own servants—that woman was Harriet Tubman." After the war, Hunter served on the military tribunal tasked with prosecuting the eight co-conspirators involved in the Lincoln assassination. He died in 1886 and is buried in Princeton, New Jersey.

**"I'M ON MY WAY TO CANADA."** Song that **Harriet Tubman** sang after arriving at the train station in **Niagara Falls**, Ontario, Canada, with **freedom seekers Joe Bailey**, Bill Bailey, **Eliza Manokey**, and **Peter Pennington** around 1 December 1856. Written by Joshua McCarter Simpson (ca. 1820–1877), an African American **abolitionist**, poet, composer, and herbalist, the song was a popular tune on the antislavery lecture circuit during the 1850s, where Tubman would have heard it performed. The song was sung to the tune of "Oh Suzannah!" and here is Tubman's slightly altered version of Simpson's original:

I'm on my way to Canada,
That cold and dreary land;
The sad effects of slavery,
I can't no longer stand.

I've served my master all my days,
Without a dime's reward;
And now I'm forced to run away,
To flee the lash abroad.

Farewell, ole master, don't think hard of me,
I'll travel on to Canada, where all the slaves
  are free.

The hounds are baying on my track,
Ole master comes behind.
Resolved that he will bring me back,
Before I cross the line;

I'm now embarked for yonder shore,
There a man's a man by law;
The iron horse will bear me o'er,
To shake the lion's paw.

Oh, righteous Father, wilt thou not pity me,
And aid me on to Canada where all the
  slaves are free.

Oh, I heard Queen Victoria say,
That if we would forsake
Our native land of slavery,
And come across the lake;

That she was standin' on the shore,
With arms extended wide,
To give us all a peaceful home
Beyond the rolling tide.

Farewell, ole master, don't think hard of me,
I'll travel on to Canada, where all the slaves
  are free.

**INDENTURED SERVITUDE.** An inequitable economic contract between a free person and an employer where the free person signs a no-wage labor contract for a term of years in return for some monetized benefit. For instance, poorer European immigrants during the seventeenth and eighteenth centuries chose this system as a means of establishing themselves in the colonies. Typically, they signed seven-year indenture contracts in return for the high cost of sailing to North America. Wealthy planters, ship captains, and businesspeople paid for the workers' passage in return for their free labor. Young children were often indentured until adulthood. Once the contract term was over, the worker was then free to earn and keep their own wages. The indenturing of orphaned or poor white children often required a contract ensuring the employer housed, fed, and clothed the child and taught them a trade. The indenturing of free Black children by whites became commonplace, often against the wishes of their free parents. This contract system denied parents of their rights to their own children and the benefits of the child's labor. After the **Civil War** and **Emancipation**, the indenturing of formerly enslaved children by former enslavers proliferated as a means to keep their free labor and that of formerly enslaved parents. **Harriet Tubman**'s brother **Robert Ross** had two young sons, John Ross Jr. and **Moses Ross**, who were indentured by **Thomas Haddaway** and his wife, **Sarah**, when the state of Maryland outlawed slavery on 1 November 1864. After the **Civil War**, **John Bowley** secretly took the two boys from the Haddaway plantation in Talbot County, Maryland, and sent them to Auburn, New York, in the late 1860s where Ross was then living a new life as **John Stewart Sr.**

# J

**JACKSON, DINAH BELL (ca. 1799–ca. 1873).** A free African American woman, likely born in the **White Marsh** and **Peter's Neck** area of **Dorchester County, Maryland**. She married **Jacob Jackson** in the early 1830s. She and her husband ran a farm, raised several children of their own, and took in orphaned children of free neighbors and relatives. They raised sheep, and Dinah spun the wool and possibly dyed the yarn for sale. She knew **Harriet Tubman** and her family. After Jacob's death, she struggled to maintain ownership of their 140-acre farm. By 1870 she lost the property to creditors. She died sometime in 1873. Dinah and Jacob Jackson's former homesite is part of the Harriet Tubman Underground Railroad National Historical Park in **Dorchester County, Maryland**.

**JACKSON, JACOB (ca. 1795–1864).** Born enslaved near **Madison, Maryland**, in the mid-1790s, Jackson became free when his enslavers, the John Jones family, **manumitted** him in the early 1830s. He married **Dinah Bell**, a free woman. Jackson owned land in the **White Marsh** area south of **Madison** and near **Malone's African Methodist Episcopal Church** and later purchased about 150 acres west of Madison near Parson's Creek. He and Dinah raised their free born and adopted children and operated a small farm and raised sheep for wool and meat, and Jacob served as a respected veterinarian to Black and white residents in the **Madison** area. Literate, Jackson knew **Harriet Tubman** and her family and assisted her efforts to liberate her brothers, **Robert, Ben**, and **Henry Ross** during **Christmas Day 1854**. With the help of a friend in Philadelphia, Tubman sent a letter to Jackson, using a code they agreed upon at some point prior to 1854. Caution on their part proved necessary because the suspicious **Madison, Maryland**, postmaster read Jackson's mail. In the letter Tubman asked Jackson to "read my letter to the old folks, and give my love to them, and tell my brothers to be always watching unto prayer, and when the good old ship of Zion comes along, to be ready to step aboard." Tubman had the letter signed "William Henry Jackson," the name of one of Jackson's adopted sons who had left **Dorchester County** some years before, to disguise her identity. When questioned by the authorities, Jackson denied knowing what the letter meant and threw it away, but he quickly contacted Tubman's brothers who were working for landowners in **Peter's Neck** near Jackson's home, informing them she was coming for them. He died in 1864 at the age of about sixty-nine years old. Dinah and Jacob Jackson's former homesite is part of the Harriet Tubman Underground Railroad National Historical Park and is located along the **Harriet Tubman Underground Railroad Byway and All-American Road** in Dorchester County, Maryland.

**JACKSON, PETER (ca. 1826–unknown).** Born in **Dorchester County, Maryland**, Peter was enslaved by George Winthrop, a farmer who lived near **Cambridge, Maryland**. His parents were free, his mother **manumitted** sometime after Peter's birth. He escaped from Winthrop on 21 November 1850 but returned or was captured. His enslaved friend **Sam Green Jr.** escaped from Dr. **James Muse** in August 1854. Green sent a letter from Canada to his father Reverend **Samuel Green Sr.** in which he wrote, "Tell P. Jackson to come on Joseph Baley com on." Peter fled with **Harriet Tubman** and her brothers **Ben Ross Jr.**, **Robert Ross**, and **William Henry Ross** and friends **Jane Kane**, **John Chase**, and others on **Christmas Day 1854**. Josiah Bailey fled two years later. Jackson reached Canada and freedom.

**JACOBS, HARRIET** (ca. 1813–7 March 1897). Born enslaved in North Carolina, Jacobs endured sexual harassment for years from her enslaver, Dr. Norcom. In defiance of his advances, she engaged in a relationship with another white man, bearing him two children, which enraged her enslaver. In 1835 he threatened to sell the children, so she escaped by hiding for seven years in the attic of the home owned by her free grandmother in Edenton. The father of her children purchased them from Norcom and sent them to New York City. In 1842, Jacobs successfully escaped to New York and after many years settled in Rochester, New York, the home of **Frederick Bailey Douglass**, **Amy** and **Isaac Post**, and many other antislavery activists.

While living with the Posts in the mid-1850s, Jacobs's children and brother encouraged her to write her autobiography. Her friend **Lydia Maria Child** edited the final manuscript, which was published in 1861 as *Incidents in the Life of a Slave Girl* under the pseudonym Linda Brent. It was an international success. During the **Civil War**, Jacobs and her daughter Louise opened a school for African Americans in Alexandria, Virginia, with support from the local Black community and Northern antislavery activists. Jacobs and **Harriet Tubman** traveled in many of the same women's rights and abolition circles, and Tubman availed herself of Jacobs's experience running the school to help her reorganize the **National Home for the Relief of Destitute Colored Women and Children** in Georgetown, Washington, D.C., in January 1865. Under the auspices of the **New England Freedmen's Aid Society**, Jacobs and Louise left Alexandria for Savannah, Georgia, in the fall of 1865 to distribute clothing and open a school for recently freed people. They stayed for a few months and returned to New England. In 1877, they moved to Washington, D.C., where Jacobs died on 7 March 1897. She is buried in Mount Auburn Cemetery in Cambridge, Massachusetts.

**JAMES** (ca. 1810–unknown). Born enslaved in **Dorchester County, Maryland**, James (last name unknown) was enslaved by **Edward Brodess**. Brodess sold James and another enslaved person, Rhody, to **Dempsey P. Kane**, a **slave trader** from Mississippi, on 18 July 1825.

**JOHN BROWN HALL**. A large brick structure on the grounds of the **Harriet Tubman National Historical Park** in Auburn, New York, used as an infirmary and nursing home. **Harriet Tubman** purchased the building as part of a twenty-five-acre property she acquired in 1896. The property also included the **Harriet Tubman Home for the Aged and Infirm Negroes**. Tubman became a resident of John Brown Hall, where she was cared for by a nursing staff during the last two years of her life.

**JOHNSON, OLIVER** (27 December 1809–10 December 1889). Born in Vermont to Quaker parents and apprenticed as a printer, Johnson moved to Boston in the early 1830s and became close friends with **William Lloyd Garrison**. Johnson helped found the New England Anti-Slavery Society in 1832. Johnson served, on occasion, as interim editor of Garrison's *The Liberator* until 1844 when he moved to New York City to work for other antislavery publications including the *New York Tribune*. In 1853, he became associate editor of the *National Anti-Slavery Standard*, the official newspaper of the **American Anti-Slavery Society**. Working with **Sydney Howard Gay**, Johnson participated in **Underground Railroad** activities, including helping **Harriet Tubman** and some of her fellow **freedom seekers** including **Joseph "Joe" Bailey**, **William "Bill" Bailey**, **Peter Pennington**, and **Eliza Manokey**. He raised and distributed money to Tubman and other self-liberators, supplied food and housing, and arranged for travel further north. Johnson supported a number of reform causes, including women's rights, and continued to edit and write for numerous newspapers for the rest of his life. He died in 1889.

**JOHNSON, WINNIBAR (WILLIAM OR WINORY)** (ca. 1827–unknown). Born in **Madison, Maryland**, John was enslaved by **Samuel Harrington**. Harrington also enslaved Johnson's three sisters, Ann, Charlotte, and Ellen. On 10 June 1854, Johnson escaped with **Harriet Tubman**'s help. He arrived safely in Philadelphia, Pennsylvania, where he met **William Still**, an **Underground Railroad** agent. Harrington posted a reward of $250 for Johnson's capture and return to Maryland. After a brief stay, Johnson moved to New Bedford, Massachusetts, where he settled into a large Black community that included **freedom seekers** he knew from Maryland. He left behind a free wife, Catherine, and three children, who later joined him in New Bedford. Harrington sold Johnson's sisters; Ann later escaped and reached New Bedford in 1857. After the **Civil War**, Johnson posted a notice in the *Christian Recorder* inquiring for the whereabouts of his sisters Charlotte and Ellen. It is not known if he ever saw them again.

**JOLLY, HARKLESS** (ca. 1800–aft. 1870). Born in Maryland, Jolly was enslaved by the Staplefort family, living near the **Little Blackwater Bridge** in **Dorchester County, Maryland**. Jolly married **Harriet Tubman**'s sister **Linah Ross Jolly**. They had two daughters: **Kessiah Jolly Bowley** and **Harriet Jolly**. Kessiah escaped slavery in 1850, and Harriet was sold in 1852. Kessiah returned to **Dorchester County** around 1868 with her family and lived with Harkless in **Church Creek**.

**JOLLY, HARRIET** (ca. 1832–unknown). Born in **Dorchester County, Maryland**, Jolly was the daughter of **Harriet Tubman**'s sister Linah and enslaved by **Edward Brodess**. In 1849, Brodess's widow, **Eliza Ann Keene Brodess**, sold seventeen-year-old Jolly and her one-year-old daughter, **Mary Ann Jolly**, to local merchant Thomas Willis for $375. In 1852, Willis sold Jolly without Mary Ann and another daughter, two-year-old **Sarah Ann Jolly**, to **James A. Stewart** for $312.50, possibly to settle a debt. In 1855, Stewart sent her to his Texas plantation with dozens of other enslaved people. Her fate remains unknown.

**JOLLY, KESSIAH.** *See* BOWLEY, KESSIAH JOLLY.

**JOLLY, LINAH ROSS** (ca. 1808–unknown). Born enslaved in **Dorchester County, Maryland**, Jolly was the first of nine children of **Ben Ross** and **Harriet "Rit" Green Ross** and **Harriet Tubman**'s oldest sibling. Jolly was enslaved by Mary Pattison Brodess Thompson and then, after Mary's death, **Edward Brodess**. She married **Harkless Jolly** sometime before 1824. She had two children, **Kessiah Jolly Bowley** and **Harriet Jolly**. Harriet Tubman later recalled being with her sister and mother at the Polish Mills farm during the famous **Leonid meteor shower** on the night of 13 November 1833. Jolly was sold by **Edward Brodess** sometime before 1844. Her fate is unknown.

**JOLLY, MARY ANN (MARY JANE)** (ca. 1848–unknown). Born in **Dorchester County, Maryland**, Jolly was the daughter of **Harriet Jolly** and granddaughter of **Linah Ross Jolly**. They were enslaved by **Edward Brodess**. After Brodess's death in 1849, his widow, **Eliza Ann Keene Brodess**, sold Mary Ann and her mother to Thomas Willis. Her sister, **Sarah Ann Jolly**, was born in 1850. Willis sold their mother to **James A. Stewart** in 1852, who sent her to his Texas plantation in 1855. Willis kept the children until he was forced to set them free on 1 November 1864 when Maryland made slavery illegal. Mary Ann's fate remains unknown.

**JOLLY, SARAH ANN** (ca. 1850–unknown). Born in **Dorchester County, Maryland**, Jolly was the daughter of **Harriet Jolly** and granddaughter of **Linah Ross Jolly**. Her mother and sister, **Mary Ann Jolly**, were enslaved by **Edward Brodess**. After Brodess's death in 1849, his widow, **Eliza Ann Keene Brodess**, sold them to Thomas Willis. Harriet was still enslaved by Willis when she gave birth to

Sarah Ann in 1850. Willis sold Harriet to **James A. Stewart** in 1852, who sent her to his Texas plantation in 1855. Willis kept the children until he was forced to set them free on 1 November 1864 when Maryland made slavery illegal. Sarah Ann's fate remains unknown.

**JONES, HORATIO** (25 October 1772–13 March 1856). Living in Button's Neck near the **Blackwater River**, Jones was a neighbor and contemporary of **Anthony Thompson** at **Peter's Neck**. Jones enslaved **Jane Kane**, who married **Harriet Tubman**'s brother **Ben Ross Jr.** after they escaped together during the **Christmas Day 1854, escape of Harriet Tubman's brothers**. Ross brought her a suit of men's clothing to wear as a disguise. She told **William Still** in Philadelphia that Jones was "the worst man in the country." Kane later told **Benjamin Drew** that Jones was a physically violent man who beat his slaves, starved them, and took away their clothes to keep them from visiting loved ones away from his farm. He whipped Kane's brother "until his back was as raw as a piece of beef"; he beat her "until the blood ran from my mouth and my nose," then locked her in a cupboard where she almost suffocated.

**JONES, JOHN W.** (1817–1900). A **freedom seeker** from Virginia who settled in Elmira, New York, Jones was one of the most active **Underground Railroad** agents in the region. He received self-liberators sent from Philadelphia by **William Still** and forwarded them to Rochester, Buffalo, and **Niagara Falls** for transportation to Canada. It is assumed that **Harriet Tubman** was aided by Jones between 1850 and 1854. After that time, she used the **Underground Railroad** route that took her through New York City, Albany, Syracuse, Rochester, and **Niagara Falls**. Oral traditions in the Elmira community also support this view.

*JOURNAL C.* Officially called *Journal C of Station 2 of the Underground Railroad*, the journal is one of two surviving volumes maintained by **Underground Railroad** agent **William Still** and **James Miller McKim** of the **Philadelphia Vigilance Committee** from 1852 to 1857. The men recorded the names and stories of **freedom seekers** from Maryland, Delaware, Virginia, North Carolina, and several other Southern states, who arrived in their office in Philadelphia, Pennsylvania. Still and McKim also recorded the funds expended for food, shelter, transportation, clothing, and medical care for the self-liberators. The books document approximately 450 of the estimated 1,400 people the vigilance committee aided during that time. Several of **Harriet Tubman**'s missions are documented in the journal, including her rescue of her brothers **Robert Ross**, **Ben Ross Jr.**, and **Henry Ross** on **Christmas Day 1854**. The names and stories of other freedom seekers from the **Eastern Shore of Maryland** are among the many listings in the journal. Still later used the record to publish his 1872 book *The Underground Railroad*, which details more than 700 stories. The Historical Society of Pennsylvania holds the records in their collections; they are available online.

# K

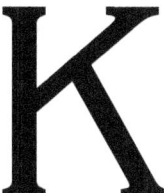

**KANE, DEMPSEY P.** Mississippi **slave trader** who roamed the **Eastern Shore of Maryland** purchasing enslaved men, women, and children to transport to **Deep South** states and resell them for a profit. Kane purchased **Harriet Tubman**'s sister **Mariah Ritty Ross** in 1825.

**KANE, JANE.** *See* STEWART, CATHERINE KANE.

**KEENE, DAWES.** An enslaved man held by **Eliza Brodess** during the 1850s. She may have inherited him from her deceased father, John Keene. She sold Keene to William Cooper and Samuel Dunnock for $300 in November 1850.

**KEENE, ELIZA ANN.** *See* BRODESS, ELIZA ANN KEENE.

**KEENE, RICHARD.** One of the enslavers who offered a reward for the capture of his enslaved person who fled with the **Cambridge 28** in October 1857.

**KELLEY, ESTHER (HESTER) (ca. 1800–unknown).** Wife of **Jonah Kelley**, Esther may have been the Quaker woman whom **Harriet Tubman** said helped her escape in 1849. *See also* KELLEY, JONAH.

**KELLEY, JONAH (ca. 1800–1873).** Kelley and his wife, **Esther**, lived on a large farm in Preston, Maryland, near **Linchester Mill**. They were opposed to slavery and were active participants in the area's **Underground Railroad** with their neighbors **Jacob, Hannah,** and **Arthur Leverton** and **Daniel Hubbard**—a landscape of more than 1,300 acres of contiguous lands that became an important zone-of-safety destination for **freedom seekers** from **Dorchester County**. Their son, William T. Kelley, wrote about their participation in the escape of **Margaret Haskins** and her family on New Year's Eve, 1857 in the Quaker publication *Friends' Intelligencer*.

*KENT.* On 21 October 1856, **Harriet Tubman** helped a young woman named "**Tilly**" flee enslavement. Unable to safely bring Tilly to Philadelphia via a northeasterly route out of Baltimore, Tubman took Tilly south, via the steamboat *Kent* to Seaford, Delaware. The steamer *Kent* docked at Dugan's Wharf in Baltimore's Inner Harbor, which is now the site of the National Aquarium Marine Mammal Pavilion at Pier 4. During the 1850s, the *Kent* made weekly round-trip excursions to the **Eastern Shore of Maryland**, carrying mail, freight, and passengers up and down the Chesapeake Bay and several of its Eastern Shore tributaries, including the **Choptank** and **Nanticoke** rivers. Tilly's story is also celebrated in Seaford, Delaware, and there is now a Network to Freedom Site at Seaford's Gateway Park along the **Nanticoke River** where the former steamboat landing and hotel once stood.

**KIAH, EMILY (ca. 1827–unknown).** Born in Maryland and enslaved by **Ann E. Craig**, Emily escaped with her husband, **William "Bill" Kiah**, in March 1857 with the famous

Dover Eight group of freedom seekers. They had to leave behind their nine-year-old daughter, Mary, also enslaved by Craig. When they successfully made it to **William Still**'s office in Philadelphia, he wrote their name as "Chion." In 1860, Emily and Bill returned to Maryland and rescued their daughter. They settled in Canada first, then Auburn, New York, during the **Civil War**.

**KIAH, ISAAC** (ca. 1790–unknown). Born in Maryland and enslaved by **Anthony Thompson** on his plantation at **Peter's Neck** in **Dorchester County**, Isaac was married to an enslaved woman held by Dorothy Staplefort on her farm at the **Little Blackwater Bridge**.

Isaac and **Ben Ross**, Harriet Tubman's father, worked together. His wife's name is unknown.

**KIAH, WILLIAM "BILL"** (ca. 1827–unknown). Born in Maryland and enslaved by **Benjamin Gaither Tubman**, Bill escaped with his wife, **Emily Kiah**, in March 1857 with the famous **Dover Eight** group of **freedom seekers**. They had to leave behind their nine-year-old daughter, Mary, who was enslaved by **Ann E. Craig**. When they successfully made it to **William Still**'s office in Philadelphia, he wrote their name as "Chion." In 1860, Emily and Bill returned to Maryland and rescued their daughter. They settled in Canada first, then Auburn, New York, during the **Civil War**.

# L

**LEASING OF SLAVES.** Also known as **hiring out**, this practice was frequently employed in the South. Enslavers would rent their enslaved people to labor for another person for a short- or long-term contract. Sometimes enslaved people were leased for a season or by the task. Some enslaved people hired out their free time to earn real wages to improve their lives or potentially buy their freedom. **Harriet Tubman** was leased by **Edward Brodess** throughout her childhood and young adulthood. She also hired herself out to masters of her choice to earn income for herself.

**LECOMPTE, CHARLES.** A **slave trader** located in East New Market, **Dorchester County, Maryland**. He sold more than one hundred enslaved people during 1827, including infants, children, and teenagers separated from their parents and young adults to traders from Mississippi and Kentucky.

**LECOMPTE, SAMUEL W. (24 November 1796–29 January 1862).** A naval captain living in **Cambridge, Maryland**, LeCompte enslaved **Joseph Cornish**, a blacksmith and a preacher in the **African Methodist Episcopal Church** who was married to a free woman and the father of five children. Cornish believed that LeCompte was going to sell him over the Christmas holiday, so with information he received from **Harriet Tubman**, he escaped on 8 December 1855 and safely made it to Canada. LeCompte enslaved twenty-four people in 1860.

**LEONID METEOR SHOWER (1833).** The Leonids are part of the cosmic debris from the Temple-Tuttle comet, which passes by the earth in mid-November. Approximately every thirty-three years, the Leonids casts tens of thousands of meteors in what is called "meteor storm." On the night of 12 November 1833, **Harriet Tubman**, then called Araminta "Minty" Ross, sneaked away in the dark to visit with her mother, **Rit Green Ross**, and her sister **Linah Ross Jolley**, who had been leased by their enslaver, **Edward Brodess**, to Polish Mills, a white neighbor near **Bucktown, Maryland**. Rit was allowed to have her two youngest children with her: **Henry Ross**, aged two or three, and **Moses Ross**, aged about one year old. Tubman risked severe punishment to visit her mother at Mills's plantation at night. Late that night, Tubman later told an interviewer in 1896, she saw the stars "all shooting whichway." The Leonids produced a rare meteor storm that night and into the next morning. One Maryland observer noted that the "light was so intense" and that the meteors "fell like snow." Another observer in Boston wrote that the sky had the "appearance of a thick shower of fire." An **Eastern Shore** resident recalled the meteor shower resembled a "snowstorm of fiery flakes." Tubman and her family believed it was a sign that the end of the world was near.

**LEVERTON, ARTHUR WHITELEY (8 February 1806–4 July 1880).** The son of **Jacob Leverton** and Elizabeth Whiteley, Arthur grew up on his father's 220-acre farm in **Preston, Maryland**, situated in an area along the border between Caroline County and Dorchester County, Maryland, and near other Quakers and a small free Black community, including millwright Daniel Hubbard who worked at the nearby Linchester Mill. After his father's death, Arthur inherited the farm.

How long he was involved in Underground Railroad activities like his father is unknown, but he and Daniel Hubbard helped Margaret Haskins and her family escape over the New Year's holiday in January 1858. The Haskins family was captured, and when it was discovered that Leverton and Hubbard had assisted the family, the two barely escaped a lynch mob before fleeing to Philadelphia and safety. Leverton hired a lawyer, who helped sell the farm. Leverton and his wife, Margaret, and seven children joined his stepmother, Hannah Leverton, and other family members in Milford, Marion County, Indiana. He died there in 1880.

**LEVERTON, HANNAH WILSON WRIGHT (2 September 1800–12 May 1866).** A radical Quaker, Hannah married Jacob Leverton in 1823. They had four children together, including Mary Elizabeth Leverton, before Jacob died in 1847. Their farm in Preston, Maryland, was situated in an area along the border between Caroline County and Dorchester County, Maryland, and near other Quakers and a small free Black community, including millwright Daniel Hubbard who worked at the nearby Linchester Mill. The Leverton farm was also near Dr. Anthony C. Thompson's 2,200-acre plantation at Poplar Neck, where Ben Ross lived from 1846 to 1857 and from where Harriet Tubman escaped in 1849. Tubman later told a friend that it was a Quaker woman who helped her on her first steps to freedom in 1849. Jacob's son, Arthur Leverton, inherited the farm. By 1850, Hannah was living close by with her daughter Ruth Leverton Noble. After Arthur was almost lynched in January 1858 when he and Daniel Hubbard came under suspicion for helping Margaret Haskins and her family escape slavery in Dorchester County, Hannah moved with other family members to a Quaker community in Milford, Indiana, where she died in 1866.

**LEVERTON, JACOB (10 March 1774–11 March 1847).** A radical Quaker born in Caroline County, Maryland, Leverton was a staunch abolitionist in a Southern slaveholding community. Married to Elizabeth Whiteley in 1804, they had one son, Arthur W. Leverton, in 1806. Elizabeth died in 1813, and Leverton married Esther Swiggett, with whom he had three more children before she died in 1821. He married Hannah Wilson Wright Leverton, and they had four children.

The Levertons lived on a 220-acre farm along the Caroline and Dorchester County, Maryland, border near Preston. A small free Black community, including millwright Daniel Hubbard, existed in the area, and with a small circle of Quakers created an important geographical area of protection through which freedom seekers could flee to Underground Railroad locations further north. In 1842, an enslaved teenager named Jane Hughes fled from William Charles and William E. Hooper. She sought help from Jacob and Hannah, who helped her escape. When questioned later, Jacob admitted he assisted Hughes. Charles and Hooper sued Jacob. He purportedly died in 1847 during court proceedings related to the lawsuit.

Hannah continued live on the farm and likely continued to play a role in the area Underground Railroad network with her stepson, Arthur, and neighbor Daniel Hubbard. The Leverton farm was also near Dr. Anthony C. Thompson's 2,200-acre plantation at Poplar Neck, where Ben Ross lived from 1846 to 1857 and from where Harriet Tubman escaped in the fall of 1849, possibly with help from Hannah.

**LEVERTON, MARY ELIZABETH (20 February 1830–unknown).** Daughter of Jacob and Hannah Leverton who married Anthony C. Thompson Jr., the son of Dr. Anthony C. Thompson, who owned a 2,200-acre plantation in nearby Poplar Neck, in 1849. Mary was disowned by the local Quaker meeting when she married Thompson because he was not a Quaker. It is unknown if Mary had any knowledge of Harriet Tubman's escape plans or local Quaker involvement.

**LIBERIA.** A state or republic in Africa established in 1821 on land acquired by the **American Colonization Society** as part of its **colonization movement** for the resettlement of formerly enslaved and free Blacks in America. Several **Dorchester County** free Black families and some enslaved people who were **manumitted** by local slaveholders moved to Liberia between 1821 and the 1850s.

**LIGHT, CHARLES ANTHONY (dates unknown).** Born in Maryland and enslaved by **Reuben Phillips**, he escaped on Saturday night, 24 July 1858, in company with **William Henry Cornish, Mary Light** (likely related), **Esther Cornish, Solomon Cornish, Thomas Rideout,** and **John Green**. Their white **Underground Railroad** conductor was an Irish immigrant and wood sawyer named **Hugh Hazlett**. The group was caught a few days later in **Caroline County, Maryland**, and brought to **Cambridge** via a steamboat, but a mob had gathered to await their arrival at Long Wharf. The sheriff feared the mob would lynch Hazlett, so he ordered the steamboat to leave Long Wharf and dock at another location upriver. Hazlett and the others were later safely secured in the **Cambridge** jail. Light was reenslaved by Phillips.

**LIGHT, GEORGE (dates unknown).** Born in Maryland and enslaved by Willis Brannock of **Cambridge**, Light fled on 24 October 1857 with his brother **Solomon Light** and twenty-six other people, famously known as the **Cambridge 28**. He was interviewed by **Underground Railroad** agent **William Still** in Philadelphia. He successfully made his way to freedom and settled in St. Catharines, Ontario, Canada.

**LIGHT, MARY.** Born in Maryland and enslaved by Reuben Phillips, she escaped on Saturday night, 24 July 1858, in company with **William Henry Cornish, Charles Anthony Light** (likely related), **Esther Cornish, Solomon Cornish, Thomas Rideout,** and **John Green**. Their white **Underground Railroad** conductor was an Irish immigrant and wood sawyer named **Hugh Hazlett**. The group was caught a few days later in **Caroline County, Maryland**, and brought to **Cambridge** via a steamboat, but a mob had gathered to await their arrival at Long Wharf. The sheriff feared the mob would lynch Hazlett, so he ordered the steamboat to leave Long Wharf and dock at another location upriver. Hazlett and the others were later safely secured in the **Cambridge** jail. Mary Light was reenslaved by Phillips.

**LIGHT, SOLOMON.** Born in Maryland and enslaved by Willis Brannock of **Cambridge**, Light fled on 24 October 1857 with his brother **George Light** and twenty-six other people famously known as the **Cambridge 28**. He was interviewed by **Underground Railroad** agent **William Still** in Philadelphia. He successfully made his way to freedom and settled in St. Catharines, Ontario, Canada.

**LINCHESTER MILL.** Preston, Caroline County, Maryland. A water-powered grist and sawmill has been operating at this site since the 1680s. Located at the headwaters of Hunting Creek in **Preston**, the Linchester Mill was ideally situated amid a secret network of **Underground Railroad** safe houses operated by the Levertons, the Hubbards, and the Kelleys on the west side and **Harriet Tubman**'s parents, **Ben Ross** and **Rit Green Ross**, at the **Poplar Neck** plantation owned by Dr. **Anthony C. Thompson** on the east side. **Daniel Hubbard**, an Underground Railroad conductor, lived less than a mile away and likely worked at the mill. The milldam provided a good crossing point over Hunting Creek for **freedom seekers** fleeing from **Dorchester County, Maryland**. Such crossing points helped **freedom seekers** to stay dry, especially in cold weather, and to avoid unwanted attention. The mill is now a historic site along the **Harriet Tubman Underground Railroad Scenic Byway and All-American Road**.

**LINCOLN, PRESIDENT ABRAHAM (12 February 1809–15 April 1865).** Lincoln was elected and sworn in as the sixteenth president of the United States just before the start of the **Civil War**. He guided the United States through the war, preserving the country as a union and ending slavery. He was assassinated soon after his second inauguration on 14 April 1865. He was responsible for enacting the **Emancipation Proclamation**, which became effective on 1 January 1863.

**Harriet Tubman** never met him in person. Early in the war she was angry that he would not allow the recruitment of African American soldiers. She famously said, "God's ahead of master Lincoln. God won't let master Lincoln beat the South till he does the right thing. Master Lincoln, he's a great man, and I am a poor negro; but the negro can tell master Lincoln how to save the money and the young men. He can do it by setting the negroes free. Suppose that was an awful big snake down there, on the floor. He bite you. Folks all scared, because you die. You send for a doctor to cut the bite; but the snake, he rolled up there, and while the doctor doing it, he bite you again. The doctor dug out that bite; but while the doctor doing it, the snake, he spring up and bite you again; so he keep doing it, till you kill him. That's what master Lincoln ought to know." Lincoln changed his mind and began encouraging the establishment of Black regiments in early 1863. After Lincoln's assassination, Tubman regretted that she never met him.

**LITTLE BLACKWATER BRIDGE.** A bridge over the Little Blackwater River in Maryland. It is situated near **Atthow Pattison**'s former plantation, where **Harriet Tubman**'s mother, **Harriet "Rit" Green**, was born and where her grandmother **Modesty** lived as an enslaved woman.

**LITTLE DIPPER.** A group of seven bright stars in the constellation **Ursa Minor** in the Northern Hemisphere night sky. The configuration of the stars is similar to a ladle or dipper with a handle—a smaller version of the **Big Dipper**. The North Star, also known as **Polaris**, is the last star on the handle of the dipper. The North Star is an important navigational tool, and **Harriet Tubman** used it to guide her on her **Underground Railroad** rescue missions.

**LOGUEN, JERMAIN W. (5 February 1813–30 September 1872).** Born enslaved in Tennessee, Loguen escaped in 1834. Living in Canada, then Syracuse, New York, Loguen studied at the Oneida Institute, an integrated radical antislavery school in Whitesboro, New York. He married a free Black woman, Caroline Storum, and with their six children ran an important and busy **Underground Railroad** station in their home in Syracuse. He worked with Unitarian minister **Samuel J. May** in managing the city's **Underground Railroad** network, sometimes openly and in defiance of the **Fugitive Slave Act**. On 1 October 1851, a **freedom seeker** named William "Jerry" Henry was arrested in Syracuse. Loguen and a group of **abolitionists** colluded to free Henry from the authorities and helped him escape to Canada. Threatened with arrest for his role in the "Jerry Rescue," Loguen fled to Canada, too, but soon returned to the city and resumed his **Underground Railroad** activities. It is estimated that Loguen and his family assisted more than 1,500 freedom seekers.

**Harriet Tubman** stopped there with her charges during some of her liberation missions from the **Eastern Shore of Maryland**. Family testimony claims that the Loguens' daughter Sarah witnessed Tubman removing buckshot from the legs of some **freedom seekers** hiding in their home. Tubman so inspired Sarah that she later became a physician. Loguen was a teacher and a minister and bishop in the **African Methodist Episcopal Zion Church (AMEZ)**. He published an autobiography, *The Rev. J. W. Loguen, as a Slave and as a Freeman, a Narrative of Real Life*, in 1859. Loguen died in 1872 in Syracuse.

**LONG, SILAS.** Born in Maryland and enslaved by Sheriff Robert Bell of **Cambridge**, Long fled on 24 October 1857 with twenty-seven other people in a group famously known as the **Cambridge 28**. He was interviewed by **Underground Railroad** agent **William Still** in Philadelphia. He successfully made his way to freedom and settled in St. Catharines, Ontario, Canada.

**LONG WHARF.** Built in 1810 in **Cambridge, Maryland**, along the **Choptank River** at the end of High Street. The shallow waters made it difficult for ships to dock along the waterfront in **Cambridge**, necessitating the building of a long wharf to deeper waters. It was dismantled in the early twentieth century after dredging made the waterfront more accessible to vessels. During the early to mid-1800s, enslaved people were bought and sold and carried on ships docking here.

On Saturday night, 24 July 1858, **William Henry Cornish, Mary Light, Charles Anthony Light, Esther Cornish, Solomon Cornish, Thomas Rideout,** and **John Green** fled their enslavers in the Town Point and **Cambridge** areas in **Dorchester County, Maryland.** Their white **Underground Railroad** conductor was an Irish immigrant and wood sawyer named **Hugh Hazlett.** They were caught a few days later in **Caroline County, Maryland,** and brought to **Cambridge** via a steamboat, but a mob had gathered to await their arrival at Long Wharf. The sheriff feared the mob would lynch Hazlett, so he ordered the steamboat to leave Long Wharf and dock at another location upriver. Hazlett was later safely secured in the **Cambridge** jail. The **freedom seekers** were reenslaved, and Hazlett was tried and convicted and sent to prison for forty-four years. The area is now a waterfront park and marina, and it is a site along the **Harriet Tubman Underground Railroad Scenic Byway and All-American Road.**

**LOWBER, PETER.** A **slave trader,** tavern keeper, and sheriff in East New Market, **Dorchester County, Maryland,** during the 1820s and 1830s. He was responsible for the sale of hundreds of enslaved people to dozens of buyers, many out-of-state slave traders from Kentucky, Georgia, Virginia, Mississippi, and other states.

**LUCAS, ALICE.** *See* BRICKLER, ALICE LUCAS.

**LUCAS, ALLEN (ca. 1874–5 May 1916).** Born and raised in Auburn, New York, by his parents **Margaret Woolford Stewart** and **Henry Lucas,** Allen was likely named after his father's long-lost brother, Allen Kelly. He had two sisters, Marguerite and **Alice Lucas Brickler.** He died in Auburn, New York, in 1916 and is buried in Fort Hill Cemetery.

**LUCAS, HENRY (ca. October 1842–13 February 1936).** Born enslaved in Richmond, Virginia, Lucas either escaped or was **manumitted** sometime before or during the **Civil War.** He moved to Auburn, New York, after the war and established a catering business. He married **Margaret Woolford Stewart,** who was related to **Harriet Tubman.** He and Margaret had three children, **Allen,** Marguerite Lucas Richardson, and **Alice Lucas Brickler.** In 1895, Lucas posted an advertisement in the *Richmond Planet* newspaper in Richmond, Virginia, looking for information regarding his brother, Allen Kelley. Henry died in 1936 and is buried in Fort Hill Cemetery.

**LUCAS, MARGARET WOOLFORD STEWART (ca. 1852 to 1854–19 May 1930).** Born free to **Isaac** and **Mary Woolford,** Margaret had a twin brother, **James;** a sister, **Sarah;** and another brother named **Moses Woolford.** Isaac and Mary lived next door to **Ben** and **Rit Ross** in the early 1850s at **Poplar Neck** in **Caroline County, Maryland.**

Sometime in 1861, **Harriet Tubman** traveled to Maryland and, according to later testimony of **Alice Lucas Brickler,** "kidnapped" Margaret from her family and brought her to Auburn, New York, where she was raised in the **William Henry Seward** home. According to Alice, some Tubman relatives resented Margaret's apparent favored status, fueling generations of speculation about Margaret's identity and rumors that she may have been Tubman's secret daughter from an unknown relationship. Margaret married **Henry Lucas,** and they had several children together, including Alice and **Allen Lucas.** In 1885, Margaret posted an advertisement in the *Christian Recorder* asking for information about her father, **Isaac Woolford,** who lived at **Poplar Neck,** and her brother Moses whom she believed had been left with an "old lady in Caroline County." The advertisement reads:

> INFORMATION WANTED OF MY FATHER, Isaac Wolford. He was raised in Poplar Neck, Caroline county Eastern Shore Md. He was probably in the army, but I do not know what regiment he was in. He left my

youngest brother with an old lady in Caroline county. Any information of him will be thankfully received by his daugther [sic]. MAGGIE E. LUCAS. 166 West Genesee St, Auburn, N. Y."

It is unknown whether Margaret was reunited with Moses. She died in Auburn, New York, on 19 May 1930.

# M

**MADISON, MARYLAND.** A village in **Dorchester County, Maryland**, on Madison Bay, a tributary of the Little Choptank River. During the nineteenth century, the village and bay were known by the name Tobacco Stick. During the late 1830s and early 1840s, Harriet Tubman worked for **John T. Stewart**, a Madison merchant and shipbuilder, bringing her back to the familial and social community near where her father lived at **Peter's Neck** and where she had been born.

**MALONE'S AFRICAN METHODIST EPISCOPAL CHURCH.** First established as African Methodist Episcopal, Malone's Church on White Marsh Road south of the town of **Madison** stands as a testament to the spiritual, economic, political, and social life of a blended pre–Civil War free and enslaved Black community. Malone's would be the first of five Black churches built in south **Dorchester County, Maryland**, between **Cambridge** and Taylor's Island soon after the **Civil War**. Named for Jeremiah Malone and his wife, Rose, freed people who deeded the land to the community in 1864, the church started with a small building in 1866, which was used for both a school and a place of worship. The congregation changed to Methodist Episcopal in 1887. In 1890, a new church building replaced the old. The church closed during the 1990s, but its historic graveyard is still in use. Harriet Tubman purportedly lived on or near Jeremiah Malone's property with her husband John during the mid-1840s. The site is located along the **Harriet Tubman Underground Railroad Scenic Byway and All-American Road**.

**MANLOVE, BARTHOLOMEW.** A **slave trader** from Bourbon County, Kentucky, who purchased enslaved people from local traders and individual enslavers in Maryland, including from **Dorchester County, Maryland**, during the 1820s and 1830s.

**MANOGA.** *See* MANOKEY.

**MANOKA.** *See* MANOKEY.

**MANOKEY, ELIZA (ca. 1814–unknown).** Born in **Dorchester County, Maryland**, Manokey was enslaved by Ann Martin Staplefort Grieves of **Church Creek**, who had inherited the enslaved woman from her first husband, John Staplefort. She was married to **Bill Banks**, who had been enslaved by **Anthony Thompson**, who also enslaved Tubman's father, **Ben Ross**. Manokey and Banks had two children, a daughter named Caroline and a son who was taken from Manokey when he was four years old. Grieves sent him to Missouri. **Bill Banks** had been **manumitted** during the early 1840s, but Manokey remained enslaved. Abused and maltreated, Manokey escaped from Grieves in January 1856, hiding in the woods with help from free Black families. "My Savior protected me, and I trusted in him. I did not even get frosted," she later told **Underground Railroad** agent **Sydney Howard Gay**.

By November 1856, Manokey found her way to Delaware, where she joined **Harriet Tubman** as she was leading **Peter Pennington** and **Josiah (Joe) Bailey** and his brother **William (Bill) Bailey** north in mid-November

1856. Bounty hunters chased the group, eager to collect the $2,600 reward for the arrest of the three men, though no reward advertisement for the capture and return of Manokey has been found. Such high rewards increased the danger of capture for the runaways. It took the group ten days to reach **Thomas Garrett** in Wilmington, Delaware, a trip that typically took only three days. **Slave catchers** forced them to proceed cautiously and remain hidden. They were "passed along by friends in various disguises" and were "scattered and separated" and led "roundabout" to a variety of **Underground Railroad** safe houses to avoid detection. Garrett learned they were trapped on the other side of the Christiana River, unable to cross the bridge into Wilmington because the authorities were watching. Garrett engaged the services of two Black bricklayers, who loaded their wagon and rode across the bridge in the morning, "singing and shouting" and greeting the police and others looking for the group. The bricklayers located Tubman and the **freedom seekers** and concealed them in a hidden compartment built into the wagon. The bricklayers proceeded back over the bridge, still "singing and shouting," successfully evading detection by the police and **slave catchers**.

One day later, on November 26, the party arrived in Philadelphia at **William Still**'s office, who instantly sent them to **Sydney Howard Gay** of the **New York Vigilance Committee** and his associate **Oliver Johnson** at the offices of the *National Anti-Slavery Standard* newspaper in New York City. Before forwarding them by train to the **Syracuse (New York) Fugitive Aid Society**, Gay recorded an interview with Eliza. The treasurer of the Syracuse Society, **W. E. Abbott**, sent them to **Samuel D. Porter** of Rochester, New York, who immediately put them on a train to the suspension bridge over the Niagara River just north of **Niagara Falls**. The **freedom seekers** settled in Ontario. Eliza Manokey's final destination remains unknown, and it is likely she returned to Maryland after the **Civil War**.

MANOKEY, JERRY (ca. 1780—bef. 1850). Born in **Dorchester County, Maryland**, Manokey was enslaved by **Anthony Thompson**. Manokey may have been born in Africa to an unidentified African woman enslaved by Thompson who died before 1783 when Manokey would have been a boy. He was enslaved with **Ben Ross** on Thompson's 1,000-acre plantation in **Peter's Neck** in **Dorchester County, Maryland**. He was one of Thompson's most valuable workers. He was married to an enslaved woman named **Polly Manokey** with whom he had at least eight children, including **Mary Manokey Ross**, who married Harriet Tubman's brother **Robert Ross**. Thompson **manumitted** Jerry and Polly before dying in 1836. In his last will and testament, Thompson left Jerry ten acres of land and a lifetime supply of wood and bread.

MANOKEY, MARY. *See* ROSS, MARY MANOKEY.

MANOKEY, POLLY (bef. 1800–bef. 1850). The circumstances of Polly's birth are unknown. She was enslaved by **Anthony Thompson** on his plantation in **Peter's Neck** in **Dorchester County, Maryland**. *See also* MANOKEY, JERRY.

MANUMISSION, MANUMIT, MANUMITTED. The act of freeing or **emancipation** of an individual or group of enslaved African Americans by legal will, purchase, lawsuit, lawful petition, or an act of legislation. Manumissions occurred from the earliest days of the enslavement of Africans in North America. Enslavers could manumit individuals as an act of religious, political, social, or personal action with no financial remuneration. The process could be executed by enslaved Africans and African Americans who could purchase their freedom with wages earned from extra paid employment or sale of manufactured goods. Free Blacks could purchase the freedom of their enslaved family or friends. Some enslaved people were manumitted through bequests and instruction in a deceased enslaver's last will and testament. A few enslaved people filed lawsuits or petitioned for their freedom through courts and legislatures. Individual states passed many laws governing the legal manumission of enslaved people, creating barriers and limiting the potential for freedom. For instance, in Maryland, beginning in the 1790s, it was illegal for enslavers to manumit an enslaved person older than forty-five years old. Some slaveholders did not want to take care of old, disabled, and dependent African Americans so they set them free to fend for themselves. Some white communities shunned this practice. The law was often ignored. Some states required that newly manumitted people leave the state immediately, forcing the separation of free and enslaved families.

**MANUSCRIPT HISTORY CONCERNING THE PENSION CLAIM OF HARRIET TUBMAN, 1866–1868.** Held at the National Archives, this manuscript was compiled and written by Auburn, New York, banker **Charles P. Wood**. The manuscript consists of a narrative history of **Harriet Tubman**'s work as a spy and scout during the **Civil War**. Wood included letters and testimony supporting Tubman's claim for remuneration for her services and submitted it to Congress. Her petition was denied. *See* appendix D.

**MARSH CREEK.** A tributary of the **Choptank River**, northwest of the village of Choptank Landing near **Poplar Neck, Caroline County, Maryland**. During the 1840 and 1850s, Marsh Creek was an important source of waterpower for milling and transportation of timber cut from Dr. **Anthony C. Thompson**'s plantation at **Poplar Neck**. **Harriet Tubman**'s father, **Ben Ross**, ran the sawmill and timber operations for Thompson there during that time period.

**MARYLAND COLONIZATION SOCIETY.** Founded in 1817, the society was a state branch of the **American Colonization Society**, whose objective was to send free Blacks to the national society's colony in **Liberia** in Africa. The Maryland Colonization Society drew support from slaveholders, nonslaveholders, and **abolitionists** alike. Maryland had the largest free Black population of all the southern states during the **antebellum period**. Maryland established a settlement at Cape Palmas in **Liberia**. Dorchester County slaveholders, including Dr. **Anthony C. Thompson**, represented a significant number of the Maryland Colonization Society's leadership, and one of the colony's first settlers and leaders was James Benson, a free Black man from **Cambridge, Maryland**. Ultimately, few freeborn or manumitted Maryland African Americans were willing to leave the homes they knew. Many had ties to enslaved family and friends, which they were unwilling to sever. By 1852, **Dorchester County** free Blacks, including Reverend **Samuel Green**, were organizing with other Marylanders in opposition to colonization efforts. The Maryland Colonization Society's efforts resulted in an average of fifty emigrants per year. Together with the **American Colonization Society** and other state organizations, only a few thousand African Americans settled in **Liberia** in Africa by the outbreak of the **Civil War**. Adjustment to the climate proved difficult, and many emigrants died of disease.

**MASON COMMITTEE.** A select committee commonly known as the Mason Committee after its chairman, Senator James Mason of Virginia, was established on 14 December 1859 by the U.S. Senate to investigate **John Brown**'s raid on **Harpers Ferry**, Virginia, in October 1859 and determine the involvement of other persons and organizations. The committee delivered a report to the U.S. Congress the following June 1860, revealing details of Brown's planned attack on the federal arsenal.

**MASON, JAMES E. (ca. 1860–unknown).** Born in Pennsylvania, Mason was an ordained minister in the **African Methodist Episcopal Zion Church**. He served as pastor of the Memorial African Methodist Episcopal Zion Church in Rochester, New York, where **Frederick Bailey Douglass** once worshiped. He presided over the funeral mass for Douglass in 1895, and in 1896, he joined the Board of Directors of the **Harriet Tubman Home for Aged and Infirm Negroes** in Auburn, New York. He published his reminiscences of **Harriet Tubman** in a coauthored pamphlet with Reverend **Edward U. A. Brooks**, *Tribute to Harriet Tubman, the Modern Amazon* (Auburn, New York: Tubman Home, 1914).

**MAY, SAMUEL J.** (12 September 1797–1 July 1871). Born in Boston, May graduated from Harvard Divinity School and spent nearly fifty years pastoring Unitarian congregations in Connecticut, Massachusetts, and New York. He met **William Lloyd Garrison** in 1830 and helped Garrison found the **New England Anti-Slavery Society**. A radical **abolitionist**, he lectured widely and campaigned for the immediate abolition of slavery. He also supported integrated schools and was a pacificist like Garrison. He participated in the famous "Jerry Rescue" with Reverend **Jermain Loguen** of Syracuse in 1851, and May's home became a stop on the **Underground Railroad** in that city. He helped **Harriet Tubman** and introduced her to other abolitionists in the central New York region who helped raise money for her **Underground Railroad** missions and to support her aging parents. During the **Civil War**, May campaigned for the enlistment of African American men in the Union Army and participated in the organizing of several relief societies to help support recently freed people in the South. After the war, he wrote *Some Recollections of Our Anti-Slavery Conflict* and donated his extensive collection of antislavery ephemera, manuscripts, and books to Cornell University in Ithaca, New York. He died in 1871.

**MCDOUGALL, CLINTON DUGALD** (19 June 1839–24 May 1914). A U.S. Representative from New York, Congressman McDougall introduced a bill, *Harriet Tubman—H.R. 2711*, in the House of Representatives of the United States, 43rd Congress, in 1874 requesting payment to **Harriet Tubman** for her service as a spy and scout during the **Civil War**. The bill failed to pass.

**MCGOWAN, JAMES A.** (4 February 1932–17 October 2008). McGowan was a highly respected historian who was an early proponent of challenging the myths surrounding **Harriet Tubman**'s life. McGowan was born and raised in Brooklyn, New York. A brilliant student, McGowan dropped out of high school at the age of sixteen despite his academic achievements. He was an exceptional athlete, and in 1951 he was hired as a first baseman for the Philadelphia Stars, a National Negro League team. The Brooklyn Dodgers expressed interest in recruiting him, but he became disabled after being stabbed on a street in Brooklyn, which ended his career in baseball. An infection from the wound eventually left him a paraplegic. A talented singer, McGowan formed the Four Fellows, a background vocal group that toured and recorded with some of the great Black performers of the 1950s, including Chuck Berry, Etta Jones, Ella Fitzgerald, Bo Diddley, and many others. He wrote of his experiences performing across the country in his memoir, *Hear Today! Here to Stay! A Personal History of Rhythm and Blues* (1979). He was later inducted into the United In Group Harmony Association Hall of Fame. He became actively involved in sports for the disabled, including wheelchair basketball, and then moved to other sports.

Living in Philadelphia, McGowan returned to school and earned a BA in liberal arts and then an MS in counseling from Temple University. In 1978 he was named chairman of the Committee for the Disabled of the Pennsylvania Governor's Council on Physical Fitness. In that role he worked to make public places accessible to the disabled and counseled mentally ill adolescents. He received the Sol Feinstone Award from Temple University, the Distinguished Service Award from Pennsylvania Governor Thornburgh, and the Equal Opportunity Award from the U.S. Postal Service. He established the first wheelchair sports competition at Temple University and founded Freedom's Wings, an organization that taught disabled people how to fly airplane gliders. He also established the first all-disabled rowing regatta on the Schuylkill River. In 1981, McGowan was the first paraplegic officially certified as the first paralyzed man to sky dive. He went on to complete twenty more dives, breaking several records along the way and earning the prestigious Star Crest Award. In 2005 he published *Walking on Air: The Memoirs of a Paraplegic Sky Diver* (2005).

In 1986, after a failed attempt to swim the English Channel, McGowan devoted his time to researching the life of Harriet Tubman. McGowan's interest in Tubman rose out of his passion for **Thomas Garrett**, a Quaker and **Underground Railroad** agent in Wilmington, Delaware, who helped Tubman on several of her rescue missions. McGowan wrote and published the first adult biography of Garrett, titled *Station Master on the Underground Railroad: The Life and Letters of Thomas Garrett* (1977), and then published an updated and expanded edition in 2005. McGowan spent three decades—1977 to his death in 2008—researching, collaborating, writing, and documenting Tubman's life. He published *The Harriet Tubman Journal*, a quarterly publication, from 1993 through 1995. McGowan was nearly finished with his own Tubman biography when he died in the fall of 2008 in Newtown, Pennsylvania. His friend and coauthor, William C. Kashatus, completed the biography, *Harriet Tubman: A Biography*, in 2011.

McGowan spoke widely about Thomas Garrett and Harriet Tubman, and he earned many honors for his work on these leaders of the **Underground Railroad**, including the Angel of Philadelphia Award given by the William Still Foundation in 2003. McGowan was the narrator and consultant for the film *Whispers of Angels: A Story of the Underground Railroad* (2007). He was instrumental in the creation of the Tubman-Garrett Riverfront Park in Wilmington and the development of the Underground Railroad Scenic Byway in Delaware, which is now part of the **Harriet Tubman Underground Railroad Scenic Byway and All-American Road**.

**MCKIM, JAMES MILLER (14 November 1810–13 June 1874).** Born and raised in Pennsylvania, Miller obtained a theological degree and was ordained in the Presbyterian Church in 1835. A radical **abolitionist** and a follower of **William Lloyd Garrison**, Miller attended the founding meeting of the **American Anti-Slavery Society** in 1833. He was close friends with **Lucretia Coffin Mott** and her husband, **James**. Miller married in 1840 and settled in Philadelphia, where he eventually became involved with the **Pennsylvania Anti-Slavery Society** and the **Philadelphia Vigilance Committee** assisting **freedom seekers** with **William Still**. He helped maintain the *Journal C* records created by Still to record the names and stories of self-liberators who found refuge with them in Philadelphia. McKim worked closely with **Thomas Garrett** of Wilmington, Delaware, who frequently corresponded with McKim alerting him to the impending arrival of **freedom seekers**.

During the **Civil War**, McKim organized relief to send resources to newly freed people in the South. He traveled to Hilton Head, South Carolina, in 1862 to observe the living conditions of the freedmen, which helped inform relief efforts in the region. He helped establish Camp William Penn outside Philadelphia where Black troops were trained. After the war, he was an early investor in the fledgling *Nation* and later became editor in chief. He died in New Jersey in 1874.

**MEDFORD'S WHARF.** A small village located along the **Choptank River** near **Preston** in **Caroline County, Maryland**, during the nineteenth century. The village prospered from the trade in timber and agricultural products and is situated just south of Dr. **Anthony C. Thompson**'s **Poplar Neck** plantation. It is now known as **Choptank Landing, Maryland**, and is a stop on the **Harriet Tubman Underground Railroad Scenic Byway and All-American Road**.

**MEREDITH, PRITCHETT (6 January 1799–10 December 1869).** A white landowner near Bucktown, Maryland, Meredith enslaved more than one dozen people, including **Thomas Elliott** and **Denard Hughes**. Elliott and Hughes successfully escaped in March 1857, with six other individuals in a group nicknamed the **Dover Eight**. Meredith, Hughes later reported, was "the hardest man around," and his wife, eighty-three years of age, "drank hard" and was "very stormy." Meredith purchased Thomas from Benjamin and Margaret Keys Elliott in April 1841. Margaret had inherited Thomas and several other enslaved Hughes family members, whom she also sold to Meredith. Meredith's "Poplar Farm" was situated about a mile from the **Bucktown** crossroads and less than two miles from the Brodess farm where **Harriet Tubman** spent portions of her childhood, and Elliott and Hughes knew

Tubman and the Ross family. In 1861, John Wesley Hughes, also enslaved by Meredith, escaped but was later caught and returned to slavery.

**MILLER, ANNE FITZHUGH (4 March 1856–1 March 1912).** Born in Peterboro, New York, Anne was the youngest child of woman suffragist Elizabeth Smith Miller and the granddaughter of **Gerrit Smith**. In 1897, Anne established the Geneva (New York) Political Equality Club, a women's rights organization that included among its members **Eliza Wright Osborne**, **Susan B. Anthony**, and **Harriet Tubman**. In late 1911, Miller interviewed eighty-nine-year-old Tubman in Auburn, New York, for an article title "Harriet Tubman" for the *American Review* magazine. It featured a few new details about Tubman's life and included an image of Tubman in a wheelchair in front of **John Brown Hall**. The article appeared posthumously in August 1912.

**MILLS, CHARLES (1821–1900).** Born in Hartford, New York, to antislavery parents, Mills attended the Oneida Institute like his father. The institute's leader was the inspirational abolitionist **Beriah Green**. The institute was desegregated, holding classes for Black and white students together, the first racially integrated institution of higher education. Mills later moved to Syracuse, New York. It was from his home there in February 1861 that Mills wrote to **David Wright** in Auburn, New York, asking him to warn **Harriet Tubman** and her family that **slave catchers** were looking for **freedom seekers** to capture and claim bounties for their arrest.

**MILLS, JOHN (ca. 1810–bef. 1859).** Landowner and merchant in **Bucktown, Maryland**, Mills owned the **Bucktown Village Store** from 1834 to 1853. It was during his tenure as shopkeeper that **Harriet Tubman** experienced a near fatal injury at the store. A slaveholder, Mills lived near **Edward Brodess**. After Brodess died in 1849, Mills loaned widow **Eliza Ann Keene Brodess** $1,000 to pay her deceased husband's debts. Appointed co-administrator of the Brodess estate, he managed the sales of several of the Brodess family's enslaved people, including **Harriet Jolley** and her children in 1849. He also posted the reward advertisement for the capture of Tubman and her brothers **Henry Ross** and **Ben Ross Jr.** after they escaped from **Poplar Neck** in **Carolina County, Maryland**, in September 1849.

**MILLS, POLISH (8 November 1808–9 September 1865).** Mills owned a farm near **Bucktown**, across from **Edward Brodess** on Greenbrier Road. In 1833, Brodess leased **Harriet Tubman**'s mother, **Rit Green Ross**, and sister **Linah Ross Jolley** to Mills to work on his farm. Rit was allowed to bring her two youngest children, three-year-old Henry and one-year-old Moses, and Linah brought her one-year-old daughter **Harriet Jolley** to the Mills farm, but no other children were allowed to join them. On the night of 12 November 1833, Tubman snuck out in the dark to visit with her mother and sister. That night, Tubman and her family witnessed the **Leonid Meteor Shower** cast thousands of meteors across the night sky, sparking fear and wonder. In 1853, Mills testified in court about Tubman and her family in a long-drawn-out lawsuit between the Pattison and Brodess families, contesting legal ownership of Rit and her children. The lawsuit ended in 1860 after most of the Ross family had escaped or died.

**MINTY.** Nickname for Araminta Ross, later known as **Harriet Tubman**.

**MITCHELL, CYRUS (ca. 1830–unknown).** Born in **Dorchester County, Maryland**, Mitchell was enslaved by James K. Lewis. Mitchell fled on 20 September 1856 in company with four other men: **Francis Molock, Joshua Handy, Charles Dutton,** and **Ephraim Hudson**. They followed instructions likely given to them by **Harriet Tubman**. After passing through **Thomas Garrett**'s home in Wilmington, Delaware, the men arrived in Philadelphia, where they were interviewed on the 29th by **William Still**. Still noted that Mitchell used John Steel as an alias. The **freedom seekers** reached Canada safely.

**MODESTY** (ca. 1750 to 1770–bef. 1820). An African woman kidnapped from Africa and sold into American slavery. She was enslaved by **Atthow Pattison** on his farm along the **Little Blackwater Bridge** in **Dorchester County**. Her exact heritage is unknown, but she arrived in Maryland sometime before 1785 and likely before the American Revolution (1776), during which the African slave trade was suspended. The Maryland colonial census recorded five unidentified enslaved people in fifty-six-year-old Pattison's household in 1776. One of them may have been Modesty, but the identities and ages of the enslaved people remain unknown. Tubman believed that Modesty had been "brought in a slave ship from Africa." She may have been **Asante**, as Tubman had been told that she was a descendant. Modesty was **Harriet "Rit" Green Ross**'s mother, though the identity of who fathered Rit is unknown. It may have been Pattison. Tubman once said that her mother's father was a white man. Dr. **Anthony C. Thompson** remembered Modesty and spoke of her in his court testimony in 1853 when ownership of Rit was being contested by the Pattison family. Modesty died sometime between 1810 and 1820.

**MOLOCK, FRANCIS** (ca. 1835–unknown). Born in **Dorchester County, Maryland**, Molock was enslaved by James Waddell of Vienna, Maryland. Molock fled on 20 September 1856 in company with four other men: **Cyrus Mitchell, Joshua Handy, Charles Dutton**, and **Ephraim Hudson**. They followed instructions likely given to them by **Harriet Tubman**. After passing through **Thomas Garrett**'s home in Wilmington, Delaware, the men arrived in Philadelphia, where they were interviewed on the 29th by **William Still**. Still noted that Molock used Thomas Jackson as an alias. Waddell offered a $300 reward for Molock's capture. The **freedom seekers** reached Canada safely. Molock settled in Owen Sound, Ontario, Canada.

**MONTGOMERY, JAMES** (22 December 1814–6 December 1871). Born in Ohio, Montgomery moved to Kansas when that territory opened for settlement in 1854 after the passage of the Kansas-Nebraska Act. He was a Free-Stater, meaning he supported the admission of Kansas into the United States as a free state. Proslavery forces hoped to create another slave state. Violence erupted between the two factions, and Montgomery led a group of men who fought against the slaveholders. A radical **abolitionist**, he was close to **John Brown**.

During the Civil War, Montgomery was commissioned a colonel in the Union Army and helped recruit men for the **Second South Carolina Colored Volunteers**, one of the earliest African American regiments of the war. He met **Harriet Tubman** in South Carolina, and they worked closely together. She led Montgomery and his men during the **Combahee River Raid** in early June 1863. Montgomery later led the regiment during the Battle of Olustee, where **Nelson Charles Davis**, Tubman's future second husband, fought with the Eighth U.S. Colored Troops. Montgomery left his command of the Second South Carolina and returned to Kansas, where he led another regiment into battle. After the war he retired and died at his home in Linn County, Kansas, in 1871.

**"MOSES GO DOWN TO EGYPT LAND."** *See* "HAIL, OH HAIL YE HAPPY SPIRITS."

**MOSES, WILLIAM J.** (1822–7 April 1895). An Auburn, New York, publisher, politician, and community leader, Moses published **Sarah Hopkins Bradford**'s 1868 biography, *Scenes in the Life of Harriet Tubman*. Moses published numerous Auburn newspapers and *The Northern Christian Advocate*, a religious weekly, over a forty-year period.

**MOTT, JAMES** (20 June 1788–26 January 1868). Born on Long Island, New York, Mott was a Quaker and **abolitionist**. A merchant, Mott married Lucretia Coffin in 1811, and they settled in Philadelphia, Pennsylvania. Together they became devoted to the antislavery cause and refused to purchase goods produced through enslaved labor. Mott stopped selling cotton and only sold wool. With Lucretia, he became actively involved in **women's rights** and their home became a stop on the **Underground Railroad**. *See also* MOTT, LUCRETIA COFFIN.

**MOTT, LUCRETIA COFFIN** (3 January 1793–11 November 1880). The daughter of a whaling captain, Mott was born on Nantucket Island, Massachusetts. A Quaker, she married James Mott in 1811 in Philadelphia. A devoted **abolitionist** like her husband, she refused to buy or use goods produced by enslaved labor. A leading member of her Quaker community, she became a minister in the Society of Friends in 1821. She and James helped found the **American Anti-Slavery Society** in 1833 with **William Lloyd Garrison**. The society did not initially allow women to be members, so Lucretia organized the Philadelphia Female Anti-Slavery Society that same year. She insisted on a diverse membership and invited Black women to join, a progressive position that not all **abolitionists** agreed with. She and James belonged to the **Pennsylvania Anti-Slavery Society**, and the couple attended the World Anti-Slavery Convention in London, England, in June 1840. While the women were forced to sit apart from the men, Lucretia met and became lifelong friends with **Elizabeth Cady Stanton**.

Eight years later, in mid-July 1848, Mott, her sister **Martha Coffin Wright**, Stanton, **Frederick Bailey Douglass**, and scores more met at the **Seneca Falls Convention**, in Seneca Falls, New York, to formulate demands and strategies for gender equality in all aspects of private and public life. Lucretia and James remained active in women's rights and antislavery work, and their home in Philadelphia, and then later their farm, called "Roadside" just north of the city, became safe houses on the **Underground Railroad**. It was in that capacity that Lucretia met **Harriet Tubman**, who once told a friend that Mott was the first white woman to help her in Philadelphia. They became close friends.

Mott introduced Tubman to her sister Martha Wright in Auburn, New York. Wright's husband David worked with **William Henry Seward** who also lived in Auburn. Through these friendships Tubman purchased her own home in 1859 from Seward, enabling her to resettle her parents, **Ben Ross** and **Rit Green Ross**, from their temporary home in St. Catharines, Ontario, Canada. Lucretia and James worked to help the newly freed people in the South during the **Civil War** and immediately afterward. Lucretia continued campaigning for women's rights and helped cofound Swarthmore College in 1864. After James's death, Lucretia kept working until her death in 1880.

**MUIR, JOHN** (28 December 1791–2 April 1861). Born in **Dorchester County, Maryland**, Muir was a wealthy planter, investor, merchant, and enslaver of dozens of people. One of Muir's enslaved men, **Nat Amby**, successfully escaped with his wife, **Elizabeth "Lizzy" Amby**, on 17 October 1857 with more than a dozen other **freedom seekers**. Muir posted a $500 reward for Nat's capture and return to **Cambridge**.

**MURRAY, ANNA.** *See* DOUGLASS, ANNA MURRAY.

**MUSE, JAMES** (17 January 1813–21 November 1867). A wealthy doctor and slaveholder in **Cambridge, Maryland**, Muse enslaved **Samuel "Sam" Green Jr.** and his sister, **Sarah Green**, the children of Reverend **Samuel Green** and **Catherine "Kitty" Green**. After Sam Jr. escaped in August 1854, he reached **William Still**'s office and **Underground Railroad** station in Philadelphia, Pennsylvania, and told Still that Muse was cruel and violent, "the worst man" in Maryland. In an act of revenge, Muse sold Sarah away from her two children to a buyer from Missouri.

**MYERS, HARRIET JOHNSON** (ca. 1810–2 September 1865). Born near Albany, New York, Harriet married **Stephen Myers** in 1827. They raised ten children together and were active in antislavery activities. Their home was a station on the **Underground Railroad**.

**MYERS, STEPHEN** (ca. 1805–13 February 1870). Born enslaved in New York, Myers was **manumitted** sometime before 1827. He married Harriet Johnson, and they moved to Albany where their home became one of the most important stations on the **Underground**

**Railroad.** Stephen published the *Northern Star*, an **abolitionist** newspaper, and raised money to aid **freedom seekers** with food, clothing, shelter, and travel expenses. **Harriet Tubman** reported to historian **Wilbur Siebert** that Meyers gave her assistance and helped get her and her **freedom seekers** on trains headed to Syracuse, Rochester, and **Niagara Falls** on their way to Canada. The Stephen and Harriet Myers Residence is a historic site owned and operated by the Underground Railroad Education Center in Albany, New York.

**MYTHS ABOUT HARRIET TUBMAN.** *See* appendix F.

**MYTHS ABOUT THE UNDERGROUND RAILROAD.** *See* appendix E.

# N

**NALLE, CHARLES** (ca. 1821–1875). Born into slavery in Virginia and eventually enslaved by **Blucher Hansbrough**, Nalle escaped in October 1858 and settled in the small city of Troy, New York. Hansbrough discovered Nalle's whereabouts in April 1860 from a lawyer who befriended Nalle in Troy and was eager to claim the reward for informing on Nalle. Empowered by the laws embedded in the **Fugitive Slave Act**, Hansbrough sent **slave catchers** to capture Nalle and bring him back to Virginia. On 7 April 1860, they captured Nalle and secured him in a Troy jail cell. A large crowd gathered and, with the help of **Harriet Tubman**, freed him from custody. The authorities battled the crowd and recaptured Nalle, only to have him liberated again and hurried off to Canada for his safety. Local **abolitionists** raised $650 and paid Hansbrough for Nalle's legal freedom.

**NANTICOKE INDIAN TRIBE.** A tribe of indigenous people living along the **Nanticoke River** in **Dorchester** and neighboring counties in Maryland and in Sussex County, Delaware. Like their neighbors, the **Choptank**, Manokin, and Pokomoke Indians of the **Eastern Shore of Maryland**, the Nanticoke spoke various dialects of Algonquin. During the mid-seventeenth century, these Indians fought European intrusion and struggled to maintain community and cultural independence. Indigenous people in Delmarva built shelters of wood, reeds, mud, and grasses and established corn agriculture during the Woodland period. Semipermanent and permanent settlements profoundly affected social and political relationships within and between villages and societies. The Nanticoke people claimed the lands along the northwest side of the Nanticoke River between Marshyhope Creek and Chicone Creek. When English explorer Captain John Smith investigated and surveyed the Chesapeake Bay and its shores during several voyages between 1607 and 1609, he recorded meeting the Nanticoke people along the Nanticoke River but failed to engage with their indigenous **Choptank** neighbors. Enslavement of Indians on the **Eastern Shore** did occur early in the 1600s, mostly the result of war and kidnapping, but Maryland outlawed the practice in 1649. **Indenture** of native people continued for decades. Disease, war, food insecurity, outmigration, and intermarriage with white colonizers and Africans diminished the size and strength of the Nanticoke people. During the eighteenth century, a small band of Nanticokes settled in marshy areas of southern Delaware, where members of the tribe survived into the twentieth century.

**NANTICOKE RIVER.** A tributary of the Chesapeake Bay, flowing from its headwaters in Kent County and Sussex County, Delaware, to Maryland. The sixty-four-mile river continues southwest into Maryland, becoming the boundary between **Dorchester County** and Wicomico County, Maryland, and is named for the **Nanticoke Indians** who lived there when European colonizers arrived in the Chesapeake in the late 1500s and early 1600s. English explorer John Smith sailed up the Nanticoke during his voyage mapping the

Chesapeake Bay region between 1607 and 1609, and he met the Indigenous Nanticoke people then. The principal ports on the Nanticoke are Vienna, Maryland, and Seaford, Delaware. **Harriet Tubman** sailed in the steamship *Kent* in October 1856 with a **freedom seeker**, **Tilly**. Pretending to be free women of color, Tubman and Tilly disembarked in Seaford and took a train to Wilmington, Delaware, where **Thomas Garrett** helped them on to Philadelphia and freedom.

**NAPOLEON, LOUIS** (1 April 1800–March 1881). Born in New York City to an enslaved mother and Jewish father, Napoleon was set free in 1823 when his wife purchased his freedom for $50. Napoleon became a furniture polisher and finisher. By the 1830s he was active in the **Underground Railroad** in the city and eventually partnered with the New York City Vigilance Committee and **Sydney Howard Gay**.

*NARRATIVE OF THE LIFE OF FREDERICK DOUGLASS, AN AMERICAN SLAVE* (1845). The first autobiography written and published by **Frederick Douglass**, which provided authentic details about his life in slavery. A best seller, it brought Douglass international fame and acclaim and secured his prominent role in the **antislavery movement**. The *Narrative* is considered a part of classic American canon and is still in print.

**NATIONAL AMERICAN WOMAN SUFFRAGE ASSOCIATION (NAWSA)**. The founding of NAWSA in February 1890 occurred with the merger of the National Woman Suffrage Association (NWSA), led by **Elizabeth Cady Stanton** and **Susan B. Anthony**, and the American Woman Suffrage Association (AWSA), led by Lucy Stone, Julia Ward Howe, and Henry Blackwell. The two organizations combined their strategies—a campaign to achieve women's voting rights through a federal constitutional amendment with a campaign for women's suffrage laws on the state level. Thirty years later, in 1920, the NAWSA successfully secured the right for women to vote through the passage of the **Nineteenth Amendment to the Constitution**. **Harriet Tubman**, a suffragist, fought for its passage but died in 1913 before she could vote.

*NATIONAL ANTI-SLAVERY STANDARD*. Established in 1840, the *Standard* was the official newspaper of the **American Anti-Slavery Society**, and it was published in New York City and Philadelphia, Pennsylvania. One of its earliest editors was **Lydia Maria Child**. Abolitionists **Sydney Howard Gay** and **Oliver Johnson** also spent several years editing the newspaper. It ceased publishing in 1870.

**NATIONAL ASSOCIATION OF COLORED WOMEN (NACW)**. In July 1896 the **National Federation of Afro-American Women** joined forces with the **National League of Colored Women** in Washington, D.C., to create the NACW in response to frustration with the segregated meetings and overt racism of the **National American Woman Suffrage Association (NAWSA)**. At that first meeting, **Harriet Tubman** was a featured speaker. Introduced to the audience as "Mother Tubman," she told them of her **Civil War** service and sang a few melodies, which, with her voice strong even at the age of seventy-four, "penetrated every portion of the large auditorium." She was asked, as the oldest member attending the meeting, to introduce **Ida B. Wells-Barnett's** newborn, "Baby Barnett," to the audience, after which she urged her fellow suffragists and civil rights activists to consider the urgent need for elder care. Donations were offered in support of Tubman's goal of establishing a home for aged and ill African Americans on the twenty-five-acre property she had purchased the year before. The association's first president was Mary Church Terrell. The NACW became the largest federation of Black women's clubs in the country. Its motto is "Lifting as We Climb."

**NATIONAL COUNCIL OF NEGRO WOMEN (NCNW)**. Founded in 1935 by educator and civil rights activist Dr. Mary McCloud Bethune, the NCNW advocates for STEM education, social justice, political action, and entrepreneurship, among other causes for the advancement of African American women. In 1943,

Harriet Tubman was a founding member of the National Association of Colored Women, a suffrage organization, in 1896. Harriet Tubman, ca. 1897. From *Tribute to Harriet Tubman, the Modern Amazon*, by James E. Mason and Edward U. A. Brooks, 1914. *Courtesy of the author*

under the leadership of Dr. Dorothy Height, the NCNW formally requested the naming of a U.S. Liberty Ship in honor of **Harriet Tubman**. The U.S. Maritime Commission granted it in the spring of 1944, and the SS *Harriet Tubman* was launched at the New England Ship Building Company in South Portland, Maine, on June 3.

**NATIONAL FEDERATION OF AFRO-AMERICAN WOMEN.** Responding to the racism they confronted in the predominantly white **National American Woman Suffrage Association (NAWSA)**, Black women founded the National Federation of Afro-American Women in Boston in 1895. Spearheaded by Josephine St. Pierre Ruffin, the founder of *Woman's Era*, the organization grew quickly. In July 1896, the National Federation joined forces with the **National League of Colored Women** in Washington, D.C., to create the **National Association of Colored Women**.

**NATIONAL HOME FOR THE RELIEF OF DESTITUTE COLORED WOMEN AND CHILDREN.** At the insistence of women activists, the Home was established in Georgetown, Washington, D.C., in 1863 by the U.S. War Department to aid Black women and their children and orphans displaced by the **Civil War**. It offered food, shelter, clothing, employment assistance, and education programs. **Harriet Tubman** joined the staff at the Home in January 1865 to replace the Home's prior manager who proved to be abusive and cruel to the Home's clients. Tubman worked with **Harriet Jacobs** and abolitionist **Julia Wilber**, who wrote about Tubman's work in Washington at the time. The Home was moved to 8th Street NW in Washington in 1866 after the property was returned to its former **Confederate** owner.

**NATIONAL LEAGUE OF COLORED WOMEN.** Founded in 1892 as an organization of African American Women's clubs, it merged with the **National Federation of Afro-American Women** in July 1896 in Washington, D.C., to form the **National Association of Colored Women (NACW)**.

**NATIONAL PARK SERVICE NETWORK TO FREEDOM PROGRAM (NTF).** The National Park Service preserves and protects historical, cultural, natural, and iconic places—the physical memory of America's history. Locations related to the **Underground Railroad** are part of the Network to Freedom Program. The program includes locations with a documentable and verifiable connection to **Underground Railroad** activity. There are more than 650 sites, facilities, and programs across the country and the Caribbean in the Network to Freedom database. See https://www.nps.gov/subjects/undergroundrailroad/index.htm.

**NATIONAL WOMAN SUFFRAGE ASSOCIATION (NWSA).** One of two national women's suffrage organizations, the NWSA was founded in May 1869 by **Elizabeth Cady Stanton** and **Susan B. Anthony** in response to disagreements with other suffragists over support for the Fourteenth and Fifteenth Amendments, which secured voting rights for African American men but no women of any race. More conservative suffragists founded the **American Woman Suffrage Association (AWSA)** in November 1869 in Boston, which supported the amendments. The NWSA and the AWSA remained in opposition until the 1890s, when both organizations reunited to form the **National American Woman Suffrage Association (NAWSA)**. **Harriet Tubman** supported **Susan B. Anthony** in her political views.

**NEW ENGLAND FREEDMEN'S AID SOCIETY.** Founded in Boston, Massachusetts, in 1862 in response to an appeal to provide humanitarian aid and educational resources to formerly enslaved people at Port Royal, South Carolina, during the American **Civil War**, the New England Freedmen's Aid Society expanded in 1864 to provide teachers and other aid for newly freed people in other Southern states. The society published a monthly journal called *The Freedmen's Record*, which was edited by **Ednah Dow Littlehale Cheney**, among others. Their extensive records, housed at the Massachusetts Historical Society in Boston, document the funds raised and distributed in support of the activities of schools, teachers, and students from 1864 through 1874, when the society disbanded. The records reveal the educational needs and challenges facing newly freed people in the South, who faced difficult conditions, including racism, discrimination, violence, poverty, and displacement. The New England Society paid **Harriet Tubman** a salary for a few months in the winter and spring of 1865, and Cheney wrote an article for *The Freedmen's Record* in March 1865 about Tubman's life and activities called "Moses."

**NEW ENGLAND SHIPBUILDING COMPANY.** On June 3, the Liberty Ship **SS *Harriet Tubman*** was launched from its berth at the New England Ship Building Company at its shipyard in South Portland, Maine.

**NEW GUINEA.** A historic Black community in Auburn, New York, identified on an 1837 map of the city as "Negro Settlement, New Guinea." **Morgan "Luke" Freeman**'s family were among the first settlers of New Guinea.

**NIAGARA FALLS.** A waterfall on the Niagara River situated on the border between the state of New York and Ontario, Canada. The falls are actually two falls, separated by Goat Island. The largest of the two is Horseshoe Falls and on the Canadian or western side of the river and island. The smaller American Falls flow on the east of the island and river. **Freedom seekers** fleeing through the region faced great challenges trying to cross the river during the **antebellum period**. Ferries and small boats provided one source of transportation. A suspension bridge was built in 1848 that carried people and wagons across the river gorge near the falls, connecting the cities of Niagara Falls, New York, and Niagara Falls, Ontario, Canada. In 1855 that bridge was replaced by a new suspension bridge with two decks, one carrying carriages and another carrying trains. In November 1856, **Harriet Tubman** rode across the river in a train with **Joseph "Joe" Bailey**, **William "Bill" Bailey**, **Peter Pennington**, and **Eliza Manokey**.

**NIAGARA FALLS UNDERGROUND RAILROAD HERITAGE CENTER.** Located in the city of Niagara Falls, New York, near the former site of the 1855 suspension bridge and in a historic train station building, the center is part of the Niagara Falls Underground Railroad Heritage Area, which includes the City of Niagara Falls; the natural, scenic, and historic resources related to the Niagara River; the Niagara Gorge; and the **Niagara Falls**. The mission of the heritage area and the heritage center is to educate and inform local, national, and international communities and visitors about the history of **abolition** and **Underground Railroad** activities in the region. The center focuses specifically on interpreting, educating, and inspiring visitors with the stories of **freedom seekers** and **abolitionist** allies in the Niagara Falls area.

**NINETEENTH AMENDMENT TO THE CONSTITUTION.** Passed by the U.S. Congress on 4 June 1919, the amendment reached its final approval and passage on 18 August 1920 when three-fourths of the states ratified it. The amendment granted women the right to vote. In many states, African American women and men remained ineligible to vote because of restrictive and discriminatory voting laws designed to deny them the franchise.

**NORTH STAR.** *See* POLARIS.

**NORTHRUP, EVA STEWART (12 May 1890–16 June 1964).** Born in St. Catharines, Ontario, Canada, to **John Isaac Stewart**, **Harriet Tubman**'s nephew and the son of her brother **William Henry Ross Stewart**. When Eva's mother, Catherine Elizabeth Garner Stewart, died shortly after her birth, John Isaac brought Eva to Auburn, New York, to be raised by Tubman. He died in 1893 and is buried next to **Nelson Charles Davis**, Harriet Tubman's second husband, at Fort Hill Cemetery. Eva's grandfather William Henry participated in raising Eva. She later moved to Philadelphia with her husband, Frank Northrup, and daughter, Mariline. Her correspondence in 1840 with **Earl Conrad** for his Tubman biography constitutes an important biographical record. Eva was chosen to launch the **SS *Harriet Tubman*** on 3 June 1943 in South Portland, Maine. Her daughter, Mariline, later donated the champagne bottle from that day, along with other Tubman family artifacts, including the shawl that **Queen Victoria** gave to Tubman, to the National Museum of African American History and Culture. Northrup died in 1964 in Philadelphia.

"OLD SHIP OF ZION." A Methodist spiritual, "Old Ship of Zion" was first published by nineteenth-century scholar William Francis Allen in 1860, who noted that the song was an African American spiritual with roots in 1830s Maryland. Tubman used the phrase "Old Ship of Zion" in a letter to freeman **Jacob Jackson** to convey a **coded message** to her brothers that she was coming to rescue them during Christmas 1854. This song was probably very familiar to Tubman and Black communities on the **Eastern Shore of Maryland**, and it is likely she and Jackson created the code specifically for themselves.

O What ship is this that will take us all home?
O glory! Hallelujah!
'Tis the old ship of Zion, Hallelujah!
'Tis the old ship of Zion, Hallelujah!

Come along, come along, and let us go home!
O glory! Hallelujah!
Our home is over Jordan, Hallelujah!
Our home is over Jordan, Hallelujah!

Do you think she will be able to take us all home?
O glory! Hallelujah!
No doubt she will be able, Hallelujah!
No doubt she will be able, Hallelujah!

She has landed many thousands, and can land as many more!
O glory! Hallelujah!
She has landed them in heaven, Hallelujah!
She has landed them in heaven, Hallelujah.

"ON JORDAN'S STORMY BANK." Spiritual written by Samuel Stennett and published in 1787. *See* "BOUND FOR THE PROMISED LAND."

**ORPHANS COURT RECORDS, DORCHESTER COUNTY, MARYLAND.** Consists of probate and estate records including last will and testaments; inventories of deceased's assets, both liquid and real; and more. These records from the colonial period through the nineteenth century are important resources in tracing African American genealogy. The records are available at the Maryland State Archives in Annapolis, Maryland.

**OSBORNE, ELIZA WRIGHT (3 September 1830–18 July 1911).** Born in Cayuga County, New York, Osborne was the daughter of suffragist and **abolitionist Martha Coffin Wright** and **David Wright**. Osborne's mother and aunt, **Lucretia Coffin Mott**, in company with **Elizabeth Cady Stanton** and **Frederick Bailey Douglass**, were part of the small group of reformers who organized and conducted the first **Seneca Falls Convention** in 1848. Three years later she married David Munson Osborne, a farm equipment manufacturer in Auburn, New York. Eliza and David had four children and devoted their lives to abolition, women's suffrage, and other community and national reform issues.

Through her mother, Eliza became close to **Harriet Tubman**, and after her mother's death in

1874, Eliza provided occasional financial support when Tubman needed it. David Osborne's company, **D. M. Osborne**, provided employment for many of the **freedom seekers** Tubman brought north, including her own brother **John Stewart**. After the **Civil War**, Eliza helped sponsor fund drives for the freedmen in South Carolina, collecting clothing, school supplies, books, and more for newly freed people and for Tubman's nephew **James A. Bowley**. Eliza's sister, Ellen Wright, married **William Lloyd Garrison II**, the son of **William Lloyd Garrison** of Boston, Massachusetts. Eliza was witness to some of Tubman's epileptic seizures and wrote about them to family and friends, providing valuable firsthand accounts of what may have been **temporal lobe epilepsy**. Eliza frequently held women's suffrage meetings in her home, where Tubman was a welcome guest. In 1902, **Susan B. Anthony** wrote, "This most wonderful woman—*Harriet Tubman*—is still alive. . . . All of us were visiting at the Osborne's, a real love feast of the few that are left and here came *Harriet Tubman*!" When Osborne died in 1911, she left a $50 yearly bequest to Tubman.

**OSGOOD, LUCY.** A Boston **abolitionist**. In 1859, Osgood wrote to **Lydia Maria Child** about a recent appearance by **Harriet Tubman** at an intimate meeting in the home of **Ednah Dow Littlehale Cheney** in Boston. She reported: "Her name is Harriet. She is coal black & was a slave only three years ago, but within that time she has taken leg bail herself, & assisted no fewer than fifty others to do the same. Two or three times she has returned to the very plantation where she had served, & brought away with her companies of her relatives & friends. Her old father & mother she had helped out of bondage, & the object of this gathering was to assist her to buy a little place for them in Auburn. Her course had not been always smooth." Tubman, she continued, "went for her husband. . . . She had carefully provided herself with clothing to make him, she said, fit to be seen among folks—Lo! However, the recreant had taken to himself another helpmeet & strongly advised her to give up the nonsense of freedom, & 'I had his clothes' said she, 'but no husband.'—Mrs. Follen & Mrs. Putnam shouted at her comic pathos—They dubbed her Moses the deliverer, instead of Harriet."

**OTWELL, THOMAS.** A free Black farmer living in Kent County, Delaware, who worked as an **Underground Railroad** agent during the 1850s and 1860s. He helped **Harriet Tubman** one or more times before March 1857, when he betrayed a group of **freedom seekers** called the **Dover Eight**. Tubman had instructed the group to contact Otwell, believing he would guide them to the next stops on the **Underground Railroad** north to Wilmington, Delaware. Otwell deceived them when he conspired with a white man, **James Hollis**, and lured the group into the Dover jail so he could collect the $3,000 reward for the **freedom seekers'** capture. The group became suspicious and, after an altercation with the sheriff, made a bold and dangerous escape from the jail. Another Black **Underground Railroad** agent who had also worked with Tubman, **William Brinkley**, successfully ferried the group in his wagon thirty-eight miles to **Thomas Garrett's** home in Wilmington, Delaware. Garrett forwarded them to **William Still** in Philadelphia. They eventually made their way to freedom in Canada where they joined Harriet Tubman and other friends from **Dorchester County, Maryland**. Otwell may have endured disdain from his neighbors, and he may have continued helping **freedom seekers**. His fate remains unknown.

**OVERLAY, THOMAS.** A **slave trader** who advertised in the **Cambridge, Maryland**, newspapers during the late 1820s and early 1830s when demand was high for enslaved labor in the **Deep South**.

# P

PARKER, HARRIET ANN. *See* STEWART, HARRIET ANN PARKER.

PARKER, JOHN D. (ca. 1804–1868). Born in Maryland, Parker may have been hired by **Anthony Thompson** as an overseer or plantation manager in the late 1820s and 1830s. An aging Thompson, with hundreds of acres of agricultural lands and vast tracks of timber and nearly forty enslaved people, may have required the assistance of a younger white man to manage his property. Though **Ben Ross** was considered a supervisor or foreman for Thompson's timber business, Thompson's substantial landholdings and large enslaved community population probably required the employ of a professional overseer. When Thompson died in 1836, John D. Parker seemingly continued to manage the plantation operations for Dr. **Anthony C. Thompson** and his brother Dr. **Absalom Thompson**. Parker purchased some of Thompson's property from the estate in 1837 and then several more parcels from the heirs of **Joseph Stewart** during the late 1840s. He also began acquiring enslaved workers.

Parker remained intimately connected to the extended Ross family and other free and enslaved Black families in this area throughout the 1840s, 1850s, and 1860s. In 1853, Dr. **Anthony C. Thompson** sold two young children, George and Charlotte Brown Parker; their recently freed mother, Sophia, lived nearby. **Simon Ross**, a free Black who lived on Harrisville Road near the Thompson plantation, and who was likely closely related to **Ben Ross**, spent years trying to get his children, eight-year-old Benjamin, six-year-old David, and three-year-old Charles back from John D. Parker, who had indentured them without Ross's permission in May 1857. He finally reclaimed them with the help of the **Freedmen's Bureau** in 1869.

PARKER, SARAH (ca. 1784 to 1800–February 1890). A formerly enslaved person born in Maryland. Her history before arriving in New York state after the **Civil War** is unknown. In 1875, she was living with **Harriet Tubman**. Blind, Parker needed care and Tubman provided it, keeping her in her home on South Street in Auburn, New York, until she died in 1890. The *Auburn Bulletin* newspaper reported that for years, Parker "has been unable to assist herself and has depended entirely on the kindness of her benefactress who has been all that a daughter could be. It was quite affecting to witness the grief manifested by Miss Tubman over the death of the old woman." Local newspapers reported that Parker was 106 years old when she died. She is buried in Soule Cemetery in Auburn.

PARKER, THEODORE (24 August 1810–10 May 1860). Born in Lexington, Massachusetts, Parker became a Unitarian minister, social reformer, writer, and radical **abolitionist**. He was a member of the **Boston Vigilance Committee**, and he participated in **Underground Railroad** activities and sheltered **freedom seekers** in his home. He supported **John Brown** and was a member of Brown's **Secret**

Harriet Tubman with family and friends. Left to right: Harriet Tubman, daughter Gertie Davis, husband Nelson Davis, neighbor Lee Cheney, boarder John "Pop" Alexander, orphan Walter Green, boarder Sarah Parker, and great niece Dora Stewart. Photo by William Chaney, ca. 1887. *Schomburg Center for Research in Black Culture, Photographs and Prints Division*

Six. His congregation in Boston grew to more than two thousand, a remarkable number of followers. Highly influential in Boston's antislavery and women's rights circles, he died in 1860 of tuberculosis in Florence, Italy, where he had sought a cure.

**PARSON'S CREEK.** *See* STEWART'S CANAL.

**PATTISON, ATTHOW (ca. 1720–1797).** Born in **Dorchester County, Maryland**, Pattison was a modest tobacco farmer and merchant, operating his businesses on his 265-acre farm on the east side of the **Little Blackwater River**. He enslaved **Harriet Tubman**'s grandmother **Modesty** and mother, **Rit Green Ross**. In 1776 and on the eve of the American Revolution, John Pattison, Atthow Pattison's father, died, leaving six enslaved adults to his children, including a woman named "Bess" to Atthow. That same year, the Maryland colonial census recorded five unnamed enslaved people in fifty-six-year-old Atthow's household. One of them is surely Bess, but the identities of the other enslaved people remain unknown. It is likely they were Africans whose purchase is unrecorded, as was the custom at that time. When Atthow died in 1797, he gifted Rit to his granddaughter Mary Pattison Brodess Thompson. Atthow's daughter, **Elizabeth Pattison**, inherited his farm and lived there with her husband and first cousin, William Pattison; daughter Mary; Gourney Crow Pattison; and other children. When Atthow wrote his will on 18 January 1791, eight years before he died, he instructed his heirs to **manumit** each enslaved female in his estate, including Rit Ross, when they reached the age of forty-five.

**PATTISON, ELIZABETH (1765–1832).** Born in **Dorchester County, Maryland**, Elizabeth was the daughter of **Atthow Pattison**. She married her first cousin William Pattison in 1780 and had at least six children, including **Mary Pattison Brodess**, the mother of **Edward Brodess**. Elizabeth enslaved **Harriet Tubman**'s grandmother **Modesty**. When Atthow died in 1797, Elizabeth inherited his 297-acre farm near the **Little Blackwater Bridge**, and her daughter Mary inherited Tubman's mother, **Rit Green Ross**, from his estate.

**PATTISON, SAMUEL (1801–1877).** A wealthy **Dorchester County, Maryland**, planter, Pattison enslaved more than a dozen people, including entire families. On the night of 24 October 1857, sixteen successfully escaped along with twelve other people enslaved by **Jane Cator**, **Reuben Phillips**, Reverend **Levi D. Travers**, Willis Brannock, and Richard Keene. The large group was later called the **Cambridge 28**. Among those who escaped from Pattison included **Susan Viney**, her four young children, and her husband, **Joe Viney**; Joe's older sons, Henry, Tom, and Joe Jr.; **Christopher "Kit" and Leah Anthony** and their three children; and **Joseph Hill** and his sister **Sarah**. Pattison offered an extraordinary reward of $3,100 for their capture. He was unsuccessful despite many **slave catchers** pursuing the families for the high reward money. Joe Viney described Pattison and his wife to **William Still**, who recorded the comments in his *Journal C*. Pattison, Viney said, was "a great big man . . . who drank pretty freely . . . [and Mrs. Pattison was] mean, sneaking, and did not want to give half enough to eat."

**PAYNE, SERENO E. (26 June 1843–10 December 1914).** Born in Hamilton, New York, Payne earned a law degree and set up his practice in Auburn, New York. He served in various city administrative posts and later became a U.S. congressman from the district. In that capacity, he helped **Harriet Tubman** successfully petition the federal government for a widow's pension as the spouse of her deceased husband, **Nelson Charles Davis**, a **Civil War** veteran. Payne and other Tubman supporters were dissatisfied that Tubman did not receive a pension of her own as a spy and scout during the war. The prospects for such a pension for Tubman seemed dim, so in December 1897, Payne introduced a bill to Congress requesting a pension for Tubman as a nurse during the war at the monthly rate of $25 per month. After two years of negotiating, the bill finally passed, awarding Tubman $12 per month for her service as a nurse, plus the $8 she was already receiving as a widow. It did not bring any further acknowledgment from the government, however, for her military service as a scout and spy. *See also* UNITED STATES ARMY MILITARY INTELLIGENCE CORPS HALL OF FAME.

**PENNINGTON, PETER (ca. 1827–18 September 1884).** Born enslaved in Sussex County, Delaware, Peter was brought to **Dorchester County, Maryland**, by his enslaver **Turpin Wright** to Wright's farm at Oyster Shell Point on the **Choptank River** when he was two years old. Peter, in company with **Joe Bailey** and his brother **Bill Bailey** and **Eliza Manokey**, fled slavery with the help of **Harriet Tubman** in mid-November 1856. The Bailey brothers knew about **Harriet Tubman** and her rescue missions to the region to bring **freedom seekers** north. After **Joe** was assaulted and whipped by his enslaver, **William Hughlett** of Talbot County, the brothers decided to escape. Bill was enslaved by **John Campbell Henry** of **Cambridge, Maryland**, but had been leased to Hughlett to operate his steam mill.

One evening in the fall of 1856, Joe rowed six miles up the **Choptank River** from Hughlett's plantation on Jamaica Point to **Poplar Neck** in **Caroline County** where **Harriet Tubman**'s free father, **Ben Ross**, lived and worked as timber foreman for Dr. **Anthony C. Thompson**. Joe informed him that he and the others were ready to escape the next time Tubman arrived from the North. On 15 November 1856, Tubman led them north into Delaware. Bounty hunters chased the group, eager to collect the $2,600 reward for their arrest, including **Turpin Wright**'s offer of $800 for the capture of twenty-five-year-old Peter. Such high rewards increased the danger of capture for the runaways. It took the group ten days to reach **Thomas Garrett** in Wilmington, Delaware, a trip that typically took only three days. **Slave catchers** forced them to proceed cautiously and remain hidden. They were "passed along by friends in various disguises" and were "scattered and separated" and led "roundabout" to a variety of **Underground Railroad** safe houses to avoid detection. Garrett learned they were trapped on the other side of the Christiana River, unable to cross the bridge into Wilmington because the authorities were watching. Garrett engaged the services of two Black bricklayers, who loaded their wagon and rode across the bridge in the morning, "singing and shouting" and greeting the police and others looking for the group. The bricklayers located Tubman and the **freedom seekers** and concealed them in a hidden compartment built into the wagon. The bricklayers proceeded back over the bridge, still "singing and shouting," successfully evading detection by the police and **slave catchers**.

One day later, on November 26, the party arrived in Philadelphia at **William Still**'s office, who instantly sent them to **Sydney Howard Gay** of the New York Vigilance Committee and his associate **Oliver Johnson** at the offices of the *National Anti-Slavery Standard* newspaper in New York City, who forwarded them by train to the **Fugitive Aid Society of Syracuse, New York**. The treasurer of the Syracuse society, **W. E. Abbott**, sent them to Samuel D. Porter of Rochester, New York, who immediately put them on a train to the suspension bridge over the Niagara River just north of **Niagara Falls**. Joe Bailey's prominent facial scar, described in the runaway reward notice, made him easily recognizable and compromised the group's safety. Bounty hunters had continued to track them. They safely made it across the suspension bridge to freedom. The **freedom seekers** settled in Ontario.

In the spring of 1858, Tubman introduced Pennington and other **freedom seekers** from **Dorchester County** to **John Brown**. Though they initially agreed to join Brown on his raid on **Harpers Ferry**, they decided not to follow him in the fall of 1859. Peter moved west to Sarnia, in Lambton County on the west side of Ontario, near the Canadian border with Michigan. Peter established himself as a fish dealer, probably a similar profession to his work tasks while enslaved by **Turpin Wright**, who owned a fishery in **Dorchester County**. When Pennington died in 1884, he left his $1,000 estate to four churches in Sarnia. He is buried in Lakeview Cemetery.

**PENNSYLVANIA ANTI-SLAVERY SOCIETY.** In 1775, **abolitionists** in Pennsylvania organized the Society for the Relief of Free Negroes Held in Bondage, which was later reorganized by Benjamin Franklin as the Pennsylvania Abolition Society in 1787. In 1837, the society reorganized again and was renamed the Pennsylvania Anti-Slavery Society. The society helped raise funds to purchase the freedom of some enslaved people, engaged in lawsuits over the status of people wrongfully held in slavery, protected free Blacks from violence, established Black schools, and lobbied the state and federal governments to end slavery. Its membership included **Thomas Garrett**, **James** and **Lucretia Coffin Mott**, **William Still**, Passmore Williamson, **Robert Purvis**, and many others. The society's papers are held by the Historical Society of Pennsylvania.

**PERCY, ALGERNON (1823–1876).** A resident of Vienna, Maryland, Percy enslaved **Maria Ennals** and her children when they escaped with **Stephen Ennals** in November 1860. **Harriet Tubman** guided them north when she returned to **Dorchester County, Maryland**, to rescue her sister **Rachel Ross**. Rachel had died, so Tubman helped the Ennals family instead. Tubman brought them to Auburn, New York, where **Martha Coffin Wright** and her family sheltered them on 29 December 1860 before they moved on to Canada.

**PERRY, JESSE (dates unknown).** A free Black who betrayed **freedom seekers** for the reward money. In late July 1858, seven enslaved people fled from near **Cambridge, Maryland**, in **Dorchester County** with the help of **Hugh Hazlett**, an Irish immigrant. After the group made their way through **Caroline County**, they were captured between Henderson and Templeville in the northeast corner of the county along the border with Queen Anne's County, Maryland, and Kent County, Delaware. Perry, in collusion with a group of white men, set an ambush for them. After their capture, Hazlett and the others were brought to **Denton** and placed in the county jail next to the courthouse. Several of the **freedom seekers** were related to members of the **Cambridge**

28, who had fled in October 1857. Hazlett and the **freedom seekers** were returned by steamboat down the **Choptank River** to **Cambridge**, where Hazlett was nearly lynched. The **freedom seekers** were reenslaved, and Hazlett was tried and convicted and sent to prison for forty-four years. Perry and his cohorts shared more than $1,000 reward.

**PETER'S NECK, MARYLAND.** Peter's Neck is a loosely defined region south of **Madison** and the town of **Woolford**, east of Parson's Creek and west of Harrisville Road, between the Little Choptank and the **Blackwater rivers**. Peter's Neck includes many specific sites associated with Tubman, her family, and the **Underground Railroad**, including the southern portions of Parson's Creek and White Marsh Road below **Malone's Church**, Harrisville Road, and **Anthony Thompson**'s plantation where Tubman was born and where her father later occupied ten acres as a free man after 1840. Peter's Neck also includes portions of the historic White Marsh free Black community landscapes dating from the turn of the nineteenth century.

**PHILADELPHIA VIGILANCE COMMITTEE.** Founded in 1852 to formally organize resistance to the **Fugitive Slave Act of 1850** and help **freedom seekers** in the city through a network of **Underground Railroad** agents and supporters. The members of the committee included **William Still**, **Charles Bustill**, **Nathaniel W. Depee**, and **James Miller McKim**. The committee managed and coordinated efforts to provide shelter, food, clothing, medicine, and transportation for nearly 1,400 self-liberators, including **Harriet Tubman**, enabling them to navigate their way to freedom through Philadelphia to New York, New England, and Canada.

**PHILLIPS, REUBEN E. (1805–unknown).** A wealthy planter from Town Point, near **Cambridge, Maryland**, Phillips enslaved eleven people in 1852. His stepdaughter, **Jane Cator**, enslaved eight people or more at that time. On 24 October 1857, many of them escaped in a large group of twenty-eight people, including **Daffney Cornish** and six of her eight children and her husband, **Aaron Cornish**, who was enslaved by Reverend **Levi D. Travers**. The other twenty people were enslaved by **Samuel Pattison**, Richard Keene, and Willis Brannock, all of **Dorchester County**. Cator, Phillips, Pattison, and Brannock posted a $3,100 reward for the capture of their enslaved people. This escape, in addition to another escape of a group of sixteen a week earlier, prompted newspaper headlines describing the unusual activity as a Stampede of Slaves. Local slaveholders increased their surveillance and successfully thwarted additional escapes over the next two years.

**PHILLIPS, WENDELL (29 November 1811–2 February 1884).** Born into wealth in Boston, Massachusetts, Phillips attended Harvard and obtained a law degree in 1833. Deeply influenced by his progressive parents and **William Lloyd Garrison**, Phillips became an ardent **abolitionist** and used his skills as a lawyer and orator to argue passionately for the antislavery cause. He met **Harriet Tubman** in Boston during the mid-1850s and became a close friend and supporter. They shared stages together during conventions and rallies for abolition and women's rights. Phillips was a member of the **American Anti-Slavery Society** and the **Boston Vigilance Committee**, helping protect **freedom seekers**. After the **Civil War**, Phillips campaigned for passage of the **Fourteenth** and **Fifteenth Amendments**. He continued to send financial support to Tubman in Auburn, New York, when she needed it. He died in Charlestown, Boston, Massachusetts, in 1884.

**PLOWDEN, WALTER D. (unknown–ca. 1893).** Born enslaved in Washington County, Maryland, Plowden was **manumitted** as a young adult. He moved to New York City prior to the **Civil War** and joined the Forty-seventh New York Volunteers as the servant of the regimental surgeon, but curiously he also enrolled in the Thirteenth New York Militia. Neither regimental rosters show Plowden mustered in. He followed the Forty-seventh to South Carolina, where he became a freelance civilian supporting Union efforts in the Hilton Head district. In early June, he testified at the court-martial trial of Private **John E. Webster**, who was accused of embezzling food and other supplies illegally from the commissary stores.

He became a scout for the U.S. Army and was a member of **Harriet Tubman**'s team who spied on **Confederate** forces and relayed information to Union officers. The other scouts were **Isaac Hayward**, **Mott Blake**, **Peter Burns**, **Sandy Sellers**, **George Chisholm**, **Solomon Gregory**, **Gabriel Cahern**, and river pilots **Charles Simmons** and **Samuel Hayward**. Under Tubman's command, the group was considered by General **Rufus Saxton** to be among "the most valued scouts and pilots in the Gov't employ in" Hilton Head, South Carolina.

Plowden was captured by a **Confederate** force in December 1863 while on a scouting mission and imprisoned for eighteen months before being liberated by Union forces. In 1868, Plowden petitioned the U.S. Congress for unpaid wages as a spy and scout during the war. On 1 March 1869 he was awarded $1,000, while at the same time Congress refused to consider a similar petition from **Harriet Tubman** regarding her unpaid work. In 1873, Plowden returned to Congress and demanded an additional $4,000 in unpaid wages, but he was denied. During the 1870s, Plowden worked as a claims agent, writing appeals for war veterans and their widows seeking pensions because of disability or death. He was charged with fraud because he robbed some of the veterans and their dependents of their claims money. He died in disgrace in Washington, D.C., in the early 1890s.

**POLARIS.** A bright star in **Ursa Minor**, a constellation of stars visible in the Northern Hemisphere. Ursa Minor is also known as the **Little Dipper**. It contains Polaris, also known as the North Star. Its position is extremely close to the north celestial pole, rising above the Earth's North Pole. Visible to the naked eye, it is used for navigation. Tubman traveled by night, using the North Star and instructions from white and Black helpers to find her way to freedom. She later said, "God . . . gave me my strength, and he set the North Star in the heavens; he meant for me to be free."

**POMEROY, THEODORE** (31 December 1824–23 March 1905). Lawyer, politician, **abolitionist**, and banker in Auburn, New York. Pomeroy was **David Wright**'s law partner and later became a U.S. congressman and then mayor of Auburn. He hired **Harriet Tubman** to perform domestic services, including child care. Friends noted she deeply mourned his death in 1905.

**POPLAR NECK, MARYLAND.** A neck of land along the **Choptank River** between Skillington Creek to the north and **Marsh Creek** to the South, near **Preston, Maryland**, in Caroline County. It was the site of Dr. **Anthony C. Thompson**'s plantation from 1846 to 1857. **Harriet Tubman** escaped from there in the fall of 1849 and conducted several escape missions during the 1850s from this area. Tubman's father, **Ben Ross**, was active in the **Underground Railroad** from his home here, assisting Tubman, her brothers, and others who escaped on **Christmas Day 1854**.

**PORTER, MARIA G.** (8 October 1805–13 December 1896). Born in Maine, Porter moved to Rochester, New York, in 1836 where she ran a boarding house. An **abolitionist**, she became the treasurer for the **Rochester Ladies Anti-Slavery Sewing Society**. Her home was a stop on the **Underground Railroad**, and **Harriet Tubman** stayed at her home with her parents, **Ben Ross** and **Rit Green Ross**, after bringing them north in the late spring of 1857. Porter recorded funds raised and expended in aid of **freedom seekers** and advocated for the abolition of slavery. Her brother, Samuel D. Porter, was also an **abolitionist** and **Underground Railroad** agent. According to newspaper articles, Tubman visited Porter shortly before Porter's death in 1896.

**POST, AMY KIRBY** (20 December 1802–29 January 1889). A Quaker, activist, and reformer, Post was a devoted **abolitionist** and champion of women's rights. Married to **Isaac Post**, they lived in Rochester, New York. Amy joined the group of women, including **Elizabeth Cady Stanton**, **Martha Coffin Wright**, and **Lucretia Coffin Mott**, who met at the **Seneca Falls Convention** in July 1848. Post was among the sixty-eight women and thirty-two men who signed the Declaration of Sentiments calling for equality for women in law and society. With Isaac, Amy opened their home as an **Underground Railroad** station, and they were longtime friends and supporters of **Frederick Bailey Douglass** and **Anna Murray Douglass**. They were all part of the **Underground Railroad** network that helped **Harriet Tubman** when she traveled through central New York State and Rochester on her way to Canada with her **freedom seekers**.

**POST, ISAAC** (26 February 1798–April 1872). A Quaker, Post married Amy Kirby in 1828. The couple were radical **abolitionists** and women's rights activists. *See also* POST, AMY KIRBY.

**PREDEAUX, HENRY** (ca. 1830–unknown). Born enslaved on the **Eastern Shore of Maryland**, Predeaux escaped on 7 March 1857 with **Thomas Elliot** and **Denard (Denwood) Hughes** from **Dorchester County, Maryland**. They were joined by **Emily Kiah**, **William Kiah**, **James and Lavinia Woolford**, and an unidentified eighth man with the surname Tubman. A Black **Underground Railroad** conductor and a friend of **Harriet Tubman** named **Thomas Otwell** betrayed the group and lured them into the Dover, Delaware, jail for the collective $3,000 reward for their capture. Predeaux, described by **William Still** as a "giant of a man," helped the group break out of the jail by scattering burning embers from the fireplace across the floor, frightening the sheriff and his family. He used a hot poker from the fireplace to break the window so that his fellow **freedom seekers** could escape. They successfully made their way to Philadelphia, where they were forwarded on to Canada.

**PRESTON, MARYLAND.** A town in **Caroline County**. Originally called Snow Hill, the town was renamed in 1856. Quakers established Marshy Creek Meeting in the area in 1727 and built a meeting house near the headwaters of **Marsh Creek** on the west side of **Preston** and west of **Linchester Mill** in the mid-1700s. **Abolitionists** and **Underground Railroad** agents **Jacob** and **Hannah Leverton** and **Jonah** and **Esther Kelley** were members. In 1849, the meeting house and cemetery were sold to the local **Preston** Black community, who later built a new church called Mt. Pleasant Church. The site is now a stop on the **Harriet Tubman Underground Railroad Scenic Byway and All-American Road**. One **freedom seeker** testified that **Harriet Tubman** used a cemetery as a meeting place for her rescue missions.

**PURVIS, ROBERT** (4 August 1810–15 April 1898). Born to a free Black woman and a British man, Purvis was sent to Philadelphia, Pennsylvania, and then Massachusetts to be educated. An **abolitionist**, he joined **William Lloyd Garrison** and others to found the **American Anti-Slavery Society** in 1833. He settled in Philadelphia and helped organize the Vigilant Association of Philadelphia to help protect **freedom seekers** from **slave catchers**. His home became a stop on the **Underground Railroad**. He and his wife, Harriet Forten, the daughter of James Forten—a wealthy sailmaker and **abolitionist**—were active in antislavery and women's rights causes. A member of the Pennsylvania Anti-Slavery Society, Purvis helped organize a new vigilance group called the **Philadelphia Vigilance Committee**. Purvis, who served as chairman of the committee, helped manage and coordinate the society's efforts to provide shelter, food, clothing, medicine, and transportation for nearly 1,400 self-liberators, including **Harriet Tubman**. He remained active in reform movements until he died in 1898.

**QUILT CODE MYTH.** *See* appendix E.

# R

**RECONSTRUCTION ERA (1865–1877).** Refers to the period of dramatic political, social, and economic change after the American **Civil War** that included the period of physically rebuilding the war-torn South. During these years, the **Thirteenth, Fourteenth,** and **Fifteenth Amendments to the Constitution** were passed, ensuring freedom and citizenship rights to Black women and men and voting rights to Black men. Policies considered radical for the time period included efforts to create a more equal, multiracial society, especially in former **Confederate** states. Progressives called Radical Republicans fought former **Confederate** southerners to create a more democratic society. The **Freedmen's Bureau** was established during this period, bringing education and federal protection to newly freed people. The U.S. Congress passed the Reconstruction Acts in 1867, which divided the South into five military districts and helped create new governments that included Black men. **Harriet Tubman**'s nephew **James A. Bowley** was elected to the South Carolina state legislature during this period. White resistance to equality fueled violence against Blacks, terrorizing communities throughout the South. Federal troops stationed in the South helped stop some of the violence, but after 1877, when the troops left, white southerners reasserted their power. Discrimination and racism, codified through newly enacted laws throughout the South, kept Blacks segregated and disfranchised for another one hundred years.

*THE REFUGEE: OR THE NORTH-SIDE VIEW OF SLAVERY.* During the spring and summer of 1855, **abolitionist**, journalist, and teacher **Benjamin Drew** of Massachusetts visited fourteen cities and towns in Ontario, Canada, then known as Canada West, and interviewed African American **freedom seekers** who had fled from southern enslavers in the United States. Drew selected 114 of those interviews for publication in his book *The Refugee* in November 1855. The book offers important personal details of lives spent in slavery and the paths taken to reach freedom in Canada. Drew interviewed **Harriet Tubman**. She told him that "slavery is the next thing to hell."

**RELIGIOUS FAITH OF HARRIET TUBMAN.** Tubman's religious faith was rooted in powerful Methodist evangelical teachings invigorated by a mystical and deeply personal spiritual experience. The seizures she experienced due to her head injury reinforced her notions of a powerful spiritual being guiding and protecting her through divine instruction. Tubman "used to dream of flying over fields and towns, and rivers and mountains, looking down upon them 'like a bird.'" The visions Tubman experienced were central to her inner spirituality and reinforced religious beliefs nurtured through strong African cultural traditions and powerful evangelical thought.

Dr. **Anthony C. Thompson**, Anthony Thompson's son, practiced medicine but was also an ordained Methodist minister. He forced Tubman and other enslaved people under his control to attend his services. **Ben** and **Rit**

Ross claimed Thompson was just "pretending to preach" and was nothing but "a wolf in sheep's clothing." Though they attended Thompson's periodic services, Tubman and her family were influenced by Episcopal, Baptist, and Catholic teachings. Tubman and her family likely integrated different religious practices into their daily lives. Tubman and her parents fasted on Fridays, a practice then typical of Catholics, though some Methodists and Episcopalians also followed this habit. Tubman said her father did "it for conscience; we was taught to do so down South. He says if he denies himself for the sufferings of his Lord an' Master, Jesus will sustain him."

In the early years of the nineteenth century, slaveholders became increasingly concerned about the possible subversive messages preached by Black ministers and required their enslaved people, like Tubman and her family, to attend their Christian services. In **Bucktown**, oral tradition and local lore suggests that Tubman, her family, and many of the area's free and enslaved Blacks attended two possible sites of worship. One is the current site of **Bazel Methodist Episcopal Church**, located on Bucktown Road, slightly southwest of the **Bucktown** crossroads, and only half of a mile southeast of the Brodess property. In the years following Nat Turner's Rebellion, when gatherings of free and enslaved people were strictly monitored or forbidden, it is unlikely that Tubman's family attended services in the clearing by the woods near that location during the **antebellum period** unless a white overseer supervised their services. The first church structure was built in 1876. Tubman and her family attended **Camp Meetings**.

Wherever Tubman worshiped, her faith was deep and founded upon strong religious teachings, whether these were specifically Methodist, Catholic, Episcopal, Baptist, or of African origin. **Thomas Garrett**, a Quaker in Wilmington, Delaware, felt that he "never met with any person, of any color, who had more confidence in the voice of God, as spoken direct to her soul . . . and her faith in a Supreme Power truly was great." When Tubman settled in Auburn, New York, she attended services at Presbyterian, **African Methodist Episcopal (AME)**, African Methodist Episcopal Zion **(AMEZ)**, and Baptist churches. She spent her final years as a member of **Thompson Memorial AMEZ Church** on Parker Street in Auburn, New York.

**RESCUE MISSIONS OF HARRIET TUBMAN.** *See* appendix A.

**RIDEOUT, THOMAS.** Born in Maryland and enslaved by Anne M. Dixon, Thomas escaped on Saturday night, 24 July 1858, in company with **Mary Light, Charles Anthony Light, William Henry Cornish, Esther Cornish, Solomon Cornish,** and **John Green**. Their white **Underground Railroad** conductor was an Irish immigrant and wood sawyer named **Hugh Hazlett**. The group was caught a few days later in **Caroline County, Maryland**, and brought to **Cambridge** via a steamboat, but a mob had gathered to await their arrival at Long Wharf. The sheriff feared the mob would lynch Hazlett, so he ordered the steamboat to leave Long Wharf and dock at another location upriver. Hazlett and the others were later safely secured in the **Cambridge** jail. Rideout was reenslaved by Dixon.

**RIDGEWAY, MARTHA.** Harriet Tubman's nurse at **John Brown Hall** beginning in 1911. Ridgeway was at Tubman's side when she died on 10 March 1913.

**ROBINSON, JOHN BELL.** A proslavery writer from Philadelphia. In 1860 he wrote that **Harriet Tubman** had been featured as "A Female Conductor on the **Underground Railroad**" at a women's suffrage meeting in Boston in July. He was horrified, he told his readers, that she was applauded for bringing her parents "away from ease and comfortable homes" where they had been "caressed and better taken care of . . . around the plentiful board of their master." He argued further that Tubman's "cruelty" to her parents was "a thousand times worse than to sell young ones away!"

**ROCHESTER LADIES' ANTI-SLAVERY SEWING SOCIETY.** Founded in 1851 in Rochester, New York, by a small group of women, including **Maria G. Porter**, the society raised funds to promote abolition and support **Underground Railroad** activities in the city and greater central New York networks and provide financial resources to individual **freedom seekers** including **Harriet Tubman**. The society grew over time and conducted successful antislavery fairs where they sold products and donated the receipts to the society. **Frederick Bailey Douglass** and **Gerrit Smith** donated ticket sales from their lectures to the group, and later the society held its own lecture series. The society also helped financially support Douglass's newspapers when he ran short of funds. Their records reveal payments for travel, food, clothing, medicine, and shelter for self-liberators and also the costs for burial for a **freedom seeker** who died in their care. The society's account books and letters are held by the William L. Clements Library at the University of Michigan.

**ROCK, JOHN STEWART** (13 October 1825–3 December 1866). Born free in Salem, New Jersey, Rock became an **abolitionist**, teacher, and one of the first Black men to earn a medical degree. While living in Boston and working with other antislavery activists and **Underground Railroad** agents, he hosted **Harriet Tubman** in his home during the late 1850s.

**ROSS, ANGERINE** (ca. 1847–aft. 1864). Enslaved by **Edward Brodess** and his family, Angerine was the daughter of **Harriet Tubman**'s sister **Rachel Ross** and an unidentified man. After Rachel's death in 1859, Tubman attempted to rescue Angerine and her brother, **Ben Ross**, but failed because she did not have $30 to bribe an unidentified courier to bring the children to Tubman's hiding place. Angerine and Ben remained enslaved by the Brodess family. Angerine was emancipated by law on 1 November 1864. Her fate remains unknown.

**ROSS, ARAMINTA "MINTY."** See TUBMAN, HARRIET ROSS.

**ROSS, BEN** (ca. 1849–aft. 1864). Enslaved by **Edward Brodess** and his family, Ben was the son of **Harriet Tubman**'s sister **Rachel Ross** and an unidentified man. Emancipated by law on 1 November 1864, his fate remains unknown. *See also* ROSS, ANGERINE.

**ROSS, BENJAMIN "BEN"** (ca. 1780 to 1783–19 November 1871). Born enslaved around 1780, Ben Ross's ancestry remains unknown, though there is evidence of possible siblings and other relatives living in the county, both free and enslaved. In 1783, **Anthony Thompson** paid taxes on four enslaved people—three boys under the age of eight and one boy between eight and fourteen years old. When, where, and how Thompson acquired them—through purchase, inheritance, comingling of family or marriage assets, or if they were the sons of a deceased enslaved woman or one sold away—is not known, and their names remain unknown, too. Ben Ross, though, could be one of the boys under the age of eight. There are no bills of sale, deeds, or chattel records documenting Thompson's purchase of any of the enslaved people he was taxed for that year.

Thompson married Mary "Polly" King in 1786. They had three sons: Dr. **Anthony C. Thompson**, Dr. **Absalom C. Thompson**, and **Edward Thompson**. Polly died ca. 1801, and in 1803, Thompson married widow **Mary Pattison Brodess**. Mary moved six miles from her home near her mother, **Elizabeth Pattison**, at the **Little Blackwater Bridge** to Thompson's plantation at **Peter's Neck** along the **Blackwater River** and Thompson's Creek. Thompson lived in a log home at the time on the plantation, but between 1800 and 1810, he supervised the construction of a large federal-style wood-frame home. It was certainly built with the labor of Ross, a skilled carpenter and timber foreman. Mary brought her toddler son, **Edward Brodess**, and several enslaved people, including **Harriet "Rit" Green** and three men, **Shadrack**, **Frederick**, and **Samuel**, with her.

By 1808, Green and Ross had married and started their own family. At least five of their nine children were born here: Linah, Mariah Ritty, Soph, Robert, and Ben Jr. Around 1810, Mary died, leaving eight-year-old Edward and her enslaved people under Thompson's guardianship. Rit worked for Thompson or was hired out by him for the benefit of young Edward's future inheritance, enabling Rit and Ben to maintain a family life together on the Thompson plantation. Between 1823 and 1824, Edward left his stepfather's house and moved to his own inherited farm near **Bucktown**, taking Rit and her children with him and away from Ben. Thompson enslaved more than forty people, including entire families whose surnames include Manokey, Kiah, Bowley, Tyler, Ross, Saunders, and Young, among others, some of whom may be related to Ben Ross. As Thompson lay dying in 1836, he dictated his last will and testament. He **manumitted** each of his forty-three enslaved people according to a specific timetable, ranging from immediate emancipation to the longest possible limited term of service of forty-four years. Ben was set free and given ten acres of land in Peter's Neck. He leased Rit and several of the Ross children, including **Harriet Tubman**, so that they could live with him. In 1846, Rit moved with Ben to **Poplar Neck** in **Caroline County** to work for Dr. **Anthony C. Thompson**.

In April 1857, Ben was suspected of aiding **freedom seekers** along the **Underground Railroad** and risked arrest. Tubman raced to Maryland to rescue her parents and brought them to St. Catharines, Ontario, Canada, where she settled them in a house on North Street. Ben was reluctant to leave Maryland, however. He had vowed he would not leave Maryland "so long as any of his children remain in bondage," but they had to leave **Rachel Ross** and her children and **Mary Manokey Ross**, the wife of **Robert Ross**, and their children behind. Tubman found it difficult to continue her rescue missions and take care of her parents. She purchased a small farm from **William Henry Seward** in Auburn, New York, in 1859 so they could be supported by Tubman's many friends there. Ben died there in 1871, and Rit passed in October 1879.

**ROSS, BEN, JR. (BROTHER OF HT).** *See* STEWART, JAMES (BROTHER OF HT).

**ROSS, HARRIET "RIT" GREEN (ca. 1785– 13 October 1879).** Born enslaved around 1785, Rit's mother was **Modesty**, an African woman held in bondage by **Atthow Pattison**. When Pattison died in 1797, he bequeathed Rit to his granddaughter **Mary Pattison Brodess Thompson**. In 1803, after the death of her first husband, **Joseph Brodess**, and her marriage to **Anthony Thompson**, Mary moved six miles from her home near her mother, **Elizabeth Pattison**, at the **Little Blackwater Bridge** to Thompson's plantation at **Peter's Neck** along the **Blackwater River** and Thompson's Creek. She brought her toddler son, **Edward Brodess**, and several enslaved people, including Rit and three men, **Shadrack**, **Frederick**, and **Samuel**, with her.

As a result of the marriage, Rit and **Ben Ross** became members of the same household, eventually marrying and starting their own family around 1808. Over the next twenty-five years, Rit and Ben raised nine children: **Linah Ross Jolly** was born in 1808, **Mariah Ritty** around 1811, **Soph Ross** in 1813, **Robert Ross** in 1816, **Araminta "Minty" Ross** (aka **Harriet Tubman**) in 1822, **Ben Ross Jr.** in 1823, **Rachel Ross** in 1825, **Henry Ross** in 1830, and **Moses Ross** in 1832. Mary died around 1810, leaving her eight-year-old son Edward and her enslaved people under Thompson's guardianship. Rit worked for Thompson or was hired out by him for the benefit of young Edward's future inheritance, enabling Rit and Ben to maintain a family life together on the Thompson plantation.

Between 1823 and 1824, Edward left his stepfather's house and moved to his own inherited farm near **Bucktown**, taking Rit and her children with him and heartlessly separating the Ross family. Rit and Ben struggled to protect them. Brodess sold Mariah Ritty, Linah, and Soph, and they were never heard from again. When he tried to sell Moses, Rit hid Moses in a nearby swamp and threatened Brodess with a knife. In 1840 Ben was set free. He leased Rit and several of the Ross children, including **Harriet Tubman**, so that they could live with him at **Peter's Neck**. In 1846, Rit moved with Ben to **Poplar Neck** in **Caroline County** to work for Dr. **Anthony C. Thompson**.

Rit had understood that **Atthow Pattison** had instructed his heirs to set Rit free when she turned forty-five years old, but she remained enslaved. After **Edward Brodess** died in 1849, ownership of Rit was contested. **Eliza Keene Brodess**, Edward's widow, sold Rit to Ben in 1855 for $20. By then, their four sons, Harriet Tubman, and several grand- and great-grandchildren had escaped slavery. In April 1857, Ben was suspected of aiding **freedom seekers** along the **Underground Railroad** and risked arrest. Tubman rescued her parents and brought them to St. Catharines, Ontario, Canada, where she settled them in a house on North Street. They changed their surname to Stewart. Tubman found it difficult to continue her rescue missions and take care of her parents. She purchased a small farm from **William Henry Seward** in Auburn, New York, in 1859 so they could be supported by Tubman's many friends there. She tried to rescue Rachel and her children, but Rachel died in 1859 and the children remained enslaved. Ben died in 1871, and Rit passed in October 1879.

**ROSS, HARRIET "RITTY"** (24 December 1854–unknown). The daughter of **Mary Manokey Ross** and **Robert Ross**, Ritty was born on Christmas Eve near **Madison, Dorchester County, Maryland**. That night, **Harriet Tubman** was waiting forty miles away in **Poplar Neck, Caroline County** to lead Robert and their brothers **Ben Ross** and **Henry Ross** and others to freedom in Canada. Mary had gone into labor and delivered Ritty; Robert was conflicted. Should he choose freedom or stay enslaved and risk being sold to satisfy debts accrued by the estate of **Edward Brodess**? He chose freedom, leaving Mary, Ritty, and his two sons, **John Henry Ross** and **Moses Ross**.

**ROSS, HENRY (BROTHER OF HT)**. See STEWART, WILLIAM HENRY, SR. (BROTHER OF HT).

**ROSS, JOHN HENRY.** See STEWART, JOHN HENRY.

**ROSS, JOHN ISAAC.** See STEWART, JOHN ISAAC.

**ROSS, LINAH.** See JOLLY, LINAH ROSS.

**ROSS, MARIAH RITTY** (ca. 1811–unknown). The enslaved sister of **Harriet Tubman**, Mariah Ritty was the second child of **Ben** and **Rit Green Ross**. She was sold by **Edward Brodess** in 1825 when Tubman was three years old. It is likely that **Dempsey P. Kane**, a Mississippi slave trader, purchased her and took her to the **Deep South**. Her fate remains unknown.

**ROSS, MARY MANOKEY** (ca. 1832–unknown). The daughter of **Jerry** and **Polly Manokey**, Mary married **Harriet Tubman**'s brother **Robert Ross** sometime around 1850. Enslaved by **Anthony Thompson**, she was part of his estate property when he died in 1836. His son Dr. **Anthony C. Thompson** inherited her. Mary and Robert had three children: **John Henry Ross**, **Moses Ross**, and **Harriet "Ritty" Ross**. After Robert escaped on **Christmas Day 1854**, Mary married another man by the name of Wells, with whom she had children. In 1856, Dr. Thompson signed a **manumission**, setting Mary free in 1862. A year later, Thompson sold Mary to his daughter **Sarah Catherine Haddaway** in Talbot County.

**ROSS, MOSES.** For Harriet Tubman's nephew, see STEWART, MOSES.

**ROSS, MOSES (BROTHER OF HT)** (ca. 1832–unknown). The last of nine children born to **Ben Ross** and **Rit Green Ross** and Harriet Tubman's youngest sibling. According to testimony given to **Samuel Gridley Howe** by his brother **William Henry Ross Stewart** in St. Catharines, Ontario, Canada, in 1863, their mother, Rit, threatened to kill **Edward Brodess**'s neighbor **John Scott** when he attempted to trick her into revealing where she had hidden Moses to prevent Brodess from selling him to a **slave trader** from Georgia in 1844. Brodess did not sell Moses, but he did sell Tubman's sister **Soph Ross** instead. Moses escaped with Tubman's help in 1851. His fate remains unknown, but he was presumed dead by 1865.

**ROSS, RACHEL** (ca. 1825–1859). The sixth of nine children born to **Ben Ross** and **Rit Green Ross** and Harriet Tubman's youngest sister. Enslaved by **Edward Brodess**, Rachel had two children: **Angerine Ross** and **Ben Ross**. Tubman made several attempts during the 1850s to liberate Rachel and her children and bring them to freedom in the North. The Brodess family separated Rachel from her children, and she refused to escape without them. In 1859 Rachel died. Tubman discovered her death when she returned to **Dorchester County, Maryland**, in November 1860 to rescue her and the children. Lacking $30 to bribe someone to bring the children to her hiding place, Tubman had to leave them enslaved. She brought **Stephen** and **Maria Ennals** and their children to freedom instead.

**ROSS, ROBERT (BROTHER OF HT).** *See* STEWART, JOHN (BROTHER OF HT).

**ROSS, SIMON (ca. 1800–aft. 1870).** Born free and may have been a blood relative to **Ben Ross**, **Harriet Tubman**'s father. He lived with his family near the **Anthony Thompson** plantation in **Peter's Neck** in **Dorchester County, Maryland**, in an area populated by many free Black families from 1820 to 1870. Married to a free woman, possibly named Eliza, his children were free born. In 1857, a white neighbor, **John D. Parker**, petitioned the county court to indenture Ross's sons—eight-year-old Benjamin, six-year-old David, and three-year-old Charles. Ross spent years trying to reclaim his children. Black parents were nearly powerless to prevent indentures of their children. Despite their ability to support them and teach their children trades, many Black families found the local courts indifferent to their rights to their own children. Parker owned the former Thompson home site and hundreds of acres of Thompson's former lands. The boys were still living in Parker's household in 1860, along with nine enslaved people. After the **Civil War**, Ross asked the **Freedmen's Bureau** to help him get his children from Parker. In 1867, eighteen-year-old Benjamin, sixteen-year-old David, and thirteen-year-old Charles were still indentured to Parker. Parker kept fighting the **Freedmen's Bureau** and kept the children indentured, depriving Ross the right to live with and educate his children and benefiting from their contributions to the whole family's standard of living. Ross succeeded in liberating them in 1868. He died sometime after 1870.

**ROSS, SOPH (ca. 1813–aft. 1844).** The third of nine children born to **Ben Ross** and **Rit Green Ross** and one of **Harriet Tubman**'s older sisters. Enslaved by **Edward Brodess**, Soph had one daughter, **Ann Marie Stewart Elliott**, with an unidentified man in 1844. According to testimony given to **Samuel Gridley Howe** by her brother **William Henry Ross Stewart** in St. Catharines, Ontario, Canada, in 1863, Soph was sold away from her three-month-old daughter in 1844 to a **slave trader** from Georgia. Her husband had hidden her to prevent the sale, but a minister whom he trusted (possibly Dr. **Anthony C. Thompson**) betrayed him. As Brodess lay dying in 1849, he could not look at then five-year-old Ann and asked she be taken out of his sight. Soph's fate remains unknown.

**RUNAWAY.** Once commonly used to describe a **freedom seeker**. According to the **National Park Service Network to Freedom Program**, terms "such as 'runaway' and 'escapees' refer to freedom seekers. These terms tend to disparage the freedom seeker. 'Runaway' conjures up the image of a discontent adolescent, while 'escapee' is linked to 'fugitive,' evoking the image of a guilty law breaker deserving of capture and punishment."

# S

**SALEM CHAPEL, BRITISH METHODIST EPISCOPAL CHURCH.** Located on the corner of Geneva and North Streets in St. Catharines, Ontario, Canada, the chapel was built between 1853 and 1855. Its congregation included many **freedom seekers** from the United States, including **Harriet Tubman** and her family and friends from Maryland. Tubman's rented log home on North Street (ca. 1858–1859) sat within a few hundred feet of the church. The church helped raise funds for newly arrived **freedom seekers**, hosted antislavery lectures, and provided educational resources to the growing Black community in the city. In 1999, Canada designated Salem Chapel a National Historic Site. The congregation conducts tours by appointment and still holds services every Sunday morning.

**SAMUEL.** A man enslaved by Mary Pattison Brodess Thompson. He was identified in **Anthony Thompson**'s guardian's account for the years 1821–1822 for his stepson, **Edward Brodess**. Samuel's full identity and fate remains unknown.

**SANBORN, FRANKLIN B.** (15 December 1831–27 February 1917). Born in Hampton Falls, New Hampshire, Sanborn became a noted **abolitionist**, author, editor, teacher, reformer, and civil rights activist. During the 1850s, he was actively involved in the antislavery movement, working with some of the giants of abolition in New England, including **Wendell Phillips** and **William Lloyd Garrison**. Sanborn supported revolutionary **abolitionist** John Brown and became one of a small group of activists called the **Secret Six** who backed John Brown's raid on **Harpers Ferry**, Virginia, in the fall of 1859. Sanborn met **Harriet Tubman** sometime around 1858 or earlier in Boston. They became lifelong friends. Sanborn wrote the earliest biography of Tubman for *The Commonwealth* newspaper on 17 July 1863. Sanborn maintained contact with Tubman until her death in 1913, and he published a tribute to her in the *Springfield Republican* newspaper on 19 March 1913. Sanborn lived the majority of his adult life in Concord, Massachusetts. He died in 1917 in New Jersey and is buried in Sleepy Hollow Cemetery in Concord, Massachusetts.

**SAXTON, RUFUS** (19 October 1824–23 February 1908). Born in Massachusetts to parents active in **abolition** and women's rights, Saxton graduated from the U.S. Military Academy at West Point in 1849. During the **Civil War** in 1862, Saxton was appointed brigadier general and military governor of the **Department of the South**. He directed the recruitment and organization of the first Black regiments of Black soldiers and appointed his **abolitionist** friend **Thomas Wentworth Higginson** colonel of the First South Carolina Colored Volunteers.

Saxton knew and respected **Harriet Tubman** and supported her work as a spy and scout for the Union Army. She lived part of the time in Beaufort, South Carolina, at the Savan House across from the Arsenal and close to General Saxton's headquarters and the local "contraband" and military hospitals. Saxton

Harriet Tubman remained lifelong friends with many of New England's abolitionists, including Franklin Sanborn, who included her in his memoir, *Recollections of Seventy Years*. Photo, Boston, ca. 1886, published in *Recollections of Seventy Years* (Boston: Gorham Press, 1909). *Courtesy of the author*

planned the festivities celebrating the **Emancipation Proclamation** on 1 January 1863 on Hilton Head Island, South Carolina. In the spring, Tubman unwittingly purchased stolen sugar from Private **John E. Webster**, who was in charge of the commissary. When she became suspicious, she immediately reported him to Saxton. Webster was arrested, tried, and convicted of theft in a military court. Saxton believed her to be one of "the most valued scouts" employed by the **Department of the South**. After the war he argued for civil rights for African Americans. Saxton also supported Tubman's petition for unpaid wages for her service as a spy and scout during the war. He remained in the military until his retirement in 1888 and is buried in Arlington National Cemetery in Arlington, Virginia.

*SCENES IN THE LIFE OF HARRIET TUBMAN.* Book by **Sarah Hopkins Bradford**. Published by **William J. Moses** in November 1868 in Auburn, New York, *Scenes* was the first full biography of Harriet Tubman. Based on interviews conducted by Bradford during the spring of 1868, and material already published by **Franklin Sanborn** in the *Commonwealth* newspaper in July 1863 and **Ednah Dow Littlehale Cheney** in the *Freedman's Record* in March 1865, it set Tubman's early life permanently in the historical record. Bradford also included letters from **Frederick Bailey Douglass, Gerrit Smith, Thomas Garrett, William Henry Seward**, and **Wendell Phillips** attesting to Tubman's character and detailing some of her activities. General **Rufus Saxton** wrote attesting to Tubman's **Civil War** service. Though Bradford made several material errors in recording Tubman's story, her biography has served as an important record and foundation for further research into Tubman's life. Two more versions of this biography appeared, slightly altered with additional details included in 1886 and 1901 as *Harriet, the Moses of Her People*. *Scenes* is still in print.

**SCOTT, JOHN (18 February 1799–21 October 1863).** A wealthy planter and slaveholder who lived near **Edward Brodess** near **Bucktown, Maryland**. According to testimony given to **Samuel Gridley Howe** by **Harriet Tubman**'s brother **William Henry Ross Stewart** in St. Catharines, Ontario, Canada, in 1863, their mother, Rit, threatened to kill Scott when he colluded with Brodess and an unidentified enslaved person in an attempt to trick her into revealing where she had hidden her son Moses, whom Brodess hoped to sell to a **slave trader** from Georgia in 1844. Her threat had an impact—Brodess did not sell Moses.

**SECOND SOUTH CAROLINA COLORED VOLUNTEERS.** In January 1863, Colonel **James Montgomery** was authorized to raise a regiment of African American troops, including both free and refugee, who would serve under the command of white officers to fight for the United States Union Army during the **Civil War**. He organized the regiment in Beaufort and Hilton Head, South Carolina, and by May the men were mustered into service as the Second South Carolina Volunteer Infantry. **Harriet Tubman** was attached to the regiment, performing scouting and spying service and leading Montgomery and his men up the **Combahee River** on an armed raid. They raided plantations, routed out **Confederate** forces, and freed more than 750 enslaved people. In February 1864, the regiment was reorganized as the Thirty-fourth United States Colored Troops Infantry.

**SECRET SIX.** A group of abolitionists devoted to **John Brown** and dedicated to advancing Brown's plans to destroy slavery. In 1856 Brown began formulating his plans to attack the federal arsenal at **Harpers Ferry**, Virginia. An associate, **Franklin Sanborn** of Massachusetts, introduced Brown to wealthy and powerful **abolitionists** in Boston. Impressed with Brown's passion and vision to end slavery through armed attack and resistance, they secretly funded his efforts to raise a small army. These men—**Gerrit Smith, Thomas Wentworth Higginson, Samuel Gridley Howe, Franklin B. Sanborn, George L. Stearns**, and **Theodore Parker**—became known as the Secret Six. The group also supported **Harriet Tubman** and hoped she would be at Brown's side when he attacked the arsenal. After Brown's raid failed in October 1859, the group went into hiding because their role in supporting Brown was exposed, putting them at risk of arrest for treason. Smith voluntarily committed himself to a psychiatric institution; Sanborn, Stearns, and Howe fled to Canada; and Parker was already in Italy. Higginson stood his ground and refused to be intimidated. In 1860 Sanborn was arrested at his home in Concord, Massachusetts, but townspeople prevented federal marshals from taking him to Washington, D.C.

**SELLERS, SANDY (dates unknown).** Born enslaved in South Carolina, Sellers escaped and became a scout and spy who aided the U.S. Army during the **Civil War**. He was a member of **Harriet Tubman**'s team who spied on **Confederate** forces and relayed information to Union officers. The other scouts were **Isaac Hayward, Mott Blake, Peter Burns, George Chisholm, Solomon Gregory, Gabriel Cahern, Walter D. Plowden**, and river pilots **Samuel Hayward** and **Charles Simmons**. Under

Tubman's command, the group was considered by General **Rufus Saxton** to be among "the most valued scouts and pilots in the Gov't employ in" Hilton Head, South Carolina.

**SENECA FALLS CONVENTION 1848.** Held at the Wesleyan Chapel in Seneca Falls, New York, in July 1848, it is traditionally referred to as the first women's rights convention in the United States. Conceived and planned by **Elizabeth Cady Stanton, Lucretia Coffin Mott,** and **Martha Coffin Wright**, among others, the convention produced a "Declaration of Rights and Sentiments," outlining demands for equal civil, social, political, and religious rights of women, including the right to vote. The convention did spark annual meetings around the country, which helped organize women over many decades. Women's Rights National Historical Park is located in Seneca Falls.

**SEVERANCE, CAROLINE (1820–1914).** An **abolitionist** and woman suffragist. Severance helped organize a woman's suffrage meeting held at the Melodeon Hall in Boston on 4 July 1860, where **Harriet Tubman** spoke. During the **Civil War**, Severance traveled to South Carolina to observe New England **abolitionists'** work with the newly freed people. She met **Harriet Tubman**, who was then working for General Terry. Tubman told her that she had recently been robbed, so Severance promised to take her savings and send them to Auburn for Tubman's family. After the war, Severance worked with **Susan B. Anthony** to establish women's suffrage organizations and campaign to have the word "male" struck from the **Fourteenth Amendment to the Constitution**, a position shared by Tubman and many other women.

**SEWARD, FRANCES MILLER (25 September 1805–21 June 1865).** The daughter of Elijah and Hannah Miller, Frances was born in the family home on Cayuga Lake near Auburn, New York. Her father's success as a lawyer and real estate investor afforded the family the opportunity to move to a mansion in Auburn in 1817. She and her sister, **Lazette Miller Worden**, received good educations. In 1824, she married **William Henry Seward**, a young lawyer. They lived in her father's mansion on South Street and had five children together including Frederick, William, and Fanny.

Committed to political and social reform activities, Frances was an **abolitionist** and women's rights activist, and she sheltered **freedom seekers** in their home. Through her relationship with **Martha Coffin Wright**, whose husband David was William Henry's law partner, Frances met **Harriet Tubman**. By 1859, Tubman was in need of a home for her aged parents, whom she had brought to Canada from Maryland in the spring of 1857. Tubman knew the antislavery community in Auburn would help take care of her parents while she traveled widely to raise money for her rescue missions. Frances had inherited multiple properties from her father, so with her husband's consent and assistance from her son William she arranged to sell a seven-acre farm on the Fleming and Auburn line for $1,200. Tubman paid on the mortgage periodically over the next fourteen years when Frances's son Frederick closed the mortgage and turned the property over to Tubman. Tubman and Frances were very close—like-minded and independent women, their friendship nurtured their advocacy for equality and justice. Tubman mourned deeply when Frances died in 1865 and when the Sewards' daughter Fanny died unexpectedly a little more than a year later in 1866.

**SEWARD, WILLIAM HENRY (16 May 1801–10 October 1872).** A lawyer and politician, Seward was born in Orange County, New York, to a wealthy, slaveholding family. (New York State abolished slavery in 1827.) He joined the law practice of Elijah Miller in Auburn, New York, and married Miller's daughter Frances in 1824. Seward held various local and state political positions and was elected governor of New York in 1839. By then, he and Frances had become **abolitionists**. As governor, he encouraged the passage of laws protecting **freedom seekers** from **slave catchers** on New York soil and signed legislation guaranteeing the immediate **emancipation** of enslaved people brought into the state by their enslavers.

He also supported immigration and universal public education for all residents.

In 1846, Seward defended a mentally ill Black man, William Freeman, who had murdered four people. Seward used the insanity defense successfully to spare Freeman's life, though he died shortly afterward in prison. In 1849, Seward was elected to the Senate, where he served for the next twelve years until 1861. The Sewards participated in the region's **Underground Railroad** network by sheltering **freedom seekers** in their home during the 1850s. Frances and William Henry likely met **Harriet Tubman** through friend **Martha Coffin Wright** and her husband, **David Wright**, Seward's law partner in Auburn. In May 1859, the Sewards sold Tubman a seven-acre farm in Fleming, New York, just over the Auburn line. Tubman was technically still enslaved and considered a fugitive from the law, making the real estate transaction risky for the Sewards, who could have been charged with a crime.

In 1860, Seward ran for the presidency as a Republican, but he lost his bid to the newcomer **Abraham Lincoln**. Seward supported Lincoln and helped campaign for him. Lincoln appointed Seward secretary of state in 1861, who hoped he could negotiate a compromise with southern states then seceding from the union. Seward was severely wounded by Lewis Powell, John Wilkes Booth's co-conspirator, on the night of 14 April 1865 when Booth assassinated President Lincoln. He recovered slowly and endured the unexpected death of his wife, Frances, in June and his daughter Fanny the following year. He continued in his position under Lincoln's successor, Andrew Johnson, and in 1867 negotiated the purchase of the state of Alaska from Russia. In 1870, he began his memoirs and died on 10 October 1872. Harriet Tubman grieved his death, sending flowers to adorn his coffin. He is buried with Frances and their daughter Fanny in Fort Hill Cemetery. *See also* SEWARD, FRANCES MILLER.

**SHADRACH (dates unknown).** A man enslaved by Mary Pattison Brodess Thompson. He is identified in the **Anthony Thompson's** guardian's account for the years 1821–1822 for his stepson, **Edward Brodess**. Shadrack's full identity and fate remains unknown.

**SHAW, ROBERT GOULD (10 October 1837–18 July 1863).** Born in Boston to an **abolitionist** family, Shaw accepted an appointment as commander of the **Fifty-fourth Massachusetts Voluntary Infantry Regiment**, the second Black regiment officially authorized during the **Civil War**. Advanced to colonel in the spring of 1863, Shaw led his regiment to South Carolina where they saw their first action. Shaw disapproved of Col. **James Montgomery**'s military tactic of burning **Confederate** property. Famously, Shaw would lead his men into combat at Fort Wagner during July 1863. **Harriet Tubman** served Shaw his last meal before the battle. The courage and valor displayed by the men during the assault on the fort earned them respect across the nation and put to rest the racist belief that Black soldiers could not fight as well as white soldiers. Shaw died during the battle on July 18. He was buried by victorious **Confederate** soldiers in a mass grave with his fallen men as a sign of disrespect for the officer. Shaw's family, however, was proud that he was buried with fellow Black soldiers. After the war the Union Army disinterred the bodies and moved them to a new gravesite in Beaufort, South Carolina; they insisted he remain with his men.

**SHIMER, ANTHONY.** *See* GOLD SWINDLE.

**SIEBERT, WILBUR (30 August 1866–2 September 1961).** Siebert was a professor of history at Ohio State University during the 1890s when he embarked on a years-long project documenting the history of the **Underground Railroad**. He conducted interviews and corresponded with hundreds of informants—former **abolitionists** and **Underground Railroad** agents and conductors and their children and associates from the **antebellum period**. He interviewed **Harriet Tubman** in April 1897 in Cambridge, Massachusetts. In 1898 he published his findings in *The Underground Railroad from Slavery to Freedom*. His extensive research collections are housed at Houghton

Library at Harvard University and at the Ohio State Archives.

**SIMMONS, CHARLES (dates unknown).** Born enslaved in South Carolina, Simmons was a river pilot who aided the U.S. Army during the **Civil War**. He was a member of **Harriet Tubman**'s team who spied on **Confederate** forces and relayed information to Union officers. The other scouts were **Isaac Hayward, Mott Blake, Peter Burns, Sandy Sellers, George Chisholm, Solomon Gregory, Gabriel Cahern, Walter D. Plowden,** and **Samuel Hayward,** also a river pilot. Under Tubman's command, the group was considered by General **Rufus Saxton** to be among "the most valued scouts and pilots in the Gov't employ in" Hilton Head, South Carolina. Simmons and Hayward were vital to safe navigation along heavily mined waters in the Hilton Head district.

**SLATTER, HOPE HULL (1790–1853).** Born in Georgia, Slatter became one of America's largest **slave traders** during the 1830s through the 1850s. Based on Pratt Street in Baltimore, Slatter and other dealers made the city one of the busiest domestic slave trade markets in the south.

**SLAVE AUCTIONS.** Events where enslaved people were sold to the highest bidder. Auctions of enslaved people occurred in communities all over the South in designated market exchanges in commercial zones, in front of courthouses and other public buildings, or on the premises of **slave traders** such as **Hope Hull Slatter** of Baltimore. **Harriet Tubman**'s niece **Kessiah Jolley Bowley** was sold to the highest bidder at an auction at the **Dorchester County Courthouse** in 1850.

**SLAVE CATCHERS.** Also known as "man hunters" and "negro catchers," professional, freelance, and part-time slave catchers and bounty hunters roamed the countryside, cities, and towns, hunting **freedom seekers** to take them back into slavery and receive a monetary reward. After the passage of the **Fugitive Slave Act** in 1850, slave catchers searching in the North were given the power to force cooperation from local authorities for the return of their sought-after enslaved property even though slavery had long been outlawed in those states. The financial rewards paid by slaveholders proved lucrative especially for landless white men and some free African Americans and made successful escapes more unlikely. They were often at liberty to travel far beyond their communities. Reward advertisements were printed in local and regional newspapers, and individual handbills were posted at train stations and other public places, enticing men to search for **freedom seekers**. Some slaveholders privately hired freelance bounty hunters, paying travel expenses in addition to a dollar reward if the enslaved person was caught. Some southern communities enacted laws in support of government-sponsored slave patrols to monitor neighborhoods for illicit activity or illegal gatherings of enslaved people, as well as escape plots. These patrols engaged the services of local men, who formed groups to patrol areas deemed at risk for escapes or insurrection. They were less effective at catching **freedom seekers** but were a clear deterrent to escape. Some slave patrols in the **Deep South** engaged the services of enslaved men, too, creating a difficult and dangerous environment within enslaved communities who could no longer trust their fellow bondspeople for fear of betrayal.

**SLAVE TRADE, TRANS-ATLANTIC.** The trans-Atlantic slave trade encompassed the trade in enslaved African peoples from many African regions and transported to North and South America between the sixteenth and nineteenth centuries. The trade is characterized by a triangular trading system transporting enslaved people, crops, and manufactured goods between England, West Africa, and the Caribbean and the Americas, or between New England colonies, Africa, and the Caribbean. The trans-Atlantic slave trade is also characterized by the deadly Middle Passage, the portion of the trans-Atlantic voyage where millions of captive Africans, poorly fed and chained in crowded, unhealthy conditions below deck died before reaching the Americas.

Great Britain banned the trans-Atlantic trade in 1807; the United States followed the next year. Despite significant criminal penalties, illegal trading continued for decades.

**SLAVE TRADE, U.S. INTERSTATE.** The trade in enslaved people from one state or region of the United States to another, particularly after the banning of the **trans-Atlantic slave trade** in 1808. The expansion of the U.S. territories through land acquisition and the planting of cotton throughout the **Deep South** and Midwestern states put pressure on the supply and demand for enslaved labor. Historians estimate that in the sixty years before the **Civil War**, more than one million enslaved people were sold away from their families and forced to move from the **Upper South** and Chesapeake Bay region to newly opened territories and states in the **Deep South**. It is also known as the domestic slave trade.

**SLAVE TRADE, U.S. INTRASTATE.** The trade in enslaved people within the boundaries of one state.

**SLAVE TRADERS.** People engaged in the business of buying and selling enslaved people.

**SMEDLEY, DR. ROBERT C. (1832–2 January 1883).** Born in Chester County, Pennsylvania, Smedley obtained a medical degree in 1860. Married to a Quaker woman, Smedley was well versed in the region's **Underground Railroad**. Many of his neighbors were **abolitionists** and actively involved in helping **freedom seekers**. His interest in the actions of his neighbors inspired him to interview many of them during the early 1880s and record their stories. Before he died in January 1883, Smedley turned his unfinished manuscript over to **Underground Railroad** agent Robert Pervis and Marianna Gibbons, a member of an important family that aided self-liberators in Chester County. In June 1883, they published Smedley's book as *The History of the Underground Railroad in Chester and Neighboring Counties of Pennsylvania*. It remains a vital resource for historians and remains in print.

**SMITH, ANN FITZHUGH (11 January 1805–6 March 1875).** Born in Maryland to a wealthy slaveholding family, Ann moved in 1817 to Groveland, New York, where her father, William Fitzhugh, had purchased land. Five years later she married **Gerrit Smith**, the heir to a vast real estate fortune. They settled in Peterboro, New York, and together they became active in social and political reform movements of the day, especially **abolition**. They used their great wealth to support antislavery leaders and organizations. At Ann's request, Gerrit purchased the freedom of Harriet Sims and Samuel Russel and their five children, a family once enslaved by the Fitzhughs. Supportive of women's rights, Ann did not take a leadership role in the movement, preferring to remain in the background. She was close to **Lucretia Coffin Mott**, **Susan B. Anthony**, **Lydia Maria Child**, and her husband's cousin **Elizabeth Cady Stanton**. Her daughter, Elizabeth Smith Miller, and granddaughter **Anne Fitzhugh Miller** were both prominent suffragists. Ann managed a busy household in Peterboro, including maintaining an active **Underground Railroad** station helping hundreds of **freedom seekers**, including **Harriet Tubman**. She died less than three months after Gerrit passed away. They are buried in the Peterboro Cemetery.

**SMITH, CHARLES A. (December 1844–21 November 1924).** Born in Pennsylvania, Smith joined Company C of the **Fifty-fourth Massachusetts Voluntary Infantry Regiment**, one of the first Black regiments formed during the **Civil War**, in March 1863 in Pennsylvania. He fought in the Battle of Fort Wagner in July 1863. He met **Harriet Tubman** in one of the colored hospitals while stationed in Beaufort, South Carolina. After the war, Smith became a minister and eventually moved to Auburn, New York, to lead worshipers at **Thompson Memorial African Methodist Episcopal Zion Church** on Parker Street in Auburn, New York. Smith and his wife, **Frances**, became actively involved in the establishment of the **Harriet Tubman Home for the Aged**, and they both served on the home's Board of Managers. Charles and Frances were at Tubman's bedside when she died on 10 March 1913. Smith died in 1924 and is buried next to his wife at Fort Hill Cemetery in Auburn, New York.

**SMITH, FRANCES** (April 1851–14 April 1947). Born in New York, Frances was married to **Charles A. Smith**, a minister at **Thompson Memorial African Methodist Episcopal Zion Church** on Parker Street in Auburn, New York. Frances became actively involved in the establishment of the **Harriet Tubman Home for the Aged**, and she and Charles served on the home's Board of Managers. The couple was at Tubman's bedside when she died on 10 March 1913. Smith died in 1947 and is buried next to her husband at Fort Hill Cemetery in Auburn, New York.

**SMITH, GERRIT** (6 March 1797–28 December 1874). Politician, **abolitionist**, social reformer, women's rights advocate, and philanthropist, Smith was born in Utica, New York. He moved to his family's 50,000-acre estate in Peterboro, New York, in 1807. His father, Peter Smith, made a fortune in real estate and in partnership with businessman John Jacob Astor. Gerrit took over his father's business around 1820 and vastly increased the family wealth. He married Ann Fitzhugh in 1822 and they had seven children; only two, Elizabeth and Greene, survived childhood. Smith spent his life involved in various social reform activities. Antislavery and civil rights, though, dominated his efforts.

In 1834, he established a school for African Americans in Peterboro and financially supported other Black and integrated educational institutions. He founded the Liberty Party in 1840 to promote political candidates dedicated to abolition. The party nominated him as a presidential candidate in 1848. He was elected to the U.S. House of Representative in 1852; he served only a year before leaving in disgust due to the outsized influence of slaveholders in Congress. His home was a stop on the **Underground Railroad**, helping hundreds of **freedom seekers**, including **Harriet Tubman**. She visited their home frequently, and she and Gerrit became lifelong friends.

During the 1840s, he started giving fifty-acre lots to property-less people and **freedom seekers**, enabling them to vote. Many settled on Smith's 120,000 acres in the Adirondack Mountains near Lake Placid and North Elba. The Smith home served as a gathering place for the leading **abolitionists**, writers, politicians, and reformers of the day, including **Frederick Bailey Douglass**, **William Lloyd Garrison**, and **Wendell Phillips**, among others. A supporter of **John Brown**, Gerrit was a member of Brown's **Secret Six**. After Brown's failed raid on the arsenal at **Harpers Ferry**, Virginia, in October 1859, Smith suffered a mental health crisis and was hospitalized for several weeks. He believed in gender equality and was advised by his cousin, suffragist **Elizabeth Cady Stanton**. He gave away millions of dollars during his lifetime in support of social, political, economic, and educational reform. He suffered a stroke and died in December 1874. The Gerrit Smith Estate is a National Historic Landmark. *See also* SMITH, ANN FITZHUGH.

**SPENCE, ARA.** A Maryland District and Court of Appeals judge. He enslaved **Henry Predeaux**, who fled with seven other people known as the **Dover Eight** in March 1857.

**SS *HARRIET TUBMAN*** (3 June 1944–1972). A U.S. Maritime Commission cargo ship built during WWII and named in honor of Tubman. The **SS *Harriet Tubman*** was the first Liberty Ship, out of thousands built during the war, named for a Black woman and only one of eleven named for an African American. The **National Council of Negro Women** formally requested the naming of the ship in honor of her, and the Maritime Commission granted it in the spring of 1944. On June 3, the **SS *Harriet Tubman*** was launched from its berth at the New England Ship Building Company in South Portland, Maine. The **National Council of Negro Women** sponsored a War Bond drive with the slogan, "Buy a Harriet Tubman War Bond for Freedom." Tubman's great-niece, **Eva Stewart Northrup** of Philadelphia, christened the ship. Alida Stewart Johnson and Thelma Frazier, both great-nieces, were matrons of honor. Twenty-two Tubman relatives attended the festivities, including members of the Bowley, Stewart, Keene, Cornish, Proctor, Thompson, Bryant, Brickler, and Wilkins families. The **SS Harriet Tubman** served through several wars and was decommissioned in 1972.

**STANLEY, CAROLINE AND DANIEL.** An enslaved couple from **Cambridge, Dorchester County, Maryland**, who escaped together and successfully fled on 17 October 1857 with their six children and a group of nine other **freedom seekers**, including **Nat and Lizzy Amby**, Hannah Peters, William Griffen, Henry Moore, James Camper, Noah Ennals, and Levin Parker. Daniel Stanley was enslaved by Robert Callender, but Caroline and the children were held by **Samuel W. LeCompte**. John Augusta, an African American barber and **Underground Railroad** agent in Norristown, Pennsylvania, hid them before sending them to **William Still** in Philadelphia. The Stanley family later reached Ontario, Canada, and settled in the outskirts of St. Catharines.

**STANLEY INSTITUTE.** Located in a historic Black community called Christ Rock near **Cambridge, Maryland**, the Stanley Institute was one of several African American schools established in the immediate post–**Civil War** period. In 1867, the community acquired an unused school building in nearby **Church Creek** and moved it to Christ Rock to serve as a church and school. Originally called the Rock Elementary School and referred to as "Colored School No. 3" on maps from the late nineteenth century, the community changed the name to Stanley Institute in honor of a local leader and school board president, Ezekiel Stanley. The community established Christ Rock Methodist Church across the street in 1875. The school was used until 1966 when **Dorchester County, Maryland**, finally integrated its public schools. Stanley Institute is one of the few surviving African American schools from the postwar period. The institute and the church are a historic site and are a stop on the **Harriet Tubman Underground Railroad Scenic Byway and All-American Road**, which highlights the story of the **Cambridge 28** and Stampede of Slaves in October 1857.

**STANTON, ELIZABETH CADY (12 November 1815–26 October 1902).** Born in Johnstown, New York, Elizabeth Cady was raised in a privileged household and received an excellent education, something denied most women of the period. She spent time with her cousin **Gerrit Smith**, who influenced her positions on abolition and women's rights. She married Henry B. Stanton in 1840, and together they attended the World's Anti-Slavery Convention in London, where they met **William Lloyd Garrison** and **Lucretia Coffin Mott**. Mott inspired her passion for gender equality, and together with **Martha Coffin Wright** and others, she planned the **Seneca Falls Convention** and was a leading contributor to the Declaration of Rights and Sentiments demanding gender equality.

She met **Susan B. Anthony** in 1851. They became lifelong friends and collaborators, and together they wrote the *History of Woman Suffrage*, highlighting their roles in the fight for women's voting rights over those of other suffragists. The women's rights movement split into factions in 1869 over the issue of supporting the **Fifteenth Amendment to the Constitution**, which gave Black men the right to vote but not women of any race. Stanton and Anthony organized the **National Woman Suffrage Association (NWSA)** to organize around a campaign to achieve women's voting rights through a federal constitutional amendment. Fellow suffragists Lucy Stone, Julia Ward Howe, and Henry Blackwell who supported the **Fifteenth Amendment** created the **American Woman Suffrage Association (AWSA)**, which focused on campaigning for woman suffrage laws on the state level. **Harriet Tubman** was friends with and supported **Susan B. Anthony** and the NWSA. Tubman's relationship with Stanton appears negligible. In 1890, the two associations merged to create the **National American Woman Suffrage Association (NAWSA)**. Thirty years later, in 1920, the NAWSA successfully secured the right for women to vote through the passage of the **Nineteenth Amendment to the U.S. Constitution**. Stanton, Anthony, and Tubman died before the passage of the amendment.

**STEARNS, GEORGE L.** (8 January 1808–9 April 1867). A Boston merchant and manufacturer, Stearns was born in Medford, Massachusetts. In 1843, he married Mary Elizabeth Preston, the niece of **Lydia Maria Child**. An early **abolitionist**, Stearns used his home in Medford as an **Underground Railroad** station aiding **freedom seekers**. He helped support the settlement of Kansas as a free state. Through that activity he met **John Brown** and Col. **James Montgomery** and later became one of Brown's **Secret Six** financial backers. He also supported **Harriet Tubman**, who thanked him in a letter she sent to **Franklin Sanborn** in June 1863 from Beaufort, South Carolina. Stearns was instrumental in helping to recruit soldiers for the **Massachusetts Fifty-fourth Regiment**. He is buried in Mount Auburn Cemetery in Cambridge, Massachusetts, and his twenty-six-acre estate, "Evergreen" in Medford, was gifted to Tufts University in 1920 and remains part of the school's campus today.

**STERLING, DOROTHY** (23 November 1913–1 December 2008). Journalist and historian, Sterling published more than three dozen children's books on topics such as abolition, women's and civil rights, and important African American historical figures, including the 1954 fictionalized biography called *Freedom Train: The Story of Harriet Tubman*. The biography is still in print.

**STEWART, CATHERINE KANE** (ca. 1835–ca. 1877). Born **Jane Kane** in Dorchester County, Maryland, and enslaved by **Horatio Jones**, she escaped from Jones's plantation on **Christmas Eve 1854**. Kane was at the time the fiancé of **Harriet Tubman's** brother **Ben Ross Jr.** They planned to escape together. She used a disguise—men's clothing—to flee unrecognized. When they reached safety in Philadelphia, Ross took the name **James Stewart** and Jane took the name Catherine. They married shortly after arriving in Canada. Her escape is one of the few first-person narratives dictated to and published by abolitionist **Benjamin Drew** in Canada in 1855. Catherine and James had three children, **Elijah Ross Stewart**, Hester Stewart, and Adam Stewart. The family moved to Auburn, New York, during the **Civil War** and lived in **Harriet Tubman's** home. After James's death around 1863, Catherine married Andrew Winslow and had a child, Albert. She died in Auburn before 1880. Catherine's escape story is featured on the **Harriet Tubman Underground Railroad Scenic Byway and All-American Road** and in the **National Underground Railroad Network to Freedom Program**.

**STEWART, CHARLES** (1880–1969). Born in Auburn, New York, Charles was **Harriet Tubman's** great-nephew, the grandson of her brother **William Henry Ross Stewart**. Charles was at Tubman's bedside when she died on 10 March 1913.

**STEWART, ELIJAH ROSS** (1856–1932). Born in 1856 in Chatham, Ontario, Canada, he was the son of **Harriet Tubman's** brother **James Stewart** (née Ben Ross Jr.) and his wife **Catherine Kane Stewart** (née **Jane Kane**). Elijah, his mother, and his sister Hester moved to Auburn, New York, in the spring of 1861 and lived in Tubman's home for several years. His father died in Canada before 1863. His mother remarried in 1863 to Andrew Winslow. Stewart attended Auburn schools and married a woman named Georgia around 1879. They had two children, Edith and Benjamin, and moved to Boston around 1886, where he secured employment with the railroad. He became a U.S. citizen in October 1889. What became of Georgia and the children is unknown. In 1893 he married an Irish immigrant, Mary Brathwaite. They had eight children together. **Harriet Tubman** stayed with Elijah and his family when she traveled to Boston in the 1890s and early 1900s. She gave him the sharpshooter's rifle she carried during the **Civil War**. He died in 1932.

**STEWART, ELIZA SMITH** (1855–ca. 1890). Wife of **Harriet Tubman's** nephew **John Stewart Jr.** Eliza and John raised three children, Dora, Clarence "Dye," and Gertrude. John died in 1880, and Eliza died around 1890 in Auburn, New York.

**STEWART, EVA "KATY."** *See* NORTHRUP, EVA STEWART.

**STEWART, HARRIET ANN PARKER** (ca. 1832–27 December 1916). Born free near Smithville and Slaughter Creek in west **Dorchester County, Maryland**, to free parents Isaac and Julia Parker, Harriet married **Harriet Tubman**'s brother **William Henry Stewart Sr.** (née Henry Ross) around 1850. After William Henry escaped to St. Catharines, Ontario, Canada, with Tubman's help during **Christmas Day 1854**, Tubman returned the following spring and helped Harriet and her son **William Henry Stewart Jr.** make their way to Canada. William and Harriet had nine more children, including **John Isaac Stewart** and eight daughters. Harriet lived on their farm in Grantham, on the outskirts of St. Catharines, until her death in 1916.

**STEWART, HARRIET "RIT."** *See* ROSS, HARRIET "RIT" GREEN.

**STEWART, JAMES A.** (24 November 1808–3 April 1879). Merchant, real estate developer, planter, shipbuilder, lawyer, proslavery politician, and circuit court judge, Stewart was born in **Dorchester County, Maryland**, the son of **Joseph Stewart** and Rachel Linthicum Stewart. James A. Stewart knew **Harriet Tubman** and her family for decades. His brother **John T. Stewart**, then living in the family's ancestral home in **Madison, Maryland**, leased Tubman from **Edward Brodess** in the mid-1830s after she suffered a near fatal head injury at the **Bucktown Village Store**. John managed the family's shipbuilding and merchant business. James hired Tubman's father, **Ben Ross**, to supervise the family lumber business and timber operations in **Peter's Neck** in Dorchester County.

In 1837, James purchased hundreds of acres of **Anthony Thompson**'s plantation after Thompson's death in 1836. One of the land transactions identifies the property as "down by ol' Ben's," the location of **Ben Ross**'s cabin and ten-acre farm plot, now an archaeological site referred to as "Ben's 10." A land speculator and investor, James acquired immense wealth in addition to the property and money he inherited from his parents. His father, Joseph, and uncle Levin Stewart had arranged for the **manumission** of many of their enslaved people, including **John Bowley**—who married Tubman's niece **Kessiah Jolly**—Bowley's parents, siblings, and others. Bowley and his brothers trained in the shipbuilding trades, and once free they established their own shipbuilding company in **Cambridge, Maryland**. James enslaved more than forty people and owned ships, farms, and forested land throughout the **Eastern Shore** and sat on boards of banks and businesses. He was a powerful and influential attorney and later a circuit court judge.

Sometime during the late 1840s, Tubman likely asked him to investigate the probate records for **Atthow Pattison**, the enslaver who directed his heirs in 1797 to manumit her mother, **Rit Green Ross**, at the age of forty-five around the year 1830. **Edward Brodess**, Pattison's great-grandson, never liberated Rit. Tubman had no legal rights to press a lawsuit, but in July 1849, other Pattison heirs hired Stewart to file a complicated suit against the widow **Eliza Ann Keene Brodess** claiming their rights to a share of the value of Rit and the Ross children. In 1852, while the lawsuit continued its path through the courts, Stewart bought those rights and title to Rit and her children from the Pattison heirs for $105—a speculative investment indicating his confidence the court would find in his favor. The complicated case weaved its way through the courts for the next ten years and was finally dismissed. The records from the lawsuit provide some of the most important genealogical documentation for Tubman's family. Stewart also purchased Tubman's niece, **Harriet Jolley**. He sent her to Texas in 1855 to work on plantations he had acquired there, taking her away from her two children. By the mid-1850s, Stewart's political career was flourishing, and he was elected to the U.S. Congress in 1855, where he voted for proslavery legislation. He died in 1879.

**STEWART, JAMES (BROTHER OF HT)** (ca. 1823–ca. 1863) (NÉE ROSS, BEN, JR. [BROTHER OF HT]). Enslaved by **Edward**

Brodess and his family, he was the sixth of nine children born to **Ben Ross** and **Rit Green Ross**. He escaped slavery with **Harriet Tubman** and their brother **Henry Ross (William Henry Stewart Sr.)** on 17 September 1849 from **Poplar Neck** in **Caroline County, Maryland**. Confused about which way to go and who to trust, they returned. Tubman then fled on her own. The Brodess family wanted to sell Stewart, so he escaped with Tubman's help on **Christmas Day 1854**. Stewart's fiancé, **Jane Kane**, joined them, along with **John Chase** and **Peter Jackson**. When they reached safety in Philadelphia, he took the name James Stewart, and Jane took the name Catherine. They married and settled in Chatham, Ontario, Canada. Catherine and James had three children, **Elijah Ross Stewart**, Hester (Esther) Stewart, and Adam Stewart. Catherine and the children moved to Auburn, New York, in 1861 to live in Tubman's home on South Street. James died in Canada ca. 1863.

**STEWART, JAMES ISAAC.** *See* STEWART, JOHN ISAAC.

**STEWART, JOHN (BROTHER OF HT)** (ca. 1816–19 November 1889) (NÉE ROSS, ROBERT [BROTHER OF HT]). Enslaved by **Edward Brodess** and his family, he was the fourth of nine children born to **Ben Ross** and **Rit Green Ross**. He married **Mary Manokey** in about 1850, and they had three children: **John Henry Ross [Stewart]**, **Moses Ross [Stewart]**, and **Harriet "Ritty" Ross**. Hearing that he was going to be sold by the Brodess family, John decided to escape with the help of his sister, **Harriet Tubman**, on **Christmas Day 1854**. He was forced to leave his wife and children behind; Mary had just given birth to their daughter Harriet, making the decision to escape more difficult. He escaped with several others, including his brothers **Henry Ross (William Henry Stewart Sr.)** and **Ben Ross Jr. (James Stewart)**, and Ben's fiancé, **Jane Kane**, as well as **John Chase** and **Peter Jackson**. When the brothers reached safety in Philadelphia, he took the name John Stewart. He settled in St. Catharines, Ontario, Canada. He moved with his parents to Auburn, New York, from 1859 to 1861. He married Amelia "Millie" Hollis in Auburn in 1863. After the Civil War, **John Bowley** found Stewart's sons John Henry and Moses **indentured** to **Thomas and Sarah Haddaway** in Talbot County, Maryland, and brought them secretly to Auburn to be reunited with their father. Stewart lived near Tubman for the rest of his life. He died in 1889 and is buried next to his wife Millie in Soule Cemetery in Auburn.

**STEWART, JOHN HENRY, JR.** (15 June 1851–ca. 1881). Born enslaved in **Dorchester County, Maryland**, John Henry was the son of **Mary Manokey Ross** and **Harriet Tubman**'s brother **John Stewart** (née **Robert Ross**). He had a brother, **Moses Stewart** (née **Moses Ross**), and a sister, **Harriet Ross**. John Henry was enslaved by Dr. **Anthony C. Thompson**. When Robert escaped slavery with Tubman's help on **Christmas Day 1854**, he left Mary and the children behind. After Maryland outlawed slavery on 1 November 1864, Thompson indentured John Henry and Moses to **Thomas Haddaway** in Talbot County, Maryland. After the **Civil War**, Robert asked **John Bowley** to secretly liberate the boys and bring them to Auburn, New York, where he was living. John Henry and Moses joined their father, who had taken the name John Stewart. The sons took Stewart as their surname, too. John Henry married a woman named Eliza Smith, and they had three children before he died: Dora, Clarence "Dye," and Gertrude.

**STEWART, JOHN ISAAC** (ca. 1855 to 1857–2 March 1893). Born free in **Dorchester County, Maryland**, John Isaac was the son of **Harriet Tubman**'s brother **William Henry Stewart Sr.** (née **Henry Ross**) and **Harriet Parker**, a free Black woman. After his father escaped on **Christmas Day 1854**, Tubman returned to Dorchester County in the spring of 1855 and led Harriet, **William Henry Jr.**, and possibly John Isaac (his exact birth date is unknown) to St. Catharines, Ontario, Canada, to reunite with **William Henry Sr.** John Isaac—sometimes called James Isaac—remained in St. Catharines, where in 1888 he married Catherine Elizabeth Garner. They had one child, Eva "Katy"

Stewart, around 1892. Garner died shortly afterward. John Isaac moved to Auburn, New York, to live with his father, who had left St. Catharines and purchased a home near Tubman. He died in 1893 and is buried next to Tubman's second husband, **Nelson Charles Davis**, in Fort Hill Cemetery in Auburn. Tubman helped raise Eva to adulthood.

**STEWART, JOHN T.** (10 May 1816–6 October 1882). Merchant, farmer, and shipbuilder, Stewart was born in **Dorchester County, Maryland**, the son of **Joseph Stewart** and Rachel Linthicum Stewart. Stewart knew **Harriet Tubman** and her family for decades. He lived in his family's ancestral home in **Madison, Maryland**, and leased Tubman from **Edward Brodess** in the mid-1830s after she suffered a near fatal head injury at the **Bucktown Village Store**.

Stewart managed the family's shipbuilding and merchant businesses in **Madison**. Tubman's work assignments may have varied considerably while working for Stewart. The Stewart family's 225-acre plantation sat upon the north side of Madison Bay and extended along the shoreline where goods were loaded and unloaded on their wharves. They owned a shipyard, a store, a windmill, a warehouse, and two blacksmith shops. The Stewarts' mercantile, farm, shipbuilding, and lumbering businesses required the labor of many people, including enslaved and free Blacks with varying skills, including blacksmiths, like **John Bowley** and his brothers, ship carpenters and sail makers, sawyers and timber inspectors, stevedores and drivers, and farm laborers. In 1826, Joseph Stewart inherited his brother **Levin Stewart**'s enslaved people, who were promised their freedom through **manumission** once they became adults. Joseph honored those manumission agreements, as did John T. after Joseph died in 1839. Tubman worked for John T. as a domestic, then as a field worker, and then as a stevedore on the docks, packing and hauling goods. She eventually became part of Stewart's timber gang, cutting trees in the forests in **Peter's Neck**.

**STEWART, JOSEPH** (25 March 1779–4 August 1839). Merchant, farmer, and shipbuilder, Stewart lived in Tobacco Stick, now called **Madison, Dorchester County, Maryland**. He and his family owned considerable property and business enterprises along Madison Bay. In 1809, Joseph and **Anthony Thompson** were among the seven commissioners appointed by the Maryland state legislature to oversee the construction of the **Blackwater and Parson's Creek Canal Company**, commonly referred to as **Stewart's Canal**, to ease the extraction of timber from the area. Construction required a tremendous amount of enslaved and free labor. The workers carved the seven-mile canal out of the forests and marshland, from the headwaters of Parson's Creek south to the head of the **Blackwater River**, and extended northeast to connect Madison Bay near Stewart's shipyard and wharves. The canal still exists and is a stop on the **Harriet Tubman Underground Railroad Scenic Byway and All-American Road**.

**STEWART, LEVIN** (24 October 1780–25 April 1825). Born in **Madison, Dorchester County, Maryland**, Levin became a ship builder. He eventually moved to Georgetown, Washington, D.C., to expand his business. He left his enslaved people behind in **Madison**, but on 28 July 1817, he returned to **Dorchester County** and recorded a deed in the courthouse providing for the **manumission** of his enslaved people. Some received their freedom immediately, while children were required to wait until they turned thirty years old. **John Bowley**, his parents, and siblings were among those set free. When Stewart died in 1825, his brother **Joseph Stewart** inherited some of Levin's enslaved people and honored the manumissions as required in the court document.

**STEWART, MARGARET.** See LUCAS, MARGARET WOOLFORD STEWART.

**STEWART, MOSES** (15 January 1853–26 July 1895). Born enslaved in **Dorchester County, Maryland**, Moses was the son of **Mary Manokey Ross** and Harriet Tubman's brother **John Stewart** (née Robert Ross). He had an older brother, **John Henry Stewart** (née John Henry Ross) and a sister, **Harriet Ross**.

Moses and his siblings were enslaved by Dr. **Anthony C. Thompson**. When their father, Robert, escaped slavery with Tubman's help on **Christmas Day 1854**, he left Mary and the children behind. After Maryland outlawed slavery on 1 November 1864, Thompson indentured John Henry and Moses to **Thomas Haddaway** in Talbot County, Maryland. After the **Civil War**, Robert asked **John Bowley** to secretly liberate the boys and bring them to Auburn, New York, where he was living. John Henry and Moses joined their father, who had taken the name **John Stewart**. The sons took Stewart as their surname, too. Moses married an unidentified woman and had four children with her in Auburn. In October 1884, Moses was arrested and convicted of petty larceny and served twenty days in jail. He and a friend drowned in Owasco Lake near Auburn in July 1895.

**STEWART, WILLIAM HENRY, JR.** (ca. 1851–1906). Born free in **Dorchester County, Maryland**, William Henry Jr. was the son of **Harriet Tubman**'s brother **William Henry Ross Stewart Sr.** (née Henry Ross) and Harriet Parker, a free Black woman. After his father escaped on **Christmas Day 1854**, Tubman returned to **Dorchester County** in the spring of 1855 and led Harriet, William Henry Jr., and possibly his brother **John Isaac Stewart** (exact birthdate is unknown) to St. Catharines, Ontario, Canada, to reunite with **William Henry Sr.** William Henry Jr. moved to Auburn, New York, in the 1870s, living for a short time with Tubman and other family members. He married Emma Moseby in 1879, and they had three children: Charles, Alida, and Emma Stewart. William died in 1906 and is buried next to **Harriet Tubman** in Fort Hill Cemetery.

**STEWART, WILLIAM HENRY, SR. (BROTHER OF HT)** (ca. 1830–19 July 1912) (**NÉE ROSS, HENRY [BROTHER OF HT]**). Enslaved by **Edward Brodess** and his family, he was the eighth of nine children born to **Ben Ross** and **Rit Green Ross**. He escaped slavery with **Harriet Tubman** and their brother, **Ben Ross Jr.** (**James Stewart**), on 17 September 1849 from **Poplar Neck** in Caroline County, Maryland. Confused about which way to go and who to trust, they returned. He married a free woman, **Harriet Ann Parker (Stewart)** in about 1850. The Brodess family wanted to sell him, so he escaped with Tubman's help on **Christmas Day 1854**. He was forced to leave his pregnant wife and son, **William Henry Stewart Jr.**, behind. He escaped with several others, including his brothers, **Robert Ross (John Stewart)** and **Ben Ross Jr. (James Stewart)**, and Ben's fiancé, **Jane Kane**, as well as **John Chase** and **Peter Jackson**. When the brothers reached safety in Philadelphia, he took the name William Henry Stewart. He settled in St. Catharines, Ontario, Canada. Several months later, Tubman brought Harriet Ann, **William Henry Jr.**, and newborn **John (James) Isaac Stewart** to St. Catharines. Stewart and Harriet Ann purchased a farm in Grantham, near St. Catharines, and raised several more children: Caroline, Mary, Julia, Mary A., Amanda, Martha, Alice, and Gertrude. He later moved to Auburn, New York, with his son, **William Henry Jr.**, and purchased property. Harriet Ann did not join him. William helped raise his granddaughter, **Eva Stewart Northrup**, in Auburn. He died in 1912 and is buried in Fort Hill Cemetery in Auburn.

**STEWART'S CANAL.** Also known as Parson's Creek and Coursey Creek, the canal is a small tributary on the south side of the Little Choptank River, just east of Slaughter Creek and Taylor's Island along Route 16 and west of the **Jacob Jackson** homesite west of **Madison, Maryland**. Situated along the **Harriet Tubman Underground Railroad Scenic Byway and All-American Road**, the creek serves as the entry/exit point for Stewart's Canal. Originally named St. Stephen's Creek for Stephen Gary, the first European landowner in 1662, and renamed Parson's Creek after the Reverend Thomas Thompson acquired the land and lived there during the early to mid-1700s, the creek served as an entry and exit point for a seven-mile canal built by white and free and enslaved Black labor between 1810 and the 1840s. Original financial backers included **Joseph Stewart** and **Anthony Thompson**, who benefited from the canal that eased transportation of their timber and crops to market. The canal connected Parson's Creek to the head of the **Blackwater River** to help move timber and agricultural products quickly and efficiently out of the region. Partially completed in 1832, the canal eventually connected Madison Bay via an additional branch that rerouted the canal between Parson's Creek and **Blackwater River** to **Madison**'s sawmills, wharves, and waiting vessels.

**STILL, WILLIAM (7 October 1821–14 July 1902).** Born in Burlington County, New Jersey, to Levin Still and Sydney Still, a **freedom seeker** from **Carolina County, Maryland**, William became one of the most important agents of the **Underground Railroad**. His mother's sacrifice to secure freedom for herself and her children deeply shaped the course of his life. Sydney and Levin were once enslaved in Caroline County, but Levin was **manumitted** in 1798, while Sydney remained enslaved by Alexander "Saunders" Griffith. After Levin moved to New Jersey between 1804 and 1806, Sydney escaped with their four children—Peter, Levin Jr., Mahala, and Kitty—but **slave catchers** caught her near Greenwich, New Jersey, and returned her to Griffith. After locking her in the attic of a nearby brick home for three months as punishment, Griffith let her out. She fled again, taking Mahala and Kitty but leaving Peter and Levin Jr. behind. In retaliation, Griffith sold the two boys to Kentucky. Levin Jr. later died. Levin and Sydney—who changed her name to Charity—lived safely in Burlington County, New Jersey, where they raised fourteen more children. William was their last. He received some education, enabling him to move to Philadelphia, and in 1847 he was hired as a clerk for the Pennsylvania Anti-Slavery Society and then, later, as secretary for the **Philadelphia Vigilance Committee.** It was there that, through a fortuitous series of events, he met his long-lost brother Peter whom Griffith had sold forty years before. He reunited Peter with his mother and siblings in New Jersey.

In his role as secretary of the committee, Still managed the city's busy **Underground Railroad** network. In 1852, after meeting his brother Peter, he began recording the names and histories of the **freedom seekers** aided by the committee in an account book called *Journal C*. It was his family's tragic separation that informed William's decision to record the names of **freedom seekers** so that separated family members could reunite at a later date. He married Letitia George in 1847, and they had four children together. They operated their home as an **Underground Railroad** safe house. He worked with other **Underground Railroad** operatives, including **Thomas Garrett, Harriet Tubman, James Miller McKim, Sarah Buchanon, Sydney Howard Gay,** and many others. Fearful that **slave catchers** and police authorities might discover his *Journal C*, he hid it and other documents in a cemetery for a period of time.

Active in antislavery politics, Still became a leader in the city's African American community and during the **Civil War** opened a successful coal and stove business. In 1871, Still published the stories from *Journal C* as *The Underground Railroad: A Record of Facts, Authentic Narratives, Letters, &c., Narrating the Hardships, Hairbreadth Escapes and Death Struggles of the Slaves in their efforts for Freedom.* He died in 1902 and is buried with his wife in Eden Cemetery in Collingwood, Delaware County, Pennsylvania.

**SUKE (dates unknown).** Likely born in Africa, Suke was enslaved by **Atthow Pattison**. When Atthow died in 1797, he gave Suke and another enslaved woman, **Bess,** to his daughter, **Elizabeth Pattison.** It is likely these enslaved women were related to **Harriet Tubman**'s mother, **Rit Green Ross.** According to Pattison's will, his heirs were legally bound to set Bess, Suke, and Rit free when they reached the age of forty-five years old. Rit was not **manumitted,** and the fates of Bess and Suke remain unknown.

# T

**TALBERT, MARY MORRIS BURNETT (17 September 1866–15 October 1923).** Born in Oberlin, Ohio, Talbert attended Oberlin College, graduating in 1886. Active in antilynching campaigns and civil rights, she became a leader in the Black women's suffrage club movement through Buffalo's Phyllis Wheatley Club and the National Association of Colored Women's Clubs. Talbert moved to Buffalo, New York, during the early 1890s, and in 1905 hosted the first meeting of the Niagara Movement, which later became the National Association for the Advancement of Colored People.

Talbert met **Harriet Tubman** through their mutual passion for women's rights and equality. As the president of the **Empire State Federation of Women's Clubs**, Talbert helped raise funds to pay for Tubman's care during the last two years of her life. Talbert was visiting Tubman a month before her death in March 1913, when Tubman clasped her hand and said, "Tell the women to stand together for God will never forsake us," a clear reference to the racial division within the larger **women's rights movement**. The Empire State Federation raised the money in 1915 to pay for a headstone for Tubman's grave at Fort Hill Cemetery in Auburn, New York. In 2005, Talbert was inducted into the National Women's Hall of Fame in Seneca Falls, New York.

**TAPPAN, LEWIS (23 May 1788–21 June 1873).** Staunch New York **abolitionist**, Tappan founded the American Missionary Society, which established antislavery Congregational churches in America. In 1833, he joined **William Lloyd Garrison** to establish the **American Anti-Slavery Society**, but by 1840 he split with that organization over the issue of allowing women to be elected to and hold official positions within the society, which he opposed. In protest he established the **American and Foreign Anti-Slavery Society**. Tappan assisted some **freedom seekers** who arrived in New York and was instrumental in raising funds to purchase the freedom of members of the Weems family in 1852. During the fall of 1855, Tappan met **Harriet Tubman** when she asked him for financial support for her next rescue mission to Maryland. He wrote about her courage in a letter dated 17 November 1855. *See* appendix C.

**TATLOCK, HELEN WOODRUFF (14 November 1870–12 October 1957).** Tatlock lived in Auburn between 1880 and 1898, where she met and interacted with **Harriet Tubman**. In 1939, author **Earl Conrad** interviewed Tatlock for his biography of Tubman. She told Conrad that Tubman was an exceptional storyteller, and she revealed some interesting stories that Tubman told her, including details about the Quaker woman who helped her escape to freedom from **Poplar Neck** in **Carolina County** in 1849; that Tubman liked butter in her tea; that while working for **John T. Stewart** as a domestic, Tubman used to fluff up the feather beds and jump into them; and how Tubman gave crying babies paregoric to keep them quiet while traveling along the **Underground Railroad**.

**TELFORD, EMMA (1851–26 January 1920).** Journalist and lecturer, Telford grew up in Auburn, New York. She interviewed **Harriet Tubman** ca. 1904–1905 for a lecture she delivered in 1905 in Auburn. She combined work by **Sarah H. Bradford** with information she gleaned from stories Tubman told her. The lecture, "Harriet: The Modern Moses of Heroism and Visions," is in the archives of the Cayuga Museum in Auburn. Telford died in California in 1920 and is buried in Arizona.

**TEMPORAL LOBE EPILEPSY (TLE).** A medical condition that stems from seizures emanating from the temporal lobes of the brain, located on each side of the head by the temples. The seizures can last for a few seconds or up to two minutes and vary in intensity and type. Patients experience a wide variety of symptoms, including visual and auditory hallucinations, semiconsciousness, and more. **Harriet Tubman** may have suffered from TLE due to the traumatic brain injury she endured as a young teenager at the **Bucktown Village Store**. Tubman told interviewers that when she had a seizure, she sometimes felt like she was flying above the earth or could hear music, singing, and other voices, which she attributed to God telling her what to do. She witnessed bright lights and fire and heard water rushing sometimes. She experienced seizures while working in the fields, in the woods, and in the house and while executing her rescue missions. Tubman received no treatment for her disability. Today, TLE patients can access a variety of treatments, including medications, surgery, or brain stimulation.

**THIRTEENTH AMENDMENT TO THE CONSTITUTION.** Passed by the U.S. Congress on 31 January 1865, during the final months of the **Civil War**, it was ratified by the states 6 December 1865. The amendment abolished slavery. "Neither slavery nor involuntary servitude, except as a punishment for crime whereof the party shall have been duly convicted, shall exist within the United States, or any place subject to their jurisdiction."

**THOMPSON, ABSALOM (21 July 1789–October 1842).** The son of **Anthony Thompson** and Mary "Polly" King, Dr. **Anthony C. Thompson**'s brother, and stepbrother to **Edward Brodess**. He lived in Talbot County, Maryland. He inherited a portion of his father's estate in 1836, including many enslaved people, whom he **manumitted** upon his death in 1842.

**THOMPSON, ALBERT (ca. 1831–unknown).** Born in Oneida County, New York, Thompson joined Company G Eighth United States Colored Troops in July 1863. He fought during the **Civil War** with fellow soldier **Nelson Charles Davis**, **Harriet Tubman**'s second husband. After the war, Thompson moved to Auburn, New York, to work in the factories there. Nelson Davis followed him and boarded in Tubman's home.

**THOMPSON, ANTHONY (7 April 1762–May 1836).** A descendant of founding families of **Dorchester County, Maryland**, Thompson married Mary "Polly" King, daughter of John King in October 1786. They had five children: Dr. **Anthony C. Thompson**, Dr. **Absalom Thompson**, Thomas Thompson, Edward Thompson, and Samuel Thompson. Anthony enslaved **Ben Ross**, **Harriet Tubman**'s father. After his wife Polly died ca. 1801, Thompson married widow **Mary Pattison Brodess** in October 1803. She moved with her two-year-old son, **Edward Brodess**, to Thompson's plantation at **Peter's Neck** along the **Blackwater River**. She also brought **Harriet Tubman**'s enslaved mother, **Harriet "Rit" Green**, and three enslaved men, **Shadrack, Frederick**, and **Samuel**. By 1808, Rit and Ben were married.

Thompson owned about 1,000 acres of fields and forests and enslaved more than forty people, many of them family groups. See appendix B. Mary died around 1810, leaving custody of young Edward to his stepfather. As guardian, Thompson managed Brodess's inheritance, which included a small unimproved farm in **Bucktown** and enslaved people including Rit, the children she bore with Ben, and the three men Shadrack, Frederick, and Samuel. Thompson recorded some of the management of Brodess's inheritance in guardian's accounts, later submitted to the Maryland Court of Appeals during an extensive lawsuit, *Brodess v. Thompson*, filed in 1823. Brodess sought redress from the court because Thompson used the majority of Brodess's financial assets to build a house on Brodess's farmstead in **Bucktown**, leaving him financially insolvent when he reached the age of majority in 1823. The lawsuit strained their relationship. Thompson lost all appeals and was forced to repay the funds he expended on Brodess's behalf. Thompson died in May 1836 at his home in **Peter's Neck**, leaving a substantial estate consisting of real and personal property, including **Ben Ross** and dozens of enslaved people. In his will, he instructed the executors of his estate to manumit all of his enslaved people according to a specific schedule over many years into the future, ensuring his heirs would benefit from the free labor for decades.

**THOMPSON, ANTHONY C. (8 August 1793–1868).** The son of **Anthony Thompson** and Mary "Polly" King, Dr. **Absalom Thompson**'s brother, and stepbrother to **Edward Brodess**. Dr. Thompson employed **Ben Ross** after Ross was **manumitted** in 1840. With his brother Absalom, Dr. Thompson inherited his father's estate in 1836, and the two men shared in the sale of the family plantation at **Peter's Neck** and claimed ownership of their father's enslaved people. In 1847, Thompson purchased a 2,200-acre plantation at **Poplar Neck** in **Caroline County, Maryland**, where Ross managed timbering operations. **Harriet Tubman** worked for Thompson and lived with her parents at **Poplar Neck** from 1847 until her escape in the late fall of 1849. Dr. Thompson **manumitted** several of the enslaved people he inherited and also sold some of them, something his father never did. Thompson sold his **Poplar Neck** plantation and moved back to his home in **Cambridge, Maryland**. He died there in 1868 after a long illness.

**THOMPSON, ANTHONY C., JR. (15 March 1825–11 January 1897).** The son of Dr. **Anthony C. Thompson**, Anthony married **Mary Elizabeth Leverton**, **Jacob** and **Hannah Leverton**'s daughter, in November of 1849. The Levertons lived near Dr. Thompson's property at **Poplar Neck**; it is very likely that young Anthony met Mary Elizabeth while he comanaged his father's business with his brother **Edward Thompson**. Mary, a Quaker, was "disowned" by the local Quaker Meeting in 1850 because she married a non-Quaker and had failed to attend required meetings. Mary and Anthony Thompson moved to Anne Arundel County in early 1850, where Anthony became a merchant, and by the end of the decade had moved to Indiana where Mary's brother, **Arthur Leverton**, and mother, **Hannah Leverton**, had moved after Arthur was suspected of helping **freedom seekers** escape in 1858.

**THOMPSON, EDWARD.** Son of Dr. **Anthony C. Thompson** who managed his father's operations at **Poplar Neck** in **Caroline County** with his brother **Anthony C. Thompson Jr.** during the late 1840s and early 1850s. **Ben Ross** worked with the young men in Thompson's timber business.

**THOMPSON, JOHN K. (16 April 1817–5 December 1883).** Thompson was the son of Dr. **Anthony C. Thompson** and Mary Kersey Thompson and the grandson of **Anthony Thompson**. A physician like his father, John, his wife, and their children left Maryland around 1857 and settled in Tippecanoe, Indiana.

**THOMPSON MEMORIAL AFRICAN METHODIST EPISCOPAL ZION (AMEZ) CHURCH.** Built in 1891 across from Fort Hill Cemetery on Parker Street and one mile from the **Harriet Tubman Home** in Auburn, New York. The first **AMEZ** church in Auburn was established in 1838 and located on Washington Street. In 1891, the Zion Church moved to a newly built church on Parker Street and renamed it Thompson Memorial in honor of Henry Thompson, the first local AME Zion bishop and a former **freedom seeker**. **Harriet Tubman** pledged $500 for its construction. For many Black women of the late nineteenth century, the church served as not only a spiritual sanctuary but also a social and political haven

After funeral services held at the Thompson Memorial AME Zion Church on 13 March 1913, Harriet Tubman was buried at Fort Hill Cemetery, Auburn, New York. *Collection of the Smithsonian National Museum of African American History and Culture, gift of Charles L. Blockson*

where they could forge strong networks in support of racial, gender, economic, and educational advancement. Tubman's wake and funeral were held here on 13 March 1913. The active congregation moved to another site in Auburn in 1993, and Thompson Memorial is now owned by the National Park Service and a part of the **Harriet Tubman National Historical Park**.

**TILGHMAN, TENCH.** Alias used by **freedom seeker** Peter Jackson, who fled with **Harriet Tubman**'s brothers **Robert Ross** and **Henry Ross** and others on **Christmas Day 1854**.

**TILLY.** On 21 October 1856, Harriet Tubman helped a young woman named "Tilly" flee enslavement in Baltimore, Maryland. Unable to safely bring Tilly to Philadelphia via a northeasterly route out of Baltimore, Tubman took Tilly south, via the steamboat *Kent*, to Seaford, Delaware. The steamer *Kent* docked at **Dugan's Wharf** in Baltimore's Inner Harbor. During the 1850s, the *Kent* made weekly round-trip excursions to the **Eastern Shore of Maryland**. The steamboat sailed up the **Nanticoke River**, stopping at Vienna, Maryland, then moving along to Seaford.

Tubman and Tilly took the newly established Delaware Railroad to Camden, eventually finding their way to Wilmington, where **Underground Railroad** agent **Thomas Garrett** documented their arrival and helped them on to Philadelphia and freedom. According to Garrett, who wrote of Tubman's mission to **Eliza Wigham** in Scotland, Tubman

> had gone from Philadelphia with the captain of a steam boat, trading through the Delaware and Chesapeake canal, & had taken the precaution to get from him a certificate of her being a resident of Philadelphia, & free. She knew she could not bring a strange woman from Baltimore to Philadelphia, either by railroad or steam boat, without giving bonds in 500 dollars, and therefore took passage for herself & companion to Seaford, on the eastern shore of Maryland, in the steamboat, & delivering the Captain her passport from Philadelphia to Baltimore, and he, knowing the captain of the boat that took her to Baltimore, was prevailed on to give her a certificate, also. When the boat arrived at Seaford, she boldly went to the Hotel & called for supper & lodging. Next morning when they were about to leave, a dealer in such stock attempted to arrest them, but on showing the captain's certificate, the landlord interfered & the women went to the railroad & paid their passage to Camden, some 50 miles below here, & then came up in private conveyance. I asked her if she was not frightened when arrested. "Not a bit," she said.

Tubman biographer **Sarah H. Bradford** also wrote about Tilly. This rescue mission is celebrated today in Seaford and on Pier 4, and both sites are in the Network to Freedom Program.

**TINDLE, MILES** (dates unknown). A **slave trader** in **Dorchester County, Maryland**. Tindle purchased Susan, the daughter of **Jerry** and **Polly Manokey**, from William V. M. Edmundson of East New Market and then illegally sold her to an out-of-state buyer. Susan was supposed to remain in Maryland under directives noted in the 1836 last will and testament of **Anthony Thompson**.

**TOBACCO STICK, MARYLAND.** *See* MADISON, MARYLAND.

**TOWNSEND, MARTIN I.** (6 February 1810–8 March 1903). An attorney and **abolitionist**, Townsend was involved in the **Charles Nalle** rescue in Troy, New York, in 1860. After Nalle had been captured by agents of **Blucher Hansbrough**, his enslaver, Townsend obtained a writ of habeas corpus, which required that Nalle be brought before a judge so that Townsend could argue for his release. In front of a large crowd, **Harriet Tubman** rescued Nalle from the courthouse, and, according to Townsend, "exposed herself to the fury of the sympathizers with slavery, without fear, and suffered their blows without flinching."

**TRAVERS, LEVI D.** (21 November 1828–26 May 1907). A Dorchester County, Maryland, minister who enslaved **Aaron**, the husband of **Daffney Cornish**. Aaron was one of the **Cambridge 28**, who successfully escaped from **Dorchester** on 24 October 1857. Travers offered a $300 reward for his capture and return to **Cambridge, Maryland**.

*TRIBUTE TO HARRIET TUBMAN, THE MODERN AMAZON.* (Auburn, New York: Tubman Home, 1914.) A pamphlet coauthored by Reverend **James E. Mason** and Reverend **Edward U. A. Brooks** as a memorial to Tubman and fundraiser to support the work of the **Harriet Tubman Home for the Aged and Infirm Negroes** in Auburn.

**TRUTH, SOJOURNER** (ca. 1797–26 November 1883). Born enslaved in New York, Truth escaped with her infant daughter in 1826. An outspoken **abolitionist**, suffragist, and spiritual leader, Truth spent years traveling the country lecturing for freedom and equality. She met **Harriet Tubman** sometime in the late summer or early fall of 1864 during the **Civil War** in Boston. Tubman told Rosa Belle Holt that Truth had told her that President **Abraham Lincoln** was a good man, but Tubman disliked him and refused to meet him because he took too long to allow the recruitment of Black troops. But, she said, "I is sorry now I didn't see Master Lincoln and thank him."

**TUBMAN, BENJAMIN GAITHER** (12 September 1831–22 March 1879). Was living in **Cambridge, Maryland**, when his enslaved man **William "Bill" Kiah** escaped with his wife, **Emily Kiah**, in March 1857. The Kiahs escaped with six others in a group known as the **Dover Eight**. Benjamin offered a $400 reward for Bill's capture and return to **Cambridge**.

**TUBMAN, EVANS** (ca. 1820–unknown). Born free to free parents in **Dorchester County, Maryland**, he was **Harriet Tubman's** brother-in-law. During the 1850s and 1860s, Evans worked seasonal jobs in Baltimore and **Dorchester County**.

**TUBMAN, HARRIET ROSS** (ca. February or March 1822–10 March 1913). Born enslaved in **Dorchester County, Maryland**, Tubman was the fifth of nine children of **Ben Ross** and **Harriet "Rit" Green Ross**. She was named Araminta "Minty" Ross. Her enslaver, **Edward Brodess**, began leasing Tubman to other masters when she was only six years old. See other entries for her life as an enslaved person, her family, community, education, marriage, escape and work as an **Underground Railroad** conductor, **Civil War** activities, home life, suffrage, early biographies and documentation, death, and legacy.

**TUBMAN, JOHN** (ca. 1818–30 September 1867). Born free to free Black parents, Thomas and Priscilla Tubman, in the White Marsh Road area of Peter's Neck south of **Madison, Maryland**. A day laborer working in the woods and fields in **Dorchester County**, John met and married Minty Ross sometime around 1844. Minty changed her name to **Harriet Tubman** at that time. According to oral tradition, the couple lived on or near the site of **Malone's African Methodist Episcopal Church** on White Marsh Road.

As a free man, John forfeited all his rights to any children he fathered with Harriet. Because she was enslaved, any offspring would legally belong to **Edward Brodess**, her enslaver. Brodess died in March 1849, setting in motion the dissolution of Harriet's family and her marriage with John Tubman. According to interviews with Harriet during the 1850s and 1860s, John did not want to leave with her when she fled slavery in the fall of 1849. He was free, with free parents and siblings. If he fled with Harriet and they were caught, his punishment would have meant imprisonment and sale into slavery.

On 4 January 1850, after Harriet had run away, John Tubman went to the courthouse and requested a certificate of freedom attesting to his free status enabling him to travel outside the county. The certificate of freedom reads: "Negro Man John Tubman aged about 32 years, 5 feet 9 ½ inches high, dark mulatto complexion with small scar on back of left hand, and also one other near top of calf of left leg, was born free and raised in Dorchester County. Identified by James Smith S.C. [Slaughter Creek]." John may have sought seasonal work in Baltimore, where his free brothers **Evans** and **Thomas "Tom" Tubman** worked.

In 1851, Harriet returned to **Dorchester County**, and she hoped John would leave and follow her to Philadelphia. He refused. He had remarried, a free woman named Caroline with whom he had four children: Thomas (b. 1855), Ann (Angerine, b. 1857), William (b. 1860), and Alexander (b. 1863). In October 1857, John purchased a ten-acre farm along Aireys Road. He also owned a racehorse named "Fly." In September 1867, John Tubman was murdered by his white neighbor, **Robert Vincent**. Vincent was put on trial, but after deliberating less than ten minutes, the jury found Vincent not guilty. Two witnesses to the murder, John's thirteen-year-old son Thomas and Rachel Camper, a neighbor, were not allowed to testify because they were Black and Vincent was a white man.

**TUBMAN, THOMAS "TOM"** (ca. 1813–bef. 1900). Born free to free parents in **Dorchester County, Maryland**, Tom was **Harriet Tubman's** brother-in-law. During the 1850s and 1860s, Tom worked seasonal jobs in Baltimore and **Dorchester County**. Harriet later revealed that she received **Underground Railroad** aid from Tom, whom she referred to as "cousin," in Baltimore during the 1850s.

**TWELFTH BAPTIST CHURCH, BOSTON.** Founded in 1840, its membership was notable for their active antislavery and **Underground Railroad** activities. Members included **Lewis** and Harriet **Hayden**, John S. Rock, and many other Black **abolitionists**. In early January 1862, **Harriet Tubman** spoke here while raising money for her assignment in the **Department of the South** early in the **Civil War**.

# U

**UNDERGROUND RAILROAD (UGRR).** According to the **National Park Service Network to Freedom Program (NTF)**,

> The Underground Railroad—the resistance to enslavement through escape and flight, through the end of the Civil War—refers to the efforts of enslaved African Americans to gain their freedom by escaping bondage. Wherever slavery existed, there were efforts to escape. At first to maroon communities in remote or rugged terrain on the edge of settled areas and eventually across state and international borders. These acts of self-emancipation labeled slaves as "fugitives," "escapees," or "runaways," but in retrospect freedom seeker is a more accurate description. Many freedom seekers began their journey unaided and many completed their self-emancipation without assistance, but each subsequent decade in which slavery was legal in the United States, there was an increase in active efforts to assist escape.

Individuals like **Harriet Tubman** who helped lead **freedom seekers** were identified as "conductors," and those like **Thomas Garrett**, who helped shelter and provide food, medicine, and protection, were called "stationmasters." Though the decision to aid in the escape of an enslaved person may have been spur-of-the-moment, the UGRR became, over time and especially during the antebellum period, purposely and regionally organized. It was "a covert and sometimes informal network of routes, safehouses, and resources spread across the country that was used by enslaved African Americans to gain their freedom." Participation in UGRR networks was illegal but still attracted people of all backgrounds. According to the NTF, **freedom seekers** escaped "in many directions—Canada, Mexico, Spanish Florida, Indian territory, the West, Caribbean islands and Europe."

**UNDERGROUND RAILROAD MYTHS.** *See* appendix E.

***THE UNDERGROUND RAILROAD: A RECORD OF FACTS, AUTHENTIC NARRATIVES, LETTERS, &C., NARRATING THE HARDSHIPS, HAIRBREADTH ESCAPES AND DEATH STRUGGLES OF THE SLAVES IN THEIR EFFORTS FOR FREEDOM.*** Book written by **William Still** and published in 1872. As chairman of the **Philadelphia Vigilance Committee**, William Still recorded the testimony of **freedom seekers** who arrived in Philadelphia, one of the largest and most important **Underground Railroad** hubs in the country, in a series of bound journals. The details recorded in Still's *Journal C* provide firsthand dramatic stories of life under slavery and about individual and collective efforts to reach freedom. After the **Civil War**, Still gathered what remained of his papers (some had been lost) and published them in *The Underground Railroad* (1872), the most comprehensive compendium of the **Underground Railroad**'s mechanisms and networks and the people who escaped along the eastern seaboard. **William Still**'s papers and

*Journal C* are held by the Historical Society of Pennsylvania in Philadelphia.

**UNION ARMY.** *See* UNITED STATES ARMY DURING THE CIVIL WAR.

**UNITED STATES ARMY DURING THE CIVIL WAR.** The regular federal and volunteer armed forces of the twenty-three states that comprised the United States after the thirteen **Confederate** states seceded in the winter and spring of 1861. Generally referred to as the Union Army, the force was comprised of more than two million soldiers, including 200,000 African Americans. The Union Army defeated the Confederate army, which surrendered on 9 April 1865 at Appomattox Court House, Virginia.

**UNITED STATES ARMY MILITARY INTELLIGENCE CORPS HALL OF FAME.** Established on 1 July 1988, the Military Intelligence Corps Hall of Fame honors soldiers and civilians who provided exceptional intelligence service to the military. Located in headquarters for the United States Army Intelligence Center of Excellence at Fort Huachuca, the Hall of Fame recommends outstanding individuals be recognized. In a lengthy vetting process, a final selection is made for induction into the hall. Both living and deceased professionals are eligible. In June 2021, **Harriet Tubman** was inducted into the hall for her outstanding service as a spy and scout during the **Civil War**.

**UNITED STATES COLORED TROOPS (USCT).** On 22 May 1863, the U.S. War Department issued General Order No. 143, which officially established African American regiments into the U.S. armed forces. These regiments were called United States Colored Troops (USCT) and were led by white officers. At least three Union Army regiments of Black troops had been created in 1862, and the First South Carolina Colored Volunteers under the leadership of **Thomas Wentworth Higginson** started operations that fall. After the **Emancipation Proclamation** was enacted on 1 January 1863, more regiments were organized. By May, the **Fifty-Fourth Massachusetts Voluntary Infantry Regiment** and the **Second South Carolina Colored Volunteers** had been created. Some white officers mistreated their men, and because of racism, some had low expectations of the men's ability to fight. Initially the men were paid $10 per month minus $3 for clothing and equipment for a total of $7, while white soldiers received $13 with no deductions. After protests, Congress equalized the pay in June 1864 and retroactively paid the Black soldiers the balance. Over the course of the war, 200,000 African Americans fought for the United States, exhibiting extraordinary courage and valor.

**UPPER SOUTH.** The region of the United States including Maryland, District of Columbia, Virginia, Delaware, North Carolina, Tennessee, and Kentucky.

**URSA MAJOR.** A constellation of stars visible in the Northern Hemisphere and also known as the **Big Dipper**. Two of its seven stars, Merak and Dubhe, are known as the pointer stars because they direct viewers to **Polaris**, also known as the North Star.

**URSA MINOR.** A constellation of stars visible in the Northern Hemisphere and also known as the **Little Dipper**. It contains **Polaris**, also known as the North Star.

# V

**VICTORIA, QUEEN OF ENGLAND (24 May 1819–22 January 1901).** During her sixtieth anniversary—her Diamond Jubilee—as monarch, the Queen sent Harriet Tubman a fine lace shawl and a silver Jubilee medal in 1897. She had read **Sarah H. Braford**'s biography, *Harriet, the Moses of Her People*, and felt moved to honor Tubman for her courage and accomplishments. The shawl is now on display at the National Museum of African American History and Culture in Washington, D.C.

**VINCENT, ROBERT (ca. 1811–aft. 1868).** A farmer in **Dorchester County, Maryland**, and a neighbor to **John Tubman**, the estranged husband of **Harriet Tubman**. In September 1867, John Tubman was murdered by Robert Vincent after a brief argument on the side of the road. Vincent was arrested and put on trial. After deliberating less than ten minutes, the jury found Vincent not guilty. Two witnesses to the murder, John's thirteen-year-old son Thomas and Rachel Camper, a neighbor, were not allowed to testify because they were Black and Vincent was a white man.

**VINEY, JOE AND SUSAN.** An enslaved couple who escaped with their four young children, Lloyd, Frank, Albert(a), and nine-month-old J. W.; Joe's three older sons, Henry, Joe, and Tom; and several other families enslaved by **Samuel Pattison** and others during the night of 24 October 1857. The **freedom seekers**, later known as the **Cambridge 28**, included **Aaron and Daffney Cornish** and six of their eight surviving children, **Kit and Leah Anthony** and their three children, **Solomon Light, George Light, Marshall Dutton**, and **Silas Long**, among others. They were chased by **slave catchers** seeking to cash in on the thousands of dollars in reward money posted for their capture. They successfully eluded arrest and made their way through Delaware, Pennsylvania, and New York. They safely settled in St. Catharines, Ontario, Canada. This escape came just one week after the escape of **Lizzy and Nat Amby, Caroline and Daniel Stanley**, Hannah Peters, William Griffen, Henry Moore, James Camper, Noah Ennals, and Levin Parker on 17 October 1857. Together, these two large escapes became known as the Stampede of Slaves.

**WASHINGTON, BOOKER T. (5 April 1856–14 November 1915).** Born enslaved, Washington emerged as a powerful Black leader and educator and helped dramatically expand Tuskegee Institute (now University) in Alabama from the 1880s through the 1910s. He advocated for vocational and industrial training for African Americans as an alternative to advanced academic studies. In June 1914, Washington was invited to Auburn, New York, to participate in the memorial plaque unveiling ceremonies for a tablet gifted by the citizens of Auburn to the city in honor of **Harriet Tubman**. He urged fellow African Americans to stand together for mutual benefit and advancement, remarking that they would be "measured by the great life of Harriet Tubman and by her great life all the country is watching you."

**WATERMEN, AFRICAN AMERICAN.** See BLACK JACKS.

**WEBB, JAMES H. (ca. 1822–unknown).** A free African American farmer living in **Preston** during the 1850s. In 1852, he built a hand-hewn, one-room log home with a loft, which still stands on Grove Road and is featured on the **Harriet Tubman Underground Railroad Scenic Byway and All-American Road**. Webb's wife and children were enslaved but able to live with him. **Harriet Tubman**'s father and mother, **Ben** and **Rit Ross**, lived nearby and likely lived in a similar structure at nearby **Poplar Neck**.

**WEBSTER, JOHN E. (ca. 1823–24 June 1864).** Joined Company G, Forty-seventh Pennsylvania Volunteers in September 1861. Stationed in South Carolina during the **Civil War**, he was assigned to the superintendent position at Beaufort, allocating work tasks to newly freed people in staffing the docks and warehouses, cutting and hauling wood, and building structures important for the functioning of military in the occupied city. He was also responsible for doling out rations of food and other supplies from the commissary but was caught embezzling items and selling them for profit to **Harriet Tubman** and **Walter Plowden**, among others. Both testified at Webster's court-martial trial in early June 1863, shortly after the **Combahee River Raid**. Webster was reprimanded and not court-martialed. He died in Baton Rouge, Louisiana, in June 1864 during the Red River Campaign.

**WELLS-BARNETT, IDA B. (16 July 1862–25 March 1931).** One of the founders of the National Association for the Advancement of Colored People (NAACP), Barnett was a renowned journalist, suffragist, and civil rights activist. She risked her life documenting lynchings in America and then publishing her report in *Southern Horrors: Lynch Law in All Its Phases* in 1892. She was a featured speaker at the founding convention of the National Association of Colored Women's Clubs in Washington, D.C., in July 1896. There, she shared the stage with **Harriet Tubman**, introducing her to the crowd as "Mother Tubman."

**WIGHAM, ELIZA (23 February 1820–3 November 1899).** A British **abolitionist** and woman suffragist, Wigham and her sister Mary Edmundson supported American antislavery activities and helped fund **Underground Railroad** work. **Thomas Garrett** of Wilmington, Delaware, solicited money from Wigham to help **Harriet Tubman**. He wrote Wigham frequently, detailing some of Tubman's risky but successful rescue missions to Maryland. Garrett told Wigham he was proud of his acquaintance with Tubman and that he marveled at her devotion to her family and friends at the risk of her own health and liberty. Garrett knew that Wigham and her sister would be moved and compelled to send as much money as they could to further Tubman's and his work liberating **freedom seekers**.

**WILBUR, JULIA** (8 August 1815–6 June 1895). A Quaker **abolitionist** who lived in Rochester, New York, she supported the career and activities of **Frederick Douglass** and was a member and secretary of the **Rochester Ladies' Anti-Slavery Sewing Society**. In that role she aided **freedom seekers** and helped raise funds in support of the regional **Underground Railroad**. She kept extensive diaries during the **Civil War**, including entries mentioning **Harriet Tubman**. In March 1865 she recorded Tubman speaking at a rally at **Henry Highland Garnet**'s church in Washington, D.C., following President **Abraham Lincoln**'s inauguration. She was a devoted suffragist, working with **Susan B. Anthony** for decades until her death in 1895.

**WILKINS, HORATIO W.** (dates unknown). Horatio Wilkins (also known as Wilkinson) was born in **Dorchester County, Maryland**, and enslaved by Thomas Hodson. He escaped during the winter of 1858 and passed through **William Still**'s office in Philadelphia in February; he told Still that Hodson (Still spelled it Hodges) had visited Canada and, upon returning, told his enslaved people that Canada was "the meanest part of the globe" he had ever seen. Hodson told them that he had not seen one Black person; a "custom-house" official informed him that all the runaway slaves had been sent "round Cape Horn" and sold. Just in case his slaves still doubted him, Hodson told them "the suffering from deep snows and starvation was fearful." Horatio told Still he knew it was all a lie. Wilkins settled in St. Catharines, Ontario, Canada. He cofounded the **Fugitive Aid Society of St. Catharines** in 1861 with **Harriet Tubman** and **Christopher "Kit" Anthony**, among others.

**WILKINSON, HORATIO W.** See WILKINS, HORATIO W.

**WILLIAM STILL INTERPRETIVE CENTER.** Located along the **Harriet Tubman Underground Railroad Scenic Byway and All-American Road** near Denton, Caroline County, Maryland, the center celebrates the struggles of **William Still**'s family to secure freedom from bondage through escape, resettlement in New Jersey, and then **Underground Railroad** activity. Housed in a historic one-room "cottage" from 1820, the center features a period "slave cabin" interior, exhibits, and a "garden patch" highlighting foodstuffs common in gardens cultivated by **Eastern Shore** enslaved people.

**WILLIAMS, EMILY.** See KIAH, EMILY.

**WILLIAMS, WILLIAM.** See KIAH, WILLIAM.

**WILMER, GEORGE** (ca. 1810–unknown). Born in Kent County, Maryland, Wilmer was enslaved by Eben Welch, a wealthy man with a large farm along the Sassafras River, a strategic path to upper Delaware and freedom in the North for Maryland runaways. Wilmer was one of nearly twenty enslaved people working for Welch in the 1850s, but, living so close to the Delaware border, he also ran a clandestine **Underground Railroad** operation in the area. In late December 1855, **Thomas Garrett** of Wilmington, Delaware, wrote fellow **Underground Railroad** agent **William Still** of Philadelphia, Pennsylvania, that Wilmer was a "forwarder of slaves . . . some twenty-five within four months." The following September, Still recorded Wilmer in his *Journal C* ledger assisting **William Cornish** of **Dorchester County** to Philadelphia. Welch never seemed to suspect Wilmer of such illegal activities. After Welch died in 1858, Wilmer was freed

During the early 1900s, Harriet Tubman maintained a high-profile public image and campaigned for women's rights. Photo: Tarby Studios, ca. 1905. *Collection of the Smithsonian National Museum of African American History and Culture, gift of Charles L. Blockson*

and, according to provisions in Welch's will, awarded three acres of land to farm. With his wife, Margaret, Wilmer settled in Wilmington, Delaware, instead, likely continuing his **Underground Railroad** activities with his neighbors who worked with Garrett.

**WINTHROP, GEORGE.** Enslaver of **Peter Jackson**, who fled with **Harriet Tubman**; her brothers **Robert Ross**, **Henry Ross**, and **Ben Ross**; and their friends on **Christmas Day 1854**.

*WOMAN'S ERA* (March 1894–January 1897). Founded in Boston by Josephine St. Pierre Ruffin, *Woman's Era* was the first American newspaper established for and by African American women. Its readership and subscriber base included members of Black women's clubs around the nation. It advocated for women's suffrage and reported on suffrage meetings and conventions. It also promoted anti-lynching campaigns. In its July 1896 issue, **Harriet Tubman** was featured as one of America's most "Eminent Women."

**WOMEN'S RIGHTS MOVEMENT, AMERICAN** (traditionally 13 July 1848–18 August 1920). The decades-long campaign waged by activists demanding the right to vote for American women. From the **Seneca Falls Convention** in 1848 to the ratification of the **Nineteenth Amendment to the Constitution** in August 1920, generations of America women fought for equal rights and suffrage. **Lucretia Coffin Mott**, **Martha Coffin Wright**, **Susan B. Anthony**, **Elizabeth Cady Stanton**, and **Harriet Tubman** among others were early activists. Like these other women, Tubman died before she could vote.

**WOOD, CHARLES P.** (ca. 1818–7 December 1878). A resident of Auburn, New York, Wood was a banker and investor in D. M. Osborne Manufacturing Co., in Auburn, New York. Wood recruited soldiers to fight for the Union Army and participated in relief efforts for local central New York families suffering from the loss of family members during the **Civil War**. He was the compiler and author of the **Manuscript History Concerning the Pension Claim of Harriet Tubman**, which Wood used to help **Harriet Tubman** petition the federal government for payment for her services as a spy during the war. He died in Auburn, New York, in 1878 and is buried in Fort Hill Cemetery.

**WOODSON, CARTER G.** (19 December 1875–3 April 1950). American historian, journalist, and civil rights leader often referred to as the father of Black History Month. Born and raised in Virginia, the son of formerly enslaved people, Woodson went on to graduate from Berea College, University of Chicago, and later, in 1912, he became the second African American to earn a PhD from Harvard University. His specialty included the history and culture of the African Diaspora. His early academic career was spent teaching in segregated high schools and then on the faculty at Howard University, where he eventually became dean. Woodson founded the Association for the Study of African American Life and History (1915); published the *Journal of Negro History* (1915), now called the *Journal of African American History*; and established **Associated Publishers** in 1920 to publish works by Black authors and for African American readers.

Early in his career as a publisher he believed that only African Americans should research and write about Black subjects. Woodson also created Black History Week (1926), now known as Black History Month (1970), to encourage the public to learn more about African American history and culture. **Associated Publishers** published **Earl Conrad**'s 1943 biography of **Harriet Tubman**. Woodson published many books, pamphlets, articles, and curriculum guides on Black history and culture. He died of a heart attack on 3 April 1950 at his home in Washington, D.C. His legacy lives on in the inclusion of African American history and culture in social studies classrooms across America today.

**WOOLFLEY, JAMES AND LAVINIA.** *See* WOOLFORD, JAMES AND LAVINIA.

**WOOLFOLK, AUSTIN AND JOHN.** Brothers and Baltimore slave traders beginning in the early 1810s through the 1830s. For a time, they were the largest traders in the region, buying enslaved people in the Chesapeake region and selling them to Georgia, Louisiana, and other Deep South states. By 1830, the brothers opened a branch office in Cambridge, Maryland, where they competed with other traders such as Thomas Overlay, Hope Slater, and Henry Boyce, whose ready cash proved attractive to Eastern Shore slaveholders eager to pay off their debts. The Woolfolks were responsible for tearing apart thousands of enslaved families during more than thirty years of business.

**WOOLFORD, ISAAC** (ca. 1825–28 July 1865). Born in Dorchester County, Maryland, Isaac Woolford lived in Peter Simpson Jr.'s home, three households away from Ben and Rit Ross, according to the 1850 Poplar Neck census. He married a woman named Mary soon thereafter. She may have been the twenty-five-year-old woman named "Mary" living in the Ross household in 1850, suggesting a potential connection between the families (*see also* Mary Woolford). The couple had four children: twins James and Margaret (*see also* Margaret Woolford Stewart Lucas), Moses, and Sarah. Between 1860 and 1861, Mary, James, and Sarah died, probably as a result of an epidemic. During that time period, Harriet Tubman secretly returned to Poplar Neck and took Margaret from her family and brought her to Auburn, New York. During the Civil War, Isaac joined Company I, Twenty-ninth United States Colored Troops in Easton, Maryland, on 20 September 1864. He died of scurvy in the U.S. Army Post Hospital in Brazos, Santiago, Texas, on 18 July 1865. In 1885, his daughter Margaret posted an advertisement in the *Christian Recorder* asking for information about her father, Isaac, and her brother Moses.

**WOOLFORD, JAMES** (ca. 1852 to 1854–ca. 1861). Born and raised at Poplar Neck, near Preston in Caroline County, Maryland, to parents Mary and Isaac Woolford, James lived with his twin sister, Margaret Woolford Stewart Lucas; younger brother, Moses; and sister Sarah. He died sometime around 1861 along with his mother and sister Sarah, presumably due to an epidemic.

**WOOLFORD, JAMES AND LAVINIA** (dates unknown). Born enslaved in Dorchester County, Maryland, the Woolfords escaped slavery on 8 March 1857 with friends Thomas Elliott, Denard Hughes, Henry Predeaux, Bill and Emily Kiah, and an unidentified man. The group became known as the Dover Eight. They used instructions to follow a particular Underground Railroad route given to them by Harriet Tubman. They sought help from Reverend Samuel Green in East New Market, Maryland, and then from Tubman's father, Ben Ross, at Poplar Neck in Caroline County. The group was instructed to contact a Black Underground Railroad agent, Thomas Otwell, then living somewhere outside of Dover, Delaware. Otwell was supposed to guide them to the next stops on the Underground Railroad north to Wilmington, Delaware, but Otwell betrayed them when he conspired with a white man, James Hollis, and lured the group into the Dover jail so they could collect the $3,000 reward for the freedom seekers' capture. After an altercation with the sheriff, Woolford and the rest broke out of the jail. A trustworthy Black Underground Railroad agent, William Brinkley, successfully ferried the group in his wagon thirty-eight miles to Thomas Garrett's home in Wilmington, Delaware. Garrett forwarded them to William Still in Philadelphia. James and Lavinia became separated before reaching Still's office. While James and the other freedom seekers were sent on to Canada, Lavinia stayed hidden for several months in Delaware or Pennsylvania. She eventually made her way to Still's office with another freedom seeker, Ann Johnson. Still recorded Woolford as Woolfley. She was sent on to Canada and reunited with her husband.

**WOOLFORD, MARGARET.** See LUCAS, MARGARET WOOLFORD STEWART.

**WOOLFORD, MARY** (ca. 1825–ca. 1861). Mary's birthplace or parentage is unknown, though she was probably born free or manumitted at a young age. She married **Isaac Woolford** between 1850 and 1851 in **Caroline County, Maryland**. According to the 1850 U.S. Census, Isaac was living three households away from **Ben** and **Rit Ross**. That same year, a twenty-five-year-old woman named "Mary" was living in the Ross household, suggesting a potential connection between the families. According to **Harriet Tubman**'s own testimony, on the evening that she escaped slavery in the late fall of 1849 from Dr. **Anthony C. Thompson**'s plantation at **Poplar Neck**, she tried to tell "Mary" that she was running away but was interrupted by the arrival of Dr. Thompson. This "Mary" is likely the woman who married Isaac. The couple had four children: twins **James** and **Margaret**, **Moses**, and **Sarah**. Between 1860 and 1861, Mary, James, and Sarah died, probably during an epidemic, leaving Isaac, Margaret, and Moses alone. During that time period, **Harriet Tubman** secretly returned to **Poplar Neck** and took Margaret from her family and brought her to Auburn, New York.

**WOOLFORD, MARYLAND.** A village located on a tributary of the Little Choptank River two miles west of **Church Creek** along present-day Route 16 in **Dorchester County, Maryland**. Originally called Loomtown, then Milton, the town hosted shipyards and commercial wharves.

**WOOLFORD, MOSES (1857–aft. 1880).** Born and raised at **Poplar Neck**, near **Preston** in **Caroline County, Maryland**, to parents **Mary** and **Isaac Woolford**, Moses lived with twin siblings, **Margaret Woolford Stewart Lucas** and **James**, and a younger sister, **Sarah**. After his mother, brother James, and sister Sarah died, his sister Margaret was taken to Auburn, New York, to live with **Harriet Tubman**. His father, Isaac, joined the Union Army in 1864, leaving Moses to be raised by **Gracie Chase Friend** and her son **Harrison Friend**. His whereabouts remain unknown after 1880.

**WOOLFORD, SARAH (1859–ca. 1861).** Born and raised at **Poplar Neck**, near **Preston** in **Caroline County, Maryland**, to parents **Mary** and **Isaac Woolford**, Sarah lived with twin siblings, **Margaret Woolford Stewart Lucas** and **James**, and brother **Moses**. She died sometime around 1861 along with her mother and brother James, presumably due to an epidemic.

**WORDEN, LAZETTE MILLER (1 November 1803–3 October 1875).** Born in Cayuga County, New York, Worden was the sister of **Frances Miller Seward**, the wife of **William Henry Seward**. After her husband, Alvin Worden, died in 1856, Lazette returned to Auburn and became active in local antislavery and **Underground Railroad** activities. She also helped manage the Seward household when the **Civil War** started. In early 1862, **Harriet Tubman** entrusted nine-year-old **Margaret Woolford Stewart Lucas** to her care. Worden helped raise Margaret in the Seward household. Worden died in 1875 and is buried in Fort Hill Cemetery in Auburn, New York.

**WRIGHT, DAVID (18 March 1806–24 February 1897).** Born in Bucks County, Pennsylvania, Wright was educated in Quaker schools before moving to Aurora, New York, in 1826. While apprenticing in a law office he met **Martha Coffin Pelham**, a widow with a four-year-old daughter, and they married in 1829. They eventually moved to nearby Auburn, where Wright became law partners with **William Henry Seward**. In addition to Martha's daughter, the couple raised six children of their own, including **Eliza Wright Osborne** and **Ellen Wright Garrison**. The Wright home became a stop on the **Underground Railroad**. They became friends with **Harriet Tubman** through an introduction from Martha's sister, **Lucretia Coffin Mott** of Philadelphia. After the **Civil War**, David tried to help Tubman file a lawsuit after she had been forcibly ejected from a railroad car because she was African American. Wright died in 1897 and is buried in Fort Hill Cemetery in Auburn, New York.

**WRIGHT, ELLEN.** *See* GARRISON, ELLEN WRIGHT.

**WRIGHT, MARTHA COFFIN PELHAM (25 December 1806–4 January 1875).** Born in

Boston to Quaker parents, Thomas and Ann Coffin, Wright moved to Philadelphia as a small child with her family, including sister **Lucretia Coffin Mott**. Educated in Quaker schools, Wright lived in a strict Quaker household. She fell in love with Captain Peter Pelham, a naval officer from a slaveholding Kentucky family, and married him in 1824 after overcoming her family's strong objections. They had one child, a daughter, but in 1826 Pelham died, leaving her a young widow with few resources. She moved to Aurora, New York, to teach in a Quaker school; there she met **David Wright** and married him in 1829. They eventually moved to nearby Auburn, where Wright became law partners with **William Henry Seward**. In addition to Martha's daughter, the couple raised six children of their own, including **Eliza Wright Osborne** and **Ellen Wright Garrison**.

The Wright home became a stop on the **Underground Railroad**. Martha and her sister Lucretia became active **abolitionists** and suffragists and deeply involved in the fledgling **women's rights movement**. The women, along with feminist **Elizabeth Cady Stanton**, organized the First Women's Rights Convention at Seneca Falls in July 1848. Martha, Lucretia, and Stanton were among the sixty-eight women and thirty-two men who signed the Declaration of Sentiments calling for equality for women in law and society. The Wrights became friends with **Harriet Tubman** through an introduction from Lucretia, who met Tubman in Philadelphia after she escaped slavery. During the 1850s, Martha and her family became close to Tubman and her family, providing material, financial, and personal support when Tubman needed it. Wright died from typhoid fever in 1876 and is buried in Fort Hill Cemetery in Auburn, New York.

**WRIGHT, TURPIN (1793–1869).** Born in Delaware, Wright was a ship captain, **slave trader**, and farmer with land and enslaved people in Seaford, Delaware, and **Dorchester County, Maryland**. In 1833, Wright petitioned the Delaware State Legislature for permission to transfer nineteen enslaved people he jointly owned with his brothers Jacob and Charles Wright to **Dorchester County**. The brothers owned twelve hundred acres of woods, peach orchards, and agricultural fields, in addition to waterfront property along the **Choptank River** and the **Nanticoke River** where they operated fisheries harvesting crabs, oysters, and fish and merchant sailing businesses. One of Wright's enslaved people, **Peter Pennington**, escaped with friends **Josiah "Joe" Bailey**, **William "Bill" Bailey**, and **Eliza Manokey** in May 1856, accompanied by **Harriet Tubman**, who guided them safely to Canada.

**WYMAN, ELIZABETH "LILLIE" BUFFIN CHASE (10 December 1847–10 January 1929).** Born in Rhode Island to **abolitionist** parents who operated an **Underground Railroad** station in their home, Wyman was an American reformer active in the women's suffrage movement, labor reform, and civil rights. An author, she published fiction and nonfiction books, essays, articles, and biographical sketches of activists and reformers, including **Harriet Tubman**. She was an early member of the National Association for the Advancement of Colored People, founded in 1909. She died in 1929 in Newton, Massachusetts.

# Appendix A

## Harriet Tubman's Underground Railroad Rescue Missions

**Approximate total number of people:** 67
**Number of trips:** 13

Tubman also gave instructions to almost seventy more people, including the two groups constituting the Stampede of Slaves, the **Dover Eight**, and more, who found their way to freedom without her direct leadership.

### DECEMBER 1850

**Kessiah Jolley Bowley** (Tubman niece)
James Alfred Bowley (six years old)
Araminta Bowley (baby)
**John Bowley** (Kessiah's free husband)

### EARLY 1851

Moses Ross
Unidentified man
Unidentified man

### LATE 1851

Unidentified man called "brother"
Unidentified wife of "brother"
Unidentified
Unidentified
Unidentified
Unidentified
Unidentified
Unidentified
Unidentified

Unidentified
Unidentified

### FALL 1852

Unidentified
Unidentified
Unidentified
Unidentified
Unidentified
Unidentified
Unidentified
Unidentified
Unidentified

### MAY–JUNE 1854

Winnebar (Winory or William) Johnson
Jane Pennington (possible)

### CHRISTMAS 1854

**Robert Ross**, alias **John Stewart** (Tubman brother)
**Henry Ross**, alias **William Henry Ross Stewart** (Tubman brother)
**Ben Ross Jr.**, alias **James Stewart** (Tubman brother)
**Jane Kane**, alias **Catherine Stewart** (fiancée of Ben Ross Jr. above)
**Peter Jackson**, alias **Tench Tilghman**
**John Chase**, alias Daniel Lloyd
Unidentified (possibly George Ross)

# APPENDIX A

Unidentified (possibly William Thompson)
Unidentified
Unidentified

## EARLY 1855

Harriet Ann Parker Ross, alias **Harriet Ann Parker Stewart** (free wife of William Henry Ross Stewart)
**William Henry Stewart Jr.** (Tubman nephew, free)
**John Isaac Ross** (Tubman nephew, free)

## DECEMBER 1855

Henry Hooper or Cooper (possible)
**Joseph Cornish** (possible)

## MAY 1856

Ben Jackson
**James Coleman**
**Henry Hopkins**
William A. Connoway (Conoway), alias William Andrew Cook

## OCTOBER 1856

Tilly

## NOVEMBER 1856

Josiah "Joe" Bailey
William Bailey
Peter Pennington
Eliza Manokey

## MAY 1857

Harriet "Rit" Green Ross, alias **Harriet "Rit" Stewart** (Tubman's mother)
Benjamin "Ben" Ross, alias **Benjamin "Ben" Stewart** (Tubman's father)

## DECEMBER 1860

**Stephen Ennals**
**Maria Ennals**
Harriet Ennals
Amanda Ennals
baby Ennals
John Cornish, alias John Wesley Reed
Unidentified woman

## UNKNOWN DATES (LIKELY SOME OF THE "UNIDENTIFIED" ABOVE)

Margaret Woolford Stewart Lucas (Tubman relative)
Ann Marie Stewart (Tubman niece)
Amelia "Millie" Hollis Stewart
**Henry Carrol**
Unidentified twin girl
Unidentified twin girl

# Appendix B

## Anthony Thompson's Inventory of Slaves, Recorded by Dr. Anthony C. Thompson, January 1839

| Names | Time to Serve Yr. | Mo. | Relations |
|---|---|---|---|
| 1. Ben [Ross] | 1 | 4 | Wife and children belonging to Edward Brodess |
| 2. Jack [Manokey] | 14 | 4 | Wife and children free |
| 3. Bill [Banks] | 6 | 4 | Wife belonging to Mrs. Stapleford |
| 4. Aaron [Manokey] | 20 | 4 | A cripple—no wife |
| 5. Allen | 22 | 4 | Not married |
| 6. Joshua [Tyler?] | 16 | 4 | Not married |
| 7. Draper [Manokey] | 17 | 4 | Not married |
| 8. Moses [Manokey] | 17 | 4 | Wife and child belonging to Mrs. Murray |
| 9. Isaac [Kiah] | 6 | 4 | Wife belonging to Mrs. Stapleford |
| *Women and Children* | | | |
| 10. Sarah Ann [Reed] [Saunders, Spriggs] | 4 | 4 | Husband belonging to Dr. Tubman |
| 11. Jacob [Saunders] | 25 | 4 | [Sarah's child] |
| 12. Charles [Saunders] | 27 | 4 | [Sarah's child] |
| 13. Bob [Saunders or Spriggs?] | 35 | 4 | [Sarah's child] |
| 14. Rebecca [Spriggs] | 38 | 4 | [Sarah's child] |
| 15. Charity [Spriggs] | 40 | 4 | [Sarah's child] |
| 16. Sarah Jane [Young] | 17 | 4 | Husband belonging to Mr. John Crawford |
| 17. Angeline [Young] | 39 | 4 | [Sarah's child] |
| 18. Cassan[dra or Cassey] [Young Nichols] | 38 | 4 | *[notation illegible]* [Sarah's child] |
| 19. Nancy [Young] | For life | | [Sarah's child] |
| 20. Hooper [Young?] | For life | | [Sarah's child] |
| 21. Leah [Ennals Slacum?] | 8 | 4 | Husband belonging to Captain Solomon Mitchell |
| 22. Jerry [Ennals Slacum] | 39 | 4 | [Leah's child] |
| 23. Mary [Slacum] | For life | | [Leah's child] |
| 24. Infant [Eliza Jane Slacum Cane] | For life | | [Leah's child] |

# APPENDIX B

| Names | Time to Serve Yr. | Mo. | Relations |
|---|---|---|---|
| 25. Betsy [Bowley] | 14 | 4 | Husband, Major Bowley, free |
| 26. Alfred [Bowley] | 24 | 4 | |
| 27. Maria [Bowley? Manokey? Bailey] | 21 | 4 | Not married *(delicate)* |
| 28. Pheba [Tyler] | 26 | 4 | Not married, is my house girl & was raised by me <u>ACT</u> [Anthony C. Thompson] *sister to J. T.* |
| 29. Harriot | 26 | 4 | Not married |
| 30. Hanner | 28 | 4 | Husband in Talbot [Co.]—belonging to Mrs. Haddaway—[?] Hanner lives with Absalom [Thompson] |
| 31. Sophia [Green, aka Sophia Brown] | 26 | 4 | Not married |
| 32. Emeline [Manokey?] | 32 | 4 | [referring to Emeline and Charlotte together] Phillis's children and sisters to Eliza and Matilda, who belong to Absalom [Thompson] |
| 33. Charlotte [Manokey?] | 32 | 4 | |
| 34. Mary [Manokey Ross Wells] | 37 | 4 | [referring to Mary and Susan together] Old Jerry's children and are to remain with him to certain ages by the will |
| 35. Susan [Manokey] | 38 | 4 | |
| 36. Levin [Tyler] | 37 | 4 | No parents, raised in my family—<u>ACT</u> [Anthony C. Thompson] |
| 37. Pheba [Kiah Ferrare] | 38 | 4 | Isaac's child |
| 38. Jerry [Manokey] | Free | | |
| 39. Polly [Manokey] | Free | | |
| 40. Phillis [Manokey?] | Free | | |
| 41. Eliza [Manokey] | | | Awarded to Absalom [Thompson] |
| 42. Matilda [Manokey] | | | Awarded to Absalom [Thompson] |
| 43. Job | | | Awarded to Absalom [Thompson] |

Anthony C. Thompson, List of Anthony Thompson's Negroes, 1839, MS 1405. Levin Richardson Collection, 1758–1865, Maryland Historical Society, Baltimore, MD.
Notes in *italics* are additions presumably made by Anthony C. Thompson at a later date. Additions by author in [] brackets.

# Appendix C

## Famous Harriet Tubman Quotes and Speech Fragments

*Tubman on her decision to escape slavery:*
"I had reasoned this out in my mind; there was one of two things I had a right to, liberty, or death; if I could not have one, I would have the other; for no man should take me alive; I should fight for my liberty as long as my strength lasted, and when the time came for me to go, the Lord would let them take me."—Tubman to **Sarah Bradford**, 1868

*Tubman, upon reaching freedom in Pennsylvania:*
"So it was with me," she said. "I had crossed the line. I was free; but there was no one to welcome me to the land of freedom. I was a stranger in a strange land; and my home, after all, was down in Maryland; because my father, my mother, my brothers, and sisters, and friends were there. But I was free, and they should be free. I would make a home in the North and bring them there, God helping me. Oh, how I prayed then," she said. "I said to de Lord, 'I'm gwine to hole stiddy on to you, an' I know you'll see me through.'"—Tubman to **Sarah Bradford**, 1868

*Tubman on her work on the Underground Railroad:*
"It wasn't me, it was the Lord! I always told him, 'I trust you. I don't know where to go or what to do, but I always expect you to lead me' and he always did."—Tubman to **Sarah Bradford**, 1868

"God's time is always near. He set the North Star in the heavens; He gave me the strength in my limbs; He meant I should be free."—Harriet Tubman to **Ednah Dow Cheney**, circa 1859

"I didn't know the way, but there was the North Star and I followed that and hid myself all day till I got to Pennsylvania."—Harriet Tubman to Blandina Miller, 1899

*Tubman on taking freedom seekers to Canada after passage of the Fugitive Slave Act in 1850:*
"I wouldn't trust Uncle Sam with my people no longer; I brought them all clear off to Canada."—Tubman to **Sarah Bradford**, 1868

*Abolitionist Lewis Tappan to Anthony Lane, 1855, describing his meeting with Tubman:*
"I asked her what would be her feelings if she should be seized and sent to the far South into perpetual slavery. She replied calmly and resolutely, 'I shall have the consolation to know that I had done some good to my people.'"—Harriet Tubman to **Lewis Tappan**, ca. 1855

"I was the conductor of the Underground Railroad for eight years, and I can say what most conductors can't say—I never ran my train off the track and I never lost a passenger."—Harriet Tubman at a woman suffrage convention, New York, 1896

*Tubman on enslavement:*
"I grew up like a neglected weed—ignorant of liberty, having no experience of it. Then I was

not happy or contented: every time I saw a white man I was afraid of being carried away. I had two sisters carried away in a chain-gang—one of them left two children. We were always uneasy. Now I've been free, I know what a dreadful condition slavery is. I have seen hundreds of escaped slaves, but I never saw one who was willing to go back and be a slave. I have no opportunity to see my friends in my native land. We would rather stay in our native land, if we could be as free there as we are here. I think slavery is the next thing to hell. If a person would send another into bondage, he would, it appears to me, be bad enough to send him into hell, if he could."—Harriet Tubman to **Benjamin Drew**, St. Catharines, Canada, 1855

*During celebrations in Boston for British Emancipation Day in August 1859, Harriet Tubman was introduced to the audience as "Harriet Garrison" to obscure her identity because she was praised as "one of the most successful conductors on the Underground Railroad." Tubman denounced the controversial* **colonization movement** *through a parable, as reported by* **abolitionist** *and newspaper editor* **William Lloyd Garrison**:
Tubman "told the story of a man who sowed onions and garlic on his land to increase his dairy productions; but he soon found the butter was strong and would not sell, and so he concluded to sow clover instead. But he soon found the wind had blown the onions and garlic all over his field. Just so, she said, the white people had got the 'nigger' here to do their drudgery, and now they were trying to root 'em out and send 'em to Africa. 'But,' she said, 'they can't do it; we're rooted here, and they can't pull us up.'"—Harriet Tubman to the audience at the August 1859 British Emancipation Day celebration in Boston, Massachusetts, published by **William Lloyd Garrison** in *The Liberator* on 26 August 1859

*Tubman's advice to President Lincoln:*
"They may send the flower of their young men down South, to die of the fever in the summer, and the ague in the winter. (For it is cold down there, though it is down South.) They may send them one year, two years, three years, till they are *tired* of sending, or till they use up all the young men. All no use! God's ahead of master Lincoln. God won't let master Lincoln beat the South till he does *the right thing*. Master Lincoln, he's a great man, and I am a poor negro; but the negro can tell master Lincoln how to save the money and the young men. He can do it by setting the negroes free. Suppose that was an awful big snake down there, on the floor. He *bite* you. Folks all scared, because you die. You send for a doctor to cut the bite; but the snake, he rolled up there, and while the doctor doing it, he bite you again. The doctor dug out *that* bite; but while the doctor doing it, the snake, he spring up and bite you again; so he *keep* doing it, till you kill him. That's what master Lincoln ought to know."—Harriet Tubman to **Lydia Maria Child**, 1862

*Tubman witnessing the Battle of Fort Wagner:*
"And then we saw the lightning, and that was the guns; and then we heard the thunder, and that was the big guns; and then we heard the rain falling, and that was the drops of blood falling; and when we came to get in the crops, it was the dead that we reaped."—Harriet Tubman to **Albert Bushnell Hart**, 1904

*Tubman on the conditions for the wounded:*
"I'd go to the hospital, I would, early every morning. I'd get a big chunk of ice, I would, and put it in a basin, and fill it with water; then I'd take a sponge and begin. First man I'd come to, I'd thrash away the flies, and they'd rise, they would, like bees round a hive. Then I'd begin to bathe their wounds, and by the time I'd bathed off three or four, the fire and heat would have melted the ice and made the water warm, and it would be as red as clear blood. Then I'd go and get more ice, I would, and by the time I got to the next ones, the flies would be round de first ones, black and thick as ever."—Harriet Tubman to **Sarah Bradford**, 1868

*Tubman on woman suffrage:*
In 1911, **James B. Clark** interviewed Tubman. He asked her, "Do you really believe that women should vote?" Tubman responded, "I suffered enough to believe it."

Two years later in 1913, as Tubman lay dying at the Harriet Tubman Home for the Aged in Auburn, she told **Mary Talbert**, "Tell the women to stand together for God will never forsake us."

# Appendix D

## Earliest Published Interviews and Biographical Essays about Harriet Tubman

*From Civil War correspondent James Yerrington, reporting from Hilton Head, South Carolina, for the* Wisconsin State Journal, *Madison, Wisconsin, Saturday, 20 June 1863.* Colonel Montgomery's raid - The Rescued Black Chattels - A Black she "Moses" - Her Wonderful Daring and Sagacity - The Black Regiments - Col. Higginson's Mistakes - Arrival of the 54th Massachusetts, &c., &c.

Correspondent of the State Journal
Fernandina, June 6th, 1863

Affairs in this Department seem, for the moment, to indicate more vigor and activity, though perhaps in a small way. At Beaufort, a few days since, I had the satisfaction of witnessing the return of the gallant Col. Montgomery from a successful raid into the enemy's country, having with him the trophies of war in the shape of 780 black chattel, now recreated and made freemen, and thousands of dollars worth of rice and other property.

As I witnessed the moving mass of recreated black humanity on its way from the boat to the church at Beaufort, where they were quartered for the moment, with the filth and tatters of slavery still hanging to their degraded persons, my heart went up in gratitude to God for the change which had been wrought on South Carolina soil. The emblem of liberty and the nations' glory, as it floated over these poor, defenseless children of oppression, never looked to me so glorious, and never thrilled my heart with a more honest pride, and in my elation I almost anticipated the time when, "everywhere under the whole Heaven," it should be recognized as the emblem of freedom, and on its ample folds should appear the glorious inscription, "Liberty and union, now and forever, one and inseparable."

I doubt whether the church was ever before filled with such a devout crowd of worshippers—whether it was ever before appropriated to so good a purpose—whether so true a gospel had ever before been preached within its walls. I certainly never felt such swelling emotions of gratitude to the Great Ruler as at this moment.

Col. Montgomery and his gallant band of 300 hundred black soldiers, under the guidance of a black woman, dashed into the enemies' country, struck a bold and effective blow, destroying millions of dollars worth of commissary stores, cotton, and lordly dwellings, and striking terror to the heart of rebellion, brought off near 800 slaves and thousands of dollars worth of property, without losing a man or receiving a scratch! It was a glorious consummation.

After they were all fairly disposed of in the church, they were addressed in strains of thrilling eloquence by their gallant deliverer; to which they responded in a song—

"There is a white robe for thee."

A song so appropriate and so heartfelt and cordial as to bring unbidden tears.

The Colonel was followed by a speech from the black woman who led the raid, and under whose inspiration it was originated and conducted. For sound sense and real native eloquence, her address would do honor to any man, and it created quite a sensation.

And now a word of this woman - this black heroine - this fugitive slave. She is now called "Moses," having inherited the name for many daring feats she has accomplished in behalf of the bondmen and the many slaves she has set free. She was formerly a slave in Virginia - she determined upon "freedom or death," and escaped to Canada. She there planned the deliverance of all her kindred, and the nine successful trips to different slave states, effecting the escape of over 180 slaves and their successful establishment in Canada. Since the rebellion she has devoted herself to her great work of delivering the bondmen, with an energy and sagacity that cannot be exceeded. Many and many times she has penetrated the enemy's lines and discovered their situation and condition, and escaped without extreme hazard. True, she is a "nigger" at that, but in patriotism, sagacity, energy, ability, and all that elevates human character, she is head and shoulders above the many who vaunt their patriotism and boast their philanthropy, swaggering of their superiority because of the cuticle in which their Creator condescended to envelop them.

The 2nd South Carolina regiment, with the accessories gained from this raid, every man of whom is anxious to enlist for the war, will now be full, and under Col. Montgomery will achieve glory and honor for the black soldiery.

As I anticipated in my letter after the move at Jacksonville, the 1st South Carolina regiment is rendered almost useless, under the mistaken course of its Colonel [Higginson] in treating his men as more or less than human.

The 54th Massachusetts black regiment, with full ranks, arrived at Beaufort on the day after Col. Montgomery's return, and was hailed with immense enthusiasm. It is a splendid regiment, and if a chance is given, it will wipe out on South Carolina soil the insults and injuries inflicted in time past on Massachusetts seamen and citizens by her lordly slaveholding aristocracy. God speed the day!

The vessel which brought the 54th returns immediately to bring the 55th, (colored,) which is being organized. Fred. Douglass has two sons in the 54th. When it moves it will strike terror to the hearts of the rebel slaveholder . . .

\* \* \*

*On Friday, 10 July 1863,* **Franklin B. Sanborn,** *editor of* **The Commonwealth** *newspaper, published the 20 June 1863* Wisconsin State Journal *article by James Yerrington and then added his own biographical sketch of Tubman, the first detailed biography of the formerly enslaved woman:*

The above, from a correspondent of the Wisconsin State Journal, will remind many of our readers of their interviews with the heroine here mentioned, - Harriet Tubman. She has a more remarkable history than any fugitive slave we have ever met, some portions of which we will give in our next issue. She is of unmixed negro blood, was born in Maryland - not Virginia - and has brought her rescued country people chiefly from the Eastern shore of Maryland, in the neighborhood of Cambridge. Her religious experiences are as startling as those of Sojourner Truth, whose letter we printed last week.

### HARRIET TUBMAN

It was said long ago that the true romance of America was not in the fortunes of the Indian, where Cooper sought it, nor in the New England character, where Judd found it, nor in the social contrasts of Virginia planters, as Thackeray imagined, but in the story of the fugitive slaves. The observation is as true now as it was before war, with swift, gigantic hand, sketched the vast shadows, and dashed in the high lights in which romance loves to lurk and flash forth. But the stage is enlarged on which those dramas are played, the whole world now sit as spectators, and the desperation or the magnanimity of a poor black woman has power to shake the nation that so long was deaf to her cries. We write of one of these heroines, of whom our slave annals are full—a woman whose career is as extraordinary as the most famous of her sex can show.

Araminta Ross, now known by her married name of Tubman, with her sounding Christian name changed to Harriet, is the grand-daughter of a slave imported from Africa, and has not a drop of white blood in her veins. Her parents were Benjamin Ross and Harriet Greene, both slaves, but married and faithful to each other. They still live in old age and poverty, but free, on a little property at Auburn, N. Y., which their daughter purchased for them from Mr. Seward, the Secretary of State. She was born, as near as she can remember, in 1820 or in 1821, in Dorchester County, on the Eastern shore of Maryland, and not far from the town of Cambridge. She had ten brothers and sisters, of whom three are now living, all at the North, and all rescued from slavery by Harriet, before the War. She went back just as the South was preparing to secede, to bring away a fourth, but before she could reach her, she was dead. Three years before, she had brought away her old father and mother, at great risk to herself.

When Harriet was six years old, she was taken from her mother and carried ten miles to live with James Cook, whose wife was a weaver, to learn the trade of weaving. While still a mere child, Cook set her to watching his musk-rat traps, which compelled her to wade through the water. It happened that she was once sent when she was ill with the measles, and, taking cold from wading in the water in this condition, she grew very sick, and her mother persuaded her master to take her away from Cook's until she could get well.

Another attempt was made to teach her weaving, but she would not learn, for she hated her mistress, and did not want to live at home, as she would have done as a weaver, for it was the custom then to weave the cloth for the family, or a part of it, in the house.

Soon after she entered her teens she was hired out as a field hand, and it was while thus employed that she received a wound which nearly proved fatal, from the effects of which she still suffers. In the fall of the year, the slaves there work in the evening, cleaning up wheat, husking corn, etc. On this occasion, one of the slaves of a farmer named Barrett, left his work, and went to the village store in the evening. The overseer followed him, and so did Harriet. When the slave was found, the overseer swore he should be whipped, and called on Harriet, among others, to help tie him. She refused, and as the man ran away, she placed herself in the door to stop pursuit. The overseer caught up a two-pound weight from the counter and threw it at the fugitive, but it fell short and struck Harriet a stunning blow on the head. It was long before she recovered from this, and it has left her subject to a sort of stupor or lethargy at times; coming upon her in the midst of conversation, or whatever she may be doing, and throwing her into a deep slumber, from which she will presently rouse herself, and go on with her conversation or work.

After this she lived for five or six years with John Stewart, where at first she worked in the house, but afterwards "hired her time," and Dr. Thompson, son of her master's guardian, "stood for her," that is, was her surety for the payment of what she owed. She employed the time thus hired in the rudest labors,—drove oxen, carted, plowed, and did all the work of a man,—sometimes earning money enough in a year, beyond what she paid her master, "to buy a pair of steers," worth forty dollars. The amount exacted of a woman for her time was fifty or sixty dollars,—of a man, one hundred to one hundred and fifty dollars. Frequently Harriet worked for her father, who was a timber inspector, and superintended the cutting and hauling of great quantities of timber for the Baltimore shipyards. Stewart, his temporary master, was a builder, and for the work of Ross used to receive as much as five dollars a day sometimes, he being a superior workman. While engaged with her father, she would cut wood, haul logs, etc. Her usual "stint" was half a cord of wood in a day.

Harriet was married somewhere about 1844, to a free colored man named John Tubman, but she had no children. For the last two years of slavery she lived with Dr. Thompson, before mentioned, her own master not being yet of age, and Dr. T.'s father being his guardian, as well as the owner of her own father. In 1849 the young man died, and the slaves were to be sold, though previously set free by an old will. Harriet resolved not to be sold, and so, with no knowledge of the North—having only heard of Pennsylvania and New Jersey—she walked away one night alone. She found a friend in a white lady, who knew her story and helped her on her way. After many adventures, she reached Philadelphia, where she found work and earned a small stock of money. With this money in her purse, she traveled back to Maryland for her husband, but she found him married to another woman, and no longer caring to live with her. This, however, was not until two years after her escape, for she does not seem to have reached her old home in her first two expeditions. In December, 1850, she had visited Baltimore and brought away her sister and two children, who had come up from Cambridge in a boat, under charge of her sister's husband, a free black. A few months after she had brought away her brother and two other men, but it was not till the fall of 1851 that she found her husband and learned of his infidelity. She did not give way to rage or grief, but collected a party of fugitives and brought them safely to Philadelphia. In December of the same year, she returned, and led out a party of eleven, among them her brother and his wife. With these she journeyed to Canada, and there spent the winter, for this was after the enforcement of Mason's Fugitive Slave Bill in Philadelphia and Boston, and there was no safety except "under the paw of the British Lion," as she quaintly said. But the first winter was terribly severe for these poor runaways. They earned their bread by chopping wood in the snows of a Canadian forest; they were frost-bitten, hungry, and naked. Harriet was their good angel. She kept house for her brother, and the poor creatures boarded with her. She worked for them, begged for them, prayed for them, with the strange familiarity of communion with God which seems natural to these people, and carried them by the help of God through the hard winter.

In the spring she returned to the States, and as usual earned money by working in hotels and families as a cook. From Cape May, in the fall of 1852, she went back once more to Maryland, and brought away nine more fugitives.

Up to this time she had expended chiefly her own money in these expeditions—money which she had earned by hard work in the drudgery of the kitchen. Never did any one more exactly fulfill the sense of George Herbert—

"A servant with this clause
Makes drudgery divine."

But it was not possible for such virtues long to remain hidden from the keen eyes of the Abolitionists. She became known to Thomas Garrett, the large-hearted Quaker of Wilmington, who has aided the escape of three thousand fugitives; she found warm friends in Philadelphia and New York, and wherever she went. These gave her money, which she never spent for her own use, but laid up for the help of her people, and especially for her journeys back to the "land of Egypt," as she called her old home. By reason of her frequent visits there, always carrying away some of the oppressed, she got among her people the name of "Moses," which it seems she still retains.

Between 1852 and 1857, she made but two of these journeys, in consequence partly of the increased vigilance of the slaveholders, who had suffered so much by the loss of their property. A great reward was offered for her capture, and she several times was on the point of being taken, but always escaped by her quick wit, or by "warnings" from Heaven—for it is time to notice one singular trait in her character. She is the most shrewd and practical person in the world, yet she is a firm believer in omens, dreams, and warnings. She declares that before her escape from slavery, she used to dream of flying over fields and towns, and rivers and mountains, looking down upon them "like a bird," and reaching at last a great fence, or sometimes a river, over which she would try to fly, "but it 'peard like I wouldn't hab de strength, and jes as I was sinkin' down, dare would be ladies all drest in white ober dere, and dey would put out dere arms and pull me 'cross." There is nothing strange in this, perhaps, but she declares that when she came North she remembered these very places as those she had seen in her dreams, and many of the ladies who befriended her were those she had been helped by in her visions.

Then she says she always knows when there is danger near her,—she does not know how, exactly, but "'pears like my heart go flutter, flutter, and den dey may say 'Peace, Peace,' as much as dey likes, I know its gwine to be war!" She is very firm on this point, and ascribes to this her great impunity, in spite of the lethargy before mentioned, which would seem likely to throw her into the hands of her enemies. She says she inherited this power, that her father could always predict the weather, and that he foretold the Mexican war.

In 1857 she made her most venturesome journey, for she brought with her to the North her old parents, who were no longer able to walk such distances as she must go by night. Consequently she must hire a wagon for them, and it required all her ingenuity to get them through Maryland and Delaware safe. She accomplished it, however, and by the aid of her friends she brought them safe to Canada, where they spent the winter. Her account of their sufferings there—of her mother's complaining and her own philosophy about it—is a lesson of trust in Providence better than many sermons. But she decided to bring them to a more comfortable place, and so she negotiated with Mr. Seward—then in the Senate—for a little patch of ground with a house on it, at Auburn, near his own home.

To the credit of the Secretary of State it should be said, that he sold her the property on very favorable terms, and gave her some time for payment. To this house she removed her parents, and set herself to work to pay for her purchase. It was on this errand that she first visited Boston—we believe in the winter of 1858-9. She brought a few letters from her friends in New York, but she could herself neither read nor write, and she was obliged to trust to her wits that they were delivered to the right persons. One of them, as it happened, was to the present writer, who received it by another hand, and called to see her at her boarding-house. It was curious to see the caution with which she received her visitor until she felt assured that there was no mistake. One of her means of security was to carry with her the daguerreotypes of her friends, and show them to each new person. If they recognized the likeness, then it was all right.

Pains were taken to secure her the attention to which her great services to humanity entitled her, and she left New England with a handsome sum of money towards the payment of her debt to Mr. Seward. Before she left, however, she had several interviews with Captain Brown, then in Boston.

He is supposed to have communicated his plans to her, and to have been aided by her in obtaining recruits and money among her people. At any rate, he always spoke of her with the greatest respect, and declared that "General Tubman," as he styled her, was a better officer than most whom he had seen, and could command an army as successfully as she had led her small parties of fugitives.

Her own veneration for Captain Brown has always been profound, and since his murder, has taken the form of a religion. She had often risked her own life for her people, and she thought nothing of that; but that a white man, and a man so noble and strong, should so take upon himself the burden of a despised race, she could not understand, and she took refuge from her perplexity in the mysteries of her fervid religion.

Again, she laid great stress on a dream which she had just before she met Captain Brown in Canada. She thought she was in "a wilderness sort of place, all full of rocks and bushes," when she saw a serpent raise its head among the rocks, and as it did so, it became the head of an old man with a long white beard, gazing at her "wishful like, jes as ef he war gwine to speak to me," and then two other heads rose up beside him, younger than he,—and as she stood looking at them, and wondering what they could want with her, a great crowd of men rushed in and struck down the younger heads, and then the head of the old man, still looking at her so "wishful." This dream she had again and again, and could not interpret it; but, when she met Captain Brown, shortly after, behold, he was the very image of the head she had seen. But still she could not make out what her dream signified, till the news came to her of the tragedy of Harper's Ferry, and then she knew the two other heads were his two sons. She was in New York at that time, and on the day of the affair at Harper's Ferry, she felt her usual warning that something was wrong—she could not tell what. Finally she told her hostess that it must be Captain Brown who was in trouble, and that they should soon hear bad news from him. The next day's newspaper brought tidings of what had happened.

Her last visit to Maryland was made after this, in December, 1860; and in spite of the agitated condition of the country, and the greater watchfulness of the slaveholders, she brought away seven fugitives, one of them an infant, which must be drugged with opium to keep it from crying on the way, and so revealing the hiding place of the party. She brought these safely to New York, but there a new difficulty met her. It was the mad winter of compromises, when State after State, and politician after politician, went down on their knees to beg the South not to secede. The hunting of fugitive slaves began again. Mr. Seward went over to the side of compromise. He knew the history of this poor woman; he had given his enemies a hold on him, by dealing with her; it was thought he would not scruple to betray her. The suspicion was an unworthy one, for though the Secretary could betray a cause, he could not surely have put her enemies on the track of a woman who was thus in his power, after such a career as hers had been. But so little confidence was then felt in Mr. Seward, by men who had voted for him and with him, that they hurried Harriet off to Canada, sorely against her will.

She did not long remain there. The war broke out, for which she had been long looking, and she hastened to her New England friends to prepare for another expedition to Maryland, to bring away the last of her family.

Before she could start, however, the news came of the capture of Port Royal. Instantly she conceived the idea of going there and working among her people on the islands and the mainland. Money was given her, a pass was secured through the agency of Governor Andrew, and she went to Beaufort. There she has made herself useful in many ways—has been employed as a spy by General Hunter, and finally has piloted Col. Montgomery on his most successful expedition. We gave some notice of this fact last week. Since then we have received the following letter, dictated by her, from which it appears that she needs some contributions for her work. We trust she will receive them, for none has better deserved it. She asks nothing for herself, except that her wardrobe may be replenished, and even this she will probably share with the first needy person she meets.

BEAUFORT, S. C., June 30, 1863.

Last fall, when the people here became very much alarmed for fear of an invasion from the rebels, all my clothes were packed and sent with others to Hilton Head, and lost; and I have never been able to get any trace of them since. I was sick at the time, and unable to look after them myself. I want, among the rest, a bloomer dress, made of some coarse, strong material, to wear on expeditions. In our late expedition up the Combahee River, in coming on board the boat, I was carrying two pigs for a poor sick woman, who had a child to carry, and the order "double quick" was given, and I started to run, stepped on my dress, it being rather long, and fell and tore it almost off, so that when I got on board the boat, there was hardly anything left of it but shreds. I made up my mind then I would never wear a long dress on another expedition of the kind, but would have a bloomer as soon as I could get it. So please make this known to the ladies, if you will, for I expect to have use for it very soon, probably before they can get it to me.

You have, without doubt, seen a full account of the expedition I refer to. Don't you think we colored people are entitled to some credit for that exploit, under the lead of the brave Colonel Montgomery? We weakened the rebels somewhat on the Combahee River, by taking and bringing away seven hundred and fifty-six head of their most valuable live stock, known up in your region as "contrabands," and this, too, without the loss of a single life on our part, though we had good reason to believe that a number of rebels bit the dust. Of these seven hundred and fifty-six contrabands, nearly or quite all the able-bodied men have joined the colored regiments here.

I have now been absent two years almost, and have just got letters from my friends in Auburn, urging me to come home. My father and mother are old and in feeble health, and need my care and attention. I hope the good people there will not allow them to suffer, and I do not believe they will. But I do not see how I am to leave at present the very important work to be done here. Among other duties which I have, is that of looking after the hospital here for contrabands. Most of those coming from the mainland are very destitute, almost naked. I am trying to find places for those able to work, and provide for them as best I can, so as to lighten the burden on the Government as much as possible, while at the same time they learn to respect themselves by earning their own living.

Remember me very kindly to Mrs.—and her daughters; also, if you will, to my Boston friends, Mrs. C., Miss H., and especially to Mr. and Mrs. George L. Stearns, to whom I am under great obligations for their many kindnesses. I shall be sure to come and see you all if I live to go North. If you write, direct your letter to the care of C.

\* \* \*

*Ednah Dow Littlehale Cheney was the editor of the* **Freedmen's Record**, *and secretary of the education department of the Freedmen's Aid Society. She met Tubman in Boston during the 1850s, and in 1864, while visiting South Carolina, she interviewed Tubman for a sketch about her life and work during the* **Civil War**. *It was published in the* **Freedmen's Record** *in March 1865.*

## MOSES.

One of the teachers lately commissioned by the New-England Freedmen's Aid Society is probably the most remarkable woman of this age. That is to say, she has performed more wonderful deeds by the native power of her own spirit against adverse circumstances than any other. She is well known to many by the various names which her eventful life has given her; Harriet Garrison, Gen. Tubman, &c.; but among the slaves she is universally known by her well-earned title of *Moses*,—Moses the deliverer. She is a rare instance, in the midst of high civilization and intellectual culture, of a being of great native powers, working powerfully, and to beneficent ends, entirely unaided by schools or books.

Her maiden name was Araminta Ross. She is the granddaughter of a native African, and has not a drop of white blood in her veins. She was born in 1820 or 1821, on the Eastern Shore of Maryland. Her parents were slaves, but married and faithful to each other, and the family affection is very strong. She claims that she was legally freed by a will of her first master, but his wishes were not carried into effect.

She seldom lived with her owner, but was usually "hired out" to different persons. She once "hired her time," and employed it in rudest farming labors, ploughing, carting, driving the oxen, &c., to so good advantage that she was able in one year to buy a pair of steers worth forty dollars.

When quite young she lived with a very pious mistress; but the slaveholder's religion did not prevent her from whipping the young girl for every slight or fancied fault. Araminta found that this was usually a morning exercise; so she prepared for it by putting on all the thick clothes she could procure to protect her skin. She made sufficient outcry, however, to convince her mistress that her blows had full effect; and in the afternoon she would take off her wrappings, and dress as well as she could. When invited into family prayers, she preferred to stay on the landing, and pray for herself; "and I prayed to God," she says, "to make me strong and able to fight, and that's what I've allers prayed for ever since." It is in vain to try to persuade her that her prayer was a wrong one. She always maintains it to be sincere and right, and it has certainly been fully answered.

In her youth she received a severe blow on her head from a heavy weight thrown by her master at another slave, but which accidentally hit her. The blow produced a disease of the brain which was severe for a long time, and still makes her very lethargic. She cannot remain quiet fifteen minutes without appearing to fall asleep. It is not refreshing slumber; but a heavy weary condition which exhausts her. She therefore loves great physical activity, and direct heat of the sun, which keeps her blood actively circulating. She was married about 1844 to a free colored man named John Tubman, but never had any children. Owing to changes in her owner's family, it was determined to sell her and some other slaves; but her health was so much injured, that a purchaser was not easily found. At length she became convinced that she would soon be carried away, and she decided to escape. Her brothers did not agree with in her plans; and she walked off alone, following the guidance of the brooks, which she had observed to run North. The evening before she left, she wished very much to bid her companions farewell, but was afraid of being betrayed, if any one knew of her intentions; so she passed through the street singing,—

"Good bye, I'm going to leave you,

Good bye, I'll meet you in the kingdom,"—

and similar snatches of Methodist songs. As she passed on singing, she saw her master, Dr. Thompson, standing at his gate, and her native humor breaking out, she sung yet louder, bowing down to him,—

"Good bye, I'm going for to leave yon."

He stopped and looked after her as she passed on; and he afterwards said, that, as her voice came floating back in the evening air it seemed as if—

"A wave of trouble never rolled

Across her peaceful breast."

Wise judges are we of each other!—She was only quitting home, husband, father, mother, friends, to go out alone, friendless and penniless into the world.

She remained two years in Philadelphia working hard and carefully hoarding her money. Then she hired a room, furnished it as well as she could, bought a nice suit of men's clothes, and went back to Maryland for her husband. But the faithless man had taken to himself another wife. Harriet did not dare venture into her presence, but sent word to her husband where she was. He declined joining her. At first her grief and anger were excessive. She said, "she did not care what massa did to her, she thought she would go right in and make all the trouble she could, she was determined to see her old man once more"; but finally she thought "how foolish it was just for temper to make mischief"; and that, "if he could do without her, she could without him," and so "he dropped out of her heart," and she determined to give her life to brave deeds. Thus all personal aims died out of her heart; and with her simple brave motto, "I can't die but once," she began the work which has made her Moses,—the deliverer of her people. Seven or eight times she has returned to the neighborhood of her former home, always at the risk of death in the most terrible forms, and each time has brought away a company of fugitive slaves, and led them safely to the free States, or to Canada. Every time she went, the dangers increased. In 1857 she brought away her old parents, and, as they were too feeble to walk, she was obliged to hire a wagon, which added greatly to the perils of the journey. In 1860 she went for the last time, and among her troop was an infant whom they were obliged to keep stupefied with laudanum to prevent its outcries. This was at the period of great excitement, and Moses was not safe even in New-York State; but her anxious friends insisted upon her taking refuge in Canada. So various and interesting are the incidents of these journeys, that we know not how to select from them. She has shown in them all the characteristics of a great leader; courage, foresight, prudence, self-control, ingenuity, subtle perception, command over others' minds. Her nature is at once profoundly practical and highly imaginative. She is economical as Dr. Franklin, and as firm in the conviction of supernatural help as Mahomet. A clergyman once said, that her stories convinced you of their truth by their simplicity as do the gospel narratives. She never went to the South to bring away fugitives without being provided with money; money for the most part earned by drudgery in the kitchen, until within the last few years, when friends have aided her. She had to leave her sister's two orphan children in slavery the last time, for the want of thirty dollars. Thirty pieces of silver; an embroidered handkerchief or a silk dress to one, or the price of freedom to two orphan children to another! She would never allow more to join her than she could properly care for, though she often gave others directions by which they succeeded in escaping. She always came in the winter when the nights are long and dark, and people who have homes stay in them. She was never seen on the plantation herself; but appointed a rendezvous for her company eight or ten miles distant, so that if they were discovered at the first start she was not compromised. She started on Saturday night; the slaves at that time being allowed to go away from home to visit their friends,—so that they would not be missed until Monday morning. Even then they were supposed to have loitered on the way, and it would often be late on Monday afternoon before the flight would be certainly known. If by any further delay the advertisement was not sent out before Tuesday morning, she felt secure of keeping ahead of it; but if it were, it required all her ingenuity to escape. She resorted to various devices, she had confidential friends all along the road. She would hire a man to follow the one who put up the notices, and take them down as soon as his back was turned. She crossed creeks on railroad bridges by night, she hid her company in the woods while she herself not being advertised went into the towns in search of information. If met on the road, her face was always to the south, and she was always a very respectable looking darkey, not at all a poor fugitive. She would get into the cars near her pursuers, and manage to hear their plans. By day they lay in the woods; then she pulled out her patchwork, and sewed together little bits, perhaps not more than inch square, which were afterwards made into comforters for the fugitives in Canada.

The expedition was governed by the strictest rules. If any man gave out, he must be shot. "Would you really do that?" she was asked. "Yes," she replied, "if he was weak enough to give out, he'd be weak enough to betray us all, and all who had helped us; and do you think I'd let so many die just for one coward man." "Did you ever have to shoot any one" was asked. "One time," she said, "a man gave out the second night; his feet were sore and swollen, he couldn't go any further; he'd rather go back and die, if he must." They tried all arguments in vain, bathed his feet, tried to strengthen him, but it was of no use, he would go back. Then she said, "I told the boys to get their guns ready, and shoot him. They'd have done it in a minute; but when he heard that, he jumped right up and went on as well as anybody." She can tell the time by the stars, and find her way by natural signs as well as any hunter; and yet she scarcely knows of the existence of England or any other foreign country.

When going on these journeys she often lay alone in the forests all night. Her whole soul was filled with awe of the mysterious Unseen Presence, which thrilled her with such depths of emotion, that all other care and fear vanished. Then she seemed to speak with her Maker "as a man talketh with his friend;" her childlike petitions had direct answers, and beautiful visions lifted her up above all doubt and anxiety into serene trust and faith. No man can be a hero without this faith in some form; the sense that he walks not in his own strength, but leaning on an almighty arm. Call it fate, destiny, what you will, Moses of old, Moses of to-day, believed it to be Almighty God.

She loves to describe her visions, which are very real to her; but she must tell them word for word as they lie in her untutored mind, with endless repetitions and details; she cannot shorten or condense them, whatever be your haste. She has great dramatic power; the scene rises before you as she saw it, and her voice and language change with her different actors. Often these visions came to her in the midst of her work. She once said, "We'd been carting manure all day, and t'other girl and I were gwine home on the sides of the cart, and another boy was driving, when suddenly I heard such music as filled all the air;" and, she saw a vision which she described in language which sounded like the old prophets in its grand flow; interrupted now and then by what t'other girl said, by Massa's coming and calling her to wake up, and her protests that she wasn't asleep.

One of her most characteristic prayers was when on board a steamboat with a party of fugitives. The clerk of the boat declined to give her tickets, and told her to wait. She thought he suspected her, and was at a loss how to save herself and her charge, if he did; so she went alone into the bow of the boat, and she says, "I drew in my breath, and I sent it out to the Lord, and I said, O Lord! you know who I am, and whar I am, and what I want; and that was all I could say; and again I drew in my breath and I sent it out to the Lord, but that was all I could say; and then again the third time, and just then I felt a touch on my shoulder, and looked round, and the clerk said, 'Here's your tickets.'"

Her efforts were not confined to the escape of slaves. She conducted them to Canada, watched over their welfare, collected clothing, organized them into societies, and was always occupied with plans for their benefit. She first came to Boston in the spring of 1859, to ask aid of the friends of her race to build a house for her aged father and mother. She brought recommendations from Gerrit Smith, and at once won many friends who aided her to accomplish her purpose. Her parents are now settled in Auburn, and all that Harriet seems to desire in reward for her labors is the privilege of making their old age comfortable. She has a very affectionate nature, and forms the strongest personal attachments. She has great simplicity of character; she states her wants very freely, and believes you are ready to help her; but if you have nothing to give, or have given to another, she is content. She is not sensitive to indignities to her color- in her own person; but knows and claims her rights. She will eat at your table if she sees you really desire it; but she goes as willingly to the kitchen. She is very abstemious in her diet, fruit being the only luxury she cares for. Her personal appearance is very peculiar. She is thoroughly negro, and very plain. She has needed disguise so often, that she seems to have command over her face, and can banish all expression from her features, and look so stupid that nobody would suspect her of knowing enough to be dangerous; but her eye flashes with intelligence and power when she is roused. She has the rich humor and the keen sense of beauty which belong to her race. She would like to dress handsomely. Once an old silk dress was given her among a bundle of clothes, and she was in great delight. "Glory!" she exclaimed; "didn't I say when I sold my silk gown to get money to go after my mother, that I'd have another someday?" She is never left in a room with pictures or statuary that she does not examine them and ask with interest about them.

I wish it were possible to give some of her racy stories; but no report would do them justice. She gives a most vivid description of the rescue of a slave in Troy. She fought and struggled so that her clothes were torn off her; but she was successful at last. Throughout all she shouted out her favorite motto, "Give me liberty or give me death," to which the popular heart never fails to respond. When she was triumphantly bearing the man off, a little boy called out, "Go it, old aunty! You're the best old aunty the fellow ever had." She is perfectly at home in such scenes; she loves action; I think she does not dislike fighting in a good cause; but she loves work too, and scorns none that offers.

She said once, just before the war, when slavery was the one theme agitating the country—"they say the negro has no rights a white man is bound to respect; but it seems to me they send men to Congress, and pay them eight dollars a day, for nothing else but to talk about the negro."

She says, "the blood of her race has called for justice in vain, and now our sons and brothers must be taken from our hearts and homes to bring the call for justice home to our hearts." She described a storm; "but the thunder's from the cannon's mouth, and the drops that fall are drops of blood."

She was deeply interested in John Brown; and it is said, that she was fully acquainted with his plans, and approved them. On the day when his companions were executed, she came to my room finding me occupied, she said, "I am not going to sit down, I only want you to give me an address;" but her heart was too full, she must talk. "I've been studying and studying upon it," she said, "and its clar to me, it wasn't John Brown that died on that gallows. When I think how he gave up his life for our people, and how he never flinched, but was so brave to the end; its clar to me it wasn't mortal man, it was God in him. When

I think of all the groans and tears and prayers I've heard on the plantations, and remember that God is a prayer-hearing God, I feel that his time is drawing near." Then you think, I said, that God's time is near. "God's time is always near," she said; "He gave me my strength, and he set the North star in the heavens; he meant I should be free." She went on in a strain of the most sublime eloquence I ever heard; but I cannot repeat it. Oh how sanguine and visionary it seemed then! but now four little years, and Maryland is free by her own act, and the bells are ringing out the declaration, that slavery is abolished throughout the land; and our Moses may walk, no longer wrapped in darkness, but erect and proud in her native State; and the name of him who was hung on the gallows is a rallying cry for victorious armies; and the stone which the builders rejected has become the head of the corner. What shall we fear whose eyes have seen this salvation?

When the war broke out Harriet was very anxious to go to South Carolina to assist the contrabands. The only condition she made was, that her old parents should be kept from want. It was wonderful to see with what shrewd economy she had planned all their household arrangements. She concluded that thirty dollars would keep them comfortable through the winter. She went to Port Royal, and was employed by Gen. Hunter, in scouting service, and accompanied Col. Montgomery in his expedition up the Combahee river. She was afterwards engaged by Gen. Saxton, to take a number of freed women under her charge, and teach them to do the soldiers' washing. She has also been making herb medicine for the soldiers, which she gives away gratuitously, feeling it to be impossible to receive money from sick soldiers; and she has made cakes and pies for sale, in the intervals of other work.

She has had no regular support from Government; and she feels that she must have some certain income, which she wishes to apply to her parents' support. This society consider her labors too valuable to the freedmen to be turned elsewhere, and have therefore taken her into their service, paying her the small salary of ten dollars per month that she asks for. She is not adopted by any branch as she could not fulfill the condition of correspondence with them. She says, when the war is over she will learn to read and write, and then will write her own life. The trouble in her head prevents her from applying closely to a book. It is the strong desire of all her friends that she should tell her story in her own way at some future time. We think it affords a very cogent answer to the query, "Can the negro take care of himself?"

Note: Some of the statements in this sketch are taken from a notice of Harriet Tubman in *The Commonwealth* of 17 July 1863.

\* \* \*

*Charles P. Wood,* Manuscript History Concerning the Pension Claim of Harriet Tubman, *in HR 55A-D1 Papers Accompanying the Claim of Harriet Tubman (Washington, D.C.: National Archives, 1868).*

Harriet Tubman was sent to Hilton Head—she says—in May 1862, at the suggestion of Gov. Andrew, with the idea that she would be a valuable person to operate within the enemies' lines—in procuring information & scouts. She was forwarded by Col. Frank Howe—the Mass. state agent in New York, by the Gov't transport Atlantic—as sent up to Beaufort, attached to the HQrs of Gen'l Stevens—and rendered much, and very valuable service acting as a spy within the enemies' lines—and obtaining the services of the most valued Scouts and Pilots in the Gov't employ in that Department. Among the original papers in Harriet's possession—is a list of the names of the Scouts and Pilots:

"Isaac Hayward" "Mott Blake"
"Gabriel Cahern" "Sandy Sellus"
"Geo Chisholm" "Solomon Gregory"
"Peter Burns"

Pilots who know the channels of the River in this vicinity, and who acted as such for Col. Montgomery up the Combahee river:

"Chas Simmons"

"Saml Hayward"

Endorsed

R. Saxton, Brig. Gen'l

Unconscious of the great value of the official documents she had from the several officers at different times, Harriet has lost some of them—and the first documentary proof we have of her service in the Department of the South is a pass issued by Gen 'l Hunter—a copy of which is hereto appended:

FROM GENERAL HUNTER
Headq'rs Dep't of the South,
Hilton Head, Port Royal, S.C.
Feb. 19, 1863.

Pass the bearer, Harriet Tubman, to Beaufort, and back to this place, and wherever she wishes to go, and give her free passage at all times on all Government transports. Harriet was sent to me from Boston, by Gov. Andrew, of Mass., and is a valuable woman. She has permission, as a warrant of the Government, to purchase such provisions from the commissary as she may need.

D. HUNTER
Maj. Gen. Com 'g.
H. Q. Dep't of the South,
July 1, 1863.

Continued in force.
Q. A. GILLMORE,
Brig. Gen'l Com'g.

On July 6, 1863 Col. Montgomery wrote as follows:
"HdQrs Col Brigade
St. Helena Island
July 6, 1863

"Brig Genl Gilmore
Com'd'g Dept of the South
General : I wish to commend to your attention Mrs. Harriet Tubman, a most remarkable woman, and valuable as a scout. I have been acquainted with her character and actions for several years.

Walter D. Plowden is a man of tried courage and can be made highly useful.
I am, General
your most obt servt"
Signed "James Montgomery"
Col Com'd'g Beaufort
On the back is endorsed
"I approve of Col. Montgomery's estimate of the value of Harriet Tubman's services."
Signed R. Saxton
Brig Genl.

From the annexed of an original paper in Harriet's possession we find that she was still rendering valuable services at Beaufort, where she remained until the month of January or Feb 'y 1865.

FROM SURGEON DURRANT

I certify that I have been acquainted with Harriet Tubman for nearly two years, and my position as Medical officer in charge of "contrabands" in this town, and in hospital, has given me frequent and ample opportunity to observe her general deportment, particularly her kindness and attention to the sick and suffering of her own race. I take much pleasure in testifying hereby to the esteem in which she is generally held.

HENRY R. DURRANT,
Act. Ass't Surgeon U.S.A.
In charge "Contraband" Hosp'l.
Dated at Beaufort, S.C.,
this 3d day of May, 1864.
I concur fully in the above.
R. SAXTON, Brig. Gen.

When she came North on leave of absence to see her aged parents residing in this City—she was taken, sick and so failed to return to New York City within the time specified in her leave, and for that reason was refused return transportation to Hilton Head. To remedy this difficulty she went to Washington and on representing her case at the War Dep't she was promptly furnished with the following:

"Pass Mrs. Harriet Tubman (colored) to Hilton Head and Charlestown, S.C., with free transportation on a Gov't transport.
By order of Sec't of War<br>Signed Louise H. Pelonge<br>Asstś Agt. Gen'l.

To Bvt. Brig. General Van Vliet,
U.S.Q.M., N.Y."
Dated Washington, March 20, 1865.

Returning with the intention of embarking at New York - she was intercepted in Philadelphia by some members of the Sanitary Commission who persuaded her to go instead to the James River Hospitals—where there was pressing need of such service as she could give in the Gov't Hospitals. And relinquishing her plan of returning to the Dept. of the South—without a thought as to the unfortunate pecuniary result of this irregular proceeding she went to the Hospitals of the James River, and at Fortress Monroe or Hampton—where she remained until July 1865. In that month she went to Washington again to advise the Gov't of some dreadful abuses existing in one or more of the Hospitals there. And so great was the confidence of some officers of the Gov't in her that Surgeon Gen'l Barnes directed that she be appointed "Nurse or Matron" as appears by the following copy of an original paper in her possession.

"I have the honor to inform you that the Medical Director Dept. of Virginia, has been instructed to appoint Harriet Tubman Nurse or Matron at the Colored Hospital, Fort Monroe, Va.
Very Resp'y<br>Signed Your obt. servant<br>V. K. Barnes<br>Surgeon General"

To Hon. W. H. Seward
Sec. of State
Washington

and with the following pass she returned to Fortress Monroe:

"No. 663 War Department
Washington, D.C.
July 22, 1865

Permit Harriet Tubman to proceed to Fortress Monroe, Va., on Government transport free of cost.
By order of the Secretary of War<br>Signed L. H. Pelonge<br>Asst. Adj. Gen."

It does not appear that she rec'd the appointment above indicated, and soon after this date she returned to Washington - and thence home - to devote herself since the country's need had ceased to her aged Father & Mother who still survive at a very advanced age entirely dependent on her.

During the service of more than three years, Harriet states that she received from the Gov't only two hundred dollars ($200) of pay. This was paid her at or near Beaufort, and with characteristic indifference to self—she immediately devoted that sum to the erection of a wash-house, in which she spent a portion of her time in teaching the freed women to do washing—to aid in supporting themselves instead of depending wholly on Gov't aid. During her absence with an important expedition in Florida this wash-house was destroyed or appropriated by a Reg't of troops fresh from the north to make shelter for themselves but without any compensation whatever to Harriet. When she first went to Beaufort she was allowed to draw rations as an officer or soldier, but the freed people becoming jealous of this privilege accorded her—she voluntarily relinquished this right and thereafter supplied her personal wants by selling pies and root beer—which she made during the evenings and nights—when not engaged in important service for the Gov't.

The value and extent of Harriet's services to the Government seems to be sufficiently attested by the papers—copies of which are herewith, and originals now in her possession. But General Saxton certifies more explicitly under later date as follows:

"Dear Madam:

I have just rec'd your letter in regard to Harriet Tubman. I can bear witness to the value of her services rendered in the Union Army during the late war in South Carolina and Florida. She was employed in the Hospitals and as a spy. She made many a raid inside the enemy's lines displaying remarkable courage, zeal and fidelity.

She was employed by Gen'l Hunter and I think by Generals Stevens and Sherman - and is as deserving of a pension from the Government for her services as any other of its faithful servants.

Very truly yours,
Signed Rufus Saxton
Bvt. Brig. General

To Mrs. Mary Derby
Auburn, N. Y."

When in Washington in July 1865 Harriet was in need of money, and applied to Mr. Sec. Seward to present her claim to the proper Department. General Hunter being then in Washington, Mr. Seward referred the matter to him in a note, of which the annexed is a copy:

"Letter from Sec'y Seward
Washington, July 25, 1865

Major Gen'l Hunter—My Dear Sir:

Harriet Tubman, a colored woman, has been nursing our soldiers during nearly all the war. She believes she has claims for faithful services to the command in South Carolina, with which you are connected, and she thinks that you would be disposed to see her claim justly settled. I have known her long as a noble, high spirit, as true as seldom dwells in the human form. I commend her therefore to your kind attention. Faithfully your friend, WM. H. Seward Major Gen. Hunter"

But no pay whatever was obtained—and another attempt has been made since—I believe with the same result.

This letter of Mr. Seward shows the estimate of Harriet Tubman by all who know her—she is known throughout this State and New England as an honest, earnest and most self-sacrificing woman. The substance of this statement has been obtained from her lips and in making it up I have before me the original papers in her possession, which are copied.

That Harriet is entitled to several thousands of dollars pay—there can be no shadow of doubt—the only difficulty seems to be in the facts that she held no commission, and had not in the regular way and at the proper times and places, made proof and application of and for, her just compensation. On such certificates as she holds she should have it without further delay.

Charles P. Wood
Auburn, June 1st, 1868

\* \* \*

*Sydney Howard Gay's interview with Harriet Tubman, 14 May 1856.* Record of Fugitives 1855–1856. *In Sydney Howard Gay Papers, 1743–1931, edited by Columbia University: Rare Book and Manuscript Library. (Author's notes in brackets.)*

May 14th. A party of four arrived from Phila It was headed by Captain Harriett Tubman, the subordinates being Ben. Jackson & Jas. Coleman who belonged to Henry Wright [Isaac Henry Wright] of Dorchester Co. Md. Wm. A. Connoway [aka Cook]. Laban Hudson [Levin Hodson], master, & Henry Hopkins, John Houston master, of the same neighborhood. They are all young men, of an aggregate market value probably of $6000.

Harriett Tubman seven years ago was the slave of Edward Brodhurst [**Edward Brodess**] of Bucktown, Md. Her master dying, & the estate to be settled, & two of her sisters having been sold into a chain-gang, she determined to run away. She did so, & made her way to Canada. In a few months, however, she concluded to return, she went back, & sought concealment-in [p. 55] the house of a friend who had first advised her escape. She made her arrival known to her friends, & her purpose, which was "to lead them out- of Egypt." She had four brothers, & two sisters & their children, then slaves, to her old mistress. She could only accomplish the release of one child, who was seven years old, & whom she hired a man to carry. She took this to Canada. After again earning money at service, the following year she returned a second time for this child's mother. This woman, from a dread of being sold, had run away from her mistress, & for eighteen months had been in concealment, occasionally with a friend, once anchored off in a boat, in the river, for a day or two, but nearly the whole time in the woods. Harriett got messages to her, & hired a man, the necessary arrangements being made, to take her in a boat from Cambridge to Baltimore. There Harriett joined her, & they were obliged to remain there for several weeks, during the sister's confinement & recovery. When the child was 5 weeks old, she induced a free coloured man to take her to Phil<u>a</u>, as his brother's wife, who was known to be free, a friendly white man who did not know that she was not the brother's [p. 56] wife having given the necessary bonds. Harriett went on the day before & took the sister & child to Canada to the child she had rescued before. There the husband & father, who was free, soon after joined them. [This is probably the story of the rescue of **Kessiah Jolly Bowley** and her two children, **James Alfred** and baby Araminta, with the help of Kessiah's free husband, **John Bowley**, circa December 1850.]

The spring following she returned a third time. Her four brothers had been fugitives all winter, in the woods, to escape the dreaded "chain gang". The three eldest, however, had "come in" at the solicitation of a lumber-man, to whom their services were important, & who had hired them before, & who had agreed to hire them again for one year, thus securing them from being sold before the next Christmas. The youngest, however, was not included in this arrangement, & remained in the woods, tho' badly frost-bitten. Harriett, from her own place of concealment, entered into communication with him & brot. him off [probably Tubman's youngest brother, **Moses Ross**].

At "Camp Meeting time," the following summer, she again went back, & went, as before, into concealment. She had interviews with the three brothers, but they all refused to leave the man who had been so kind to them, & at his own risk of loss by hiring their time put off the day [p. 57] of sale. To leave him then would have been a loss to him of the wages of their unexpired service. She did not, however, come away empty-handed but brot. off a young man in the neighborhood, who hearing of her proposed to escape with her. At Christmas she returned again for her brothers. Their term of service with the lumberman had expired. At Christmas they were to have been sold. On Christmas eve. 1854, she & they left for Canada, where they soon after arrived safely.

XXXXXXX There still remained behind one sister & her two children, & the old father of the family, who, however, being free, can leave when he pleases, but will not so long as any of his children remain in bondage in Md. Harriett's errand, at this time, was to bring off her sister & the two children. [This is her sister **Rachel Ross** and Rachel's two children Ben and Angerine; Rachel died in 1859.] She found it, however, impracticable. But the attempt is only postponed, not abandoned. Still her mission this time is not without good fruit. The mother of the young man whom she took away, in a former visit, when she was unsuccessful in getting her brothers, informed the four young [p. 58] men who are with her today, that she had come back. They made the necessary arrangements & a fortnight ago, on Saturday, the five started, Harriett leading the company. They traveled by night, & on foot to New Castle, Del. On the way or there, they learned that the hue & cry was after them. Along the Railway, at all the stations, & at rail-side taverns bills were posted, describing the four men, & offering a reward of $1200 for their capture. But for Harriett they would, without doubt, have been taken. She led them safely to New Castle. There she took them to the house of a colored woman, & for one week they lay concealed there in a potatoe-hole. Braving detection for herself, she went backward & forward between New Castle & Wilmington, on the cars to get friends to carry her company further. The risk was manifestly too great, & they had to remain quiet. When she had no longer 20c to pay her passage she walked, & at last a friend consented to go for them. They were sent to Wilmington, at night, & then to Pa. at last here.

Harriett is, by profession, a cook, & when at service earns from $15 @ $16 pr. month. She has lived in N.Y. & Phil<u>a</u>, & would have remained in one or [p. 59] the other place now, only that feeling bound to get her sister & her children "next Camp Meeting Time," & thinking it may cost a good deal, she wishes to be with her brothers to secure them pecuniary aid when the time comes for her to start again.

Sent them all to Syracuse (food) [$]21

# Appendix E

## Underground Railroad Myths

The history and interpretation of the Underground Railroad—the movement and networks devoted to assisting enslaved people escape bondage—long suffered from a lack of scholarly attention until the twenty-first century. Insufficient attention to historical sources during the late nineteenth century and throughout the twentieth century fostered and enabled the proliferation of myths, misinterpretations, and misconceptions. Using long-neglected sources, modern-day scholars have been uncovering and interpreting previously ignored or discounted historical records, including thousands of well-documented slave narratives and primary historical sources. This work has highlighted the names of freedom seekers, the places they fled from and where they settled, the people who gave them aid, and the methods they employed, as well as the names of those who tried to thwart the efforts to achieve freedom.

The myths, or substitutes for actual history, are often a mixture of fact, folklore, speculation, and creative fakelore. The secrecy that helped to protect the workings of the Underground Railroad proved to be fertile ground to seed these unsubstantiated stories. The myths are sometimes deliberate fabrications, while others are merely fanciful substitutes for unknown or as-yet-unresearched and documented histories. For instance, historians frequently encounter sites cherished by local communities because of their purported ties to the Underground Railroad but often have little to no connection to that powerful movement. Claims sometimes rest on vague oral traditions alleging the existence of once-functioning underground tunnels emanating from the structure to some distant place but which are now gone. Attic rooms, root cellars, old cisterns, and unspecified structural anomalies are often stand-ins for Underground Railroad documentation. Sometimes these claims include homes or structures that were built after the Civil War and the Underground Railroad was no longer functioning. These myths, among others, are often the result of good-intentioned but misguided efforts to reimagine people, events, and landscapes, and link them to a positive history. Ultimately, myths deter dedicated research documenting accurate and truthful histories of Underground Railroad sites. For myths associated with Harriet Tubman, see appendix F.

The most well-known and persistent myths include the following.

### THE QUILT CODE

*Myth:* A series of quilt patterns and designs created and used to convey directions and other instructions to freedom seekers along the Underground Railroad during the antebellum period.

*Fact:* The Quilt Code is a late-twentieth-century story first reported in the 1999 book *Hidden in Plain View*. The book is based exclusively on the claims of one woman, Ozella Daniels, a quilt maker who sold her quilts to tourists in a Charleston, South Carolina, market in the

1990s. She claimed that intricate quilt patterns created by free and enslaved African Americans before the Civil War secretly incorporated maps to freedom. According to Daniels, the intricate quilts were hung outside at night for freedom seekers to find and read. By counting the knots and stitches, which represented the number of miles, or longitude and latitude, of an escape route, self-liberators could decipher directions that mapped out a path to freedom. Daniels claimed the code involved a dozen different quilt block designs, which also included other secret instructions. No such quilts are known to exist, nor has any reference to them been found in the thousands of documented histories of the Underground Railroad and testimonies of freedom seekers and formerly enslaved people. The majority of the quilt patterns promoted by Daniels were post–Civil War designs and therefore were unknown to early to mid-nineteenth-century quilters. Historians and antique quilt experts have debunked the story.

## "FOLLOW THE DRINKING GOURD" SONG

*Myth:* A coded song with instructions to freedom seekers on navigating from the south to freedom in northern states.

*Fact:* The song was first published in 1928 in the Texas Folklore Society Bulletin by H. B. Parks, a botanist, who claimed its words secretly guided freedom seekers to the North. The song describes a journey from Mobile, Alabama, to the Ohio River and freedom. Parks asserted that "drinking gourd" was code for Ursa Major, also known as the Big Dipper, the constellation that points to Polaris, or the North Star. Traditionally, a drinking gourd was a hollowed out and dried squash used to cup water or other liquids. The vessels have been found in cultures throughout the world for thousands of years. None of those cultures identify Ursa Major as a drinking gourd. Parks claimed to have heard the song performed by three different elderly African Americans in North Carolina, Kentucky, and Texas between 1912 and 1918. Despite having no musical training nor expertise in history or folklore, Parks determined that the song was a code for the Underground Railroad. The words of the song, however, are very specific about navigating north along the Tombigbee River in Alabama to Ohio and therefore would not have had any relevance to freedom seekers in other Southern states. Moreover, enslaved people escaping from Alabama generally fled south to Mexico and Central America, not north. Alabama folklorists never documented the song. Twenty-five years after Parks published the song, folk singer Lee Hayes rewrote the words and music. In 1951, it became an American hit folk tune, and by the 1960s, it had become a standard song of the American civil rights movement. The song remains popular in the twenty-first century. For more information about the cultural and historical origins of the song, see http://www.followthedrinkinggourd.org/.

## AFRICAN AMERICAN JOCKEY OR GROOMSMAN STATUE

*Myth:* An ornamental iron sculpture used to identify a safe house on the Underground Railroad.

*Fact:* Colloquially known as a "lawn jockey," these statues became popular in the United States during the early to mid-twentieth century. First manufactured for the Southern residential market after the Civil War, the statue depicts a Black figure dressed as a jockey or groomsman, with an outstretched hand. Variations include the figure holding a lantern. The groomsman was a position previously held by enslaved men and boys on the plantations and properties of wealthy white people. The first mention of the statue's use on the Underground Railroad is by Wilbur Siebert, in his 1951 book *The Mysteries of Ohio's Underground Railroads*. Siebert's book includes a picture of the statue used by the descendant family of 19th-century federal judge Benjamin Piatt of Logan County, Ohio. The statue, Siebert was told, was used to signal freedom seekers approaching their home for help during the 1850s. The jockey figure, however, is a model manufactured well after the end of the Civil War and therefore could not have been used as an Underground Railroad signal. Siebert, a professor of European history at Ohio State University, was renowned for his first book, *The Underground Railroad in Slavery and Freedom*, published more than fifty years earlier in 1898. Using correspondence and interviews he conducted with former abolitionists, Underground Railroad activists, and freedom seekers, as well as multiple primary sources, Siebert collected a large database of firsthand testimonies authenticating Underground Railroad activities east of the Mississippi during the 1880s and 1890s. Siebert's original research documented the Piatt family as proslavery zealots who colluded with slave catchers to capture freedom seekers during the 1850s. It is unclear why Siebert eschewed those primary sources in favor of the statue story as told to him by an unidentified member of the Piatt family living in the house a century later.

## "WADE IN THE WATER" SONG

*Myth:* An African American spiritual used to tell people to wade in water while escaping slavery so that hunting dogs would lose traces of their scent.

*Fact:* The gospel song, written by an unknown composer, was sung during musical performances featuring the Fiske University Jubilee Singers starting in 1871. The group performed traditional Christian spirituals, African American vernacular music, popular antebellum and post–Civil War tunes, and original compositions. "Wade in the Water" was not originally associated with the Underground Railroad and was not widely popular until the 1920s. By the mid-twentieth century, it had been reinterpreted and featured as a song of freedom during the American civil rights movement. Other songs, for example, "Swing Low, Sweet Chariot," composed by an African American Cherokee man after the Civil War, were popularized by the Jubilee Singers and much later linked to the Underground Railroad. No evidence has been uncovered to corroborate these claims. Harriet Tubman did, however, use songs to relay information. See the entries for the Methodist spirituals "Bound for the Promised Land" and "Hail, Oh Hail Ye Happy Spirits."

## UNDERGROUND TUNNELS

*Myth:* Networks of tunnels, both short and long, built and maintained underneath homes, yards, roads, cemeteries, and other structures, and used to secretly move freedom seekers from one place to another without being seen.

*Fact:* Claims of underground tunnels emerged during the early to mid-twentieth century, long after the Civil War. There is only one documented underground tunnel associated with an Underground Railroad stop. The Milton House, a former stagecoach inn and tavern in Milton, Wisconsin, features a tunnel leading from the basement of the tavern to the property owner's personal cabin a few feet behind the inn. It was used specifically for the convenience of the innkeeper, Joseph Goodrich, a known abolitionist, and pressed into service in support of freedom seekers during the 1840s and 1850s.

# Appendix F

## Myths about Harriet Tubman

*Myth:* Harriet Tubman rescued 300 people in 19 trips.

*Fact:* According to Harriet Tubman's own words, in combination with extensive documentation on her Underground Railroad missions, she rescued about seventy people—family and friends—in approximately thirteen trips to Maryland. During public and private meetings in 1858 and 1859, Tubman repeatedly told people that she had rescued fifty to sixty people in approximately eight or nine trips. This was before her last mission, in December 1860, when she brought away seven people. Sarah Bradford exaggerated the numbers in her 1868 biography *Scenes in the Life of Harriet Tubman*. Bradford never claimed that Tubman told her the higher numbers; rather, Bradford estimated them based on conversations with unidentified individuals. Other people close to Tubman, including Franklin Sanborn, specifically contradicted those numbers. In addition to the family and friends, Tubman also gave instructions to another seventy or so freedom seekers from the Eastern Shore who found their way to freedom on their own.

*Myth:* Harriet Tubman was born in about 1820 in Bucktown, Dorchester County, Maryland, on the farm of Edward Brodess.

*Fact:* According to primary documents, Tubman was born in late February or early March 1822 on the plantation of Brodess's stepfather, Anthony Thompson, located in Peter's Neck in Dorchester County, Maryland. Brodess removed Tubman, her mother, and siblings to Bucktown sometime after 1824.

*Myth:* Harriet Tubman had a $40,000 "dead or alive" bounty for her capture.

*Fact:* The only reward for Tubman's capture is in the 3 October 1849 advertisement for the return of "Minty" and her brothers "Ben" and "Harry," in which their mistress, Eliza Brodess, offered $100 for each of them if caught outside of Maryland. Slaveholders on the Eastern Shore of Maryland had no idea it was Harriet Tubman (or Minty Ross, as they knew her) who was helping and inspiring people to run away. The $40,000 bounty figure was made up by Sallie Holley, a former antislavery activist in New York, who wrote a letter to a newspaper in 1867, arguing for support for Tubman in her pursuit of back pay and pension from the Union Army. In the 1868 biography *Scenes in the Life of Harriet Tubman*, Sarah Bradford claimed the reward was $12,000. When Bradford published the second edition, *Harriet, the Moses of Her People*, in 1886, she claimed the reward was $40,000. To put this in perspective, the U.S. government offered $50,000 for the capture of John Wilkes Booth, who murdered President Lincoln in 1865. The sum of $40,000 is equivalent to several million dollars in U.S. dollars today, and for that amount every newspaper in the nation would have posted the advertisement and Tubman would have been captured.

*Myth:* Harriet Tubman rescued people from throughout the South.

*Fact:* Tubman returned only to Maryland to bring away loved ones—family and friends she loved and trusted. It was too dangerous for her to go places where she was unfamiliar with the people and the landscape.

*Myth:* Harriet Tubman used the quilt code to follow the Underground Railroad.

*Fact:* Harriet Tubman never used the quilt code because the quilt code is a late twentieth-century myth. Tubman used various methods and paths to escape slavery and then go back and rescue others. She relied on trustworthy people, Black and white, who hid her, told her which way to go, and informed her of who she could trust. She used disguises; she walked and rode horses and wagons; she sailed on boats; and she rode on trains. She used songs to relay information, including the Methodist spirituals "Bound for the Promised Land" and "Hail, Oh Hail Ye Happy Spirits." She sent letters, written for her by someone else, to trusted individuals like Jacob Jackson, and she used direct communication with people. She bribed people. She followed rivers that snaked northward. She used the stars and other natural phenomenon to lead her north. She also trusted her instincts and faith to guide and comfort her in difficult and unfamiliar territory and times.

*Myth:* Harriet Tubman carried a rifle on the Underground Railroad.

*Fact:* Harriet Tubman carried a small pistol with her on her rescue missions, mostly for protection from slave catchers, but also to prevent frightened freedom seekers from turning back and risking the safety of the rest of the group. Tubman carried a specialized sharpshooters rifle during the Civil War.

*Myth:* Harriet Tubman sang "Swing Low, Sweet Chariot," "Wade in the Water," and "Follow the Drinking Gourd" as signals on the Underground Railroad.

*Fact:* Tubman told interviewers she sang two Methodist spirituals during her rescue missions. Both are listed in Sarah Bradford's biography *Scenes in the Life of Harriet Tubman*—"Bound for the Promised Land" and "Hail, Oh Hail Ye Happy Spirits" (also known as "Go Down Moses"). Tubman said she changed the tempo of the songs and some of the words to indicate whether it was safe to come out of hiding. "Follow the Drinking Gourd" became popular in 1951, and it was rewritten and performed by Lee Hayes and the Weavers, a white folk group. "Swing Low, Sweet Chariot" and "Wade in the Water" became popular after the Civil War. *See* appendix E.

# Bibliography

"20 Dollars Reward." *Cambridge Chronicle*, 24 June 1827.

"$1000 Reward." *Cambridge Democrat*, 22 May 1852.

Abrahams, Roger D. *Singing the Master: The Emergence of African American Culture in the Plantation South*. New York: Penguin, 1992.

Adams, George Worthington. *Doctors in Blue: The Medical History of the Union Army in the Civil War*. Baton Rouge: Louisiana State University Press, 1996.

Adams, Samuel Hopkins. *Grandfather Stories*. New York: Random House, 1947.

"[Advertisement]." *Cambridge Chronicle*, 9 January 1836.

Andrew, John Albion. *John A. Andrew Papers, 1772–1895*. Boston: Massachusetts Historical Society, 1982.

Anne Arundel County Court. "Land Records." Anne Arundel County Court Records, 1653–1851, Maryland State Archives, Annapolis.

"At Church of Zion. Body of Harriet Tubman Davis Will Lie in State." *Auburn Citizen*, 12 March 1913.

"Aunt Harriet Was Very Old." *Auburn Daily Advertiser*, 12 March 1913.

"Aunt Harriet's Funeral." *Auburn Daily Advertiser*, 13 March 1913.

Bailie, Helen Tufts. "Helen Tufts Bailie Journal, 1886–1936." Helen Tufts Bailie Papers, Sophia Smith Collection, Smith College, Northampton, Massachusetts.

Bancroft, Frederick. *Slave Trading in the Old South*. Columbia: University of South Carolina Press, 1996.

Bangs, Nathan. *The Life of the Rev. Freeborn Garrettson: Compiled from His Printed and Manuscript Journals, and Other Authentic Documents*, 4th ed. New York: T. Mason and G. Lane, 1838.

Baptist, Edward E. *The Half Has Never Benn Told: Slavery and the Making of American Capitalism*. New York: Basic Books, 2014.

"Bazel's Chapel (Bazel's Methodist Episcopal Church), D-274." Maryland Inventory of Historic Properties (MIHP). Crownsville: Maryland Historical Trust, 2005.

Beckert, Sven. *Empire of Cotton: A Global History*. New York: Alfred A. Knopf, 2014.

Bent, Robert. "Research Correspondence." South Portland, ME: Spring Point Museum, 1998.

Berlin, Ira. *Generations of Captivity: A History of African American Slaves*. Cambridge, MA: Belknap Press of Harvard University Press, 2004.

Berlin, Ira, et al., eds. *Freedom: A Documentary History of Emancipation, 1861–1867, Series I, Vol. 1, The Destruction of Slavery*. Cambridge: Cambridge University Press, 1985.

Bernier, Celeste-Marie, Andrew Taylor, and Frederick Douglass. *If I Survive: Frederick Douglass and Family in the Walter O. Evans Collection: A 200-Year Anniversary*. Edinburgh: Edinburgh University Press, 2018.

Berry, Daina Ramey, and Leslie M. Harris. *Sexuality and Slavery: Reclaiming Intimate Histories in the Americas*. Athens: University of Georgia Press, 2018.

Bethune, Mary McLeod. "Letter, Mary Mcleod Bethune to Mrs. Caroll Johnson, May 4,

1844." Bryant Family Scrapbook, private collection, Auburn, New York.

Bill of Complaint, Original Equity Papers, Case 249 [1853]. "Gourney C. Pattison, William Pattison, and Others vs. Eliza Brodess, Eliza Brodess, and John Mills, Administrators of Edward Brodess and Thomas Willis." Dorchester County Circuit Court (Equity Papers), Maryland State Archives, Annapolis.

"Bills Menace Historic Church." *Syracuse Post Standard*, 28 January 1982.

Blassingame, John W. *The Slave Community: Plantation Life in the Antebellum South*, 2nd ed. New York: Oxford University Press, 1979.

———, ed. *Slave Testimony: Two Centuries of Letters, Speeches, Interviews, and Autobiographies*. Baton Rouge: Louisiana State University Press, 1977.

Blight, David W. *Race and Reunion: The Civil War in American Memory*. Cambridge, MA: Harvard University Press, 2001.

Blockson, Charles L. *The Underground Railroad: Dramatic Firsthand Accounts of Daring Escapes to Freedom*. New York: Berkley Books, 1987.

Blondo, Richard Albert. "In Search of Samuel Green." *Archivists' Bulldog*, 30 April 1990.

———. *Samuel Green: A Black Life in Antebellum Maryland*. Master's thesis, University of Maryland, 1988.

Bolster, W. Jeffrey. *Black Jacks: African American Seaman in the Age of Sail*. Cambridge, MA: Harvard University Press, 1997.

Bourne, Michael O., and Christopher Weeks. *Between the Nanticoke and the Choptank: An Architectural History of Dorchester County, Maryland*. Baltimore, MD: Johns Hopkins University Press, 1984.

Bowditch, T. Edward. *Mission from Cape Coast Castle to Ashantee, with a Statistical Account of That Kingdom, and Geographical Notices of Other Parts of the Interior of Africa*. London: J. Murray, 1819.

"[Bowers]." *Easton Gazette*, 3 July 1858.

Bowley, Harkless. "Harkless Bowley Letters." Earl Conrad/Harriet Tubman Collection, Schomburg Center for Research in Black Culture, New York Public Library.

Bowley, James Alfred. "Letter, James A. Bowley to 'Aunt' [Harriet Tubman]." Harriet Tubman Collection, Harriet Tubman Home Museum, Auburn, New York.

Brackett, Jeffrey R. *The Negro in Maryland. A Study of the Institution of Slavery*. New York: Negro Universities Press, 1969 [1889].

Bradford, Sarah H. *Harriet, the Moses of Her People*. New York: Geo. R. Lockwood & Sons, 1886.

———. *Harriet, the Moses of Her People*. New York: J. J. Little & Co., 1901.

———. *Scenes in the Life of Harriet Tubman*. Auburn, NY: W. J. Moses, 1869.

Bragg, George F. *Heroes of the Eastern Shore*. Baltimore, MD: G. F. Bragg, 1939.

———. *Men of Maryland*. Baltimore, MD: Church Advocate Press, 1925.

Brawley, Benjamin G. *Negro Builders and Heroes*. Chapel Hill: University of North Carolina Press, 1937.

———. *Women of Achievement. Written for the Fireside Schools of the Women's American Baptist Home Mission Society*. Chicago: Women's American Baptist Home Mission Society, 1919.

Brickler, Alice. "Letter, Alice Lucas Brickler to Earl Conrad, August 14, 1939." Earl Conrad/Harriet Tubman Collection, Schomburg Center for Research in Black Culture, New York Public Library.

———. "Letter, Alice Lucas Brickler to Earl Conrad, July 19, 1939." Earl Conrad/Harriet Tubman Collection, Schomburg Center for Research in Black Culture, New York Public Library.

Broady, Robert. "Run Away from the Subscriber Living near Choptank Bridge." *Pennsylvania Gazette*, 19 November 1761.

Brodess, Edward. "Estate Papers of Edward Brodess, #0-482." Cambridge, MD: Dorchester County Register of Wills, 1849.

Brodess, Eliza Ann. "Three Hundred Dollars Reward." *Cambridge Democrat*, 3 October 1849.

Brodess, Elizabeth. "Public Sale [Harriet Jolly and Child]." *Cambridge Democrat*, 27 June 1849.

# BIBLIOGRAPHY

"Brodess Farm, D-746." Maryland Inventory of Historic Properties (MIHP). Crownsville: Maryland Historical Trust, 2005.

"Brooks Farm, D-36." Maryland Inventory of Historic Properties (MIHP). Crownsville: Maryland Historical Trust, 1975.

Brown, Vaughan W. *Shipping in the Port of Annapolis, 1748–1775*. Annapolis, MD: U.S. Naval Institute, 1965.

Brugger, Robert J. *Maryland, a Middle Temperament, 1634–1980*. Baltimore, MD: Johns Hopkins University Press, 1988.

Buckmaster, Henrietta. *Let My People Go*. New York: Harper & Brothers, 1941.

"Bucktown Village Store, D-80." Maryland Inventory of Historic Properties (MIHP). Crownsville: Maryland Historical Trust, 2005.

Burton, Orville Vernon. *In My Father's House There Are Many Mansions: Family and Community in Edgefield, South Carolina*. Chapel Hill: University of North Carolina, 1985.

Burton, Thomas W. *History of the Underground Railroad, American Mysteries, and Daughters of Jerusalem*. Springfield, OH: Whyte Printing Co., 1925.

Butchart, Ronald E. *Schooling the Freed People: Teaching, Learning, and the Struggle for Black Freedom, 1861–1876*. Chapel Hill: University of North Carolina Press, 2010.

Butler, Jon. *Awash in a Sea of Faith: Christianizing the American People*. Cambridge, MA: Harvard University Press, 1990.

Camp, Stephanie M. H. *Closer to Freedom: Enslaved Women and Everyday Resistance in the Plantation South*. Chapel Hill: University of North Carolina Press, 2006.

"Capture." *Cecil Whig*, 7 August 1858.

"Capture." *Easton Gazette*, 9 January 1858.

Carowan, Glenn A., and John Statsko, eds. *Comprehensive Conservation Plan Approval for Chesapeake Marshlands National Wildlife Refuge Complex (Including Blackwater River)*. Washington, D.C.: Department of the Interior, U.S. Fish and Wildlife Service, 2006.

Carroll, James. "James Carroll's Day Book." Box 41, Folder 1, Maryland Province Archives, Booth Family Center for Special Collections, Georgetown University.

Carroll, Kenneth. *Quakerism on the Eastern Shore*. Baltimore: Maryland Historical Society, 1970.

———. "Voices of Protest: Eastern Shore Abolition Societies, 1790–1820." *Maryland Historical Magazine* 84 (1984).

"Cash." *Cambridge Chronicle*, 25 December, 1830.

Cayuga County Clerk. "Harriet Tubman Home, Certificate of Incorporation." Auburn, NY: Cayuga County Clerk's Office, 1896.

Cecelski, David S. *The Waterman's Song: Slavery and Freedom in Maritime North Carolina*. Chapel Hill: The University of North Carolina Press, 2001.

Cheney, Ednah Dow Littlehale. "Moses." *Freedmen's Record*, March 1865, 34–38.

Christianson, Scott. *Freeing Charles: The Struggle to Free a Slave on the Eve of the Civil War*. Urbana: University of Illinois Press, 2010.

"Christ Episcopal Church and Cemetery, D-140." Maryland Inventory of Historic Properties (MIHP). Crownsville: Maryland Historical Trust, 1983.

"Christ Methodist Episcopal Church at Aireys, D-82." Maryland Inventory of Historic Properties (MIHP). Crownsville: Maryland Historical Trust, 2011.

"Christ Rock Methodist Church, D-585." Maryland Inventory of Historic Properties (MIHP). Crownsville: Maryland Historical Trust, 2013.

Cimbala, Paul A., and Randall M. Miller, eds. *The Freedmen's Bureau and Reconstruction: Reconsiderations*. New York: Fordham University Press, 1999.

Clark, James B. "An Hour with Harriet Tubman." In *Christophe: A Tragedy in Prose of Imperial Haiti*, edited by William Edgar Easton. Los Angeles: Grafton Publishing Company, 1911.

Clemens, Paul G. E. *The Atlantic Economy and Colonial Maryland's Eastern Shore: From Tobacco to Grain*. Ithaca, NY: Cornell University Press, 1980.

"Clement Waters House (Aka Thomas M. Meredith House, Lewis House), D-81." Maryland Inventory of Historic Properties

(MIHP). Crownsville: Maryland Historical Trust, 2012.

"Concerning Women." *The Woman's Journal*, 17 April 1897.

Conrad, Earl. *General Harriet Tubman*, 2nd ed. Washington, D.C.: Associated Publishers, 1990.

———. "Interview with Helen W. Tatlock [Mrs. William Tatlock] [1939]." Earl Conrad/ Harriet Tubman Collection, Schomburg Center for Research in Black Culture, New York Public Library.

———. "Research Correspondence." Earl Conrad/ Harriet Tubman Collection, Schomburg Center for Research in Black Culture, New York Public Library.

"Cost of Trial." *Baltimore Sun*, 7 December 1849, p. 2.

Council of Maryland. "Calendar of Maryland State Papers: The Black Books." *Proceedings of the Council of Maryland, 1732–1753*, pp. 262–64, Maryland State Archives, Annapolis.

———. "Papers Relating to Affairs in Maryland, 1701–1714: An Account of Negroes Imported into Maryland." *Proceedings of the Council of Maryland, 1732–1753*, p. 257, Maryland State Archives, Annapolis.

Curry, Dennis C. "Aboriginal Ossuaries in Maryland: An Update." *Maryland Archaeology* 44, no. 1 (2008): 1–10.

———. "Birdstones: Some Clarifications from Maryland." *Pennsylvania Archaeologist* 80, no. 2 (2010): 50–60.

Custer, Jay F. "Coastal Adaptations in the Middle Atlantic Region." *Archaeology of Eastern North America* 16 (1988): 121–35.

———. "New Perspectives on the Delmarva Adena Complex." *Midcontinental Journal of Archaeology* 12, no. 1 (1987): 33–53.

Dail, William B. "Sheriff's Sale." *Cambridge Chronicle*, 24 December 1842.

Darnall, Robert. "Run Away from the Subscriber." *Pennsylvania Gazette*, 10 November 1763.

Darrin L. Lowery, John Seidel, and John S. Wah. *Archaeological Survey of the Fishing Bay and the Fairmont Wildlife Management Area within Dorchester and Somerset County, Maryland*. Chestertown, MD: Washington College, 2005.

Darrin L. Lowery, Torbin Rick, Michael Barber, John S. Wah, and Michael Madden. "Meadowood South of the Mason-Dixon Line: An Early Woodland Meadowood Presence on the Delmarva Peninsula." *Archaeology of Eastern North America* 43 (2015): 39–60.

Davidson, Thomas E. *A Cultural Resource Management Plan for the Lower Delmarva Region of Maryland*. Charleston, SC: NOAA, 1997.

"Davis." *Cayuga County Independent*, 18 October 1888.

Davis, Harriet Tubman. "Papers for Harriet Tubman Davis." Records of the U.S. House of Representatives, Record Group 233, 1892–1899, National Archives, Washington, D.C.

"Death of Aunt Harriet, 'Moses of Her People.'" *Auburn Daily Advertiser*, 11 March 1913.

Diggins, Milt. *Stealing Freedom Along the Mason-Dixon Line: Thomas Mccreary, the Notorious Slave Catcher from Maryland*. Baltimore: Maryland Historical Society, 2015.

Dorchester County Board of Commissioners. "Assessment Record [1852]." Maryland State Archives, Annapolis.

———. "Assessors Field Book [1852]." Maryland State Archives, Annapolis.

———. "Dorchester County Levy Book [1859–1900]." Maryland State Archives, Annapolis.

Dorchester County Chattel Records, 1847–1851. "William O. Cooper and Samuel Dunnock from Eliza Brodess." In Liber WJ, No. 3, p. 286, Maryland State Archives, Annapolis.

Dorchester County Circuit Court. "Certificates of Freedom." Dorchester County Circuit Court Records, 1806–1864, Maryland State Archives, Annapolis.

———. "Court Papers. 1861–1863, Criminal Judgements." Maryland State Archives, Annapolis.

———. "Equity Papers 249 [1852]." Maryland State Archives, Annapolis.

———. "Equity Papers 394 [1855]." Maryland State Archives, Annapolis.

———. "Equity Records, 1811–1966." Maryland State Archives, Annapolis.

———. "Trader's Licenses, 1829." Dorchester County Circuit Court Papers 1813–1937, Maryland State Archives, Annapolis.

Dorchester County Court. "Anthony C. Thompson to Wm. V.M. Edmundson." Chattel Records, 1842–1847, p. 436, Maryland State Archives, Annapolis.

———. "Dorchester County Short Judgments, 1818–1827." Dorchester County Court Records, Maryland State Archives, Annapolis.

———. "Land Records." Dorchester County Court Records, 1669–1984, Maryland State Archives, Annapolis.

———. "Major Bowley to John Bowley, Richard Bowley, John T. Stewart." Chattel Records, 1847–1851, pp. 62–63, Maryland State Archives, Annapolis.

Dorchester County Orphans Court. "Orphans Court Records, Vol. T.H.H. 1 [1852]." Registrar of Wills, Cambridge, Maryland.

Douglass, Frederick. *Life and Times of Frederick Douglass*. Scituate, MA: Digital Scanning, 2001 [1882].

———. *Narrative of the Life of Frederick Douglass, an American Slave*, 6th ed. Edited by Benjamin Quarles. Cambridge, MA: Belknap Press, 1971 [1845].

Drake, Frank C. "The Moses of Her People. Amazing Life Work of Harriet Tubman." *New York Herald*, 22 September 1907.

Drew, Benjamin. *The Refugee: A North-Side View of Slavery*. Edited by Tilden G. Edelstein. Reading, MA: Addison-Wesley, 1969 [1855].

Duncan, Russell. *Where Death and Glory Meet: Colonel Robert Gould Shaw and the Fifty-Fourth Massachusetts Infantry*. Athens: University of Georgia Press, 1999.

Eastern Shore Court of Appeals. "Edward Brodess in Account with Anthony Thompson His Guardian for the Years 1821 and 1822." *Edward Brodess Jr. v. Anthony Thompson*, 1828. Maryland State Archives, Annapolis.

"Edward Brodess to Dempsey P. Kane [July 1825]." Dorchester County Land Records, Vol. Liber 9 ER 624, p. 625, Maryland State Archives, Annapolis.

Eltis, David. "The Volume and Structure of the Transatlantic Slave Trade: A Reassessment." *William and Mary Quarterly* 58, no. 1 (2001): 17–46.

Eltis, David, Stephen D. Behrendt, David Richardson, and Herbert S. Klein, eds. *The Trans-Atlantic Slave Trade Database*. Cambridge: Cambridge University Press, 1999–2010.

"Escape and Recapture." *Easton Gazette*, October 16, 1858.

Eshelman, Ralph E., and Carl W. Scheffel Jr. "Maryland's Lower Choptank River Cultural Resource Inventory." Crownsville, Maryland, 2002.

———. "Maryland's Upper Choptank River and Tuckahoe River Cultural Resource Inventory." Crownsville, MD: Choptank River Heritage, 1999.

"Excitement at Cambridge." *New York Tribune*, 7 August 1858.

"Execution of Henny, in Cambridge, in 1831 [1908]." Dorchester County Historical Society, Vertical Files, Cambridge, Maryland.

"Fears of Insurrection." *The National Era*, 26 April 1855.

Fields, Barbara Jeanne. *Slavery and Freedom on the Middle Ground*. New Haven, CT: Yale University Press, 1985.

Finkelman, Paul. *Slavery and Founders: Race and Liberty in the Age of Jefferson*. Armonk, NY: M. E. Sharp, 1996.

Fitzgerald, Joseph R. *The Struggle Is Eternal: Gloria Richardson and Black Liberation*. Lexington: University Press of Kentucky, 2018.

Foner, Eric. *Forever Free: The Story of Emancipation and Reconstruction*. New York: Vintage Books, 2005.

———. *Gateway to Freedom: The Hidden History of America's Fugitive Slaves*. Oxford: Oxford University Press, 2015.

———. *Reconstruction: America's Unfinished Revolution, 1863–1877*. New York: Harper & Row, 1988.

———. *The Story of American Freedom*. New York: W. W. Norton, 1998.

Foner, Philip S., ed. *Frederick Douglass: Selected Speeches and Writings*. Abridged and adapted by Yuval Taylor. Chicago: Lawrence Hill Books, 1999.

Footner, Geoffrey M. *Tidewater Triumph: The Development and Worldwide Success of the Chesapeake Pilot Schooner.* Centreville, MD: Tidewater Publishers, 1998.

Forten, Charlotte L. *A Free Negro in the Slave Era: The Journal of Charlotte L. Forten.* Edited by Ray Allen Billington. New York: Collier Books, 1961.

Franklin, John Hope, and Loren Schweninger. *Runaway Slaves: Rebels on the Plantation.* New York: Oxford University Press, 1999.

"Free Negroes." *Annapolis Gazette*, 18 March 1858.

Freedmen's Bureau. "Freedmen's Bureau Bank Records [1866–1876]." Church of the Latter Day Saints, Salt Lake City, Utah.

Frey, Sylvia, and Betty Wood. *Come Shouting to Zion: African American Protestantism in the American South and British Caribbean to 1830.* Chapel Hill: University of North Carolina Press, 1998.

Fuke, Richard Paul. *Imperfect Equality: African Americans and the Confines of White Racial Attitudes in Post-Emancipation Maryland.* New York: Fordham University Press, 1999.

Gallivan, Martin. "The Archaeology of Native Societies in the Chesapeake: New Investigations and Interpretations." *Journal of Archaeological Research* 19, no. 3 (2011): 281–325.

———. *The Powhatan Landscape: An Archaeological History of the Algonquian Chesapeake.* Gainesville: University Press of Florida, 2018.

Garrett, Thomas. "Letter, Thomas Garrett to Eliza Wigham, December 16, 1855." Wilmington, Delaware.

———. "Letter, Thomas Garrett to J. Miller McKim, December 29, 1854." Wilmington, Delaware.

Garrison, Agnes. "Letter, Agnes Garrison to Ellen Wright Garrison, December 1, 1899." Garrison Family Papers, Sophia Smith Collection, Smith College, Northampton, Massachusetts.

———. "Letter, Agnes Garrison to Ellen Wright Garrison, November 24, 1899." Garrison Family Papers, Sophia Smith Collection, Smith College, Northampton, Massachusetts.

———. "Letter, Agnes Garrison to Ellen Wright Garrison, November 26, 1899." Garrison Family Papers, Sophia Smith Collection, Smith College, Northampton, Massachusetts.

Garrison, Ellen Wright. "Letter, Ellen Wright Garrison to Martha Coffin Wright, December 26, 1868." Garrison Family Papers, Sophia Smith Collection, Smith College, Northampton, Massachusetts.

Garrison, George. "Letter, George Garrison to William Lloyd Garrison Jr., February 10, 1864." Garrison Family Papers, Sophia Smith Collection, Smith College, Northampton, Massachusetts.

Garrison Jr., William Lloyd. "Scrapbooks Vol. IX: 'The Anti-Slavery Struggle' [1897]." Garrison Family Papers, Sophia Smith Collection, Smith College, Northampton, Massachusetts.

Garrison, Lucy McKim. *Slave Songs of the South.* Edited by William Francis Allen and Charles Pickard Ware. New York: A. Simpson & Company, 1867.

Gaspar, David Barry, and Darlene Clark Hine, eds. *More Than Chattel: Black Women and Slavery in the Americas.* Bloomington: Indiana University Press, 1996.

Gavin, Savin. "How Ezekiel's Wheel Helped Turn African Americans into Christians: Unique Evidence Discovered by UMD Archaeologists." *UMaryland Right Now* (2016). https://umdrightnow.umd.edu/news/how-ezekiel%E2%80%99s-wheel-helped-turn-african-americans-christians-unique-evidence-discovered-umd.

Gay, Sydney Howard. "Record of Fugitives 1855–1856." Sydney Howard Gay Papers, 1743–1931, Rare Book and Manuscript Library, Columbia University.

Genovese, Eugene D. *Roll, Jordon, Roll: The World the Slaves Made.* New York: Vintage Books, 1976.

George, Christopher. *Terror on the Chesapeake. The War of 1812 on the Bay.* Shippensburg, PA: White Mane Books, 2000.

Giddings, Paula J., and Janell Hobson, eds. "Special Issue on Harriet Tubman." *Meridians: Feminism, Race, Transnationalism* 12, no. 2 (2014).

Glymph, Thavolia. "Fighting Slavery on Slaveholders' Terrain." *OAH Magazine of History* 23, no. 2 (2009): 37–41.

———. *Out of the House of Bondage: The Transformation of the Plantation Household*. Cambridge: Cambridge University Press, 2012.

Gomez, Michael A. *Exchanging Our Country Marks: The Transformation of African Identities in the Colonial and Antebellum South*. Chapel Hill: University of North Carolina Press, 1998.

Graham, Willie, Carter L. Hudgins, Carl R. Lounsbury, Fraser D. Neiman, and James P. Whittenburg. "Adaptation and Innovation: Archaeological and Architectural Perspectives on the Seventeenth-Century Chesapeake." *William and Mary Quarterly* 64, no. 3 (2007): 451–522.

Green, Rebecca. *History of Harriet Tubman and Her Brick House*. Ithaca, NY: Cornell University, 1998.

Greenberg, Kenneth S. *The Confessions of Nat Turner and Related Documents*. New York: Bedford Books, 1996.

Griffith, Dennis. "Map of the State of Maryland: Laid Down from an Actual Survey of All the Principal Waters, Public Roads, and Divisions of the Counties Therein; Describing the Situation of the Cities, Towns, Villages, Houses of Worship and Other Public Buildings, Furnaces, Forges, Mills, and Other Remarkable Places; and of the Federal Territory; as Also a Sketch of the State of Delaware Shewing the Probable Connexion of the Chesapeake and Delaware Bays June 20th, 1794."

Grundset, Eric G. *Forgotten Patriots: African American and American Indian Patriots in the Revolutionary War: A Guide to Service, Sources, and Studies*. Washington, D.C.: National Society of the Daughters of the American Revolution, 2008.

Guida, Patricia C. *Arthur W. Leverton, Underground Railroad Agent, and His Family: The Levertons, Whiteleys and Wrights*. Denton, MD: Caroline County Historical Society, Inc., 2007.

Guterman, Benjamin. "Doing 'Good Brave Work': Harriet Tubman's Testimony at Beaufort, South Carolina." *Prologue* 42, no. 3 (Fall 2000).

Guy, Anita Aidt. *Maryland's Persistent Pursuit to End Slavery, 1850–1864*. New York: Garland Publishing, 1997.

"Hampton Hospital. Harriet Tubman's Statements Contradicted." *New York Independent*, 3 August 1865.

Harding, Vincent. *There Is a River: The Black Struggle for Freedom in America*. New York: Harcourt, Brace, Jovanovich, Publishers, 1981.

"Harriet Tubman Is Dead." *Auburn Citizen*, 11 March 1913.

"Harriet Tubman, New Liberty Ship, Launched in Maine." *Auburn Citizen Advertiser*, 3 June 1944.

Harrington, Samuel. "$250 Reward." *Cambridge Democrat*, 17 June 1854.

Harris, J. William. *The Hanging of Thomas Jeremiah: A Free Black Man's Encounter with Liberty*. New Haven, CT: Yale University Press, 2009.

Harrison, Samuel. "Meteor Shower." Harrison Collection, MS 432, Maryland Historical Society, Baltimore.

"Harrisville Colored School, D-816." Maryland Inventory of Historic Properties (MIHP). Crownsville: Maryland Historical Trust, 1981.

Hart, Albert Bushnell. *Slavery and Abolition, 1831–1841. The American Nation: A History, Vol. 16*. New York: Harper & Brothers, 1906.

Haynes, Elizabeth Ross. *Unsung Heroes*. New York: DuBois and Dill, 1921.

Heinegg, Paul. *Free African Americans of Maryland and Delaware from the Colonial Period to 1810*. Baltimore, MD: Clearfield Company, 2000.

———. "Free African Americans of Virginia, North Carolina, South Carolina, Maryland and Delaware from the Colonial Period to 1810." http://freeafricanamericans.com/.

Hewitt, Nancy A. *Women's Activism and Social Change: Rochester, New York, 1822–1872*. Ithaca, NY: Cornell University Press, 1984.

Heyrman, Christine Leigh. *Southern Cross: The Beginnings of the Bible Belt*. Chapel Hill: University of North Carolina Press, 1997.

Higginbotham, Evelyn Brooks. *Righteous Discontent: The Black Women's Movement in the Black Baptist Church, 1880–1920*. Cambridge, MA: Harvard University Press, 1993.

Hine, Darlene Clarke, and Kathleen Thompson. *A Shining Thread of Hope: The History of Black Women in America*. New York: Broadway Books, 1998.

Hoffman, Ronald. *A Spirit of Dissension: Economics, Politics, and the Revolution in Maryland*. Baltimore, MD: Johns Hopkins University Press, 1973.

Holt, Rosa Belle. "A Heroine in Ebony." *The Chautauquan*, July 1896.

Horton, Lois E. *Harriet Tubman and the Fight for Freedom: A Brief History with Documents*. Boston: Bedford/St. Martin's, 2013.

Howard, James H. "The Nanticoke-Delaware Skeleton Dance." *American Indian Quarterly* 2, no. 1 (1975): 1–13.

Howland, Emily. "Emily Howland Diaries [1901–1905]." Howland Family Papers, Friends Historical Library, Swarthmore College, Swarthmore, Pennsylvania.

Huelle, Walter E. *Footnotes to Dorchester History*. Cambridge, MD: Tidewater Publishers, 1969.

"Hughes Chapel, Trinity Methodist Episcopal Church, Nause-Waiwash Longhouse, D-282." Maryland Inventory of Historic Properties (MIHP). Crownsville: Maryland Historical Trust, 2005.

Humez, Jean. *Harriet Tubman: The Life and Life Stories*. Madison: University of Wisconsin Press, 2003.

Hynson, Jerry M. *Free African Americans of Maryland, 1832: Including Allegany, Anne Arundel, Calvert, Caroline, Cecil, Charles, Dorchester, Frederick, Kent, Montgomery, Queen Ann's, and St. Mary's Counties*. Westminster, MD: Willow Bend Books, 2000.

———. *Maryland Colonization Society Manumission Book, 1832–1860. Maryland Freedom Papers, Vol. 3*. Westminster, MD: Heritage Books, 2010.

Jackson, Luther P. "The Educational Efforts of the Freedmen's Bureau and Freedmen's Aid Societies in South Carolina, 1862–1872." *Journal of Negro History* 8, no. 1 (January 1923).

"Jefferson Memorial Church, D-597." Maryland Inventory of Historic Properties (MIHP). Crownsville: Maryland Historical Trust, 1969.

Jenks, A. S. *The Chorus*. Philadelphia: A.S. Jenks, 1860.

John Milner Associates. *Cultural Landscape Assessment for the Harriet Tubman Special Resource Study. Dorchester and Caroline Counties, Maryland*. Boston: National Park Service, Boston Support Office, Northeast Region, 2003.

"John Stewart [1889]." North Street Cemetery Records, Cayuga County Historian's Office, Auburn, New York.

Johnson, Walter. *The Chattel Principle: Internal Slave Trades in the Americas*. New Haven, CT: Yale University Press, 2005.

———. *Soul by Soul: Life inside the Antebellum Slave Market*. Cambridge, MA: Harvard University Press, 1999.

Johnson, Winory. "Information Wanted." *Christian Recorder*, 7 July 1866.

Jones, Elias. *The History of Dorchester County, Maryland*. Baltimore, MD: Williams and Wilkins Company Press, 1902.

Jones, Jacqueline. *Labor of Love, Labor of Sorrow: Black Women, Work, and the Family from Slavery to the Present*. New York: Vintage Books, 1986.

Jones-Rogers, Stephanie E. *They Were Her Property: White Women as Slave Owners in the American South*. New Haven, CT: Yale University Press, 2019.

Joyner, Charles. *Down by the Riverside: A South Carolina Slave Community*. Urbana: University of Illinois Press, 1984.

Kashatus, William. *Just over the Line: Chester County and the Underground Railroad*. West Chester, PA: Chester County Historical Society with Penn State University Press, 2002.

Keddie, Leslie and Neil. *Dorchester County, Maryland Wills Liber T.H.H. I: September 1854–February 1857, Folios 340-448*. Salisbury, MD: Family Tree Bookshops, 2002.

———. *Dorchester County, Maryland, Wills. Liber LLK No. 1, November 1861–1868, Folios 209-428*. Salisbury, MD: Family Tree Bookshop, n.d.

Keene, Richard. "Run Away from the Subscriber in Dorchester County, Ennals Ferry." *Pennsylvania Gazette*, 18 December 1766.

Keene, Samuel, of Ezekiel to Samuel Keene of Henry. "Bill of Sale; 25 H.D. 395 [1809]." Chattel Records, Dorchester County Court House, Cambridge, Maryland.

Keene, Vachel. "Ran Away from the Subscriber." *Maryland Journal and Baltimore Advertiser*, 18 August 1788.

Kelley, William T. "Underground R. R. Reminiscences." *Friends' Intelligencer*, 2 April 1898.

———. "Underground R. R. Reminiscences." *Friends' Intelligencer*, 19 April 1898.

———. "Underground R. R. Reminiscences." *Friends' Intelligencer*, 28 May 1898.

Kellogg, Jane. "Letter, Jane Kellogg for Harriet Tubman to Ednah Dow Cheney, April 9, 1894." Ms.A.10.1 no. 36, Boston Public Library Rare Book Room, Boston, Massachusetts.

———. "Letter, Jane Kellogg to Ednah Dow Cheney, June 25, 1894." Ms.A.10.1 no. 37, Boston Public Library Rare Book Room, Boston, Massachusetts.

Kimball, Hannah Parker. "Christ in the Slums." *New England Magazine*, July 1897, 631–38.

King, Wilma. *Stolen Childhood: Slave Youth in Nineteenth-Century America*. Bloomington: Indiana University Press, 2011.

Kobell, Rona. "Harriet Tubman's Sinking History." *Boston Sunday Globe*, 27 October 2019.

Kolchin, Peter. *American Slavery 1619–1877*. New York: Hill & Wang, 1993.

Kulikoff, Allan. *Tobacco and Slaves the Development of Southern Cultures in the Chesapeake, 1680–1800*. Chapel Hill: University of North Carolina Press, 2012.

Lake, Stevenson and Griffing. "An Illustrated Atlas of Talbot & Dorchester Counties, Maryland." 1877.

Larson, Kate Clifford. *Bound for the Promised Land: Harriet Tubman, Portrait of an American Hero*. New York: Ballantine Books, 2004.

———. *Harriet Tubman Underground Railroad Byway Tour Guide Training Manual*. Cambridge, MD: Dorchester and Caroline Counties Offices of Tourism, 2011.

*Laws Made and Passed by the General Assembly of the State of Maryland*. Vol. 192, Chapter 129, 28 January 1814. Annapolis: Maryland State Archives, 2002.

*Laws Made and Passed by the General Assembly of the State of Maryland*. Vol. 540, Chapter 54, 5 February 1830. Annapolis: Maryland State Archives, 2002.

*Laws Made and Passed by the General Assembly of the State of Maryland*. Vol. 3182, Chapter 111, 6 January. Annapolis: Maryland State Archives, 2002.

*Laws of Maryland at Large*. Edited by Thomas Bacon. Annapolis, MD: Jonas Green, 1766.

Leonard, R. B. *Bound to Serve: The Indentured Children of Talbot County, 1794–1920*. St. Michaels, MD: Privately printed, 1983.

Lepore, Jill. *These Truths: A History of the United States*. New York: W. W. Norton, 2018.

"Letter from Cambridge. Trial of Robert Vincent." *Baltimore Sun*, 17 December 1867.

Levine, Lawrence W. *Black Culture and Black Consciousness: Afro-American Folk Thought from Slavery to Freedom*. New York: Oxford University Press, 1977.

———. "Slave Songs and Slave Consciousness." In *African American Religion: Interpretive Essays in History and Culture*, edited by Timothy E. Fulop and Albert J. Raboteau. New York: Routledge, 1997.

Levy, Peter B. *Civil War on Race Street: The Civil Rights Movement in Cambridge, Maryland*. Miami: University Press of Florida, 2003.

Lothrop, Jonathan C., Darrin L. Lowery, Arthur E. Spiess, and Christopher J. Ellis. "Early Human Settlement of Northeastern North America." *PaleoAmerica* 2, no. 3 (2016): 192–251.

Lowery, Darrin L. *Archaeological Survey of the Little Choptank River Watershed, Dorchester Co., Md*. Crownsville: Maryland Historical Trust Library, 2005.

———. "Jack's Reef in the Chesapeake and Delmarva Region: Research into the Coastal Archaeology of the Era between Circa Cal

A.D. 480 and Cal A.D. 900." *Archaeology of Eastern North America* 41 (2013): 5–30.

———. *Terrestrial Archaeological Survey of Kingston Landing, Talbot County Maryland with Photographic Documentation and Mapping Additions*. Easton, Maryland: Talbot County Department of Public Works, 2009.

Lowery, Darrin, Stephen J. Godfrey, and Ralph Eshelman. "Integrated Geology, Paleontology, and Archaeology: Native American Use of Fossil Shark Teeth in the Chesapeake Bay Region." *Archaeology of Eastern North America* 39 (2011): 93–108.

Lowery, Darrin, Torben Rick, Michael Barber, John Wah, and Michael Madden. "Meadowood South of the Mason-Dixon Line: An Early Woodland Meadowood Presence on the Delmarva Peninsula." *Archaeology of Eastern North America* 43 (2015): 39–60.

Lucas, Maggie. "Information Wanted Ads." *Christian Recorder*, 1885.

"Lynch Law in Maryland." *Liberator*, 8 July 1858.

"The Magic and Mystery of Maryland Archeology." In *Maryland Archeology Month Booklet*, edited by Sara Rivers Cofield. Crownsville: Maryland Historical Trust, April 2019.

"Malone's Methodist Episcopal Church, D-586." Maryland Inventory of Historic Properties (MIHP). Crownsville: Maryland Historical Trust, 2012.

Marks, Carol. *Moses and the Monster and Miss Anne*. Urbana: University of Illinois Press, 2009.

Mary Means and Associates, Inc., Kittleson Associates, Tony Cohen, Kate Clifford Larson, and Andy Kalback. *The Harriet Tubman Underground Railroad Byway: Where Ordinary People Did the Extraordinary. Corridor Management Plan*. Silver Spring, MD, 2007.

Marye, William B. "Former Indian Sites in Maryland, as Located by Early Colonial Records." *American Antiquity* 2, no. 1 (1936): 40–46.

Maryland Court of Appeals. *Decisions of the Court of Appeals of Maryland. Vol. 1, 1827–1828*. Annapolis, MD: Jonas Green, 1828.

Maryland General Assembly. "An Act for Preventing Indians Disaffected to the British Interest in America from Coming into This Province as Spies, or on Any Other Evil Design [1756]." *Proceedings and Acts of the General Assembly,* Vol. 56, Maryland State Archives, Annapolis.

———. "An Act to Change the Name of William W. Williams, of Dorchester County, to That of William W. Thompson [1830]." Session Laws, 336, Maryland General Assembly, Annapolis.

———. "An Act to Prevent the Tumultuous Meetings, and Other Irregularities of Negroes and Other Slaves [1723]." *Proceedings and Acts of the General Assembly*, Vol. 34, Maryland State Archives, Annapolis.

———. "The Evil Consequences of the Shuanuo Indians Entertaining Our Runaway Negro Slaves [1722]." *Proceedings of the Council of Maryland*, Vol. 25, Maryland State Archives, Annapolis.

Maryland Province Archives. "Slavery in the Maryland Province." Georgetown University Slavery Database, Georgetown University, Washington, D.C.

Maryland State Archives. "Dorchester County Slave Purchasers, 1823–1836." Legacy of Slavery in Maryland. http://slavery.msa.maryland.gov/html/research/slavebuy.html.

Maryland State Archives and the University of Maryland, College Park. *A Guide to the History of Slavery in Maryland*. Annapolis: Maryland State Archives, 2007.

Mason, James E. *Tribute to Harriet Tubman, the Modern Amazon*. Edited by Edward U. A. Brooks. Auburn, NY: Tubman Home, 1914.

Mason, Keith. "Localism, Evangelicalism, and Loyalism: The Sources of Discontent in the Revolutionary Chesapeake." *The Journal of Southern History* 56, no. 1 (1990): 23–54.

McAllister, James A., Jr. *Indian Lands in Dorchester County, Md*. Cambridge, MD: Privately published, 1962.

McCaskie, T. C. *State and Society in Pre-Colonial Asante Society*. Cambridge: Cambridge University Press, 1995.

McCurry, Stephanie. *Women's War: Fighting and Surviving the American Civil War.* Cambridge, MA: Belknap Press of Harvard University Press, 2019.

McElvey, Kay Najiyyah. *Early Black Dorchester, 1776–1870: A History of the Struggle of African Americans in Dorchester County, Maryland, to Be Free to Make Their Own Choices.* PhD dissertation, University of Maryland, College Park, 1991.

McGill, Elaine. *Certificates of Freedom, Dorchester County Court 1806–1864.* Edited by transcriber. Privately printed, 2001.

———. *Robert Bell's Book of Slave Statistics 1864–1868.* Edited by transcriber. Privately printed, 2001.

McGowan, James. *Station Master on the Underground Railroad.* Moylan, PA: Whimsie Press, 1977.

McGowan, James, and William C. Kashatus. *Harriet Tubman: A Biography.* Santa Barbara, CA: Greenwood, 2011.

McPherson, James M. *Battle Cry of Freedom: The Civil War Era.* New York: Ballantine Books, 1988.

———. *The Struggle for Equality: Abolitionists and the Negro in the Civil War and Reconstruction.* Princeton, NJ: Princeton University Press, 1964.

Menard, Russell R. "Five Maryland Censuses, 1700 to 1712: A Note on the Quality of the Quantities." *William and Mary Quarterly* 37, no. 4 (1980): 616–26.

"Meredith/Bradshaw House/Bucktown Storekeepers House, D-774." Maryland Inventory of Historic Properties (MIHP). Crownsville: Maryland Historical Trust, 2005.

Meridith, Pritchet "$600 Reward." *Cambridge Democrat*, 18 March 1857.

Miller, Ann Fitzhugh. "Harriet Tubman." *American Review*, August 1912.

Miller, Henry M. "The Archaeology of Colonial Encounters Along Chesapeake Bay: An Overview." *Revista de Arqueología Americana*, no. 23 (2004): 231–90.

Mills, Jonathan. "Negro for Sale [Kessiah]." *Cambridge Democrat*, 5 September 1849.

Mills, Polish. "Mills Deposition [1853]." Equity Papers 249, Maryland State Archives, Annapolis.

Mitchell, Charles W. *Maryland Voices of the Civil War.* Baltimore, MD: Johns Hopkins University Press, 2007.

Morgan, Jennifer L. *Laboring Women: Reproduction and Gender in New World Slavery.* Philadelphia: University of Pennsylvania Press, 2004.

Morgan, Philip D. *Slave Counterpoint: Black Culture in the Eighteenth-Century Chesapeake and Lowcountry.* Chapel Hill: University of North Carolina Press, 1999.

Mott, Lucretia Coffin. "Letter, Lucretia Coffin Mott to Martha Coffin Wright, January 1, 1867." Garrison Family Papers, Sophia Smith Collection, Smith College, Northampton, Massachusetts.

Mowbray, Calvin W. *First Dorchester Families.* Westminster, MD: Heritage Books, 2007.

Mowbray, Calvin W., and Mary I. *The Early Settlers of Dorchester County and Their Lands.* 2 vols. Westminster, MD: Willow Bend Books, 2000.

Moxey, Debra. *Dorchester County Criminal Court Docket, 1791–1805.* Cambridge, MD: Dorchester County Historical Society, 1986.

———. *Great Choptank Parish Records.* Cambridge, MD.: Dorchester County Historical Society.

———. *Newspaper Abstracts from the American Eagle and Cambridge Chronicle 1846–1857.* Cambridge, MD: Dorchester County Historical Society, 1995.

———. "Thompson Land Records." In *Dorchester County Land Records Abstracts*, edited by James McAllister Jr. Cambridge, MD: Dorchester County Historical Society, n.d.

"Mrs. Harriet Tubman, the Colored Nurse and Scout - the Bridge Street African M.E. Church Last Evening." *Brooklyn Eagle*, 23 October 1865.

National Association of Colored Women. "Minutes of the Second Convention of the National Association of Colored Women . . . August 14th, 15th, and 16th, 1899." Paper presented at the Second Convention of the National Association of Colored Women, Chicago, Illinois, 14–16 August 1899.

"Negro Stampede." *Cecil Whig*, 31 October 1857.

"Negroes Captured." *Easton Gazette*, 7 August 1858.

Neild, Teresa M., and Clara L. Small. *They Wore Blue and Their Hearts Were Loyal: The United States Colored Troops of Dorchester County, Maryland*. Berlin, MD: Salt Water Media, 2016.

Neville, Barry Paige. "For God, King, and Country: Loyalism on the Eastern Shore of Maryland During the American Revolution." *International Social Science Review* 84, no. 3/4 (2009): 135–56.

"New Corporations." *New York Times*, 5 April 1896.

Northup, Solomon. *Twelve Years a Slave: Narrative of Solomon Northup, a Citizen of New-York, Kidnapped in Washington City in 1841, and Rescued in 1853*. Edited by David Wilson. Auburn, NY: Derby and Miller, 1853.

"Notice." *Cambridge Chronicle*, 30 August 1828.

O'Connor, Thomas. *Civil War Boston: Home Front and Battlefield*. Boston: Northeastern University Press, 1997.

Oertel, Kristen T. *Harriet Tubman: Slavery, the Civil War, and Civil Rights in the Nineteenth Century*. New York: Routledge, 2016.

"Old Trinity Church, Church Creek, Md, D-4." Maryland Inventory of Historic Properties (MIHP). Crownsville: Maryland Historical Trust, 1960.

Osgood, Lucy. "Letter, Lucy Osgood to Lydia Maria Child, June 2, 1859." Lydia Maria Child Papers, Cornell University Libraries, Ithaca, New York.

"Outrage in Talbot County. A Colored Man Murdered." *Baltimore News American*, 7 October 1867.

Papson, Don, and Tom Calarco. *Secret Lives of the Underground Railroad in New York City: Sydney Howard Gay, Louis Napoleon and the Record of Fugitives*. Jefferson, NC: McFarland, 2015.

Parker, John D. "John D. Parker [Estate] Inventory [1868]." Registrar of Wills, Dorchester County Court House, Cambridge, Maryland.

Parrish, Anne. *A Clouded Star*. New York: Harper & Brothers, 1948.

Pattison, Atthow. "Will of Atthow Pattison, Est. #0-35-E [18 January 1791]." Registrar of Wills, Dorchester County Court House, Cambridge, Maryland.

"Pattison, Gourney Crow, to William Henson [1829]." Dorchester County Chattel Records, 222, Maryland State Archives, Cambridge, Maryland.

Peden Henry C., Jr. *Revolutionary Patriots of Dorchester County, Maryland 1775–1783*. Westminster, MD: Willow Bend Books, 2000.

Penningroth, Dylan C. *The Claims of Kinfolk: African American Property and Community in the Nineteenth-Century South*. Chapel Hill: University of North Carolina Press, 2003.

Petry, Ann. *Harriet Tubman, Conductor on the Underground Railroad*. New York: Harper Collins, 1955.

Phillips, Christopher. *Freedom's Port. The African American Community of Baltimore, 1790–1860*. Urbana: University of Illinois Press, 1997.

Pratt, John P. "Spectacular Meteor Shower Might Repeat." *Meridian Magazine*, 15 October 1999.

Preston, Dickson J. *Talbot County. A History*. Centreville, MD: Tidewater Publishers, 1983.

"Prisoner # 5324 Hugh Hazlett [1858]." Maryland Penitentiary Records, Prisoner Records, Maryland State Archives, Annapolis.

Raboteau, Albert J. *American Prophets: Seven Religious Radicals and Their Struggle for Social and Political Justice*. Princeton, NJ: Princeton University Press, 2016.

———. *Slave Religion: The "Invisible Institution" in the Antebellum South*. New York: Oxford University Press, 1978.

"A Race of Harriets Would Secure the Future of the Negro, Says Bishop Blackwell." *Auburn Citizen*, 14 March 1913.

Reid, Richard M., ed. *Practicing Medicine in a Black Regiment: The Civil War Diary of Burt G. Wilder, 55th Massachusetts*. Amherst: University of Massachusetts Press, 2010.

"Reward." *Cambridge Chronicle*, 8 September 1828.

Rick, Torben C., and Darrin L. Lowery. "Accelerator Mass Spectrometry $^{14}$C Dating and the Antiquity of Shell-Tempered Ceramics from the Chesapeake Bay and Middle

Atlantic." *American Antiquity* 78, no. 3 (2013): 570–79.

Rick, Torben C., Darrin L. Lowery, Gregory A. Henkes, and John S. Wah. "A Late Holocene Radiocarbon Chronology for the Shell Middens of Fishing Bay, Maryland." *Archaeology of Eastern North America* 39 (2011): 153–67.

Ripley, C. Peter, ed. *The Black Abolitionist Papers, Vols. 1–5*. Chapel Hill: University of North Carolina Press, 1991.

"Rock School, Stanley Institute, D-43, Cambridge, Md." Maryland Inventory of Historic Properties (MIHP). Crownsville: Maryland Historical Trust, 2008.

Rodriguez, Junius, ed. *Encyclopedia of Emancipation and Abolition in the Transatlantic World*. Armonk, NY: M. E. Sharpe, 2007.

Rose, Willie Lee. *Rehearsal for Reconstruction: The Port Royal Experiment*. Athens: University of Georgia Press, 1999 [1964].

Rountree, Helen C., and Thomas E. Davidson. *Eastern Shore Indians of Virginia and Maryland*. Charlottesville: University of Virginia Press, 1997.

Rountree, Helen C., Wayne E. Clarke, and Kent Mountford. *John Smith's Chesapeake Voyages, 1607–1609*. Charlottesville: University of Virginia Press, 2007.

"Runaways." *Easton Star*, 14 August 1849, p. 2.

Runyon, Randolph Paul. *Delia Webster and the Underground Railroad*. Lexington: University Press of Kentucky, 1999.

Russo, Jean Burrell, and J. Elliott Russo. *Planting an Empire: The Early Chesapeake in British North America*. Baltimore: Johns Hopkins University Press, 2012.

Ryan, Bonnie Carey. *Archaeology of John Brown Hall at the Harriet Tubman Home: Site Report*. Syracuse, NY: Syracuse University Archaeological Research Report, 2000.

"S.S. Harriet Tubman, Named for Woman Abolitionist, Goes Down Ways at Portland, Maine." *Baltimore Afro-American*, 6 June 1944.

"Sam Green and Uncle Tom's Cabin." *Easton Gazette*, 28 August 1858.

Sanborn, Franklin. "Harriet Tubman." *The Commonwealth*, 17 July 1863.

———. "The Late Araminta Davis: Better Known as 'Moses' or 'Harriet Tubman' [1913]." Franklin B. Sanborn Papers, American Antiquarian Society, Worcester, Massachusetts.

———. "Letter, Franklin Sanborn to Friend, December 20, 1859." Anti-Slavery Collection, Boston Public Library, Boston, Massachusetts.

Schalk, Toki. "A Dream Come True." *Baltimore Afro-American*, 10 June 1944.

Schwartz, Gerald, ed. *A Woman Doctor's Civil War: Esther Hill Hawks' Diary*. Columbia: University of South Carolina Press, 1984.

Scott, Julius S. *The Common Wind: Afro-American Currents in the Age of the Haitian Revolution*. London: Verso, 2018.

"Scotts Chapel (Aka Bucktown Methodist Episcopal Church, Bucktown United Methodist Church), D-270." Maryland Inventory of Historic Properties (MIHP). Crownsville: Maryland Historical Trust, 2005.

Seidel, John L. *The 2001–2003 Archaeological Investigations at the Brodess Farm Site (18do419), the Possible Harriet Tubman Birth Site, Dorchester County, Maryland*. Chesterton, Maryland, 2004.

Sernett, Milton C., ed. *African American Religious History: A Documentary Witness*. Durham, NC: Duke University Press, 1999.

Seth, Joseph B. *Recollections of a Long Life on the Eastern Shore*. Edited by Mary W. Seth. Easton, MD: Press of the *Star-Democrat*, 1926.

Seward, John. "John Seward to Sundry Negroes, January 15, 1817." Dorchester County Court Papers, 1743–1849, Maryland State Archives, Annapolis.

Seward, William H. "Microfilm Reels 192-193." Seward Papers, Harvard University, Cambridge, Massachusetts.

Shaffer, Donald R. "'I Do Not Suppose That Uncle Sam Looks at the Skin': African Americans and the Civil War Pension System, 1865–1934." *Civil War History*, June 2000.

Sherwin, Oscar. "I'se Free 'Fo' I Die." *The Negro History Bulletin*, June 1940.

Siebert, Wilbur. *The Underground Railroad from Slavery to Freedom.* New York: Macmillan Co., 1898.

———. "The Underground Railroad: Manuscript Materials Collected by Professor Siebert, Ohio University." Vol. 40. Houghton Library, Harvard University, Cambridge, Massachusetts.

Sinha, Manisha. *The Slave's Cause: A History of Abolition.* New Haven, CT: Yale University Press, 2016.

Skinner, V. L., Jr. *Abstracts of the Debt Books of the Provincial Land Office of Maryland. Dorchester County, Vol. II Liber 21: 1766, 1767, 1770.* Baltimore, MD: Clearfield Company by Genealogical Publishing Company, 2016.

"Slavery and the War of 1812—Case Studies in Maryland." Legacy of Slavery in Maryland. http://slavery.msa.maryland.gov/html/casestudies/warcountycs.html.

Small, Sasha. *Heroines.* New York: Workers Library Publishers, 1937.

Smedley, R. C. *History of the Underground Railroad in Chester and the Neighboring Counties of Pennsylvania.* Lancaster, PA: John A. Hiestand, 1883.

Smith, Barbara Clark. "Food Rioters and the American Revolution." *William and Mary Quarterly* 51, no. 1 (1994): 3–38.

Smith, Billy G., and Richard Wojtowicz. *Blacks Who Stole Themselves: Advertisements for Runaways in the Pennsylvania Gazette, 1728–1790.* Philadelphia: University of Pennsylvania Press, 1989.

Smith, Frank R. *Muskrat Investigations in Dorchester County, Md, 1930–1934.* Washington, D.C.: U.S. Department of Agriculture, 1938.

Smith, John, and William Hole. *Virginia.* London, 1624.

Snediker, Quentin, and Ann Jensen. *Chesapeake Bay Schooners.* Centreville, MD: Tidewater Publishers, 1992.

Sobel, Michel. *The World They Made Together: Black and White Values in Eighteenth-Century Virginia.* Princeton, NJ: Princeton University Press, 1987.

"St. Paul's Methodist Episcopal Church, D-606." Maryland Inventory of Historic Properties (MIHP). Crownsville: Maryland Historical Trust, 1981.

"A Stampede." *Easton Star,* 24 October 1849, p. 2.

"Staplefort House, D-131." Maryland Inventory of Historic Properties (MIHP). Crownsville: Maryland Historical Trust,, 1991.

State of Maryland. "1783 Supply Tax, Dorchester County, Md." Sharf Collection, Maryland State Archives, Annapolis.

Sterling, Dorothy. *Freedom Train, the Story of Harriet Tubman.* New York: Doubleday, 1954.

———, ed. *Speak out in Thunder Tones: Letters and Other Writings of Black Northerners, 1787–1865.* New York: Doubleday, 1973.

Stevenson, Brenda E. "Introduction: Women, Slavery, and the Atlantic World." *Journal of African American History* 98, no. 1 (2013): 1–6.

———. *Life in Black and White: Family and Community in the Slave South.* New York: Oxford University Press, 1996.

———. "What's Love Got to Do with It? Concubinage and Enslaved Women and Girls in the Antebellum South." *Journal of African American History* 98, no. 1 (2013): 99–125.

Stewart, Levin. "Levin Stewart to Sundry Negroes [28 July 1817]." Dorchester County Court Papers, 1797–1851, Maryland State Archives, Annapolis.

Stewart, Robert G. "The Battle of the Ice Mound, February 7, 1815." *Maryland Historical Magazine* 70 (1975): 372–78.

Still, William. *Journal C of Station 2 of the Underground Railroad (Philadelphia, Agent William Still) [1852–1857].* Pennsylvania Abolition Society, Historical Society of Pennsylvania, Philadelphia.

———. *The Underground Railroad.* Chicago: Johnson Publishing Company, 1970 [1871].

———. "Vigilance Committee of Philadelphia, Accounts [1854–1857]." Pennsylvania Abolition Society, Historical Society of Pennsylvania, Philadelphia.

Sublette, Ned, and Constance Sublette. *The American Slave Coast: A History of the Slave Breeding Industry.* Chicago: Lawrence Hill Books, 2016.

Sullivan, Kristin M., Erve Chambers, and Ennis Barbery. *Indigenous Cultural Landscapes Study for the Captain John Smith Chesapeake National Historic Trail: Nanticoke River Watershed*. Annapolis, MD: National Park Service Chesapeake Bay, 2013.

"Suspicious." *Public Monitor*, 8 July 1858.

Swift, Hildegarde Hoyt. *The Railroad to Freedom: A Story of the Civil War*. New York: Harcourt, Brace & World, 1932.

Talbot County Court. "Chattel Records." Talbot County Court Records, Maryland State Archives, Annapolis.

Taylor, Amy Murrell. *Embattled Freedom: Journeys through the Civil War's Slave Refugee Camps*. Chapel Hill: University of North Carolina Press, 2018.

Taylor, Robert W. *Harriet Tubman: The Heroine in Ebony*. Boston: George E. Ellis, Printer, 1901.

Taylor, Susie King. *A Black Woman's Civil War Memoirs: Reminiscences of My Life in Camp with the 33rd U.S. Colored Troops, Late 1st South Carolina Volunteers*. Edited by Patricia W. Romero. Princeton, NJ: Marcus Wiener Publishers, 1988 [1902].

Telford, Emma P. *Harriet: The Modern Moses of Heroism and Visions*. Auburn, NY: Cayuga County Museum, 1905.

"The Terrors of Slavery!" *The National Era*, 12 April 1855.

Thomas, Hugh. *The Slave Trade: The Story of the Atlantic Slave Trade: 1440–1870*. New York: Touchstone, 1997.

Thomas, Joseph D., and Marsha McCabe, ed. *Spinner: People and Culture in Southeastern Massachusetts*. Vol. 4. New Bedford, MA: Spinner Publications, 1988.

Thompson, Anthony. "Anthony C. Thompson to John D. Parker [1853]." Dorchester County Chattel Records, Maryland State Archives, Annapolis.

———. "Last Will and Testament of Anthony Thompson." Estate No. 0-65-C, 12 May 1836, Register of Wills, Dorchester County Court House, Cambridge, Maryland.

Thompson, Anthony C. "Deposition [1853]." Chancery Papers 249, Dorchester County Court House, Cambridge, Maryland.

———. "List of Anthony Thompson's Negroes, 1839." Levin Richardson Collection, 1758–1865, Maryland Historical Society, Baltimore.

Thompson, D. F. "The Thompson Family in Dorchester County and Maryland." *Democrat and News*, 7 January 1910.

———. "The Thompsons in Dorchester." *Democrat and News*, 28 January 1910.

"Trial of Hugh Hazlett." *Easton Gazette*, 20 November 1858.

Trudeau, Noah Andre. *Like Men of War: Black Troops in the Civil War, 1862–1865*. Boston: Little, Brown & Company, 1998.

Tubman, Harriet. "Letter, Harriet Tubman to Mary Wright, May 29, 1896." Ms.A.10.1 no. 90, Boston Public Library Rare Book Room, Boston, Massachusetts.

"Tubman Home Dedicated." *Auburn Daily Advertiser*, 23 June 1908.

"Tubman Home Open and Aged Harriet Was Central Figure of Celebration." *Auburn Citizen*, 24 June 1908.

Turner, Franklin. "Proceedings of the Colored National Convention." Paper presented at the National Convention of the Colored People of the United States, Franklin Hall, Philadelphia, Pennsylvania, 16–18 October 1855.

Turner, John. "Run Away from the Subscriber Living in Dorchester County." *Pennsylvania Gazette*, 28 April 1763.

University of Maryland. "Archaeologists Find Hidden African Side to Noted 1780s Maryland Building." EurekaAlert!, 2011. https://www.eurekalert.org/pub_releases/2011-02/uom-afh020811.php.

"Unsuccessful Attempt to Capture Fugitive Slaves." *New York Tribune*, 20 March 1857.

Urban, Sylvanus. "An Account of the Number of Souls in the Province of Maryland, in the Year 1755." *Gentleman's Magazine*, 1 June 1764, 261.

U.S. House of Representatives. "Harriet [Tubman] Davis, Widow of Nelson Charles, Alias Nelson Davis, Pension Claim." HR 55A-D1 Papers Accompanying the Claim of Harriet Tubman, 1890–1899, National Archives, Washington, D.C.

U.S. National Park Service. *Harriet Tubman Special Resource Study*. Boston, MA: National Park Service, Boston Regional Office, 2008.

U.S. National Park Service and Chesapeake Bay Gateways Network. *Captain John Smith Chesapeake National Historic Trail: Join the Adventure*. Annapolis, MD: National Park Service, 2007.

U.S. National Park Service, Office of Policy. *NPS-28 Cultural Resource Management Guidelines, 1998*. https://irma.nps.gov/DataStore/DownloadFile/466037.

U.S. Naval War Records Department, Office of Naval Records and Library. *The Official Records of the Union and Confederate Navies in the War of the Rebellion*. Series 1, Vol. 4. Washington, DC: Government Printing Office, 1896.

U.S. War Department, Records and Pension Office, War Records Office. *The War of the Rebellion: A Compilation of the Official Records of the Union and Confederate Armies*. Series 1, Vol. 2. Washington, DC: Government Printing Office, 1880.

———. *The War of the Rebellion: A Compilation of the Official Records of the Union and Confederate Armies*. Series 3, Vol. 1. Washington, D.C.: Government Printing Office, 1899.

Victor, Orville, J. *History of American Conspiracies: A Record of Treason, Insurrection, Rebellion &C., in the United States of America, from 1760 to 1860*. New York: James D. Torrey, 1863.

Waldstreicher, David. "Reading the Runaways: Self-Fashioning, Print Culture, and Confidence in Slavery in the Eighteenth-Century Mid-Atlantic." *William and Mary Quarterly* 56, no. 2 (1999): 243–72.

Walker, Jesse O. *Archaeological Investigations of the Holland Point Site (18do220), Dorchester County, Maryland*. Philadelphia, PA: Temple University, 2003.

———. *Final Report: Phase I Archaeological Identification Survey and Phase II Archaeological Assessment Survey Tract 100m [Linthicum Site/Tubman State Park], Blackwater National Wildlife Refuge, Ninth Election District, Dorchester County, Maryland*. Hadley, MA: Richard Grubb & Associates, 2007.

Walsh, Lorena S. "The Chesapeake Slave Trade: Regional Patterns, African Origins, and Some Implications." *William and Mary Quarterly* 58, no. 1 (2001): 139–70.

Wells, Robert V. *Population of the British Colonies in America before 1776: A Survey of Census Data*. Princeton, NJ: Princeton University Press, 1975.

Wennersten, John R. *Maryland's Eastern Shore: A Journey in Place and Time*. Centreville, MD: Tidewater Publishers, 1992.

Weslager, C. A. "Wynicaco-a Choptank Indian Chief." *Proceedings of the American Philosophical Society* 87, no. 5 (1944): 398–402.

Wesley, John. *Thoughts Upon Slavery*. London: Joseph Crukshank, 1774.

White, Deborah Gray. *Ar'n't I a Woman? Female Slaves in the Plantation South*. New York: W. W. Norton, 1987.

Whitman, T. Stephen. *Challenging Slavery in the Chesapeake: Black and White Resistance to Human Bondage, 1775–1865*. Baltimore: Maryland Historical Society, 2007.

———. *The Price of Freedom: Slavery and Manumission in Baltimore and Early National Maryland*. Lexington: University Press of Kentucky, 1997.

Wickenden, Dorothy. *The Agitators: Three Friends Who Fought for Abolition and Women's Rights*. New York: Scribner, 2021.

Wilkie, Laurie A. "Secret and Sacred: Contextualizing the Artifacts of African-American Magic and Religion." *Historical Archaeology* 31, no. 4 (1997): 81–106.

Wilks, Ivor. *Forests of Gold: Essays on the Akan and the Kingdom of the Asante*. Athens: Ohio University Press, 1993.

Williamson, Passmore. "Passmore Williamson's Visitor's Book [1855]." Chester County Historical Society, West Chester, Pennsylvania.

Wilson, Carol. *Freedom at Risk: The Kidnapping of Free Blacks in America, 1780–1865*. Lexington: University Press of Kentucky 1994.

Windley, Lathan Algerna. *Runaway Slave Advertisements: A Documentary History* from the 1730s to 1790, Vol. 2. Westport, CT: Greenwood Press, 1983.

Wise, William G. "Subscription List [1868]." Harriet Tubman Collection, Harriet Tubman Home Museum, Auburn, New York.

Witkowski, Monica C. *Women at Law in Early Colonial Maryland*. El Paso, TX: LFB Scholarly Publishing, 2012.

Wood, Charles P. "Manuscript History Concerning the Pension Claim of Harriet Tubman." HR 55A-D1 Papers Accompanying the Claim of Harriet Tubman, 1868, National Archives, Washington, D.C.

Wood, Kirsten E. *Masterful Women: Slaveholding Widows from the American Revolution through the Civil War*. Chapel Hill: University of North Carolina Press, 2004.

"Woolford Baptist Meeting House, D-231." Maryland Inventory of Historic Properties (MIHP). Crownsville: Maryland Historical Trust, 2012.

"The Wrath of the Fearful." *The National Era*, 26 April 1855.

Wright, F. Edward. *Judgment Records of Dorchester, Queen Anne's and Talbot Counties, Maryland*. Lewes, DE: Delmarva Roots, 2001.

Wright, James Martin, ed. *The Free Negro in Maryland 1634–1860*. New York: Columbia University, 1921.

Wright, Martha Coffin. "Letter, Martha Coffin Wright to Ellen Wright Garrison, December 30, 1860." Garrison Family Papers, Sophia Smith Collection, Smith College, Northampton, Massachusetts.

———. "Letter, Martha Coffin Wright to Mariana Pelham, November 7, 1865." Garrison Family Papers, Sophia Smith Collection, Smith College, Northampton, Massachusetts.

Wyman, Lillie B. Chase. "Harriet Tubman." *The New England Magazine*, March 1896, 110–18.

Yellin, Jean Fagan. *Harriet Jacobs: A Life: The Remarkable Adventures of the Woman Who Wrote Incidents in the Life of a Slave Girl*. New York: Basic Civitas Books, 2004.

Yerrington, James. "Colonel Montgomery's Raid - the Rescued Black Chattels – a Black She "Moses" - Her Wonderful Daring and Sagacity - the Black Regiments - Col. Higginson's Mistakes - Arrival of the 54th Massachusetts, &C., &C." *Wisconsin State Journal*, 20 June 1863.

# Index

Ababco Indian tribe, 26
Abbott, William E., 3, 10–11, 92, 112
abolitionist(s), xvii–xix, xxv–xxvi, 3–6, 14, 16, 20–22, 25–26, 29, 33, 35, 37, 39–40, 46–48, 51–53, 56, 60, 69, 71, 73–74, 77, 86, 88, 94–99, 101, 104–5, 107–8, 112–15, 119, 121, 125–29, 131–32, 134, 141, 145–47, 153–54, 159, 166
abolition movement, 3–5, 52–53, 80, 94, 105, 107, 113–14, 121, 125, 128, 131–34
Adams, Rev. Nehemiah, 3, 40
Adams, Samuel Hopkins, 3
Adkins Arboretum, 3
advertisements for capture of freedom seekers, xxiv, 10–12, 18–19, 40, 47, 74, 92, 96, 130, 157, 177, 189
African American spirituals, 3, 14, 28, 59, 107, 119, 187, 190
African Methodist Episcopal (AME) Church, 4, 32, 79, 85, 91, 120, 146
African Methodist Episcopal Zion (AMEZ) Church, xx, 4, 37, 62, 88, 93, 120, 131–32, 143
Agnew, Allen and Maria, 4, 51
Alcott, family of Concord, Massachusetts, 4
Algonquin, Native peoples, 26, 101
Allen, enslaved person, 164
Allen, Rev. Richard, 4
Allen, William Francis, 107
Amby, Elizabeth "Lizzie" and Nat, 4, 6, 12, 23, 32, 47, 98, 133, 151
American and Foreign Anti-Slavery Society, 4–5, 141
American Anti-Slavery Society, 5, 26, 53, 95, 98, 113, 115
American Colonization Society, 5, 12, 87, 93
American Freedmen's Inquiry Commission, 41, 51, 73
American Woman Suffrage Association (AWSA), 5, 104, 133
Anderson, Osborne P., 5–6
Andrew, Gov. John Albion, xix, xxv, 45, 73, 75, 122, 179–80
Annapolis, Maryland, 38, 107
antebellum period, 6, 12, 24, 26–27, 55, 93, 105, 120, 129, 147, 185, 187
Anthony, Aaron, 39
Anthony, Christopher "Kit" and Leah, 6, 23, 48, 111, 151, 154
Anthony, Susan B., xxvi, 5–6, 96, 102, 104, 108, 128, 131, 133, 154
Antiquities Act, xxi, 63, 67
antislavery movement. *See* abolition movement
Asante/Ashante culture, 6–7, 97
Associated Publishers, 7, 31, 61, 156
Auburn Theological Seminary, 72
Auburn, New York, xiii, xviii–xxi, xxvi, 3–4, 15–17, 20, 25, 28, 30–31, 35–37, 41–43, 46–47, 51–54, 61–67, 72–73, 78, 80, 84, 89–90, 93, 96–98, 105, 107–9, 111–14, 120, 122–23, 126, 128–29, 131–32, 134, 138–46, 153, 156–59, 167, 170, 173–74, 176, 182
Augusta, John, 4, 7, 133
Auld, Thomas, 39
Averill, Horatio F., 7

Bailey, Frederick, 5, 9, 39. *See also* Douglass, Frederick Bailey
Bailey, Harriet, 39
Bailey, Josiah "Joe," xvii, 9–11, 20, 39, 55–56, 71, 74, 77, 80, 91, 105, 111, 159, 162
Bailey, Maria, 164

# INDEX

Bailey, William "Bill," xvii, 9–11, 20, 39, 55–56, 71, 74, 77, 80, 91, 105, 111, 159, 162
Baltimore, Maryland, xvii, 12, 15–16, 24, 33, 39–40, 53, 55–56, 68, 70, 83, 130, 145–47, 157, 171–73, 183
Banks, William "Bill," 11, 91, 163
Barnes, Joseph K., xix, 11, 46, 181
Barnett, Thomas, 11, 102
Bayley, Isaac, 12
Bayley, Maria, 11–12
Bayley, Mary Ann Thompson, 12
Bayly, Dr. Alexander, 4, 12
Bayly, Josiah, Jr., 12
Bazel, Nathaniel, 12
Bazel United Methodist Church, 65–66, 120
Beaufort, South Carolina, 29, 38, 40, 45, 125, 129, 131, 134, 153, 167–69, 174, 179–80
Bell, Dinah, 12. *See also* Jackson, Dinah Bell
Bell, Robert, 12, 88
Benson, Stephen Allen, 12
Beriah, Green, 55, 96
Bess, enslaved woman, 13, 110, 118, 139
Bethune, Dr. Mary McCloud, 102
Big Dipper, 13, 88, 150, 186. *See also* Polaris
Black Jacks, xxiv, 13
Blackwater and Parson's Creek Canal Company, 13, 139
Blackwater National Wildlife Refuge, 13, 68
Blackwater River, xxiii, 13, 18, 22, 121–22, 137–38, 139
Blackwell, Henry, 102, 133
Blake, Mott, 13–14, 22–23, 26, 57, 70, 114, 127, 130, 179
Blockson, Charles L., 144, 155
Blondo, Richard A., 14
Bloomer, Amelia, 14
Boston, Massachusetts, xviii, xx, xxvi, 3–6, 14, 25–26, 30, 40, 45, 51–54, 69, 71, 73, 80, 85, 94, 104, 108–10, 113, 120–21, 126–29, 134, 146, 156, 159, 166, 172–73, 175, 178, 180
Boston Female Anti-Slavery Society, 25–26, 52
Boston Vigilance Committee, 6, 69, 71, 73, 109, 113
"Bound for the Promised Land," spiritual, viii, 14, 28, 187, 190. *See also* "Goodbye Song"; "On Jordan's Stormy Bank," spiritual

*Bound for the Promised Land: Harriet Tubman, Portrait of an American Hero,* viii, 14–15
bounty hunters, 15. *See also* slave catchers
Bowley, Alfred, 164
Bowley, Araminta, 15–16, 161, 183
Bowley, Betsy, 164
Bowley, Binah, 15–16
Bowley, Harkless, 15, 31, 41
Bowley, Harriet, 15–16
Bowley, James Alfred, 15–16, 163, 185
Bowley, John, 15–16, 38, 78, 135–37, 163, 183
Bowley, Kessiah Jolly, 15–16, 38, 81, 130, 135, 163, 183
Bowley, Major, 15–16, 164
Bowley, Richard, 15–16
Bowley, Terry, 15–16
Boyce, Henry, 16, 155
Bradford, Sarah Hopkins, 17, 39, 165–66, 189
Bradshaw Hotel, 17
Brainard, Dorsey, 17
Brannock, Willis, 17, 87, 111, 113
Brathwaite, Mary, 134
Brickler, Alice Lucas, 17, 41, 89
Brickler, Dr. Alexander, 17
Brinkley, Nathaniel, 17–18, 33, 54
Brinkley, William, 18, 33, 40, 42, 54, 108, 159
Brodess, Edward, xv–xvii, xxiii–xxiv, 16, 18–19, 31, 38, 41–42, 46, 80–81, 85, 96, 110, 121–25, 127, 129, 135–36, 144–45, 148, 165, 184
Brodess, Eliza Ann Keene, xvi–xvii, 18–19, 81, 96, 135
Brodess, Joseph, xv, 19
Brodess Farm, 18
*Brodess v. Thompson,* 19, 83, 143
Brooks, Elizabeth, 19, 25
Brooks, Rev. Edward U.A., 20, 43, 93, 103, 146
Brown, John, xviii, xxv–xxvi, 6, 10–11, 20, 37, 42, 51, 53, 60, 71, 73–74, 97, 109, 112, 125, 127, 132, 134, 178
Brown, William Wells, 21
Buchanon, Mrs. [likely Sarah], 21, 28, 32, 72, 139
Bucktown, Maryland, xiii, xvi, xviii, 1, 11–12, 18–19, 21, 24, 26, 39, 41–42, 65–67, 74, 85, 95–96, 120, 122, 127, 135, 137, 142–43, 182, 189

210

Bucktown Village Store, 11–12, 19, 21, 66, 96, 135, 137, 142
Burns, Peter, 13, 21–23, 26, 57, 70–71, 114, 127, 130, 179
Bustill, Charles, 22, 56, 113
Buttons Creek, 22

Cabin Creek, Maryland, xvii, 23, 28, 72
Cahern, Gabriel, 13, 22–23, 26, 57, 70, 114, 127, 130, 177
Callender, Robert, 133
Cambridge, xviii, 6–7, 23, 28, 32, 34, 40, 48, 71, 83, 87–88, 111, 133, 146, 151
Cambridge, Maryland, viii, xvii–xviii, 4, 6–7, 9–10, 12, 15–17, 23, 25–26, 28, 32–34, 38, 40, 48, 54–56, 63, 65–66, 70–71, 74, 79–80, 83, 85, 87–89, 91, 93, 98, 108, 111–13, 120, 129, 133–35, 143, 146, 151, 170–72, 183
Camden, Delaware, 18, 33, 54, 145
Camper, James, 4, 6, 23, 32, 133, 151
Camper, Rachel, 145, 151
camp meeting, 23–24, 33, 35, 183–84
Canada, viii, xiii, xvii–xviii, xxv–xxvi, 3, 5–6, 11, 13, 15–16, 20–21, 24–25, 27–28, 32–33, 37, 39–40, 42, 48, 56, 60, 66, 69, 71–74, 77, 80, 82, 84, 87–88, 96–99, 101, 105, 108, 112–13, 115, 119, 122–25, 127–28, 133–36, 149, 151, 154, 159, 165, 170, 172–74, 176–78, 182–83
Cannon, Patty, 24
Cannon-Johnson gang, 24
Cape May, New Jersey, xvii, 24, 170
Cardin, Senator Benjamin L., 63–64, 67
Caroline County, Maryland, xiii, xvii–xviii, xxiv, 9–10, 24, 26–27, 32–33, 35, 37–39, 41–42, 47, 55, 66, 69–71, 73–74, 86–87, 89, 93, 111–12, 114–15, 120, 122–23, 138, 142, 147, 151, 154, 157–58
Carrol, Henry, 19, 25, 162
carte de visite, 73
Carter, Florence, 25, 41
Cassan, or Cassandra, 163
Cator, Jane, 25, 32–33, 111, 113
Catt, Carrie Chapman, 25
Cayuga County, New York, 31, 41, 107, 128, 141, 158
Cecil County, Maryland, 41
Centenary Biblical Institute, 56
Central Presbyterian Church, xix, xxvi, 25, 35, 46
certificate of freedom, 146

Chapman, Maria Weston, 25
Charles, Nelson. See Davis, Nelson Charles, Jr.
Chase, John, 25, 71, 80, 161
Chatham, Ontario, Canada, 6, 15–16, 134
Cheney, Ednah Dow Littlehale, 13, 20, 26, 104, 108, 127, 165, 175
Chesapeake Bay, 16, 23–24, 26–27, 38, 41, 68, 70, 83, 101–2, 131, 145, 157
Child, Lydia Maria, 71, 80, 102, 108, 131, 134, 166
Chion, Emily and William. See Kiah
Chisholm, George, 13, 22–23, 26, 57, 70, 114, 127, 130, 179
Choptank Indian Tribe, 26–27, 101
Choptank Landing, 95
Choptank River, xxiv, 9–10, 23–24, 26–27, 33, 37–38, 54, 70–71, 83, 88, 93, 95, 111, 113–14, 159
Christ Rock, Cambridge, Maryland, 133
Christmas Day 1854, escape of Harriet Tubman's brothers, xxv, 4, 25, 27, 59, 71, 80, 82, 114, 123, 136–37, 145, 156
Church Creek, Maryland, 9–10, 22, 27, 31, 43, 67–68, 81, 91, 133, 158
Civil War, American, xviii–xx, xxv–xxvi, 3–6, 11, 13–15, 17, 20, 22–23, 26, 29–31, 35, 37–42, 45–48, 51–53, 56–57, 60, 69–75, 78, 80–81, 84, 87, 89, 91–95, 97–98, 102, 104, 108–9, 111, 113, 119, 124–25, 127–31, 133–34, 136–38, 144, 146–47, 149–50, 152–54, 157–58, 169, 175, 185–87, 190
Clarke, James B., 28, 167
Clinton, President William, 66
Cobb, Dr. Harriet, 28
coded messages, 28, 45, 59, 107, 186
Cohen, Earl, 28, 30. See also Conrad, Earl
Coleman, James, xvii, 23, 28, 31, 54, 72, 162, 182
Colleton, South Carolina, 29
colonization movement, 5, 12, 29, 87, 93
colored (contraband) hospital, Beaufort, South Carolina, 40, 166, 175, 180
colored conventions, 29
Colored hospital, Fort Monroe, Hampton, Virginia, xx, 11, 46, 166, 181
Colored Peoples Church, 29
Combahee River, South Carolina, xix, xxvi, 14, 29–30, 127, 153, 174, 179
Combahee River Raid, 1863, xix, xxvi, 14, 29–30, 97, 153, 169–70, 174, 179

# INDEX

"Come Along, Come Along," song, 29
*The Commonwealth*, newspaper, 30, 125, 127, 170, 179
Compromise of 1850, 48
Concord, Massachusetts, 4, 125, 127
Confederacy, 17, 30, 71
Confederate forces, xxvi, 13, 22–23, 26, 28, 38, 57, 70, 114, 130
Confederate States of America, 28, 30, 46, 60, 119, 150
Connoway (Conoway), William Andrew, xvii, 30, 162, 180. See also Cook, William Andrew
Conrad, Earl, xxvi, 7, 15, 17, 25, 28, 30–31, 41, 61, 105, 141
constellation, 13, 88, 114, 150, 186
contrabands, 40, 52, 125, 174–75, 179–80
Cook, James, xvi, 31, 171
Cook, William Andrew, xvii, 23, 28, 31, 54, 72, 162, 182
Cooper, Henry (Hooper), xvii, 162
Cornish, Aaron and Daffney, 23, 32–33, 39, 113, 146, 151
Cornish, Delia Ann, 32–33
Cornish, Esther (Ester), 32–33, 55, 70, 87, 89, 120
Cornish, Joseph, xvii, 32, 156, 187
Cornish, Solomon, 32–33, 55, 70, 87, 89, 120
Cornish, William, 24, 32, 35, 73, 154
Cornish, William Henry, 25, 32–33, 55, 70, 73, 87, 120
Coursey Creek, Maryland, 33, 137. See also Stewart's Canal
Cowgill, Henry, 33
Cox, John and Hannah, 4, 34, 51
Craig, Ann E., 34, 83–84

Dail, Thomas J., 33, 35
Darby, John G., 75
Davis, Gertrude "Gertie," xx, 35–37
Davis, Nelson Charles, Jr., xix–xx, xxvi, 4, 17, 25, 35–38, 45–48, 97, 105, 110–11, 136, 142
Day, William Howard, 37
*Declaration of Rights and Sentiments*, 115, 128, 133, 159
Deep South, 16, 69, 83, 108, 123, 130–31, 157
DeForest, Vincent, 65
Delaware, state of, xviii, xxi, 6, 9–10, 17–18, 23–25, 27–28, 31–33, 40, 42–43, 48, 51, 54, 60, 67, 72, 74, 82–83, 91–92, 95, 97, 101–2, 108, 111–12, 115, 120, 138, 145, 150–51, 154, 156–57, 159, 172
Denton, Maryland, 26, 37, 39, 54, 70, 112, 154
Department of the South, 37, 74, 125–26, 147, 180
Depee, Nathaniel W., 38, 113
Dependent Pension Act of 1890, 38
Dixon, Anne M., 32–33, 120
D. M. Osborne & Co., 35, 108, 156
Dorchester County Courthouse, Maryland, 16–18, 26, 130
Dorchester County Historical Society, 38–39
Douglass, Anna Murray, 3, 6, 39, 115
Douglass, Frederick Bailey, 3, 5–6, 39, 48, 53–54, 72, 80, 93, 98, 102, 107, 115, 121, 127, 132, 154
Dover Eight, xviii, 12, 18, 34, 39, 41, 55, 72, 74, 84, 95, 108, 132, 146, 157, 163
Drew, Benjamin, 40, 82, 119, 134, 166
Dugan's Wharf, Baltimore, 12, 40, 83, 145
Dunnock, Samuel, 83
Durrant, Henry K., 40
Dutton, Charles, 40, 59, 74, 96–97
Dutton, Marshall, 23, 40, 151

*Earl Conrad/Harriet Tubman Collection*, 31, 41
*Earl Conrad Papers*, 31, 41
Eastern Shore of Maryland, vii, xvii–xviii, xxiv, 14, 20, 24, 26–27, 38, 55–56, 66, 72, 82–83, 88, 101, 107, 115, 135, 145, 175, 189
Edmundson, William V. M., 143
Eighth United States Colored Troop, xix, 35, 97
Einstein, Albert, 41
Ellen Wright, 156. See also Garrison, Ellen Wright
Elliott, Ann Marie Ross (HT niece), 41–42, 124, 162
Elliott, Benjamin, 41, 89
Elliott, Margaret Keys, 41, 95
Elliott, Thomas, 20, 39, 41–42, 74, 95, 157
emancipation, meaning, 42. See also manumission, manumit, manumitted
Emancipation in Maryland, 15, 42, 74
*Emancipation Proclamation*, 42, 45, 51, 74, 126, 150
Empire State Federation of Women's Clubs, 43, 141

Ennals, Noah, 4, 6, 23, 32, 133, 151
Ennals, Stephen and Maria, 43, 112, 124, 162
Erivo, Cynthia, 60
escapee, 43, 47, 124, 149
*Essay on Woman Whipping*, 17, 44, 72

Fairbanks, Calvin, 69
fakelore, vii, 183
Fernandina, Florida, 169
Ferrare, Pheba Kiah, 164
Fifteenth Amendment to the U.S. Constitution, xix, 5, 45, 104, 113, 133
Fifty-Fifth Massachusetts Voluntary Infantry Regiment, 52
Fifty-Fourth Massachusetts Voluntary Infantry Regiment, xix–xx, xxvi, 6, 39, 45, 52, 69, 129, 131, 134, 150
First South Carolina Colored Volunteers, 74, 125, 150, 167
Fiske University, 187
Fitzgerald, Ella, 94
Fitzhugh, Ann, 131–32
Fleming, New York, xxvi, 62, 128–29
Fletcher, Benjamin, 48
Florida, state of, 13, 30, 37, 47, 66, 74, 149, 181–82
Flynn, Errol, 41
Focus Features, film company, 60
folklore, 185–87
"Follow the Drinking Gourd," song, 45, 97, 190
Folly Island, South Carolina, 52
Forten-Grimke, Charlotte, 46
Fort Hill Cemetery, Auburn, New York, xx–xxi, 37, 43, 65, 89, 105, 129, 137, 141, 143–44, 156, 158–59
Fortress Monroe, South Carolina, xix, 11, 46, 181
Fort Sumter, South Carolina, xviii, 28
Fort Wagner, South Carolina, battle of, xix, xxvi, 45, 69, 129, 131, 166
Four Fellows, singing group, 94
Fourteenth Amendment to the U.S. Constitution, xix, 5, 46, 104, 113, 119, 128
Fowler, Rev. Henry, 25, 35, 46
Franklin, Benjamin, 112
Frederick, enslaved person, 18, 46, 121–22, 142
Freedmen's Bureau, 15, 46, 73, 109, 119, 124

*Freedmen's Record*, journal, 26, 46, 104–5, 175
freedom seeker, viii, xviii, 4, 6–7, 9–14, 18–21, 23, 25, 27–29, 31–33, 35, 38–40, 42–43, 46–49, 51–54, 56, 59–60, 69–74, 77, 80, 82–84, 86–89, 92, 95–99, 102, 105, 108–9, 111–15, 119, 121–25, 128–34, 139, 141, 145, 149, 154, 157, 161, 162, 185–87, 189–90. *See also* escapee
*Freedom Train: The Story of Harriet Tubman*, 31, 47, 134
Freeman, Catherine, 47
Freeman, Morgan "Luke," 4, 47
Freeman, William, 129
Fribley, Charles, 47
Friend, Gabriel, 47–48
Friend, Gracie Chase, 47–48, 158
Friend, Harrison, 47–48, 158
Fryman, Edgar J., 48
Fugitive Aid Society, St. Catharines, Ontario, Canada, 48, 154
Fugitive Aid Society of Syracuse, New York, 3, 10–11, 48, 92, 112
fugitive slave. *See* freedom seeker
Fugitive Slave Act, 1850, xvii, 6, 48–49, 56, 60, 88, 101, 113, 130, 165

Garnet, Henry Highland, 37, 51, 154
Garrett, Rachel Mendenhall, 51
Garrett, Thomas, xvii, 9–10, 12, 28, 32, 40, 42–43, 51, 60, 72, 74, 92, 95–97, 102, 108, 111–12, 120, 127, 138, 145, 149, 154, 156–57, 172
Garrison, Agnes, 51–52
Garrison, Ellen Wright, 51, 53, 108, 158–59
Garrison, George, 52
Garrison, Helen Benson, 51, 53
Garrison, Wendel Phillips, 51–52
Garrison, William Lloyd, xviii, 3–6, 25–26, 51–53, 71, 80, 94–95, 98, 108, 113, 115, 125, 132–33, 139, 166
Garrison, William "Willie" Lloyd, II, 53
Gay, Sydney Howard, 9–11, 28, 32, 48, 53–54, 72, 80, 91–92, 102, 112, 139, 182
*General Harriet Tubman*, book, 52. *See also Harriet Tubman*, book by Earl Conrad
Geneva Political Equality Club (New York), 96
*Genius of Universal Emancipation*, newspaper, 53
Georgetown, South Carolina, 15–16, 54

# INDEX

Georgetown, Washington, D.C., xix, 80, 104, 138
Georgetown Planet, 16, 54
Georgia, state of, 17, 24, 30, 37, 80, 89, 123, 127, 130, 157
Ghana, Africa, 6
Gibbs, Abel, 18, 54. See also Gibbs, Abraham
Gibbs, Abraham, 33, 54. See also Gibbs, Abel
Gibbs, Jacob, 54
Gillibrand, Sen. Kirsten E., 63–64, 67
Gilmore, Gen. Q. A., 180
Gilpin Point, Maryland, 32, 54
Gold Swindle, xx, 54, 73, 129
"Goodbye Song," 14, 54. See also "Bound for the Promised Land," spiritual; "On Jordan's Stormy Bank," spiritual
Green, Beriah, 55, 96
Green, Catherine "Kitty," 29, 55–56, 98
Green, Harriet "Rit," 55
Green, Louisa Gray, 56
Green, Rev. Samuel, xvii, 12, 14, 29, 38–39, 42, 55–56, 80, 93, 98, 157
Green, Sam, Jr., xvii, 12, 22, 55–56
Green, Sarah Ann, 55–57
Greensboro, Maryland, 69
Gregory, Solomon, 13, 22–23, 26, 57, 70, 114, 127, 130, 179
Grieves, Ann Martin Staplefort, 9–11, 91
Griffen, William, 4, 6, 23, 32, 133, 150
Griffith, Alexander "Saunders," 139
groomsman statue (African American jockey), 186
guardian's account, 46, 125, 129, 142–43. See also Brodess v. Thompson
GWWO Architects, 68

Haddaway, Sarah Catherine Thompson, 16, 59, 123, 162
Haddaway, Thomas, 16, 59, 78, 136, 138
"Hail, oh Hail Ye Happy Spirits," spiritual, 28, 59. See also "Bound for the Promised Land," spiritual
Handy, Joshua, 40, 59–60, 74, 96–97
Hanner, enslaved person, 164
Hansbrough, Blucher, 7, 60, 72, 101, 145
Harpers Ferry, xviii, xxv, 6, 10–11, 20, 42, 60, 74, 93, 112, 125, 127, 132
*Harriet, the Moses of Her People*, book, xx, 17, 61, 72, 189
*Harriet*, 2019 movie, 60

Harriet on the Hill Day, 61, 65
*Harriet Tubman*, book by Earl Conrad, 41, 54, 61
*Harriet Tubman, Conductor on the Underground Railroad*, book, 31
Harriet Tubman Association, 61
Harriet Tubman Boosters, 63
Harriet Tubman Home, Inc., 61–65
Harriet Tubman Home for Aged and Infirm Negroes, xx, 28, 62, 80, 131–32, 146, 167
Harriet Tubman Memorial and Legacy Garden, 63, 67
Harriet Tubman Mural, 63, 67
Harriet Tubman Museum and Education Center, 63. See also Harriet Tubman Organization, Inc.
Harriet Tubman National Historical Park (HART), xx, 61–65, 80, 145
Harriet Tubman National Historical Parks Act, S247, 61, 63–65, 67
Harriet Tubman Organization, Inc., 63, 65–66, 68
Harriet Tubman Special Resources Act, 65–67
*Harriet Tubman Special Resources Study (SRS)*, 63, 65–68
Harriet Tubman Underground Railroad National Historical Monument (HATU), xxi, 63, 66–67
*Harriet Tubman Underground Railroad National Historical Monument Historic Resource Study*, 67
Harriet Tubman Underground Railroad Scenic Byway and All-American Road, 3, 19, 21, 63, 66–68, 79, 87, 89, 91, 95, 115, 133–34, 137, 153–54
Harriet Tubman Underground Railroad State Park (Maryland), 13, 22, 31, 65, 67–68
Harriet Tubman Underground Railroad State Park Visitor Center (Maryland), 13, 22, 31, 67–68
Harrington, Samuel, 69, 81
Harriot, enslaved person, 164
Harrisville, Maryland, 109, 113
Hart, Albert Bushnell, 69, 166
Haskins, Margaret, 69, 74, 83, 86
Hayden, Harriet Bell, 69
Hayden, Lewis, 69, 145
Hayes, Lee, and the Weavers folk group, 45, 184, 190
Hayward, Isaac, 13, 22–23, 26, 57, 70, 114, 127, 130, 179

# INDEX

Hayward, Samuel, 14, 22–23, 26, 57, 70, 114, 127, 130, 180
Hazlett, Hugh, 32–33, 38, 55, 70, 87, 89, 112–13, 120
Height, Dorothy, 104
Henderson, Maryland, 70, 112
Henry, John Campbell, 9–10, 25, 70–71, 111
Hicks, Thomas H., 71
Higginson, Thomas Wentworth, 71, 125, 127, 150, 169–70
Hill, Joseph "Joe," 23, 71, 111
Hill, Sarah Jane, 23, 71, 111
Hilton Head, South Carolina, xix, 6, 14, 22–23, 26, 38, 57, 70–71, 73–74, 95, 113–14, 126–28, 130, 169, 174, 179–81
hiring out of slaves, xxiv, 71, 85. *See also* leasing of slaves
Hodson, Levin, 28, 31, 72, 182
Hodson, Thomas, 152
Holley, Sallie, 71–72, 189
Hollis, James, 40, 42, 72, 108, 157
Holt, Rosa Belle, 72, 146
Hooper, enslaved child, 164
Hooper, Henry, xvii, 162. *See also* Cooper, Henry (Hooper)
Hooper, John H., 72
Hooper, Samuel, 55
Hopkins, Henry, xvii, 23, 28, 31, 54, 72, 162, 182
Hopkins, Samuel Miles, 17, 44, 72
Houston, John, 28, 31, 72, 182
Howard, Gregory Allen, 60, 83
Howe, Frances Edward, 73
Howe, Julia Ward, 73, 102, 133
Howe, Samuel Gridley, 5, 123–24, 127
Howland, Emily, 73
Hubbard, Daniel, 69, 73–74, 83, 86–87
Hudson, Ephraim, 40, 59, 74, 96–97
Hughes, Denard Denwood, xviii, 20, 39, 42, 74, 95, 115, 156
Hughes, Jane, 86
Hughes, John Wesley, 95
Hughlett, William, 9–10, 74, 111
Humez, Jean, 31
Hunter, Gen. David, 45, 74–75, 174, 179–80, 182
Hutchinson Family Singers, 29

*Incidents in the Life of a Slave Girl*, book, 26, 80
indentured servitude, 16, 42, 77–78, 109, 124, 136–37

"I'm on My Way to Canada," song, 77

Jackson, Dinah Bell, 12, 79
Jackson, Jacob, 28, 66, 79, 107, 138, 190
Jackson, Peter, 25, 27, 56, 145, 156, 163
Jacobs, Harriet, 26, 80, 104
Jamaica Point, Talbot County, Maryland, 9–10, 111
James, enslaved person, 80
Jerry's Rescue, 88, 94
John Brown Hall, xx, xxvi, 62–64, 69, 80, 96, 120
Johnson, Alida Stewart, 41, 132
Johnson, Ann, 157
Johnson, Oliver, 9, 11, 53–54, 80–81, 92, 102, 112
Johnson, Winnebar (William or Winory), xvii, 9, 69, 81, 161
Jolly, Harkless, xvi, 15–16, 81
Jolly, Harriet, xvi, 81, 96, 135
Jolly, Kessiah, 81. *See also* Bowley, Kessiah Jolly
Jolly, Linah Ross, xiii, xvi, 15–16, 81, 85, 96, 122
Jolly, Mary Ann (Mary Jane), 81
Jolly, Sarah Ann, 81–82
Jones, Horatio, 22, 134
Jones, John W., 82
*Journal C*, 82, 95, 111, 139, 149–50, 154
Juneteenth, commemorative day, 12

Kane, Dempsey P., xvi, 80, 83, 123
Kane, Jane, 25, 27, 80, 82–83, 134. *See also* Stewart, Catherine Kane
Kansas-Nebraska Act, 20, 97
Kashatus, William C., 95
Keene, Dawes, 83
Keene, Eliza Ann, xvi, 83. *See also* Brodess, Eliza Ann Keene
Kelley, Esther (Hester), 74, 83, 115
Kelley, Jonah, 33, 74, 83, 115
Kelly, Abby, 4–5
Kelly, Allen, 89
Kennedy Farm, Washington County, Maryland, 60
Kennett Square, Chester County, Pennsylvania, 4, 34
*Kent*, steamship, 12, 40, 70, 83, 102, 145
Kent County, Delaware, 70, 108
Kent County, Maryland, 17–18, 25, 33, 40–41, 51, 54, 112, 154

Kiah, Emily, 18, 34, 39, 42, 74, 83–84, 115, 146, 157
Kiah, Isaac, 84, 163
Kiah, William "Bill," 18, 34, 39, 42, 74, 83–84, 115, 146, 157
kidnapping, of free and enslaved people, 14, 24, 101
King, Mary "Polly," 121. *See also* Thompson, Mary "Polly" King

Leah, enslaved person, 163
leasing of slaves, xvi, xxiii–xxvi, 9–11, 16, 19, 32–33, 42, 73–74, 85, 96, 111, 122, 135–36, 146
LeCompte, Charles, 85
LeCompte, Samuel, W., 32, 85, 133
Lemmons, Kasi, 60
Leonid Meteor shower, xvi, 81, 85, 96
Leverton, Arthur W., 33, 69, 74, 83, 85–86, 143
Leverton, Jacob and Hannah, 74, 83, 85–86, 115, 143
Leverton, Mary Elizabeth, 86–87
Lew, Jack, U.S. Secretary of the Treasury, xxi
*The Liberator,* newspaper, 3, 5, 25, 52–53, 80, 166
Liberia, country in Africa, 5, 12–13, 29, 51, 55, 87, 93
Light, Charles Anthony, 32–33, 55, 70, 87, 89, 120
Light, George, 17, 23, 87, 89, 151
Light, Mary, 32–33, 55, 70, 87, 89, 120
Light, Solomon, 17, 23, 87, 89, 151
Linchester Mill, 73, 83, 86–87, 115
Lincoln, President Abraham, xviii–xix, 28, 42, 51, 74–75, 87–88, 129, 146, 154, 166, 189
Lindsley, Harvey B., 36
Little Blackwater River, 18–19, 26, 31, 82, 88, 110
Little Blackwater River Bridge, 88
Little Choptank River, 91, 113, 138, 158
Little Dipper, 13, 88, 114, 150
Loguen, Jermain, 3, 48, 54, 88, 94
Long, Silas, 23, 88, 151
Long Wharf, Cambridge, Maryland, 32–33, 55, 67, 70, 87–89, 120
Loomtown, Maryland, 158
Lowber, Peter, 89
Lucas, Alice, 89. *See also* Brickler, Alice Lucas
Lucas, Allen, 89

Lucas, Henry, 89
Lucas, Margaret Woolford Stewart, 47, 89–90, 137, 157–58, 162
Lucas, Marguerite, 89
lynching, 31–32, 86, 113, 141, 156

Madison, Maryland, xv–xvii, xxiii–xxiv, 11, 24, 66, 79, 81, 91, 113, 123, 135, 137–39
Malone, Jeremiah and Rose, 91
Malone's African Methodist Episcopal Church, 79, 91, 113, 146
Manlove, Bartholomew, 91
Manoga. *See* Manokey
Manoka. *See* Manokey
Manokey, Aaron, 163
Manokey, Charlotte, 164
Manokey, Draper, 163
Manokey, Eliza, xvii, 9–11, 71, 74, 77, 80, 91, 105, 111, 159, 164
Manokey, Emeline, 164
Manokey, Jerry, 92, 123, 145, 162
Manokey, Polly, 92, 123, 145, 162
Manokin Indian tribe, 26, 101
manumission, manumit, manumitted, xvi, xxiv, 13, 15–16, 33, 38, 47, 79, 91–93, 98, 110, 113, 122–23, 135–39, 142–43
*Manuscript History Concerning the Pension Claim of Harriet Tubman,* 93, 156, 179
Marsh Creek, Maryland, 24, 27, 33, 35, 93, 114–15
Maryland Colonization Society, 93
Maryland State Archives, 14, 38, 107
Mason Committee, 93
Mason, James E., 20, 43, 103, 146
Massachusetts, xviii–xx, xxv–xxvi, 4, 6, 19–21, 25, 37, 39, 45, 52–53, 69–71, 73, 75, 80–81, 94, 98, 104, 108, 113, 115, 119, 125, 127, 129, 134, 150, 159, 169–70
May, Samuel J., 88, 94
McDougall, Clinton Dugald, 94
McGowan, James A., 31, 94–95
McKim, James Miller, 38, 52, 82, 95, 113, 139
McKim, Lucy, 52
Medford's Wharf, 27, 95
Melodeon Hall, Boston, Massachusetts, 128
Meredith, Pritchett, 39, 41–42, 74, 95–96
Meredith, Thomas, 12
Merriam, Francis Jackson, 74
midwife, xv, xxiii
Mikulski, Senator Barbara A., 63, 67

Miller, Anne Fitzhugh, 96, 131
Miller, Blandina, 165
Miller, Elizabeth Smith, 96, 131
Mills, Charles, 96
Mills, John, 96
Mills, Polish, xvi, 81, 85, 96
Milton House, Milton, Wisconsin, 31
Minty, xv–xvi, xxiii–xxiv, 19, 85, 96, 121–22, 144, 189. *See also* Ross, Araminta "Minty," later known as Harriet Tubman
Missouri Compromise (1820), 20
Mitchell, Cyrus, 40, 59, 74, 97
Modesty, HT's enslaved grandmother, xiii, xv, 88, 96–97, 110, 122
Molock, Francis, 40, 59, 74, 96–97
Montgomery, Col. James, xix, xxv, 20, 29–30, 71, 97, 127, 134, 169–70, 174, 179–80
Moore, Henry, 4, 6, 23, 32, 133, 151
Morris Island, South Carolina, 45
Moseby, Emma, 138. *See also* Stewart, William Henry, Jr.
Moses, William J., 97, 126
"Moses Go Down to Egypt Land," spiritual, 28, 97. *See also* "Bound for the Promised Land," spiritual
Mott, James, 97–98, 112
Mott, Lucretia Coffin, xvii, 5, 95, 97–98, 107, 112, 115, 128, 131, 133, 156, 158–59
Moyamensing Prison, 29
Muir, John, 4, 98
Murray, Anna, 98. *See also* Douglass, Anna Murray
Murray, Bambara, 39
Murray, Mary, 39
Muse, James, xvii, 55–56, 80, 98
muskrats, xxiii, 31
Myers, Harriet, 3, 48, 98
Myers, Stephen, 3, 48, 54, 98–99

Nalle, Charles, xviii, 7, 60, 72, 101, 145
Nanticoke Indian Tribe, 26, 101–2
Nanticoke River, Maryland, 27, 38, 83, 101–2, 145, 159
Napoleon, Louis, 53–54, 102
*Narrative of the Life of Frederick Douglass, An American Slave*, 102
National American Woman Suffrage Association (NAWSA), 25, 102, 104, 133
National Antislavery Standard, 10–11, 25, 80, 92, 102, 112

National Aquarium Marine Mammal Pavilion, Baltimore, Maryland, 40, 83
National Association for the Advancement of Colored People (NAACP), 42, 66, 153
National Association of Colored Women (NACW), 19, 102–4, 153
National Council of Negro Women (NCNW), 102, 132
National Defense Authorization Act (NDAA), 64–65, 67
National Federation of Afro-American Women, 104
National Home for the Relief of Destitute Colored Women and Children, 104
National League of Colored Women, 104
National Park Service Network to Freedom Program (NTF), 46, 48, 104, 149
National Woman Suffrage Association (NWSA), 5, 102, 104, 133
New Bedford, Massachusetts, xviii, 19–20, 25, 39, 81
Newburyport, Massachusetts, 53
New Castle, Delaware, 28, 31, 72, 183
New England Anti-Slavery Society, 53, 80, 94
New England Freedmen's Aid Society, 26, 46, 80, 104, 175
New England Shipbuilding Company, 105
New Guinea, Auburn, New York, settlement, 47, 105
*New York Independent*, newspaper, 46, 52
New York Vigilance Committee, 9–10, 54, 92, 102, 112
Niagara Falls, 3, 10–11, 54, 56, 77, 82, 92, 99, 105, 112
Niagara Falls Underground Railroad Heritage Center, 105
Niagara Movement, 42, 141
Nichols, Henry, 55
Nineteenth Amendment to the U.S. Constitution, xxi, 25, 45, 102, 105, 133, 156
Norristown, Pennsylvania, 4, 7, 133
North Elba, New York, 20, 132
Northrup, Eva Stewart, 105–6, 132
North Star, 105. *See also* Polaris

Obama, Barack, 63–67
Oberlin College, 37, 139
"Oh Suzannah!," song, 77
Olustee, Florida, Battle of, 45, 47, 97
Oneida Institute, 55, 80, 96

"On Jordan's Stormy Bank," spiritual, 14, 107
Ontario, Canada, xiii, xvii–xviii, xxv, 3, 5–6, 10–11, 15–16, 20, 23, 32, 40, 42, 48, 56, 60, 73, 77, 87–88, 92, 97–98, 105, 112, 119, 122–25, 127, 133–38, 150, 154
Orphans Court records, 19, 107
Osborne, David Munson, 35, 107–8
Osborne, Eliza Wright, xxvi, 6, 72, 96, 107–8, 156, 158–59
Osgood, Lucy, 108
Otwell, Thomas, xviii, 18, 40, 42, 72, 108, 157
Overlay, Thomas, 108, 157
Owen Sound, Ontario, Canada, 60, 97
Oyster Shell Point, Dorchester County, Maryland, 9–10, 111

paregoric, 43, 139
Parker, Harriet Ann, 109. *See also* Stewart, Harriet Ann Parker
Parker, Isaac and Julia, 135
Parker, John D., 109, 124
Parker, Sarah, 109–10
Parker, Theodore, 109, 127
Parson's Creek, 13, 43, 79, 113, 137–39
Pattison, Atthow, xv, xvii, xxiv, 13, 18, 88, 97, 110, 122, 135, 139
Pattison, Elizabeth, xv, 13, 18, 110, 121–22, 139
Pattison, Gourney Crow, 110
Pattison, Samuel, 6, 23, 71, 111, 113, 148
Payne, Sereno E., 111
Pennington, Peter, xvii, 9–11, 20, 71, 74, 77, 80, 91, 112, 159, 163–62
Pennsylvania, state of, xviii, xxi, 4–7, 23, 27, 32, 34, 38, 51, 56, 70, 81–82, 93, 95, 97–98, 102, 112, 115, 131, 133, 139, 150–51, 153–54, 157–58, 165, 171
Pennsylvania Anti-Slavery Society, 1, 95, 98, 139
Pension Claim, Harriet Tubman, xxvi, 38, 93, 182
Percy, Algernon, 43, 112
Perry, Jesse, 70, 112–13
Peterboro, New York, 96, 131–32
Peters, Hannah, 4, 6, 23, 32, 133, 151
Peter's Neck, Dorchester County, Maryland, xv–xvi, xxiii, 11, 78–79, 82, 84, 91–92, 113, 121–22, 124, 135–36, 142, 146–47, 189
Petry, Ann, 31, 61

Phelps, Dr. Francis, 69
Philadelphia, Pennsylvania, xvii–xviii, xxi, xxv, 4–5, 7, 9–10, 15–16, 18, 21–22, 24, 27–29, 32–33, 38, 40, 42, 46, 51, 53–54, 56, 60, 71–72, 74, 79, 82–84, 86–88, 92, 94–98, 102, 105–6, 112–13, 115, 120, 132–34, 139, 145, 147, 149–50, 154, 157–59, 171–72, 176, 181
Philadelphia Vigilance Committee, 22, 38, 82, 95, 115, 139, 149
Phillips, Rueben Eliot, 25, 32, 87, 111, 113
Phillips, Wendell, 113, 125, 127, 132
Phyllis Wheatley Club, 141
Piatt family, 186–87
Plowden, Walter D., 14, 22–23, 26, 57, 70, 113–14, 127, 130, 153, 180
Pokomoke Indian tribe, 26, 101
Polaris, 13, 88, 105, 114, 150, 186. *See also* Little Dipper; North Star
Pomeroy, Theodore, 114
Poplar Neck, Caroline County, Maryland, xvii–xviii, xxiv–xxv, 9–10, 25, 27, 33, 39, 41–42, 47, 86–87, 89, 93, 95–96, 111, 114, 122–23, 141, 143, 153, 157–58
Porter, Maria G., 6, 114, 121
Porter, Samuel D., 10–11, 92, 112
Post, Amy Kirby, 6, 80, 114–15
Post, Isaac, 6, 80, 115
Powelson, Benjamin F., 37, 73
Predeaux, Henry, xviii, 39, 42, 74, 115, 132, 157
Preston, Maryland, xvii, xxiv, 27, 47, 73, 83, 85–87, 95, 114–15, 134, 153, 157–58
Purvis, Robert, 112, 115

Quakers, Quakerism, 33, 43, 51, 53, 56, 73–74, 80, 83, 86, 95, 97–98, 114–15, 120, 131, 141, 143, 154, 158–59, 172
Queen Victoria of England, 77, 106, 151
quilt code myth, 117, 190

Rankin, John, 69
Reconstruction Era, 119
Reed, John Wesley Cornish, 43, 162
*The Refugee: A Northside View of Slavery*, book, 40, 119
reward, monetary, for capture of freedom seeker, viii, xvii, xxiv, 9–12, 18–19, 23, 31, 40, 42, 60, 70–72, 74, 77, 81, 83, 92, 96–98, 101, 108, 111–13, 115, 130, 146, 151, 157, 172, 178, 182, 189
Rhody, 80

# INDEX

Richardson, Ezekiel, 55
Richardson, Levin, 162
Richardson, Margarite Lucas, 89
Richburg, Addie, 65
Rideout, Thomas, 32–33, 55, 70, 87, 89, 120
Ridgeway, Martha, 120
Robinson, John Bell, 120
Rochester, New York, 3, 6, 10–11, 39, 48, 54, 82, 92–93, 99, 112, 114–15, 154
Rochester Ladies Anti-Slavery Sewing Society, 48, 114, 120–21, 154
Rock, John Stewart, 112, 121, 147
Rosato, Michael, 63
Ross, Angerine (HT's niece), xiii, 43, 121, 123, 183
Ross, Araminta "Minty," later known as Harriet Tubman, 85, 96, 121–22, 146, 170, 175
Ross, Ben (HT's nephew), xiii, xvii–xviii, xxv, 43, 121–22, 183
Ross, Ben, Jr. (HT's brother), xiii, 18, 25, 27, 80, 82, 96, 122–23, 134, 156, 161. *See also* Stewart, James (HT brother)
Ross, Benjamin "Ben" (Harriet Tubman's father), viii, xv–xvii, xix, xxiii–xxv, 9–13, 18, 27, 33, 39, 47–48, 81, 84, 86–87, 91–92, 111, 114, 121–24, 135–36, 142–43, 146, 157, 162
Ross, Harriet "Rit" Green, xiii, xv, 18, 55, 81, 88, 97, 121–26, 135–36, 138, 142, 146, 162
Ross, Henry (HT's brother), xiii, 4–5, 18, 41, 71, 79–80, 82, 85, 96, 105, 122–24, 127, 134–36, 138, 156, 161–62. *See also* Stewart, William Henry Ross, Sr. (HT brother)
Ross, John Henry, 123. *See also* Stewart, John (HT brother)
Ross, John Isaac, 123. *See also* Stewart, John Isaac (HT nephew)
Ross, Linah, 123. *See also* Jolly, Linah Ross
Ross, Mariah Ritty, xiii, xv–xvi, xxiii, 83, 121–23. *See also* Rhody
Ross, Mary Manokey, 59, 92, 122–23, 136–37
Ross, Moses (Brother of HT), xiii, xvi, 85, 122, 161, 183
Ross, Moses (HT nephew), 16, 78, 123, 137. *See also* Stewart, Moses
Ross, Rachel (HT's sister), xiii, xvi–xviii, xxv, 43, 112, 121–24, 182

Ross, Robert (HT's brother), xiii, 25, 27, 59, 71, 78, 82, 92, 122–23, 136–37, 156, 161
Ross, Simon, 109, 124
Ross, Soph, xiii, xv–xvi, xxiv, 41, 121–24
Ruffin, Josephine St. Pierre, 104, 156

safe houses, Underground Railroad, 9–10, 87, 92, 98, 111, 139, 149, 186
Saint-Gaudens, Auguste, xx
Salem Chapel, British Methodist Episcopal Church, 125
Samuel, enslaved person, 18, 46, 121–22, 142
Sanborn, Franklin B., 14, 30, 125–27, 134, 189
Sandtown, Kent County, Delaware, 33
Sarnia, Lambton County, Ontario, Canada, 112
Sassafras River, Kent County, Maryland, 154
Saxton, Gen. Rufus, 14, 22–23, 26, 57, 70, 114, 125–28, 130, 179–82
*Scenes in the Life of Harriet Tubman*, book, xix, 17, 37, 39, 44, 61, 72, 75, 97, 126–27, 189–90
Schomburg Center for Research in Black Culture, New York Public Library, 31, 41, 110
Schumer, Sen. Charles, 63–64, 66–67
Scott, Dred, U.S. Supreme Court case, xviii–xix
Scott, John, 123, 127
Seaford, Delaware, 40, 83, 102, 145, 159
Second South Carolina Colored Volunteers, 29, 71, 97, 127, 150, 170
Secret Six, 20, 30, 60, 71, 73, 125, 127, 132, 134
self-emancipators, 46, 48
self-liberators, 14, 23, 46, 48, 80, 82, 95, 113, 121, 131, 186
Sellers, Sandy, 13, 21–23, 26, 57, 70–71, 114, 127, 130, 179
Seneca Falls (New York) Convention, 98, 107, 115, 128, 133, 138, 156, 159
serene, 175
Sernett, Milton, 31
Severance, Caroline, 52, 128
Seward, Frances Miller, 78, 128, 158
Seward, William Henry, xviii, xxvi, 11, 25, 65, 73, 89, 98, 122–23, 127–29, 158–59, 171, 173–74, 181–82
Shadrack, enslaved person, 18, 121–22, 129, 142

Shaw, Col. Robert Gould, xix–xx, 45, 129
Shimer, Anthony, 54, 129. *See also* Gold Swindle
Siebert, Wilbur, 28, 33, 99, 129, 186–87
signals on the Underground Railroad, 14, 28, 59, 186–87, 190
Simmons, Charles, 13, 21–23, 26, 57, 70–71, 114, 127, 130, 179
Sims, Harriet, 131
Slacum, Jerry Ennals, 163
Slatter, Hope Hull, 130
Slaughter Creek, Maryland, 135, 137, 147
slave auction, xxiv, 17, 38, 130
slave catchers, 9–10, 14, 20, 23, 25, 27, 43, 49, 60, 69, 72, 96, 111–12, 115, 128, 130, 139, 151, 187, 190
slave trade, trans-Atlantic, 130–31
slave trade, U.S. interstate, 38, 131
slave traders, xvi, xxiii, 16–17, 24, 53, 80, 83, 85, 89, 91, 108, 123–24, 130–31, 157
Smedley, Dr. Robert C., 131
Smith, Ann Fitzhugh, 131–32
Smith, Charles A., 41, 131–32
Smith, Frances, 41, 131–32
Smith, Gerrit, 20, 48, 51, 96, 121, 127, 131–33, 178
Smithsonian National Museum of African American History and Culture, 30, 61, 75, 142, 153
Smyrna, Delaware, 33
songs, used as codes on Underground Railroad myth and fact and factual, 3, 14, 29, 45, 59, 107, 176, 186–87, 190
Sophia, enslaved person, 162
Soule Cemetery, Auburn, New York, 109
*Southern Horrors: Lynch Law in All Its Phases*, book, 153
Spence, Ara, 39, 42, 132
Spencer, William, 51
spirituals, 187, 190. *See also* songs, used as codes on Underground Railroad myth and fact and factual
Spriggs, Rebecca, 163
Squyer, H. Seymour, 61
SS *Harriet Tubman*, Liberty Ship, xxi, 104–6, 132–33
stampede of slaves, xviii, 6–7, 12, 17–18, 23, 32, 113, 133, 151, 161
Stanley, Caroline and Daniel, 4, 6, 23, 32, 133, 151
Stanley Institute, 133

Stanton, Elizabeth Cady, 5, 98, 102, 104, 107, 115, 128, 131–33, 156, 159
Staplefort, Dorothy, xvi, 84
Staplefort, John, 11, 91
Staten Island, New York, 53
*Station Master on the Underground Railroad: The Life and Letters of Thomas Garrett*, book, 95
stationmasters on the Underground Railroad, xxv, 28, 149
St. Catharines, Ontario, Canada, xiii, xvii–xviii, xxv–xxvi, 5–6, 10–11, 20, 23, 32, 37, 40, 48, 60, 66, 73–74, 87–88, 122–25, 127, 133, 135–38, 151, 154, 166
Stearns, George L., 127, 134, 175
Sterling, Dorothy, 31, 47
Stewart, Alida, 132, 138
Stewart, Catherine Elizabeth Garner, 105, 136
Stewart, Catherine Kane, 25, 40, 134, 161. *See also* Kane, Jane
Stewart, Clarence "Dye," 134, 138
Stewart, Dora, 134, 138
Stewart, Esther (Hester), 134
Stewart, Eva "Katy," 135. *See also* Northrup, Eva Stewart
Stewart, Gertrude, 134, 136
Stewart, Harriet Ann Parker, 135–37, 162
Stewart, Harriet "Rit," 135. *See also* Ross, Harriet "Rit" Green
Stewart, James (HT brother), xiii, 27, 40, 135–136, 161. *See also* Ross, Ben, Jr. (HT's brother)
Stewart, James A., 135
Stewart, James Isaac (HT nephew), 136. *See also* Stewart, John Isaac (HT nephew)
Stewart, John (HT brother), xiii, 16, 27, 35, 78, 108, 136–37, 161. *See also* Ross, Robert (HT's brother)
Stewart, John Henry, Jr., 123, 136. *See also* Ross, John Henry
Stewart, John Isaac (HT nephew), 37, 105, 123, 136–37, 162
Stewart, John T., xvi, xxiv, 91, 137, 141
Stewart, Joseph, 109, 137–138
Stewart, Levin, 15–16, 137
Stewart, Margaret Woolford, 17, 37, 89, 137. *See also* Lucas, Margaret Woolford Stewart
Stewart, Moses, 137–38. *See also* Ross, Moses (HT nephew)
Stewart, William Henry, Jr., 135, 137–138, 162

Stewart, William Henry Ross, Sr. (HT brother), xiii, 5, 27, 41, 48, 73, 105, 123, 127, 135–38, 162. *See also* Ross, Henry (HT's brother)
Stewart's Canal, 13, 135, 138–39. *See also* Parson's Creek
St. Helena Island, South Carolina, 29, 38, 180
Still, Charity, 139
Still, Kitty, 139
Still, Letitia George, 139
Still, Levin, 139
Still, Levin, Jr., 139
Still, Mahala, 139
Still, Peter, 139
Still, Sydney, 139
Still, William, xvii, xxv, 4, 7, 18, 21, 28, 32, 38, 40, 42, 51, 53, 60, 67, 71–72, 74, 81–82, 84, 87–88, 95–97, 108, 111–13, 115, 133, 139, 149, 154, 157
Stone, Lucy, 102, 133
Stowe, Harriet Beecher, 56
Suke, enslaved person, 13, 139
Sussex County, Delaware, 24–25, 38, 101, 111
"Swing Low, Sweet Chariot," song, 187–88
Syracuse, New York, 3, 10–11, 17, 28, 32, 48, 54, 72, 82, 88, 92, 94, 96, 99, 112, 184

Talbert, Mary Morris Burnett, 42, 141, 167
Talbot County, Maryland, 9–10, 12, 16, 27, 39, 41, 59, 64, 66–67, 72, 78, 111, 123, 136, 138, 142, 164
Tappan, Lewis, 4–5, 141, 165
Tatlock, Helen Woodruff, 41, 141
Telford, Emma, 142
Temple-Tuttle comet, 85
temporal lobe epilepsy (TLE), xvi, xxiii, 11, 21, 108, 142
Thirteenth Amendment to the U.S. Constitution, xix, 52–53, 119, 142
Thompson, Albert, xix, 35, 142
Thompson, Anthony, xv–xvii, xxiii, 11, 18–19, 22, 27, 46, 82, 84, 91–92, 109, 113, 122–25, 129, 135, 137, 138, 142–43, 145, 163–64, 189
Thompson, Anthony C., Jr., 86, 143
Thompson, Dr. Absalom, 109, 121, 142–43, 164
Thompson, Dr. Anthony C., xvii, xxiv, 9–12, 16, 25, 27, 33, 47, 59, 64–65, 87, 93, 95, 109, 114, 119, 121–24, 136, 142–41, 158, 163–64, 171, 176
Thompson, Edward, 121, 142–43
Thompson, John K., 143
Thompson, Mary Pattison Brodess, xv, xxiii, 18–19, 46, 81, 110, 121–22, 125, 129, 142
Thompson, Mary "Polly" King, 121, 142–43
Thompson Memorial African Methodist Episcopal Zion (AMEZ) Church, xx, xxii, 4, 37, 64–65, 120, 131–32, 143–45
Tilghman, Tench, 145, 161. *See also* Jackson, Peter
Tilly, enslaved person, xvii, 12, 40, 83, 102, 145, 162
Tindle, Miles, 145
Tobacco Stick, xv, xvii, 15, 91, 136. *See also* Madison, Maryland
Tombigbee River, Alabama, 186
Townsend, Martin I., 145
Trans-Atlantic Slave Trade, 130–31
Transquaking River, Maryland, 26
Travers, Addie Clash, 65
Travers, Levi D., 32, 111, 113, 146
*Tribute to Harriet Tubman, the Modern Amazon*, 20, 43, 93, 103, 146
Troy, New York, xviii, 48, 60, 72, 74, 101, 145, 178
Trusty, Henny, 51
Truth, Sojourner, 146, 170
Tubman, Benjamin Gaither, 84, 146
Tubman, Evans, 146–47
Tubman, Harriet Ross, v, vii–ix, xi, xiii, xv–xxi, xxiii–xxvii, 3–7, 9–33, 35–48, 51–57, 59–75, 77–89, 91–99, 101–15, 119–47, 149–51, 153–59, 161–63, 165–67, 169–70, 173, 175, 179–83, 185, 187, 189; adoption of Gertie, xx, xxvi, 35–36; appearance, 19; birth, vii, xv–xvi, xxiii, 146, 170–71, 175, 189; chronology, xv–xxi; death, xxi, xxvi, 4, 17, 63, 120, 132, 134, 141, 144, 145, 146; education, vii, xxiv, 15, 146, 171, 173, 179; escape, first, xvii, xxiv, 18, 96, 136, 138, 189; escape, second, xvii, xxv, 14, 83, 86, 114, 141, 143, 146, 158, 171; head injury, xvi, xxiii, 11, 21, 96, 119, 135, 137, 142, 171, 175; home, in Auburn, New York, xviii–xxi, xxvi, 15, 25, 28, 35, 41, 42, 52, 61–67, 73, 80, 93, 96, 98, 105, 108, 109, 120, 122, 123, 128–29, 134, 136, 138, 167, 171, 173, 174, 178; illnesses and health

problems, xvi, xviii, xxiii, 11, 21, 31, 108, 119, 142, 171, 174, 180; marriage to John Tubman, xvi, xxiv, 146, 171, 175; marriage to Nelson Davis, xix, xxvi, 25, 37; myths, about, vii, 28, 31, 94, 185, 189–90; name change, xvi, xxiv, 146; religious faith of, 119–20; rescue missions of, xvii–xviii, xxv, 7, 9–10, 12–13, 15–16, 24–25, 28, 39, 43, 51, 54–55, 66, 72, 82, 88, 95, 107, 112, 115, 121–24, 128, 141–42, 145, 154, 161–62, 178, 183, 190; siblings, xiii, xv–xviii, xxiv–xxv, 5, 15–16, 18, 25, 27, 35, 40–41, 43, 48, 59, 71, 73, 78, 80–83, 85, 92, 96, 105, 108, 112, 121–24, 127, 134–38, 158, 161–62, 185; singing, 14, 28, 29, 52, 59, 77, 102, 176, 190; speech, modified by Sarah Hopkins Bradford, 61
Tubman, John, xvi, xix, xxiv, 146–47, 171, 175
Tubman, Priscilla, 146
Tubman, Thomas "Tom," 147
Tuskegee, 153
Tuskegee Institute, 153
Twelfth Baptist Church, Boston, 147

Underground Railroad, vii–viii, xi–xii, xvi–xviii, xx–xxi, xxiii, xxv–xxvi, 3–4, 7, 9–10, 13–14, 16–18, 22, 24–25, 27–28, 31–34, 38–40, 42–43, 45, 47–48, 51–56, 59, 66, 68–72, 74, 80–83, 86–89, 91–92, 94–95, 98–99, 102, 104–5, 108–9, 111, 113–15, 120–23, 129, 131–34, 138–39, 145–47, 149, 153–54, 156–59, 161–62, 185–87, 189–90
Underground Railroad, reverse, 24
Underground Railroad agents, xxv, 3–4, 7, 14, 18, 25, 28, 32–33, 38, 40, 42, 48, 51–56, 71–72, 81–82, 87–88, 95, 108, 113–14, 131, 133, 145, 154, 157
*The Underground Railroad: A Record of Facts, Authentic Narratives, Letters, &c.*, 139, 149
Underground Railroad conductors, vii, xviii–xx, xxv, 28, 31–33, 53, 55, 61, 87, 89, 115, 120, 146, 149, 165–66
Underground Railroad myths, 149, 185–90
Union Army, 6, 20, 28–29, 52, 71, 73, 94, 97, 125, 127, 129, 150, 156, 158, 182, 189
United States Army during the Civil War, 74, 148. *See also* Union Army

United States Army Military Intelligence Corps Hall of Fame, 111, 150
United States Colored Troops (USCT), 17, 35, 38, 45, 47–48, 127, 142, 150, 157
United States Sanitary Commission, 73, 181
Upper South, 16, 24, 131, 150
Ursa Major, 13, 186
Ursa Minor, 13, 88, 114
U.S. Congress, xv, xix, 38, 45–46, 48, 51, 53, 61, 64, 66, 93–94, 105, 111, 114, 119, 132, 135, 142, 150, 178
U.S. Maritime Commission, xxvii, 104, 132
U.S. Sanitary Commission, 73, 181

Vienna, Maryland, 43, 77, 97, 102, 112, 145
Vincent, Robert, xix, 147, 151
Viney, Joe and Susan, 23, 111, 151
Virginia, state of, xvi, xviii–xix, xxv, 6–7, 11–12, 17, 20–21, 30, 42, 46, 56, 60, 72, 74, 80, 82, 89, 93, 101, 125–27, 132, 150, 156, 170, 181

Waddell, James, 97
"Wade in the Water," spiritual, 187, 190
Walker, AMEZ Bishop George Herbert, 65
Washington, Booker T., 153
Waterman, African American, 153. *See also* Black Jacks
Waugh Chapel United Methodist Church, Cambridge, Maryland, 65
Webb, James, 153
Webster, Delia, 69
Webster, John E., 114, 126, 153
Welch, Eben, 154, 156
Wells-Barnett, Ida B., 102, 153
Whittier, John Greenleaf, 26
Wicomico County, Maryland, 41, 101
Wigham, Eliza, 145, 153–54
Wilbur, Julia, 104, 154
Wilkins, Horatio W., 48, 154
Wilkins, Mariline Northrup, 105–6
Wilkinson, Horatio, 154. *See also* Wilkins, Horatio W.
Willard Asylum for the Insane, Ovid, New York, 42
Williams, Emily, 154. *See also* Kiah, Emily
Williams, William "Bill," 154. *See also* Kiah, William "Bill"
Williamson, Passmore, 29, 112
William Still Interpretive Center, 154
Willis, Thomas, 17, 81–82
Wilmer, George, 33, 152, 154

Wilmer, Margaret, 156
Wilmington, Delaware, 9–10, 12, 18, 28, 32–33, 40, 42–43, 51, 60, 72, 74, 92, 95–97, 102, 108, 111–12, 120, 145, 154, 156, 157, 172, 183
Winslow, Andrew, 134
Winthrop, George, 79, 156
*Woman's Era*, newspaper, 104, 169
women's suffrage movement/rights, xxi, xxvi, 53, 102, 108, 120, 128, 141, 156, 159
Wood, Charles P., 93, 156, 179, 182
Woodson, Carter G., 7, 31, 156
Woolfley, James and Lavinia, 156. *See also* Woolford, James and Lavinia
Woolfolk, Austin and John, 157
Woolford, Isaac, 47–48, 72, 89, 157, 158
Woolford, James, 47–48, 89, 157, 158
Woolford, James and Lavinia, xviii, 39, 42, 74, 115, 157. *See also* Woolfley, James and Lavinia
Woolford, Margaret, 157. *See also* Lucas, Margaret Woolford Stewart

Woolford, Mary, 47–48, 89, 157–58
Woolford, Maryland, 113
Woolford, Moses, 47–48, 89, 158
Woolford, Sarah, 47–48, 89, 158
Worcester, Massachusetts, 41
Worden, Lazette Miller, 128, 158
World Anti-Slavery Convention, 5, 98, 138
World War II, 132
Wright, David, 43, 51, 107, 128–29, 158
Wright, Isaac Henry, 28, 31, 182
Wright, Martha Coffin Pelham, xxvi, 6, 43, 51, 53, 98, 107, 112, 115, 128–29, 133, 156, 158
Wright, Turpin, 9–10, 111–12, 158
Wyman, Elizabeth "Lillie" Buffin Chase, 159

Yerrington, James, 170
Young, Angeline, 163
Young, Rosette, 55

# About the Author

Kate Clifford Larson is a best-selling author and award-winning historical consultant, specializing in U.S. women's and African American history. She earned her BA and MA degrees from Simmons University, an MBA from Northeastern University in Boston, and a doctorate in American history from the University of New Hampshire in 2003. Her dissertation on Harriet Tubman upended more than a century of myths, misinformation, and stereotypes of the famous Underground Railroad conductor and American icon. Larson's extensive research took her to archives, courthouses, and private collections from New England to the Chesapeake and New York to Canada, unearthing never-before-seen details of Tubman's life from birth into slavery in Maryland in 1822 to her death as a free woman in Auburn, New York, in 1913.

Larson's scholarship has led to award-winning consulting for public and private partnerships in tourism, historic preservation and interpretation, educational programs, the arts, and entertainment. Her work includes development, analysis, and commentary for feature film scripts—including Kasi Lemmons's *Harriet*, starring prize-winning Cynthia Erivo, and Robert Redford's *The Conspirator*—documentaries, museum exhibits, animation, augmented and virtual reality productions, tour guides, and other public history initiatives. She has served as the consultant for the Harriet Tubman Underground Railroad State and National Park in Maryland, the Harriet Tubman Home and National Historical Park in New York, and the Harriet Tubman Underground Railroad Scenic Byway and All-American Road. In 2019, Larson completed the *Harriet Tubman Underground Railroad National Monument Historic Resource Study* for the National Park Service. The University of New Hampshire awarded her a Doctor of Humane Letters (Honor Causa) in May 2016, for her work as a biographer and consultant. She has served as the Scholar-in-Residence for In My Backyard: Geographies of Slavery and Freedom, an educational program of John Brown Lives!, a freedom education and human rights project in Westport, New York, since 2014. She lectures widely and is frequently interviewed by national and international media outlets and is a Brandeis Women's Studies Research Center Visiting Scholar.

Her previous books include *Bound for the Promised Land: Harriet Tubman, Portrait of an American Hero* (2003), which was a *Wall Street Journal* best seller in 2016; *The Assassin's Accomplice: Mary Surratt and the Plot to Kill Abraham Lincoln* (2008); *Rosemary: The Hidden Kennedy Daughter* (2015), which spent ten weeks on the *New York Times* Best Seller list and received the Mass Book Award for Nonfiction from the Massachusetts Center for the Book in 2016; and *Walk with Me: A Biography of Fannie Lou Hamer* (2021).

www.ingramcontent.com/pod-product-compliance
Lightning Source LLC
Chambersburg PA
CBHW082034300426
44117CB00015B/2475